RETRO GAMING
HACKS™

Other resources from O'Reilly

RETRO GAMING
HACKS™

Chris Kohler

O'REILLY®

Beijing · Cambridge · Farnham · Köln · Paris · Sebastopol · Taipei · Tokyo

Retro Gaming Hacks™
by Chris Kohler

Copyright © 2006 O'Reilly Media, Inc. All rights reserved.
Printed in the United States of America.

Published by O'Reilly Media, Inc., 1005 Gravenstein Highway North,
Sebastopol, CA 95472.

O'Reilly books may be purchased for educational, business, or sales promotional use. Online editions are also available for most titles (*safari.oreilly.com*). For more information, contact our corporate/institutional sales department: (800) 998-9938 or *corporate@oreilly.com*.

Editor:	Brian Jepson	**Production Editor:**	Philip Dangler
Series Editor:	Rael Dornfest	**Cover Designer:**	Ellie Volckhausen
Executive Editor:	Dale Dougherty	**Interior Designer:**	David Futato

Printing History:

October 2005:   First Edition.

 This book uses RepKover™, a durable and flexible lay-flat binding.

ISBN: 0-596-00917-8
[C]

Contents

Foreword

Way back in the Paleolithic Era of computing (about 1980), I bought my first computer, an Apple][+. I still get a kick out of the clever way Apple "spelled out" the Roman numeral two with those square brackets. My][+ was totally tricked out: a whopping 48 KB of memory, two 120 KB floppies (no disk swapping for me!), a beautiful 10" black & green monitor, an Epson MX-80 dot matrix printer that lasted me far longer than any other piece of computer gear I've ever owned, and a genuine Hayes 300-baud modem (the height of "online connectivity" then) that cost $300 (just for the modem, not the whole computer!), a nice even dollar-per-baud.

Somehow I convinced my wife that we should drop well over a month's income (and we were both employed, too). I promised her I would make it pay for itself.

I guess I did.

How? Hacking.

The computer classes that existed then were for "real computers," where you typed Cobol onto punch cards and handed your deck to the "computer operator" hoping he would run your program sometime soon and give you back a big pile of paper so you could figure out the results! Real programmers didn't play with home computers.

But then, I wasn't a real programmer. We had to learn things by ourselves. I sat in front of that Apple and typed hour after hour, writing code that didn't work, then figuring out why, changing it and trying it again. Rinse. Repeat. I was just sure that I had missed the boat on becoming a programmer. All those guys with the college Fortran classes would have all the fun.

Eventually I bought and read enough books that I figured things out. And discovered that instead of being way behind the curve, I was actually ahead of it. While they were better at algorithms, I understood people, and humor, and storytelling, and character development, and all the things one learns with a humanities degree. And by hacking away at code, I could do things that "real programmers" couldn't.

So I'm especially partial to hacking.

One hack that I used in *Leisure Suit Larry 3: Passionate Patti in Pursuit of the Pulsating Pectorals,* is worth sharing. Why? Where else could I possibly share it?!

There was a 72-screen maze in that game where you got lost in a bamboo grove. The entire maze was made up of one background picture of intersecting paths in a bamboo grove that exited out all four sides of the picture. We also made 4 cells that were mostly transparent, but that contained enough bamboo to completely cover each of those exits. We overlaid them onto that picture (see Figure P-1). For example, if there was an exit to the top, we didn't add that overlay, thus you could exit out the top. So usually we added two, or sometimes only one, overlay.

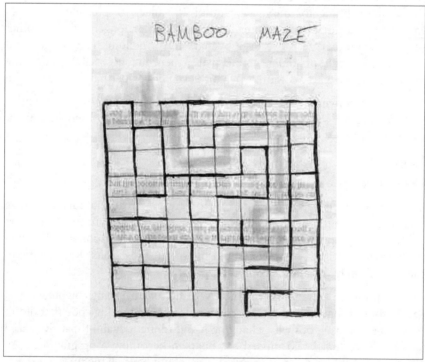

Figure P-1. The original sketch of the LSL3 Bamboo Maze

But why didn't the scenes all look identical since every picture was the same? Simple. Every time you exited one screen, we flopped everything horizontally and thus projected the picture backwards, like a slide reversed in a tray. By eliminating disk access, this technique made everything work really fast, took up little memory, and only a tiny bit of disk space.

To control it, I created a bit array that contained 4 bits for every scene. (Picture an electrical wall box with 4 light switches on it; same thing.) 72 screens times 4 bits/screen equals 288 switches. One long wall plate!

Personally, I think the hack was much more interesting than the maze itself.

But the sad part is: until now, no one ever knew just how cool a hack it was!

So enjoy Chris's book. There's plenty of fun in here for all you retro gamers. Oh, if you enjoy this, drop by my web site, *www.allowe.com* for even more inside stories...and laughs!

—Al Lowe
Creator of Leisure Suit Larry

Credits

About the Author

Chris Kohler is an editor/writer/karaoke performance artist who lives in San Francisco, where all three of those things are a dime a dozen. So like most of his friends, he has written articles about video games for *Wired*, *Official PlayStation Magazine*, *1up.com*, *IGN*, *Gamespy*, *Nintendo Official Magazine UK*, *Electronic Gaming Monthly*, and probably a few other publications.

Kohler's first book, *Power-Up: How Japanese Video Games Gave the World an Extra Life*, was published by BradyGAMES in September 2004. Kohler completed the research for Power-Up as a Fulbright scholar to Kyoto, Japan. He graduated *summa cum laude* with highest thesis honors from Tufts University, where he was Phi Beta Kappa. He has contributed to books such as *Gaming Hacks* (O'Reilly) and *High Score! Second Edition* (McGraw-Hill).

All that aside, he would most like to be remembered as having starred as the first guard after Vulcan Raven in the Easy mode of Metal Gear Solid: The Twin Snakes for Nintendo GameCube.

Contributors

The following amazing people contributed hacks to this book, often at great personal and professional risk. Give them your love.

- Simon Carless (*http://www.mono211.com/ffwd*) is Editor of *Game Developer* magazine and Gamasutra.com, the two major resources for professional video game developers. He formerly worked as a PC and console game designer for companies including Eidos Interactive and Atari, an editor for popular technology web site Slashdot, and is the author of *Gaming Hacks*, O'Reilly's previous game-related Hacks title. He lives in the Bay Area with his wife Holly and a sock-obsessed dachshund named Rollo.

- Cameron Davis (*http://www.gazunta.com*) started working in the games industry back when the Atari Jaguar was considered a good idea. However, unlike Atari, he is currently not a bastardised parody of his former self. He has written for *GameSpot*, *IGN*, *Pocket Games*, and *Official Australian Xbox Magazine* among many other publications. He is currently Lead Designer on an unannounced major character action title at Krome Studios, due for release September 2006. Davis' other credits at Krome include Designer/Assistant Producer on the GBA version of Ty the Tasmanian Tiger 2 and QA roles on a variety of other titles. He lives with his very patient wife Sabrina in Brisbane, Australia.

- Matt DelGiudice has dabbled in video game journalism since 1998, contributing reviews, photos, and FAQs to a variety of web sites and fanzines. Recently, he spent a year in Saitama, Japan as a high school English teacher, spending his free time absorbing the culture and working on independent projects. Now back in the States, he plans to marry his girlfriend of five years. Matt received his BS in Computer Science in 2004 from Clemson University in 2004, where he was a member of the Upsilon Pi Epsilon Computer Science honors society.

- Robert Ota Dieterich, when not playing old DOS games or trying to make pictures move around on his GBA, splits his time between government contracting, programming video games, and occasionally foraying into Japanese translation. His current game projects include NeonFM Dance Radio (*http://www.neonfm.com*), due out in arcades in October 2005, and Wings Templar (*http://www.hubrisoft.com/wt*), due out on PC in late 2005. He can most often be found rushing between Hampton, VA and Towson, MD with the occasional stop in Arlington, VA for a good night's rest.

- Josh Glover (*http://www.jmglov.net*) has been hacking code for as long as anyone can remember. He currently resides with his wife in scenic Columbus, Ohio, where he enjoys some of the best weather the American Midwest has to offer. He is employed as a Senior Software Engineer by Twenty First Century Communications, Inc., a telecom services and software development house. He is a product of The College of William and Mary in Virginia (where he ran with the now-legendary Group 4 crew), having earned a BS in Computer Science in 2002. He is also the Listmaster of the Tokyo Linux Users Group (TLUG), a position he has held since 2002 and will likely continue to hold until it is pried from his cold, dead hands.

- Adrian Jackson has been playing and writing interactive fiction on and off since the early eighties, for fun and profit. You'd think he'd be better at it by now. By day he works as a software developer doing the impossible with mobile phones; by night he lives in constant fear of being eaten by a grue.

- Brian Jepson is an O'Reilly editor, programmer, and coauthor of *Mac OS X Tiger for Unix Geeks* and *Linux Unwired*. He's also a volunteer systems administrator and all-around geek for AS220 (*http://www.as220.org*), a nonprofit arts center in Providence, Rhode Island. AS220 gives Rhode Island artists uncensored and unjuried forums for their work. These forums include galleries, performance space, and publications. Brian sees to it that technology, especially free software, supports that mission.

- Daniel Kohler (*http://www.settingrecords.net*) has been involved with electronics and computers from a young age. In 2003, he received his BS in Electrical Engineering with Distinction at Worcester Polytechnic Institute. While working towards his degree, he co-developed a DSP-based effects routing device for use in professional music production. When not working as an engineer, he is busy writing and producing electronic music.

- Nich Maragos (*http://www.maragos.org*) is a Louisiana-born freelance writer currently living in San Francisco, and has been published in many venues, notably *Electronic Gaming Monthly*, *Gamasutra.com*, *1UP.com*, and the book you are holding. In his spare time, he plays drums with the San Francisco Taiko Dojo and works at his own snail's pace on other books he envisions you holding someday.

- Rob "Flack" O'Hara (*http://www.robohara.com*) writes several columns for *Digital Press* (*http://www.digitpress.com*), including Extended Play, MAMExpose, and the Monday Morning MAME Club. His work has also appeared in *2600: The Hacker Quarterly*, *Digital Press' Advanced Collecting Guide*, *IGN*, and *Review to a Kill*. Rob collects retro videogame consoles, vintage computers, and full-size arcade games, which he shares with his 3-year-old son. Rob graduated from Southern Nazarene University in 2005 with a BS in Organizational Leadership, and has an Associates Degree in Journalism. He is a Senior Network Engineer for Lockheed Martin, working for the Federal Aviation Administration.

- Matt Paprocki has played video games since he was five, but he began writing about them back in 1999 with his own fanzine titled *Gaming Source*. Once the cost became too much of a burden, he found the web site Digital Press (*http://www.digitpress.com*) and has been writing reviews for them ever since. His current total is over 500, covering a variety of consoles. He also editorializes on the games industry at his blog *http://www.breakingwindows.com*. His articles have been published in *G-Fan* magazine as well as the *Toledo City Paper*.

- Adam Pavlacka is a game industry veteran and international journalist who has spent the last thirteen years covering the electronic entertainment beat for print, broadcast, and online outlets. A technology geek with a serious case of wanderlust, Adam is always on the lookout for a new toy or a reason to travel. His latest project is *Hardcore Gamer Magazine* (*http://hardcoregamermag.com*). Launched at E3 2005, HGM is a true "gamer's magazine" that focuses on the latest technology while avoiding the cookie-cutter coverage commonly found in the enthusiast press.

- Jess Ragan started his own video game newsletter in the pre-Internet boom era of 1992, when print fanzines were the preferred outlet of expression for devoted gamers. During that time, he contributed countless articles to dozens of other fanzines. Like many of his peers, Jess has since migrated to the Web, doing freelance work for the upcoming GameTap service and posting his opinions of the latest industry trends on his web site, The Gameroom Blitz (*http://grblitz.overclocked.org*).

- Luke Sandel is a serious enthusiast of all things technological and mechanical. He is typically observed in his natural environment wielding a soldering iron, Dremel, or socket wrench. A longtime lurker on several videogame-related forums, he occasionally surfaces to provide technical advice or to offload a heap of modified game systems. He is currently employed in the "web design and programming, computer-based training interface design and programming, video production and non-linear video editing, systems administration, hardware troubleshooting and repair" industry, but he is always seeking new challenges and adventures. He lives in Michigan with his wife Kristy.

- Simon St. Laurent started with a Sinclair ZX-81 in sixth grade, and moved up to a Franklin ACE 1000 that devoured many hours of his youthful time. While he regrets the frightening amount of time he spent debugging spaghetti Applesoft and assembler code because he didn't know how to structure it any better, he still spent far too many enjoyable hours playing games and writing his own. Many years later, he's turned into an editor at O'Reilly Media, Inc.

- Carol Van Epps is a long-time gaming enthusiast. She is a former Full GameMaster for one of the longest running MUDs, DragonRealms, put out by Simutronics Corp (*http://www.play.net*).

Acknowledgements

I wrote this book during an exceptionally chaotic time in my life. I'd like to take this opportunity to thank my family and friends for supporting me during this strange series of events. This goes double for Simon Carless, who steered me toward this project in the first place.

Thanks also to my editor, Brian Jepson, who has shown extraordinary resilience, bouncing back with positive ideas and a can-do attitude every time I emailed him with the news of whatever disaster had befallen the book that week.

My heart goes out to chromatic and Jiji, who served as technical editors. As I sometimes have a hard time telling a stick of RAM from a stick of licorice (my doctor can back this up), this is an exceptionally trying job.

Last but not least, my undying admiration to the many people who carved valuable chunks of time out of their lives to contribute to *Retro Gaming Hacks*. Thanks to you, this book is, if you will, a potpourri of excitement.

Preface

A few months ago, I was playing a classic Game Boy game, in all its 15-year-old monochrome glory. But the version I was playing was markedly worse than what I remembered from 1989—it ran a little slowly, had some graphic glitches, and there was no sound. And it was one of the most impressive things I'd ever seen.

Why? Because I was playing it on the Sony PSP.

It had been a pretty amazing week. Intrepid, brilliant Japanese hackers had discovered a security loophole in Sony's new portable game console that let them run executable files off of the Memory Stick media. Within days—literally *days*—they'd progressed from a simple "Hello World" display to a program that emulated the Game Boy hardware. As we went to press on this book, there were PSP programs that played games from consoles like the Neo Geo and Turbo-Grafx CD. By the time you finally read these words, there will probably be software that lets you do much more.

This volume is dedicated to the appreciation, understanding, and application of just that sort of impressive hack. And you don't even have to skirt copyright law to do it—you'll find that public domain and freeware games exist for most gaming consoles. The creation of these so-called homebrew titles is in and of itself a retro gaming hack—and a damned impressive one at that! And if you want to try your hand at creating a Game Boy title of your own, you'll find tips and tricks to help you get started right here.

As for me, I like having the actual classic game hardware. The feel of hooking up a classic NES deck, blowing on the cartridge to get it to work right, shoving it into the ancient plastic, hearing the barely-audible clicks and hum of the television as it boots up (or doesn't... and we'll show you how to fix that). Getting hand cramps from the old rectangular controllers, then throwing those controllers around the room, knowing they were so durable they'd never break. (Try that with your PSP, and you won't be playing Game Boy games or anything else.)

Retro gaming isn't about clinging to the last remaining shreds of our fleeting youth. Well, it is, but not *entirely*. The old saying "they just don't make 'em like they used to" has never rung more true. Game design has changed, some say permanently. In the never-ending quest to make games more complex, controllers have been packed full of buttons and screens filled with reams of indecipherable information. Where is the charm, the wide appeal, the elegant simplicity of the games of yesteryear?

It's out there, if you know where to look. Read this book, and you will.

Why Retro Gaming Hacks?

The term *hacking* has an unfortunate reputation in the popular press, where it often refers to someone who breaks into systems or wreaks havoc with computers. Among enthusiasts, on the other hand, the term *hack* refers to a "quick and dirty" solution to a problem or a clever way to do something. The term *hacker* is very much a compliment, praising someone as being *creative* and having the technical chops to get things done. O'Reilly's Hacks series is an attempt to reclaim the word, document the good ways people are hacking (in a good way), and pass on the hacker ethic of creative participation to a new generation of hackers. Seeing how others approach systems and problems is often the quickest way to learn about a new technology.

Not to mention the fact that hacking is often the only way to enjoy the full and complete variety of classic gaming entertainment that once so filled our lives. If you want to play retro games today, odds are you're going to have to devise some creative solution. No single book can contain all the answers you're looking for, but this one will put you into the right state of mind.

How to Use This Book

We've divided this book along various topics, not according to any sense of relative difficulty. Skip around and flip through the book; if you see an interesting title or if some paragraph catches your eye, read it! If there's a prerequisite you need to know about, a cross-reference will guide you to the right hack.

How This Book Is Organized

The book is organized into several chapters, organized by subject:

Chapter 1, *Playing Retro Games*

> Get that old Atari out of the attic! If no Atari is to be found in your attic, get one off eBay. In this chapter you'll learn about playing with the "real thing," setting up classic game systems, fixing broken hardware, and getting good deals on buying games.

Chapter 2, *Playing Neo-Retro Games*

> You don't have to fuss with classic hardware if you don't want to. The hacks in this chapter cover new hardware and software that plays old games, whether on an all-in-one joystick or on the PlayStation 2.

Chapter 3, *Playing Arcade Games on Your Computer*

> You don't have space in your apartment for three thousand arcade machines. Or do you? In this chapter we'll cover MAME—the Multiple Arcade Machine Emulator—from all the angles, learning how to play classic arcade games on PC and other platforms.

Chapter 4, *Playing Classic Console Games*

> Emulators aren't just for arcade games. You can use these clever software programs to fool your computer into thinking that it's a Nintendo Entertainment System, Sega Genesis, or practically any other retro game console imaginable.

Chapter 5, *Playing with Early Personal Computers*

> For many of us, our first retro game experience wasn't in front of a console—it was hunched over the keyboard of a classic Apple][or Atari 800XL. In this chapter, we'll bring back those classic computers, showing you how to set them up or emulate them.

Chapter 6, *Playing with Text Adventures*

> Graphics? Who needs those? Some of the first computer games created a vivid, exciting, enthralling world using only the power of words. And many text adventures—now called *interactive fiction*—are still being created even today!

Chapter 7, *Playing with DOS*

> The user-friendliness of Windows XP is all well and good, but sometimes we long for the freedom of the cold, unfeeling C:\> prompt. We'll show you how to get DOS games to work properly under modern operating systems, or even get DOS up and running again.

Chapter 8, *Playing at Game Design*

Always wanted to make a video game? It's easier than ever with modern tools that let you craft retro-style entertainment with instant results. Even programming aficionados will learn plenty from this chapter.

Chapter 9, *Playing Around with Other Neat Stuff*

Some of our brilliant ideas just don't fit into the topics covered above. In this concluding potpourri of a chapter, we'll learn things such as how to hack around inside games, exploiting glitches and bugs to our advantage.

Conventions

The following is a list of the typographical conventions used in this book:

Italics

Used to indicate URLs, filenames, filename extensions, and directory (folder) names. For example, the path for the *Applications* folder in the *Developer* directory will appear as */Developer/Applications*.

`Constant width`

Used to show code examples, the contents of files, console output, as well as the names of variables, commands, and other code excerpts.

`Constant width bold`

Used to highlight portions of code, typically new additions to old code.

`Constant width italic`

Used in code examples and tables to show sample text to be replaced with your own values.

Gray text

Gray text is used to indicate a cross-reference within the text.

You should pay special attention to notes set apart from the text with the following icons:

This is a tip, suggestion, or general note. It contains useful supplementary information about the topic at hand.

This is a warning or note of caution, often indicating that your money or your privacy might be at risk.

The thermometer icons, found next to each hack, indicate the relative complexity of the hack:

beginner   moderate   expert

Using Code Examples

This book is here to help you get your job done. In general, you may use the code in this book in your programs and documentation. You do not need to contact us for permission unless you're reproducing a significant portion of the code. For example, writing a program that uses several chunks of code from this book does not require permission. Selling or distributing a CD-ROM of examples from O'Reilly books *does* require permission. Answering a question by citing this book and quoting example code does not require permission. Incorporating a significant amount of example code from this book into your product's documentation *does* require permission.

We appreciate, but do not require, attribution. An attribution usually includes the title, author, publisher, and ISBN. For example: "*Retro Gaming Hacks* by Chris Kohler. Copyright 2006 O'Reilly Media, Inc., 0-596-00917-8."

If you feel your use of code examples falls outside fair use or the permission given above, feel free to contact us at *permissions@oreilly.com*.

How to Contact Us

We have tested and verified the information in this book to the best of our ability, but you may find that features have changed (or even that we have made mistakes!). As a reader of this book, you can help us to improve future editions by sending us your feedback. Please let us know about any errors, inaccuracies, bugs, misleading or confusing statements, and typos that you find anywhere in this book.

Please also let us know what we can do to make this book more useful to you. We take your comments seriously and will try to incorporate reasonable suggestions into future editions. You can write to us at:

O'Reilly Media, Inc.
1005 Gravenstein Hwy N.
Sebastopol, CA 95472
(800) 998-9938 (in the U.S. or Canada)
(707) 829-0515 (international/local)
(707) 829-0104 (fax)

To ask technical questions or to comment on the book, send email to:

bookquestions@oreilly.com

The web site for *Retro Gaming Hacks* lists examples, errata, and plans for future editions. You can find this page at:

http://www.oreilly.com/catalog/retrogaminghks/

For more information about this book and others, see the O'Reilly web site:

http://www.oreilly.com

Safari Enabled

 When you see a Safari® Enabled icon on the cover of your favorite technology book, that means the book is available online through the O'Reilly Network Safari Bookshelf.

Safari offers a solution that's better than e-books. It's a virtual library that lets you easily search thousands of top tech books, cut and paste code samples, download chapters, and find quick answers when you need the most accurate, current information. Try it for free at *http://safari.oreilly.com*.

Got a Hack?

To explore Hacks books online or to contribute a hack for future titles, visit:

http://hacks.oreilly.com

Where to Read More

If you get to the end of this book and find yourself wishing that it wasn't over, there's hundreds more pages of retro gaming goodness to pore through!

There are many other volumes of information out there about retro gaming, whether your interest lies in hacking, collecting, playing, or all three.

Most of these books will be found at finer booksellers, though some are best purchased directly from the publisher. In these cases, I'll give you the appropriate URL.

Supercade

Van Burnham's book, fully titled *Supercade: A Visual History of the Videogame Age 1971-1984* (published by MIT Press) is an absolutely massive coffee-table-size extravaganza of glossy color pages featuring screens and tongue-in-cheek descriptions of every major arcade game of the retro age—as well as quite a few not-so-major ones!

Sadly, the original hardcover printing of the book, which cost $49.95, weighed in at about a hundred pounds, and had to be lifted by a team of midgets (who were included with each copy), is well out of print. But you can still buy Supercade today, in paperback, for the more reasonable price of $29.95. It's well worth it for all the information, humor, and nostalgic artwork packed into this giant tome.

Arcade Fever

John Sellers' book *Arcade Fever: The Fan's Guide to the Golden Age of Video Games*, is published by Running Press and is sort of like Supercade on the Atkins diet. Though its concept is similar—glossy color pictures and text concerning a wealth of classic arcade games—the execution differs in many ways. It's a lot lighter on the wallet and the arms, for example.

Also, whereas Supercade's focus was on the art design of the book and the pictures of the games, Arcade Fever is more concerned with the game reviews themselves, which are generally more detailed and filled with relevant historical data. There are also plenty of other types of features in the book, from interviews with industry luminaries like Atari founder Nolan Bushnell to sidebars featuring trivia and campy imagery from the retro days.

Digital Retro

Gordon Laing's *Digital Retro: The Evolution and Design of the Personal Computer*, is published by Sybex Inc. and does for classic computer hardware what Supercade did for classic arcade games: it combines a history of the early personal computer industry with large, detailed photographs of every piece of classic PC hardware you could think of.

What this book doesn't offer are images of the computer programs or games that ran on the systems, so this is a book for hardware enthusiasts only. The photographs are exceptional, however. It's the next best thing to owning a collection of the machines. (Or better, if you don't have a lot of closet space).

Videogames: In The Beginning

Though much has been written in video game history books about Ralph Baer—the inventor of the Magnavox Odyssey system [Hack #2] and thus the father of video games—why not get your information right from the source? Baer has set down the story of his inventions in *Videogames: In the Beginning*, published by Rolenta Press.

But stories aren't all this book offers. Over the years, Baer has been meticulous about saving his primary source documents, from the original notebook sketches he made of his "brown box" gaming apparatus to fascinating legal documents from the many lawsuits he filed against companies who lifted his patented brainstorms. This is a must-have addition to any video game historian's library. Speaking of which, it's best to order this book directly from publisher Leonard Herman (*http://www.rolentapress.com*).

Digital Press Collector's Guide

If you browse through the collectibles section of your local bookstore, you'll probably find a few different price guides that purport to let you know the value of your game collection. But the *Digital Press Collector's Guide* is the original and best retro game collectors' guide, published by classic gaming fanzine Digital Press.

What makes the *Digital Press Collector's Guide* so appealing is that it is written entirely by true lovers of retro games, writers who have lived and breathed Atari et al. since they were the cutting edge of technology. The editors of this book are the men on the front lines of classic game fandom, organizing the Classic Gaming Expo [Hack #1] and maintaining and updating the best database of classic game release information in the world.

Even if you're not particularly into collecting, this guide is a must-have resource for its exhaustive lists of software, hardware, and accessories for every major classic system from the Odyssey to the TurboGrafx-16. And you can flip through the guide to read personal reflections on the systems as well as collectors' stories of big finds and moments of glory. Though you can find the guide on Amazon, it's best to order it directly from the Digital Press web site (*http://www.digitpress.com*).

If you're still not satisfied, poke around on Amazon.com and see if you can find other books that strike your fancy. And if you fail at that, perhaps you should consider writing a retro gaming book of your own. There are still so many stories waiting to be told.

Playing Retro Games

Hacks 1–14

Ain't nothin' like the real thing, baby. While many if not most retro gaming hackers are getting their classic console fix through emulation these days, who can resist the allure of a wood grain–paneled Atari 2600? The satisfying rubbery feel of the joystick and candy-like single button? Ripping out the cartridge when you lose and throwing it across the room, knowing that its sturdy design will keep it intact even after it crashes into the wall?

In this chapter, we'll cover the ins and outs of playing original retro game consoles. You'll learn how to buy many different classic systems and how to set them up once you've got them home. There are even hacks on finding retro games from Japan and, once you have them, tricking your American consoles into playing them.

There are hacks for every budget—you'll learn about the expensive Holy Grails of retro game collecting, but also how to save money when you go game shopping, whether on online auction sites like eBay (*http://www.ebay.com*) or in the thrift store in your church's basement.

HACK #1 Buy Retro Games

Go shopping for classic videogames, online and offline.

It used to be so easy.

Anyone who's been collecting retro games for some time now remembers the heyday of the early 1990s. For that glorious half a decade, buying retro games on the cheap [Hack #14] was like taking candy from a baby. With the advent of the Super Nintendo and Genesis hardware, the Atari 2600 and its contemporaries were two generations old. '80s retro would not come into fashion for another decade. The Internet was but a gleam in the eye of Al Gore.

Nobody had any clue that people might one day pay big bucks for their old Colecovision. It was just an obsolete hunk of plastic taking up precious closet space, ready to be unloaded at the next neighborhood yard sale. But there was never any shortage of collectors ready to scoop them up. And it was hard to resist buying multiples of the same games and hardware—how could you resist buying yet another Atari 2600 when it was only ten bucks and came with thirty games?

But as more and more games and systems entered the possession of collectors (who were far less likely to sell them off on the cheap out of their own garages), as the '80s started to become cool again, and as the advent of online auction sites started to raise the prices of retro games, Atari systems and such started to disappear from the flea market. But it's still possible to get out there and buy some classic gaming goodness, and this hack will explain some general tips.

Online Shopping

The miracle of the Internet is how it brings people together across vast distances. Nowhere is this more apparent than in e-commerce. Buyers have the ultimate choice between sellers, and sellers have multiple buyers banging down their virtual doors.

eBay. Throughout this book, you'll see hack authors constantly referring back to eBay. And how could we not? The prototypical online auction site was founded in September 1995 and quickly became one of the most-visited sites on the Web. Millions of items are posted by independent sellers on the site every day, from the mundane to the unimaginably rare. You can find anything you want on eBay, and that is especially true for classic video games. Although many eBay listings are run in the traditional seven-day auction format in which the highest bid wins, many have a "Buy It Now" option that let you purchase the item immediately for a set price.

Early eBay sellers gained a reputation for "price gouging," and it is true that the auction-style formats did in some cases tend to inflate the price that rare (and sometimes not so rare) games would fetch. But as more and more people joined eBay to sell their stuff, prices began to fall in line with real market values. You needn't be afraid of eBay; indeed, in most cases it can be the best option for finding what you want in the condition you want. eBay and its subsidiary PayPal (an online credit card payment system that most sellers accept) have extensive buyer protection policies, so in fact you can be safer when bidding on an eBay listing than buying games from an independent online retailer.

There are plenty of books available that contain all sorts of general-interest eBay tips (e.g., *eBay Hacks*, published by O'Reilly). But here are some bits of information you may want to consider when buying video games.

Know what you're looking for

Browsing through eBay listings without knowing what games you want to buy isn't very effective. If you're looking for Colecovision games, searching for `colecovision` on eBay will lead to all sorts of different auctions, but they won't be categorized or alphabetized. Best to first find some information on the system and know what games you want to buy, then search for specific game titles.

Decide what condition you want your games to be in

If a seller lists a game but doesn't mention whether it includes the original box and instruction manual, then it almost definitely doesn't. This might not make any difference to you, especially considering that the inclusion of a box and manual may drive the price of a game up. But if you do want complete titles, make sure to search for them. One common abbreviation used is "CIB," which stands for "Cartridge, Instructions, Box."

Pay attention to pictures

Pictures can show you the condition of the game you're buying, but they also might just be scans of the game's box art found on the Web. If there's no digital camera shot showing the actual item being sold, then don't presume to know anything about its condition. On the other hand, you may want to look for auctions without pictures, as they tend to end with lower prices. Of course, in this case it is always a good idea to write to the seller and get a more detailed description of the game's condition.

Online retailers. In case you'd rather not deal with the nerve-wracking excitement of auctions, there are some web-based retailers selling retro games at a fixed price. Of note are Good Deal Games (*http://www.gooddealgames.com*), whose store features a wide selection of new and pre-owned retro games for most systems as well as some original homebrew titles, and Packrat Video Games (*http://www.packratvg.com*), which specializes in Atari products.

Digital Press' Links section has a list of web retailers that site users can rate. Sites that currently have a five-star rating include *www.atariace.com*, *www.worldofatari.com*, and *www.goatstore.com*. Another well-known site, the Web home of a retail store in New Jersey, is *www.videogameconnections.com*.

Private online trading. If you really want to save money, or prefer to trade your extra games straight up for new ones, you might consider visiting some Internet message boards that are devoted to giving private citizens the opportunity to sell their games privately. Sellers have the freedom of not having to pay eBay their cut of the profits, which they will (in theory) pass on to buyers in the form of lower prices.

The disadvantages are obvious: an unscrupulous seller might just run off with your cash or your end of the trade deal, and even if the seller is on the up and up, you are entirely at their mercy if you want to return the items (or if anything gets lost or damaged in the mail). If you're feeling brave and are familiar with newsgroups, *rec.games.video.marketplace* is a good place to start (try browsing it through Google at *http://groups-beta.google.com/group/ rec.games.video.marketplace*).

Some more reputable buy/sell forums, like the ones at Digital Press (*http:// www.digitpress.com*; click the "Forums" link) and Atari Age (*http://atariage. com/forums/*), will keep forum-goers apprised of good and bad trades that have taken place, as well as keep an eye on the posts. But even the best web sites still cannot take any responsibility if any mishaps occur from trades in their forums.

Offline Shopping

As convenient as it is to shop online, there's still a lot to be said for the instant gratification and browsing opportunities you get by buying in person.

Retail stores. GameStop stores no longer buy and sell games for systems older than the PSone, but some EB Games (aka Electronics Boutique) outlets do. Still, their selection is limited and they do not buy or sell any games for retro systems other than the NES, SNES, and Genesis.

A better idea is to try searching the Web or your local Yellow Pages for independently-run game retailers. Since they are not under the thumb of wide-ranging corporate decisions, they are free to buy and sell any game or system they feel like. Well-known independent game stores that stock retro games include Multimedia 1.0 in New York City (*http://www.videogamedeals.com/ page_info.php/pages_id/2/pages_name/About%20Us*) and GameDude in North Hollywood (*http://www.gamedude.com/*).

Gaming conventions. If you can take a trip out to one of the many conventions devoted to classic video games that are held annually across the country, you'll get the best of both worlds: dealers with wide selections of wares who set up large booths on the expo floor, and "swap meets" filled with people just like you who bring boxes and backpacks full of unwanted games and hardware to sell and trade.

The most popular West Coast convention is Classic Gaming Expo (*http:// www.cgexpo.com*), which for many years took place in downtown Las Vegas but now happens every August in the San Francisco Bay Area. On the East Coast, Philly Classic (*http://www.phillyclassic.com*) has filled the Valley Forge Convention Center each spring (although the 2005 show is scheduled for the fall).

Other regional shows have included the Oklahoma Video Game Exhibition (*http://www.okge.com*), CinciClassic (*http://www.cinciclassic.com/*), Austin Gaming Exposition (*http://www.austingamingexpo.com/*), MAGFest in Virginia (*http://www.magfest.org/*), Midwest Gaming Classic in Milwaukee (*http://www.midwestgamingclassic.com/*), and Northwest Classic Games Enthusiasts Expo in Seattle (*http://www.nwcge.org/*).

Thrift stores. Think thrift stores are just a place to dump your unwanted junk? Think again. Sure, Goodwill and Salvation Army stores might not be in the cleanest or most attractive retail locations, but some people's "unwanted junk" might be in the form of retro games. The upside to thrift stores is the same as the downside—the employees pricing the items that come in usually don't have a clue what retro games are worth.

This can be good if they get in good quality stuff and price it very low—a box full of loose Sega Master System games for a quarter apiece, for example. But it can be awful if they get the idea that anything related to video games is high-tech and expensive—a shelf full of Atari 2600 commons for $6.99 each is not an unfamiliar sight. And you can't bargain them down any more than you could get a Wal-Mart cashier to knock a few bucks off your TV set.

Flea markets/Tag sales/Yard sales/Garage sales/etc. Wait, wasn't I just saying that flea markets and the like have dried up as a source of retro games? In large part, yes, but not entirely. If you've got the energy to get up early in the morning on a Saturday, driving around looking for garage sales (or just heading out to the local flea market) can reward you with some great finds. Check your local newspaper that morning or the day before to see about flea markets or yard sales in your area.

One point of advice is that you can and should bargain with your neighbors. Anyone who's held a garage sale before expects it. So go ahead and aim low. They'll meet you in the middle. Another important point of advice is, if you don't see any video games and you're at someone's residence, ask! Many people just don't imagine that their old video games might actually sell out on their front lawns.

Who knows... you might still get lucky.

Collect Original "Pong" Systems

HACK
#2   Play with two paddles and a block for maximum value.

In an early episode of "That 70's Show," the teenaged characters sit around a thirteen-inch television screen playing a game of Pong, marveling, mouths agape at the advance of high technology. Most of the modern-day audience laughed along at the concept of two lines and a dot on a TV screen being the pinnacle of scientific advance. But if you found yourself not laughing but seriously contemplating playing a game of Pong, this hack is for you. There's something appealing about breaking out the most retro of retro games, and you can still do it on the (relatively) cheap.

Odyssey

Actually, let's put "cheap" on hold for a bit to talk about the very first video game system. Invented by a brilliant engineer named Ralph Baer who had spent the last 15 years working on military projects, the Odyssey was released by Magnavox in 1972 (though Baer had completed the prototype in 1966). It played not only line-and-dot video tennis but also many other games that required only a line and dot. Magnavox failed to sell many of the systems, so the Odyssey is now a high-priced collector's item.

And it gets worse. Because Magnavox didn't think ball-and-dot gameplay on its own was enough to satisfy consumers in the age of color TV, a whole mess of accessories was included with the original Odyssey package—about three hundred pieces in all! Color overlays were included that stuck onto television sets to produce translucent "backgrounds"; some games were board games that used the television display for crude accompaniment but required stacks of Monopoly-style money; some games required sets of cards and dice. All this was included in the box with an Odyssey system, so if you do find one for sale, be sure that the asking price is commensurate with its completeness! An exhaustive list of accessories can be found at *http:// fusionanomaly.net/odyssey.html*.

There were "game cartridges" released for the Odyssey, but it is not considered to be a programmable system. The cartridges were simply circuit boards with no ROM chips that made the machine's dot-and-line setup respond differently to player controls. A light rifle, called Shooting Gallery, was available; it can fetch nearly the price of the system itself (each should go for about $100-150 in incomplete, used condition).

Will the Real Pong Please Stand Up?

If you search on eBay for pong system you'll get lots of auctions for ancient game hardware that is not, technically, Pong. The name is a trademark of Atari, who partnered with Sears to release the original home Pong system in 1975, after the success of the arcade game. That system (called Tele-Games Pong) is difficult to find, but many of the official successors to the machine (which featured more variations on the game, color graphics, and other upgrades) are a little easier to hunt down for between $20 and $40 each. Some examples of these are Super Pong, Tele-Games Pong Sports IV, Hockey-Pong, Ultra Pong, etc.

Although the original Odyssey bombed, Magnavox caught on to the Pong craze and began to release a line of scaled-down systems using the Odyssey name. The Odyssey 100, 200, 300, and 400 were released between 1975 and 1976; the 2000, 3000, and 4000 followed later. Some display in black-and-white while some display in color, and the outer shells of the system and the games they play also differ, but all play variations on TV table tennis.

But many other companies released their own Pong-inspired hardware in the years following the successful Christmas 1975 introduction of home Pong. And if you don't mind that your game of line-and-dot doesn't have the Atari name on it, you can pick one up quite cheaply. One historically significant yet not heavily sought-after line of systems is Coleco's Telstar series. Search for coleco telstar on eBay and you'll pull up all sorts of auctions that can be won for ten dollars or less. Other companies that produced their own generic Pong knockoffs include Zenith, Sharp, RadioShack, and K-Mart (!).

Being an Informed Consumer of Pong Stuff

While many "Pong" systems support AC adapters, these were usually sold as optional accessories. You may have to power them up with a bunch of C or D batteries, so be aware of this as you browse for a system to buy. Also, find out how the system hooks up to a television. Some may use standard RF connectors [Hack #3] but some (like the Odyssey systems) use proprietary hardware, so make sure a switch is included with the system when you buy it.

Also be aware of the system's controllers. The higher-priced systems back in the day didn't necessarily feature more games in the hardware, but they did have more comfortable, removable control dials. The cheaper ones had both dials attached to the body of the machine, which means that you and your sparring partner might have to get a little closer than you'd like. The prices of these cheaper systems might have originally been separated from the more expensive products by a hundred dollars or more. But today the difference is only two or three bucks, if that.

And that brings up the final point: many of these systems are for two players only! That means that you won't be able to play them alone. Some later models like the Odyssey 2000 do feature single-player modes, so be sure you're getting one that does if you plan on solitary play. If there are pictures in the auction or you are examining a unit up close in real life, look for a "Players" switch to see if it will allow you to compete against a computer-controlled paddle. Honestly, the things you kids take for granted these days...

HACK #3 Buy and Run an Atari 2600
Hook yourself up with the most classic of classics, the VCS.

Maybe you sold it at your own garage sale. Maybe your mom threw it away while you were at college. Maybe you were too young to own one in the first place. Whatever the reason, you've found yourself wanting an Atari once again. Yes, the very first video game company did produce many different consoles, but when I say "an Atari" you know what I'm talking about: the Video Computer System, a.k.a. the VCS, a.k.a. the 2600, a.k.a. the Atari.

For the purposes of this hack, I'm assuming that you're not interested in the collections for PlayStation 2 and Xbox that let you play emulated versions of classic games [Hack #16], nor are you interested in the popular standalone consoles that plug directly into your modern-day television's AV inputs and play from a selection of classic games [Hack #15]. No, you want the real thing, whether for nostalgic reasons or to play the games you remember that, for licensing reasons, will never, ever, be included on Atari Anthology, like the execrable E.T. or the 2600 versions of Pac-Man and Donkey Kong.

Well, then: here's how you're going to do it.

A Bit of History

Though the company was doing well with the success of the Pong arcade game as well as Home Pong [Hack #2] and knew that their new machine, code-named "Stella," could transform video games into an even bigger business, Atari did not have the capital to launch the new platform. So founder Nolan Bushnell decided to sell the company to Time Warner, staying on as chairman of the board.

Time Warner's corporate culture clashed with the iconoclastic Atari, but without their money it is doubtful that Stella would have become the Atari

Video Computer System. When it launched in 1977 it was not the very first programmable system (i.e., a game system in which the software was stored not within the console itself but on interchangeable cartridges that were sold separately), but it was the one that set the industry on fire.

At first, only Atari provided cartridges for the machine. But soon, some of the company's designers began to become frustrated with working conditions under Time Warner and quit to form their own startups, providing independent software support for the VCS. Once companies like Activision and Imagic blazed the trail for "third-party" software development, dozens of small-time publishers started producing Atari cartridges and accessories en masse. This makes having a "complete" Atari 2600 collection nearly impossible.

Buying an Atari

Of course, you'll need two major things—hardware and software. In each of those categories, however, you'll want to make sure you cover all your bases.

Necessary hardware parts. Here's what you'll need:

The console itself
> Although there are quite a few different revisions of the hardware with minor internal and external changes, for the purposes of this discussion I will stick with the two major versions. The original iteration of the system was shaped like a mask worn by a hypothetical duckbilled Darth Vader, with a woodgrain-paneled front (so as to fit in with the ugliness of the average 1977 living room). This is labeled with Video Computer System on its face.
>
> The second is the Atari 2600, a.k.a. the Atari 2600 Jr., a redesigned, tinier version of the system released in the late 1980s as Atari rode the coattails of Nintendo's success. Differences between the two are purely aesthetic as they play the same games, use the same power supply, etc. Ironically, although the Jr. is the rarer of the two, the original system commands a higher price. Nostalgia at its best.

A power supply
> The 2600 used a unique power supply. The part number was CO16353, and it featured 9v/500ma output and 110/120 VAC input. What distinguishes it physically from your average AC adapter is the plug it uses to connect to the 2600, which is small, like a Walkman headphone plug. It is incompatible with practically every other video game system, so be sure you are buying the right part.

A TV/Game Switch or equivalent

Unlike the power supply, the RF switch (the bit that hooks your Atari up to the television) included with the 2600 was a standard, nearly universal piece of hardware. You can buy them today for about ten dollars at brick-and-mortar RadioShack stores or online at *www.radioshack.com;* the catalog number is 15-1268. This uses the classic-style plastic switch that you have to flip yourself by reaching around the back of the television. If you'd prefer an automatic switch, you can have one for a mere three dollars more (catalog no. 15-1267).

Be aware that although the RadioShack adapters feature 75 ohm output (in layman's terms, the familiar cable that runs into the back of your TV set), the adapters that shipped with the 2600 only featured 300 ohm output (two little U-shaped bits of metal that were fitted onto screws that have since been removed from modern TV sets). So unless you're using a very old TV you will need a new adapter.

There is a slightly more elegant solution, if somewhat restrictive. RadioShack catalog number 278-255, called the Standard "F" Connector, is a tiny connector that directly links the phono plug on the 2600 and your TV's VHF input. This is a much cleaner-looking result, the downside being that you can only connect one console at a time and cannot pass your cable television connection through. If you have a television reserved for classic gaming, this may be your best bet.

Controllers of both types.

Strange as it may seem these days—when game consoles ship with a bare minimum of included accessories—the Video Computer System's standard package included two standard joysticks and a pair of "paddles" with dial controls. You'll want both to fully enjoy the system's library of games. The paddle controllers are necessary for playing Pong-style contests, and since two paddles share one controller input you can easily play doubles Pong with an extra set of paddles.

The 2600 Jr. shipped with only one standard controller. What cheapskates they had become in only a decade. Of course, the system retailed for about a sixth of the price of the VCS.

What games to buy. There are no games built into the VCS, so you will need at least one cartridge. Since so many were made, the odds are overwhelmingly in your favor that when you buy a VCS—whether online, at a thrift store, or wherever—some games will come along with it. Should you strike out on your own and want to beef up your collection with classics that are both enjoyable and very inexpensive (no more than a dollar or two for the bare cartridge), here is a starter list.

Adventure

> I would stop short of calling Adventure "the origin of video role-playing games," though many do. Regardless of how much historical and cultural significance is given to Warren Robinette's saga of a dot that defeats three dragons and recovers a chalice from a castle, it is still a fun and charming game.

Donkey Kong

> This is actually quite a terrible rendition of Shigeru Miyamoto's career-launching masterpiece of an arcade game, but worth having in your collection if only for laughs. Mario, Pauline, and DK are rendered as the formless blobs seen in Figure 1-1, and only the barest essence of the gameplay remains. It probably made Miyamoto cry.

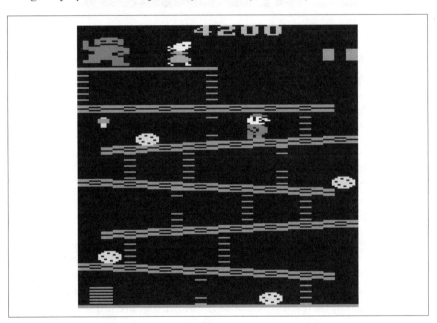

Figure 1-1. Donkey Kong for the Atari 2600

Jr. Pac-Man

> The original Pac-Man on the 2600 was afwul and probably single-handedly kicked off the great crash of 1983. But Jr. Pac-Man, released in 1987? That was some good stuff. It's interesting to see how much power designers could crank out of the 2600, seven years later (see Figure 1-2).

Yar's Revenge

> If you ever hear anyone slander Atari designer Howard Scott Warshaw for his work on E.T., wave this game in their face! Perhaps the best original title released on the 2600 (i.e., not based on an existing arcade game

or licensed property), Yar's Revenge was a fun outer-space shooter with some clever design ideas.

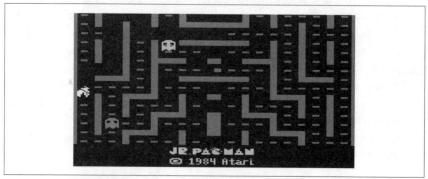

Figure 1-2. Jr. Pac-Man for the Atari 2600

What to ask the seller. If you're buying a system at a tag sale or thrift store, you're taking your chances that it won't work when you get it home. Them's the breaks. The advantage is that you'll be paying a lot less. (Or at least you should be. Ever visit a garage sale where things are marked at prices they'd be lucky to fetch on eBay? Put the pipe down!)

But if you're buying a console online, sight unseen, you do have the right and the obligation to ask the seller questions about the system's condition. Luckily, the VCS is a rather sturdily built piece of equipment, so it's rare that you'll run across one that is well and truly broken. But you should ask if the system has been tested.

Moreover, you should ask *how* it has been tested! Did the seller simply plug the system in and see if it powered up? Did he insert every controller and test them as well? Do all the switches on the machine function properly? And if it comes with an assortment of games but only one set of controllers, you should ask if there are any games in the lot that are unplayable without special controllers (the necessary controller type is written on the game labels, so the seller will be able to tell you).

Obviously, you don't want to appear to be an annoying, untrusting, perfectionist brat. Just be sure to email the seller to get a handle on how he treats his merchandise (and his customers) and you will save yourself some hassle in the long run.

Running an Atari

If you have everything listed earlier, setting up the 2600 should be a snap. You'll notice that the VCS has the wire that connects to the television switch box hardwired into the body of the unit, but the 2600 Jr. does not (so make sure that is included when you buy it as well, or it will necessitate another trip to RadioShack). Plug that into your switch box and plug the switch box into the VHF input on your television set. (If it has a manual switch, make sure it is set to GAME.) Plug the whole mess of wires into the wall socket and cross your fingers.

Common troubleshooting issues. If these steps do not immediately work, be sure that your television is set on either channel 3 or 4—that's the actual television set, *not* your VCR or cable box or satellite dish receptor or what-have-you. In these modern days, we rarely change the actual channel on our actual television sets. Go ahead and give it a try. Also, check the back of the 2600 console for a Channel 3/Channel 4 switch. If the image or sound quality is bad on one channel, try another.

If the image is in black-and-white and you're *sure* you have a color TV set, locate the Color/BW switch on the 2600 unit itself. Flip that and you should be seeing the game in three or four glorious, vivid, living colors.

Also, if you find that your paddle controllers don't seem to work properly—instead of moving smoothly, your vertical line in Pong is jittering and skipping all over the place—you can fix the paddles if you have some degree of technical expertise (or don't care if you ruin the things because they only cost a buck). See Hack 4, "Use Atari Paddles with Your PC" from *Gaming Hacks* (O'Reilly) for a brief tutorial on de-jittering your precious paddles for prettier, precision Pong play.

 Buy and Run Later Classic Consoles

HACK
#4

Get your hands on some underappreciated classics.

I'll be frank. I'm not much of an Atari 2600 fan [Hack #3]. Not that I don't enjoy a good game of E.T. every now and again, but my personal retro gaming tastes run a bit more eclectic. And hey, why restrict yourself to the VCS when there are plenty of other consoles out there for around the same price? Put in a couple hundred bucks and you could amass ten thousand 1981 dollars' worth of electronics; the fever-dream of every bellbottomed schoolboy.

 Many of the tips and pointers in the preceding hack [Hack #3] will apply to the purchase and setup of most of the consoles mentioned in this one, so I'm going to concentrate on the things that differ—non-standard accessories, unique pitfalls, etc.

Mattel Intellivision

There were other video game systems on the market when traditional toys giant Mattel threw their hat into the ring in 1979, but the Intellivision (short for "intelligent television," don't you know) was the first major competitor to the 2600. Mattel ran comparison advertisements on TV directly attacking the 2600's admittedly lesser graphics capabilities, and Atari fired back with ads demeaning the Intellivision's lack of arcade hits.

And they were both right! But they each took steps to remedy these deficiencies—Atari by introducing its RealSports line that looked and played better than their earlier efforts (but not as good as Intellivision Baseball, etc.) and Mattel by introducing some original shooters like Astrosmash. Intellivision Donkey Kong is just plain awful, though, and not in a funny way. They made Donkey Kong *green* for some reason.

The vast majority of Intellivision games shipped with "overlays," thin printed sheets of acetate that slid into the number pad on the system's controller and showed you which buttons did what. Many games are playable without the overlays, but some more complicated ones are next to impossible if you don't know the button assignments. If you're missing any, printable-quality scans of overlays are catalogued at *www.intvfunhouse.com*.

There are a multitude of different Intellivision console variations to choose from. Your best bet is to buy an original wood-and-gold Intellivision (also released by RadioShack as the Tandyvision One and by Sears as the Sears Super Video Arcade). Its power supply is internal, which means you'll have no ugly black box taking up space on your wall outlet. And the power cord—not to mention both controllers—is hardwired into the console, so there's no chance of losing them. Of course, this means that if you come across an Intellivision with broken controllers or frayed cords, you won't be able to replace them. A much later release, called the INTV System III, is nearly identical to the original but with a black and silver color scheme and an LED that indicates whether the power is on.

The black sheep of the family is the pure white Intellivision II. It leaves a much smaller footprint and the controllers are replaceable (though extras are hard to find). The disadvantages are that it is incompatible with a few games (including Donkey Kong, which maybe is not such a bad thing), and that the AC adapter is external and non-standard, meaning that you won't be able to replace it at RadioShack. Oh, and you have to hold the Power button for three seconds to turn it off, which should be a deal-breaker for easily frustrated gamers (like this author) who like having the option to *smack* the console's power off. (Why Sony adopted this vile method for the PlayStation 2 and PSP I will never understand.)

> The hard-to-find System Changer add-on hardware for the Intellivision II lets you play Atari 2600 games on the system. It is incompatible with the original Intellivision systems.

Colecovision

Of the "golden age" systems, Coleco's 1982 entry is my favorite. It was the high-end powerhouse of its day; where Atari and Intellivision claimed to replicate the arcade experience, Colecovision was the first system to really do it. Securing an exclusive license from Nintendo to port their hit arcade titles to the system, Coleco packed a copy of Donkey Kong in with each and every unit. Though it wasn't entirely faithful to the arcade title, the difference between it and the 2600 and Intellivision versions that Coleco later produced is like night and day.

Coleco didn't stop there. The company secured even more arcade hits from popular makers, publishing many of them under their own label: Data East's Bump 'n Jump and Burgertime, Sega's Congo Bongo and Space Fury, Midway's Tapper and Spy Hunter, and Universal's Mr. Do! and Ladybug. Most of these games are relatively easy to find.

Like the Intellivision, the Colecovision has a bay at the top where its controllers are stored; unlike the Intellivision the controllers are removable and replaceable. Some, but not many, Colecovision games used overlays for the controller's numerical pad. Since the system's top hits were based on arcade games that only used one or two buttons, there was little need for overlays.

The gigantic power supply is external, detachable, and proprietary, so make sure it is included when you buy the system. There were a few accessories for the system that are not especially rare: a plastic steering wheel and pedal that included Sega's Turbo arcade game, and a pair of Super Action Controllers that featured comfortable grips and large buttons and included Super Action Baseball in the box. Last but not least, Expansion Module #1 let you play all Atari 2600 games on the Colecovision.

And if you do come across an ADAM computer at a flea market, know that it can play Colecovision games. It was an awful computer even at the time of its release—it was buggy, slow, and useless—but in a pinch it can serve as a Colecovision.

Atari 5200

To defend against the onslaught of high-powered competitors, Atari released the 5200 a few months after the Colecovision in 1982. Although it occupied a much more stylized (and absolutely gigantic) form factor, the innards of the 5200 were nearly identical to Atari's line of 8-bit computers such as the 400. This resulted in a pretty high-powered system, able to more than keep up with the Colecovision graphically.

So why does it usually get little more than a footnote in gaming history? Because of its awful controllers. Like the Intellivision and the Colecovision before it, the 5200 added a numerical keypad to the controller; the games of course featured overlays, although few really needed them. But this wasn't the death knell—the analog joystick was. Though the concept was interesting (and indeed would take off when Nintendo added a stick to the Nintendo 64's controller in 1996), the 5200's stick was not self-centering, meaning that the player had to manually bring it back to the center. The market for 5200 joysticks from third-party manufacturers boomed for a while.

> If you find yourself frustrated with the standard controller, but really love your 5200, you might consider buying a new product called the Redemption 5200 (*http://www.atariage. com/store/index.php?cPath=22_76*). It is available in three versions, and lets you use 2600, Sega Master System, Sega Genesis, Atari 7800, and PC joystick controllers with the 5200, breathing new life into old games.

Although all 5200 models look alike at first glance, there is one important difference to keep in mind. Earlier models of the system, which had four controller ports, used a single cord to do two things: receive power and transmit the RF signal to the television set. This cord was, luckily, hardwired into the system; however, the special adapter that split the signal into power and RF was not, and the system is useless without it. If you find a version with two controller ports on the front, it uses separate cables for power and RF (and will work with any TV/Game switch).

What was the deal with numerical keypads and overlays, anyway? One explanation is that it made the video game system look more like a computer without the expense of adding an entire keyboard. This led parents to believe they were purchasing something that their child might someday use to learn programming. Indeed, some systems such as the Atari 2600 and Odyssey2 did feature add-on software that let users program in BASIC, but it was a tremendous chore that rarely if ever resulted in useful programs.

Thus, all the keypad really did was make the controllers awkward to hold in the hand. Amazingly, the Atari Jaguar system, released in 1996, had a numerical keypad and overlays on its oversized standard controller. (In another ill-advised throwback it even used a manual old-style TV/Game Switch.)

Atari 7800

The super-powered 7800 was intended from the beginning to be the successor to the 2600. It might have worked, too, had Atari executives not rushed out the 5200 to compete with the Colecovision and Intellivision. Work on the 7800 continued and the system was readied for a release in 1984. But Atari then made the ill-fated decision to dump video games entirely and concentrate solely on personal computers.

And then Nintendo happened, and Atari was shaken out of its lull by the fact that the video game market was now bigger than it had ever been under their watch. Looking at their stock of 2600 and 7800 merchandise that had been manufactured but never shipped, they jumped back on the bandwagon. So in 1986, Atari put its 1984 inventory on the shelves. They probably made a decent amount of money, but the 7800 didn't have a snowball's chance in hell against the onslaught of the NES.

The 7800 uses a standard TV/Game switch but a unique AC adapter, so be sure the system you're buying has one included. One advantage to the 7800 is that it is backwards compatible with 2600 cartridges without the use of an adapter. The joysticks, while notoriously painful after a few hours of play, were better than the 5200's. And though the system's software catalog was small, the games are still generally easy to find. You can order brand new, sealed 7800 titles for $5 each through O'Shea Ltd (*http://www.oshealtd. com*), though there is a minimum order of 12 games. Be sure to check out Ninja Golf!

Play with Power: Set Up an NES

Discover Nintendo-mania all over again.

If you were born during the early '80s, the hacks at the beginning of this chapter probably aroused little more than a curious interest in the back of your brain. Yes, you might have some vague memories of the Atari days. But most of your brainpower circa 1983 was probably spent mastering the complexities of toilet training and shoelace tying.

Thinking about the Nintendo Entertainment System, however, probably produces different results more akin to a burning desire to replay everything you used to have when you were a kid—then find all the games you wanted but never had enough allowance to buy. Well, good news: with some stand-out collectible exceptions, NES games are now cheaper than ever. Be aware: there is no one flawless solution for playing Nintendo games. But there are more than enough options to choose from that you should be able to find the NES hardware to suit your needs.

First, Some World History

When the Famicom (the Japanese version of the NES) was released in 1983, it looked a lot like a traditional video game system. Small cartridges plugged into the top of the unit, which was painted a toy-like red and white. This was perfectly acceptable in Japan, where the video game market was healthy, if relatively untapped—though a great number of different consoles, both imported and domestic, had been released, none had caught on like the 2600 did in the US.

But when it came time for Nintendo to launch the Famicom in the US, the industry crash of 1983 had soured retail buyers on video games. So Nintendo had to dress up the Famicom. It wasn't a video game system, it was an entertainment system. It included a light gun controller and an amusing plastic robot accessory (both sold separately in Japan). And it didn't use brightly colored cartridges that plugged into the top of the system like the Atari—it used *game paks* that slid all the way into the front of the unit, then locked down inside in a manner that, when you thought about it, vaguely resembled a....

"Toaster" NES

The gambit worked, and the original model NES (actually known as the Control Deck) became one of the hottest consumer items of the decade. As such, the so-called *toaster* model is the easiest to find today. They are abundant on eBay and stacked to the high ceiling at garage sales. They are also almost invariably broken.

As it turns out, as fun as the lock-down loading was, every time we pushed a game in it was wearing out the internal mechanism. Every NES owner knows that within a few years, the system would start to refuse to boot certain games, and soon enough nearly every attempt to put a game in would be greeted with a blinking power light and a green or blue failure screen.

Though this was sometimes by dirt on the cartridge contacts, it was more because the connectors inside the NES were beginning to bend and wear. Be aware if you do buy an original NES that it will almost certainly have this issue, which may cause you to have to attempt to boot games many times before they load. If this makes you feel incredibly nostalgic, then go ahead. If you'd rather avoid it, there is a cheap and relatively simple way to fix your NES deck for good [Hack #6].

The NES originally shipped with an automatic RF switch as well as the then very high-tech A/V cables. (Since many TV sets at this time did not feature A/V inputs, most people plugged in their NES systems through their VCRs.) It also shipped with a power adapter that is fairly easy to replace, but is so common that you should probably not bother buying a deck without one. The Control Deck was sold in a few different configurations; the robot, called ROB, is difficult to find nowadays but the Zapper light gun was included with most NES packages. The system generally shipped with two controllers.

"Toploader" NES

After the introduction of the Super Nintendo in 1991, Famicom and NES sales were still going strong; but, both the U.S. and Japanese versions of the hardware were beginning to show their age. Although the original version of the NES featured A/V output as well as RF, the Famicom did not. And U.S. toaster decks were beginning to break down more and more.

So in Japan, Nintendo introduced what they called the AV Famicom—a redesigned unit that replaced the original's RF switch with AV outputs. (For more information, see [Hack #8].) A version of the system was released in the US, but its aim was to eliminate the booting problems that older NES decks faced. Priced at a very attractive $49.99, the new Control Deck was sold until 1994, when Nintendo discontinued it.

Not that many toploader systems were sold, and in stark contrast to the price of the original NES (which started at $99.99 and has since dropped to about ten dollars or less), the new model systems routinely sell for over

$100. This is even considering the flaws of the hardware—unlike the Japanese system that spawned it, it features *only* RF output and no A/V support, and light vertical lines can be seen in the unit's video output.

Many people hunt down toploaders for reasons both practical and collectible; it is coveted as a rare piece of Nintendo merchandise and it will always reliably boot games. If you do decide to buy one, note that it originally shipped with one redesigned control pad, colloquially called a *dogbone* (probably by the same clever people who named the original system a toaster). You can have a toploader cheaper if it ships with the dirt-common normal NES controllers, but it's not complete without the "dogbone."

 Oh... and if you're one of those dirty cheaters, your Game Genie won't fit into the toploader's cartridge slot. Manufacturer Galoob did release adapters that allow its usage, but they are very rare today since they were only sent out on request when a customer complained.

Neo-Fami and Yobo

In 2004, after Nintendo stopped producing Famicom hardware, a Japanese firm called GameTech stepped up to provide their own solution. The company had already achieved some notoriety by releasing attachments that let you play your Game Boy Advance games on a television set (this was before Nintendo's own Game Boy Player let you do the same thing with much better results) and watch broadcast television on your GBA system.

Their latest product, sold in most Japanese electronics stores, was called the Neo Fami. Although the video quality of the hardware was not as sharp as the original and standard Famicom controllers could not be used with the system (it shipped with two controllers that used an Atari-style nine-pin connection), it was well received by Famicom aficionados worldwide. You can buy Neo-Fami systems in different colors at import shops, such as Play-Asia (*http://www.play-asia.com*).

If you want to play American and/or European NES games on the Neo-Fami, however, you will need an adapter. A Honeybee adapter, as described in "Buy Retro Games from Japan" **[Hack #9]**, will suffice, but they are hard to track down. Lik-Sang (*http://www.lik-sang.com*) offers its own adapters for $9.90 each at the time of this writing.

If your local shopping mall has one of those "As Seen On TV" outlet stores that have been popping up recently, you may want to look around it to see if you can find Neo Fami systems being sold under the name Yobo FC Game Console. These are also available at the Hawaii-based retailer Toys 'N Joys (*http://www.toysnjoys.com*) for the low price of $30 and include the Famicom–NES adapter in the box.

> At many shopping malls across the country, especially around Christmas, you may see kiosks selling all-in-one game systems, usually shaped like a Nintendo 64 controller, that have Famicom games built in. Do not confuse these with the legal Neo Fami units—they are illegal. They are not produced by Nintendo and therefore the makers do not have the rights to include copyrighted video game software inside the system.

HACK #6 — Make Your NES Work Like New

Defeat the "blue screen" by installing a new 72-pin connector.

In 1985, Nintendo broke into the U.S. home electronics market with the release of the Nintendo Entertainment System [Hack #5]. The NES's slick gray design blended in with existing audio-video equipment, and featured a unique front slot-loading cartridge system. Unfortunately, as many of us who were lucky enough to own an NES have come to realize, Nintendo's choice of form over function was ill-fated. Slowly but surely, NES consoles became worn-out and refused to boot cartridges, the primary symptoms of which were the infamous flashing red power light and solid blue error screen. In this hack you'll learn how to get your NES working properly.

The Dying Process

This problem starts off slowly, occurring only a small percentage of the time. During these early stages of decrepitude, blowing air into the system and the cartridge usually gets just enough dust off the contacts to allow the game to load correctly. After a while, the problem starts to show up more often, and becomes a little more difficult to fix. Blowing on the contacts begins to lose its effectiveness.

Many companies, Nintendo included, provided cleaning kits for the system that included an applicator that fit into the games and console along with an alcohol-based cleaning solution. NES Cleaning Kits were more expensive than blowing on the contacts, but were also much more effective (and safer, as the alcohol solution would not degrade the connectors over time like a person's breath would). A clean cartridge and a clean system meant that loading errors were virtually eliminated, but not for long.

Even if you took excellent care of your games and system and they never needed cleaning, NES decks would routinely break down. This is because, although dirt and dust could indeed cause loading errors, the real problem was the lock-and-load cartridge slot. The front-loading mechanism differed from earlier game systems because the cartridge was not forced directly into the system. Instead, the user gently slid the cartridge in, then locked it down with a similar gentle touch. Pushing the cartridge down locked it into position and applied some pressure between the cartridge's contacts and the 72-pin connector.

Over time, the pressure applied to the 72-pin connector began to bend the pins. The bent pins meant that the connection between the two sets of contacts was not as tight as it was when the system was brand new. Thus, while removing all traces of dirt from the contacts could sometimes help this problem, the cleaning systems became less and less effective as the pins continued to bend. Successfully loading a cartridge into the NES became an art form, and kids traded their secret techniques. One especially effective method was to wedge something in between the cartridge and the top of the slot, but of course over time this caused the pins to bend even more.

At the time, not much could be done besides buying a new system [Hack #5]. But now, luckily, there are several companies producing replacement 72-pin connectors that cost around $10. The contacts on the new connectors are made from a different type of metal that is more resistant to corrosion than the originals. The new connectors are easy to install, and will make your old NES work like new. Here are a few sites that stock new connectors. You can also find them on the Internet, and eBay, by searching for "NES 72 pin connector."

> www.estarland.com
> www.playerschoicegames.com
> www.hitgaming.com

Installing the New Connector

Although it might sound difficult, replacing the 72-pin connector is actually a quick and easy process. The only tool that you will need is a Phillips head screwdriver. Before opening your NES, make sure that all of the cables have been unplugged from the system. Also, keep in mind that static electricity can cause damage to the circuitry, so take care to ground yourself before handling any of the electronics. Here's what you need to do:

1. Remove the top system cover. Begin by turning the system upside down, as shown in Figure 1-3, to gain access to the screws. The six screws that need to be removed are recessed into the case. When all six of the screws have been removed, carefully turn the system over and remove the top cover.

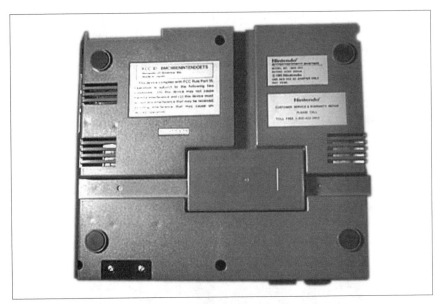

Figure 1-3. The bottom of the NES console

2. Remove the RF shield. Removing the top cover of the NES reveals the RF shield, shown in Figure 1-4, which needs to be removed to allow access to the cartridge tray. The RF shield is held in place by seven screws located around its outer edge. Once the screws have been removed, the shield needs to be slid forward slightly before it will come out.

Figure 1-4. The metal RF shield covers the innards of the NES

3. Remove the tray cartridge screws. There are six screws that hold the tray cartridge in place. Two of these screws are slightly longer than the other four (and usually a different color) and will need to be placed back in the correct spot when reassembling the unit, so pay attention to where each screw comes from.

4. Remove the RF unit screws. Before removing the tray cartridge and replacing the 72-pin connector, you need to remove the two screws near the RF unit. After removing these screws, you will be able to move the main circuit board.

5. Remove the cartridge tray. Now that the main circuit board is free, you can remove the cartridge tray, shown in Figure 1-5. Simply slide the tray forward and lift the front edge of the tray. You may have to lift the main circuit board slightly to remove the tray.

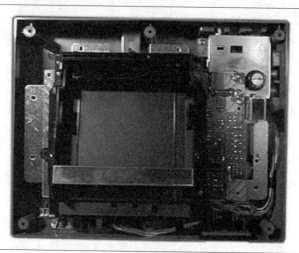

Figure 1-5. The main cartridge tray exposed

6. Replace the 72-pin connector. With the cartridge tray removed, the 72-pin connector is now ready to be replaced. There are no screws to remove on the existing connector—you just need to slide it off of the main circuit board. You will have to lift the circuit board slightly so there is enough clearance for the connector to come off. The fitting is usually tight, so be careful. Grip the connector from the points shown in Figure 1-6 and push towards the back of the system. Once the old connector has been removed, it may be beneficial to clean the circuit board contacts with some rubbing alcohol and a Q-Tip before installing the new connector. After verifying that the new connector is oriented correctly, slide it onto the main circuit board.

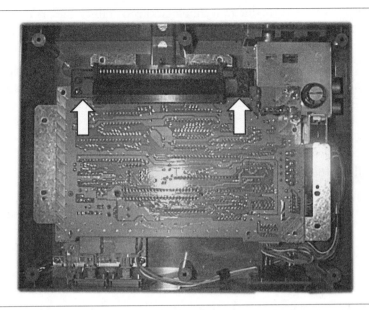

Figure 1-6. Grip the connector from the points shown

7. Reassemble the system. Now that you have successfully replaced the 72-pin connector, it is time to reassemble the system. To reassemble, follow the disassembly steps in reverse order. Note that when reinstalling the cartridge tray, there is a plastic tab that must slip underneath the main circuit board.

After you have finished replacing the 72-pin connector in your NES, it is important to clean your games before inserting them into the system. Remember, the main cause of loading errors is dirty contacts. Inserting a dirty cartridge into your system will result in a dirty system, which will be prone to future loading errors. A common suggestion for cleaning cartridges is to use a Q-Tip dipped in rubbing alcohol. By keeping your games clean, you will in turn keep your system clean, and can enjoy hassle-free gaming for years to come!

—Dan Kohler

Take Your NES Games on the Go

HACK
#7

Play your favorite NES titles in the car, on the train, or on a desert island.

Ever since the 1989 launch of the Game Boy ushered in the era of portable gaming, it was the dream of NES owners worldwide: a console that would let them play their beloved home games on the go, in vivid color. Sadly, it never happened, mostly due to technological constraints, the price of portable hardware, and the fact that the NES carts were just so darned big as to make any possible form factor a total failure from a design standpoint.

But that hasn't stopped other companies from giving it a go and trying to pack the Famicom hardware into a portable shell. In this hack, I explore a few different systems that allow you to play Famicom and NES games portably. Bear in mind that none of them are perfect, but you may find one solution that strikes your fancy.

Official Re-released Games

If you jump ahead to Chapter 2, you'll find hacks that discuss the two ways Nintendo has devised thus far to let you play certain NES titles on your Game Boy Advance. The GameCube title Animal Crossing lets you download certain emulated NES games to your GBA's memory [Hack #19], and a line of NES Classics cartridges [Hack #16] has been released on the GBA. Read those hacks to find a list of the games that are available.

Game Axe Color

This first attempt at a portable Famicom was released throughout Asia as early as 1995. It was gigantic, even exceeding the size of giant portables like the Sega Game Gear and NEC Turbo Express. It drained six AA batteries in two hours and on top of that the LCD screen was awful; it scratched all too easily and colors were severely washed out. Game Axe Color is most likely no longer being made, and that is to your benefit. I found one on eBay selling for around $150, far less than what the system used to sell for, but considering what can be had for far cheaper it is hardly worth it.

Game Theory Admiral

Sporting one of the clumsiest product names ever devised, the Game Theory Admiral sprung onto the retro gaming scene a year or so ago. It featured a form factor quite similar to that of the Game Boy Advance and was much smaller than the Game Axe Color. In fact, it was so small that Famicom games could not even fit into the unit's cartridge slot! A special adapter (included) fit into the unit and held the cartridge at a 90 degree angle protruding towards the player, hanging over the system like an awning.

The GTA (note the familiarity of the abbreviation—coincidence or carefully crafted marketing?) also featured A/V output; cables were included in the box. Thus, you could hook the unit up to your television set. When online retailer National Console Support (*www.ncsx.com*), who sold the units for a time, tested one, they found the television display to be "perfect." The bright, backlit TFT screen was also found to be much nicer than the Game Axe's.

And the price was right at just over $50. The only drawbacks were that Mystery, the company that released the system, apparently didn't stick around long enough to release an AC adapter or an adapter to run NES cartridges. You might try using the adapters found on Lik-Sang [Hack #5], but because of the way the cartridges hang over the system, this setup would be unstable at best. Most of the retailers who carried the GTA are long out of stock, although I found some on eBay selling for between $50 and $75.

PokeFami

The PokeFami is a portable Famicom-compatible system from the makers of the NeoFami [Hack #5]. This is the newest such system, having been released in 2004 by GameTech. It is sold in most major Japanese hardware stores and is generally made of tougher stuff than the Admiral. It features a 2.5" LCD screen and takes 3 AA batteries. Of course, it costs more: I found different retailers selling them for anywhere between $70 and $130.

Like the systems mentioned earlier, the PokeFami includes A/V output to a television screen. Its cartridge slot is far better than the Admiral's, since Famicom cartridges slide into the unit—although some reports indicate that the slot is too wide, thus enabling the player to accidentally shake a cartridge free during gameplay. An adapter is required for NES gameplay. At the time of this writing many different online retailers, including Lik-Sang (*http://www.lik-sang.com*) and Play-Asia (*http://www.play-asia.com*), stock the Pokefami.

AdoFami (Time Machine)

You might imagine that the PokeFami is your best bet for portable Famicom/NES playing, and you might be right. But if you own a Game Boy Advance SP system, you might want to consider the AdoFami, also called the Time Machine by English-language retailers. It plugs into the GBA SP's bottom half, overlapping a little on each side.

In layman's terms, the AdoFami contains the same hardware as a PokeFami, but uses the GBA SP's screen. It does require its own set of 4 AA batteries, and outputs sound through its own speaker and headphone output. You can change brightness, hue, and saturation by hitting the GBA's Select button while a game is in progress. A slot on the bottom of the unit allows you to play GBA cartridges while the device is attached. NES-to-Famicom adapters do work with the system, which is available for about $50 from most stores that sell the PokeFami.

The Shape of Famiclones to Come

If this hack has taught you anything, it's that it will almost assuredly be out of date by the time it is printed. Perhaps the PokeFami will be replaced with another, more compact portable Famiclone. Perhaps an AdoFami-style device that draws its power from the GBA SP's rechargeable battery will be developed. And perhaps one day a system will run NES games without the need for an adapter.

Well... maybe two out of three.

Buy a Famicom from Japan

Import Nintendo's first breakout hit game system from the exotic Orient.

It would be a very different world today if the Famicom were never released. Sure, at some point the post-Atari U.S. video game market would have been revitalized. But the American gaming industry might have remained under the total control of American companies. Or, Sega might have climbed unimpeded to the top of the Japanese game industry, then proceeded to dominate the rest of the world.

But in 1983, Nintendo did release the Family Computer—quickly dubbed the Famicom for short by abbreviation-happy Japanese consumers—and within months it was a smash success in Japan. It was such a success that Nintendo decided to bring it to the United States as the Nintendo Entertainment System. The rest, as they say, is history.

With the Famicom's crucial role in revitalizing the U.S. game business, and since it is Nintendo's best-known product, it's not surprising that game collectors in the West want to get their hands on one, even if they don't generally collect imports. There's just something about the Famicom's fun design and historical importance that calls to them.

That, and the fact that there are all sorts of games on the Famicom that don't have U.S. equivalents. This is especially true when you consider the Famicom Disk System, a magnetic-disk-based add-on drive that was never released in the US. Add all this together and the Famicom becomes a pretty desirable piece of kit. But it's tough to know how to go about getting one [Hack #9], and which model of the system you should go for. In this hack, I'll run down the pros and cons of the different Famicom systems you might consider buying, and what important things to watch for when you do.

In general, this hack will not cover the question of *where* you should buy Famicom hardware. It's not that I don't like you or anything, it's because this information is already given (albeit in a more general sense) in other hacks in this chapter—namely, "Buy Retro Games from Japan" **[Hack #9]** and "Play with Power: Set Up an NES" **[Hack #5]**.

Family Computer

The original design of the Famicom, as shown in Figure 1-7, didn't change much from its release in 1983 until about a decade later.

Figure 1-7. The Family Computer, or Famicom for short

If you want to find a complete Famicom system, it should contain the following items:

- The console, with two non-removable controllers
- A white RF switch
- A black AC adapter
- Pink and white instruction manual
- A small comic book about the system; the title roughly translates to "This is the Family Computer!"

This is the original version of the Famicom, and is not especially difficult to find today. After all, millions upon millions of them were mass-produced in Japan. The Famicom is not rare by any stretch of an eBay seller's imagination. You shouldn't pay more than $80 for a loose, complete system or $100 for a boxed one.

This is especially true as this model of Famicom almost definitely won't work on your U.S. television set. As you can see from the list of parts, it only features RF output, and then only using 300 ohm leads (those little screw things that used to be on the back of all TV sets but are no longer).

And even if you could hook the Famicom up to your TV, odds are you won't see anything. Japan and the United States both use NTSC television standards, but the RF frequencies are different. Some people have reported getting Famicom games running on channel 96 with no sound, but I have never been able to get one working.

I understand, of course, if you want an original Famicom for your collection even if you can't use it. But if you do want one that you can actually use to play games, you have a few other options.

> I lied a little bit when I said the original Famicom design didn't change much. The very first design of the system was indistinguishable from later models except for the fact that the A and B buttons were square and made out of a mushy sort of material. Most of these were recalled due to an unrelated hardware issue, and the next run featured the round, concave A and B buttons we know and love. Of course, collectors consider the ultra-rare square-button version to be the "true" original Famicom.

AV Famicom

In 1993, Nintendo released the AV Famicom (Figure 1-8) in Japan. As you might guess from its name, this was done in response to the same complaint that you probably have about the original Famicom: no AV output. Nintendo actually manufactured these machines up through the year 2004, if you can believe it.

The convenience of having AV ports made the AV Famicom a highly sought out item, and it is difficult to find today despite being a much more contemporary product. Thus, you can expect to pay upwards of $150. If you do buy one, note that it only includes the following inside the box:

- The AV Famicom console
- Two detachable controllers, same as late model NES controllers
- Instruction manual

That's right—the AV Famicom was sold without AV cables or an AC adapter. Nintendo sold both of those separately. This isn't as harsh as it sounds, as Nintendo was simply assuming that customers already owned the

Figure 1-8. The AV Famicom in all its redesigned glory

new 16-bit Super Famicom system, which was released three years prior and used the same AC adapter and AV cables.

But this money-saving measure might not work well with Americans. Yes, you can use your AV cables that came with the American Super NES, Nintendo 64, or even GameCube with this system. But you'll need to track down the AC adapter that was used for the Super Famicom. You can try using your American SNES power supply, although you may be running the risk of sending too much voltage into your poor little AV Famicom and frying its insides.

Famicom Disk System

In 1986, Nintendo had an interesting idea: put games on floppy disks, which were cheaper to produce and could be rewritten with new games (at licensed Nintendo retailers) when players got tired of the old ones. It didn't work out for a variety of reasons, but they gave it their all for a while. This resulted in many exclusive Disk System games. The Legend of Zelda, Metroid, and Castlevania, among other series, made their debut on the Famicom Disk System (Figure 1-9).

It is, as you might imagine, another coveted collector's item. There are, of course, a few caveats for would-be collectors. First and foremost is that the Disk System, though it can hook up to any Famicom system—even some of the third-party Famicom portable systems in [Hack #7]—requires its own power supply. Amazingly, the default option that Nintendo gave to gamers

Figure 1-9. Famicom Disk System (below) attached to the Famicom

who bought the unit was to use six (6) "C" batteries (not included)! A power adapter was available separately; it is quite rare. (Yes, American "C" batteries will work fine!)

You should expect to pay [Hack #9] around $100 for a working Disk System. And I stress the word *working*. Disk Systems were notorious for breaking down; the drive belt inside would turn brittle and crack with age. Nintendo used to do cheap repairs on these at their Kyoto offices, but have discontinued the practice. So make absolutely sure that when you buy one, the seller warrants that the drive belt is new and has been replaced or else you are almost assuredly buying broken hardware.

If you hook the Disk System up and turn it on, you will always see an opening screen with the Nintendo logo and Mario and Luigi telling you to "Please Set Disk Card." This does not mean the system is working. You must successfully load a disk game before you can call it a success, so be sure that when the system is described as "tested" that this is what the seller means!

> The Disk System itself is a cool retro gaming hack. It plugged into the Famicom through an adapter that fit into the cartridge slot, and when you turned the game on a ROM inside the adapter tricked Famicom into thinking it was playing a regular old cartridge game.

Twin Famicom

An easy (but not cheap!) all-in-one solution is the delicious-looking Twin Famicom (Figure 1-10), which was produced by Sharp under license from Nintendo. It has everything you could possibly want from a Famicom system—*everything* meaning AV outputs and Disk System functionality. Sure, the controllers are hardwired in and the cords are way too short, but you can't have everything.

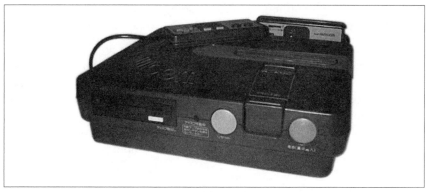

Figure 1-10. The black model of the Twin Famicom

These retail for around $100 in Japan; if you're buying one from an American auction site it will almost assuredly run you $200. And at that price you'd best make sure that the disk drive works, because otherwise you're stuck with an expensive cartridge-only Famicom system.

Famiclones

As near as I can figure, the patent on the Famicom expired in 2004. That was around the time that Nintendo stopped manufacturing the AV Famicom and all sorts of unlicensed Famicom clones (shortened by the abbreviation-happy American gaming community to "Famiclones") started popping up in Japanese retail stores.

I discuss these in a previous hack [Hack #5]. Note that most of these do feature AV ports and will work with the Disk System. The one problem with the clone machines is that they use non-standard joystick ports. Luckily there aren't that many third-party Famicom joysticks anyway (since the original machine used hardwired controllers), so this isn't a big deal.

Hopefully, between all these different versions of the system you can find some Famicom setup that fits your needs. No matter what, however, you'll need to make a tradeoff between originality, convenience, and price.

Buy Retro Games from Japan
#9   Get games early or get ones that were never released in the West.

Contrary to the domestic classic gaming scene, it's easier to snap up retro imports now than it was when they were brand new. Back in the days of the Super NES, importing games meant dealing with some fly-by-night company that advertised in black-and-white in the back pages of video game magazines, paying exorbitant prices, waiting forever, and sometimes not even receiving what you ordered.

This can still happen to you today—but only if you're not shopping smart. There are plenty of reliable, reputable importers who are upfront and honest about providing you all the information you'll need before you order. And the prices can be better than you think; in great part the days of exorbitant markups are over. So if you're curious about acquiring exotic games from foreign lands, I'm going to discuss two ways you can do it—through online retailers and through auction sites like eBay. Both have their pros and cons.

Online Import Game Sellers

Most of the businesses listed below deal primarily in contemporary game releases, but since this is *Retro Gaming Hacks*, I'll pay more attention to their back catalogs of classic games.

National Console Support (*http://www.ncsx.com*). Based in New York City, NCS is widely renowned as one of the most reliable import game retailers around. NCS posts daily news updates on the current state of the Japanese game market, listing release dates as they are announced and posting box art and screenshots of the games that come in that day. Even those who don't import many games read NCS's daily news posts.

In the "Orphanage" section of their shopping site, NCS lists brand new games for the Super Famicom, Virtual Boy, Game Boy Color, Mega Drive, PC Engine, and Sega 32X. Pickings are understandably slim, but highlights of their stock as of this writing include Fatal Fury Special for the Mega CD, a Nintendo 64 Action Replay device that lets you play import games on your U.S. system and V-Tetris for the Virtual Boy (which is a different game than Tetris 3D, which was only released in the United States).

Separate sections feature games for the Saturn, PlayStation, and Neo Geo hardware (cartridge and CD-ROM both). And that's not all—every few weeks or so, NCS will dig through its decade-plus warehouse storage containers and unearth all sorts of classic games, merchandise, and toys and offer them for sale on a first-come-first-serve basis in the daily news posts. (Yet another reason to read them regularly.)

Yamatoku (*http://www.yamatoku.jp*). When I lived in Kanazawa, Japan, there was a small shop near downtown that specialized in secondhand games. I noticed that the store rarely had any especially rare merchandise, though, and I soon found out why. I was searching on eBay for a copy of the Final

Fantasy music CD Celtic Moon that was located in Japan, and found one being sold by the store, Yamatoku. Bear in mind that this was in early 2000, so I was impressed with the store's brave leap into the age of Internet sales.

Five years later (note to self: I am aging rapidly), you can still get big deals from the tiny store. Only now they are certified eBay power sellers with nearly seven thousand positive feedback ratings. Their rarer items are still sold on their eBay store (*http://stores.ebay.com/Used-Video-Game-Shop-Yamatoku*), but the online shop at *http://www.yamatoku.jp* is home to hassle-free shopping for more common games. That's the great thing about Yamatoku—they won't rip you off by selling a dirt-common game as "rare."

Some of the games available on the site as of this writing (all second-hand) are Final Fantasy III for the Famicom (NES), unreleased in the US, for $45; Nobunaga's Ambition for the Famicom for $12; Fatal Fury Special for the Neo Geo for $20; and Valis III for the Mega Drive (Genesis) for a mere $2.

And if you can't find what you want, Yamatoku offers an online request form (*http://www.yamatoku.jp/request/request.asp*) where you can ask them to hunt down titles especially for you. Of course, this will cost you more money, but if you've got nowhere else to turn it could make your dreams come true.

Play-Asia (http://www.play-asia.com). Hong Kong-based retailer Play-Asia is the import retailer of choice for many gamers, offering low prices, fast and inexpensive international shipping, occasional low-price deals, and a great selection of brand new retro titles to boot. They offer the Neo Fami hardware (a new Japanese clone of the original Famicom system) in two different color schemes, as well as the PokeFami (a new portable Famicom-compatible system).

Unfortunately, they don't have any Famicom titles for sale, but do offer a selection of new and preowned games for the Super Famicom, Mega Drive, PC Engine (TurboGrafx-16), and other systems. You can also find the Action Replay 4M Plus that will let you play import Sega Saturn games, and as of this writing they have new copies of the ultra-rare Virtual Boy titles Insmouse no Yakata ($74.90) and Jack Bros. ($49.90).

Online Auction Sites

What do people do when they find a little bit of retro gold lurking in their attic? If they don't plug it into their TV and get hooked on the game, they might just try to unload it online.

eBay (*http://www.ebay.com*). It's a familiar refrain: would-be import gamers post on online message boards asking where they can buy a certain rare item—"and don't say 'eBay'," they warn their would-be helpers. And why not? While it's true that eBay tended to artificially inflate the prices of items coming from Japan in years past, as more and more sellers living in Japan start to post auctions, prices have begun to fall in line with what you'd pay on the streets of Tokyo.

So although you shouldn't fear eBay shopping, you should keep some tips and tricks in mind when shopping for Japanese games.

Check the seller's location
> You'd think this would be obvious. But remember, though auctions located in Japan might have lower final bid prices, the shipping will be higher. (You may also have to deal with customs duties.) Decide what your priority will be—saving a few bucks by going with a Japanese seller or the convenience of buying local. You'll also want to make sure that the seller will ship the item to the country where you live.

Check the shipping price listed in the auction
> Some sellers may offer low Buy It Now prices, then make up the money with exaggerated shipping prices. Do the research beforehand and find out what you should expect to pay for express (EMS) international shipping versus standard airmail.

Remember that games have different names in Japan
> The game you're looking for might be listed under its English name, but it might also be listed under a transliteration of its Japanese name. And that might be misspelled. In the early days of eBay I got some deals by searching for famicon, a less popular Romanization of the name of the Famicom.

Yahoo! Japan Auctions (*http://auctions.yahoo.co.jp/*). There are some items that are so rare you can't even find them on eBay. In that case, you might want to turn to Yahoo! Japan Auctions, which is the preferred online auction site of the Japanese (although there is a Japanese version of the eBay site, Yahoo! hit it big in the country before eBay did).

But, uh, there's one problem. In general, if a Japanese seller wants to deal with international, English-speaking bidders, he'll post his items on eBay. If they're up on Yahoo! Japan, you can bet that they only want to sell to Japanese-speaking buyers with mailing addresses inside Japan.

And yet, the miracle of the Internet can solve anything! Proxy services such as the one at PhotoGuide Japan (*http://photojpn.org/proxy/yahoo.html*) or Rinkya (*http://www.rinkya.com/faq_url.php*) will bid on auctions for you, buy the items, and ship them to you—for a markup, of course. Rinkya's site will even automatically translate Yahoo! Japan's menus and listings.

Of course, this solution can be pricey and complicated—not to mention the fact that it could take upwards of a month to get your items. I'd only recommend it if you absolutely can't find what you're looking for anywhere else.

Or Just Go to Japan

Hey, it's not as crazy as it sounds. Economy plane tickets to Japan are getting cheaper and cheaper these days (a travel agency in San Francisco's Japantown, at the time of this writing, is advertising a $399 round-trip ticket), and there are plenty of English-speaking hotels that cater to young travelers on a budget. Then you can just head to the game shops of the major cities and stock up on classic Japanese games at the lowest prices possible. And hey, if you want to know where to go for games once you get there, I just happen to have covered all that in my book *Power-Up: How Japanese Video Games Gave the World an Extra Life* (BradyGAMES). (You knew I had to get that plug in here somewhere.)

H A C K #10 Find, Fix, Play, and Emulate the Vectrex

Play real vector graphics arcade games, right in your own home.

The Vectrex is one of the "holy grails" of classic video game collectors, the centerpiece of any collection. Not bad for a system that was an abject market failure as soon as it hit store shelves in 1982, finding itself in the clearance bins just a year later. Released by a company called GCE or General Consumer Electronics (that was swiftly purchased by Milton Bradley during the age when every toy, movie, and candy manufacturer wanted to get a finger into the video games pie), the Vectrex was the first and only home console to use a vector graphics display.

Vector graphics were already all the rage in arcades, having been used for such popular games as Asteroids and Battlezone. Vector graphic displays produced sharper, cleaner graphics because the beam in the monitor would draw the images based on specific sets of X/Y coordinates (i.e., vectors).

Atari's home versions of their vector games for the 2600, although they may have replicated the gameplay, couldn't have replicated the graphics because home systems that hook up to a television set all use raster graphics, drawn by a beam that scans horizontally across each row of pixels, from the top down.

But the Vectrex included its own built-in vector monitor, so it didn't need to be hooked up to a TV. Thus, it was marketed as portable, although its heaviness and large size (and requirement of a wall socket to plug into) probably precluded it from that sort of use. The monitor only displayed in black and white, because a color vector display would have been prohibitively expensive for a consumer product, but tinted acetate overlays provided with each game cartridge added some color and background graphics to the games.

Collecting the Vectrex

Vectrex systems can be had on eBay for between $70 and $100, depending on condition. If you're looking to go the cheaper route and scour flea markets and garage sales…good luck. If you do manage to find one, though, take comfort in the fact that it's probably complete as is, since all the necessary bits were built in. Just make sure the attached power cord and controller haven't been hacked off. The joystick conveniently snaps into a bay underneath the monitor.

There's even a game built into the hardware, an Asteroids knockoff known as Minestorm. About thirty additional games were produced in total during the system's lifespan, ranging from the relatively common to the obscenely rare; also falling into the latter category are some accessories such as a pair of 3D goggles and a light pen that let you draw on the screen. Some relatively inexpensive Vectrex games that a beginning collector might try to track down are:

Armor Attack
> You're a tiny little square jeep, and tanks and helicopters are firing on you. As you view the action from the top down, you'll have to use your armor-piercing gun and the barriers around you to evade and shoot down the enemy vehicles.

Star Trek: The Motion Picture
> Hop into your X-Wing and drop bombs on the Death Star! No, wait, I'm thinking of a different vector graphics arcade game. This isn't as fun as the other one, but it's still a relatively easy-to-find first-person space shooter. Actually, I think I have two copies of this. Anybody want one?

Spike!
> Yes, it's actually a vector graphics platform game. Your little spiky girlfriend is kidnapped and you have to negotiate platforms and ladders and such to get her back. It even uses speech synthesis!

In addition to the originally released games, there is also a vibrant Vectrex homebrew scene. Many Vectrex games were created by John Dondzila, including clones of games like Space Invaders and Tetris. You can buy the cartridges for $20 each from his web site, *http://www.classicgamecreations. com/*. Other homebrew games, like Vec Sports Boxing, have been released from Good Deal Games (*http://www.gooddealgames.com*).

Fixing the Vectrex

Inspired by collectors' stories that I'd read online or in the Digital Press Collector's Guide, I hunted in vain for a Vectrex (as well as pretty much any old console I didn't have) for years, but never did see one at a yard sale. Once I had pretty much given up on ever finding one, my father came home and said he'd found a Vectrex on the side of the road.

Plugging it in, we discovered why it was there in the first place—it didn't work. Specifically, it had a problem that I soon discovered was evident in most Vectrex systems. When powered on, it just displayed a single white dot in the center of the monitor.

We never did get around to fixing it, but I did find all the information we needed. At some point in 1998, the original Vectrex troubleshooting guide and repair manual—the documents that GCE sent out to licensed Vectrex dealers—were located, scanned, and converted to PDF file format for easy viewing in Adobe Acrobat Reader. You can download it from *http://www. playvectrex.com/shoptalk_f.htm* and download the reader from *www.adobe. com*. Note that both guides assume knowledge of electronics and that you have certain general tools used in television repair.

As for the white dot issue, the Vectrex FAQ (*http://www.classicgaming.com/ museum/faqs/vectrexfaq.shtml*) has this to say on the subject:

> There is 1 common problem that will cause this symptom. Inside the unit there is a 4-wire power connector connecting the side board to the bottom board. Often units with no picture have bad solder joints on this connector. Try resoldering the pins and see if that helps.

Emulating the Vectrex

If you're curious—but not a hundred dollars curious—as to what Vectrex games played like, you might try emulating the system on your PC. We'll talk much, much more about emulation in Chapters 3 and 4 of this book, but I'm including Vectrex emulation in this hack for one specific reason: it's perfectly legal. The owners of the games have granted users the right to download and distribute all the Vectrex games for free, provided they do not use them to make a profit.

There are two different emulators that run Vectrex games, both of which are available at Spike's Big Vectrex Page (*http://www.classicgaming.com/vectrex/*). One of them is called DVE, and there are two versions of the program. Version 2.0 comes in two Zip files that are 1.8 MB and 1.3 MB large, and it contains all the Vectrex game software as well as the emulator files. Version 1.40 is a group of smaller Zip files, and the emulator software is not as advanced (there is no GUI and no joystick support). It is meant for slower, older PC hardware [Hack #69].

The other emulator that runs Vectrex games is called MESS, short for Multi Emulator Super System [Hack #59]. One advantage to using MESS is that it will let you play the Vectrex 3D games if you have a standard pair of red and blue anaglyph 3D glasses, like the kind that used to come with comic books. You can also adjust the color settings to be able to play the 3D games in 2D.

You can download a Zip file containing all the games at Spike's Big Vectrex Page. There are actually two files: one optimized for DVE and one for MESS. The Zip file contains all commercially released games, homebrews, and demos.

Collect Classic Handhelds

HACK #11
Put retro gaming power into the palm of your hand.

Collecting home console games—as described in most of the other hacks in this very chapter—can be fun, but there's another side of classic game collecting out there that might be more up your Alleyway. Handheld games have been popular since the late 1970's—just about as long as home games. Of course, the games were never as powerful as the home games of the time; but then again, if you only cared about the most advanced gaming technology, you wouldn't be reading this book!

In this hack, I'll talk about some of the most popular lines of handheld games, give you some idea of what they played like, and how difficult it is to collect them [Hack #1]. But first, here are some reasons to get into handheld collecting, as well as some web sites to visit.

Why Handhelds?

Most of us have fond (or less-than-fond) memories of playing LCD handheld games when we were far away from our home consoles, in the car or on vacation. Many of them were patterned after successful home games of the time, and usually adorned with artwork and fancy form factors to distract from the fact that the games were ultra-simple and oftentimes not that much fun. Still, there are plenty of advantages to collecting handheld games over consoles.

Handheld games are small
> This one's a no-brainer. Handheld games were meant to fit into a pocket, or at least be small and light enough to be portable. So storing them isn't nearly as painful as stacking away boxes of console games.

Handheld games are self-contained
> You never have to worry about hooking a handheld game up to a TV. And they run on batteries, so there are no messy wires to store and get

tangled up. Everything you need to play them, anytime you feel like it, is right there in the hardware. (Provided you keep an ample supply of batteries around, that is.)

Handheld games are colorful display pieces

Display your Atari 2600 collection on a shelf and it'll look like a black box with a bunch of smaller black boxes stacked up next to it. But put your collection of handhelds on display, and it'll be a symphony of colors, artwork, and interesting shapes, all reflective of the toy design sensibilities of the time.

Web Sites of Note

http://www.handheldmuseum.com/

Run by handheld game supercollector Rik Morgan, the Handheld Museum is his attempt to photographically catalog every handheld game ever made, a great deal of which he personally owns. He's doing quite the job of it too, with photos of and information on hundreds of games, categorized by manufacturer and with a handy search function on the front page.

http://www.handhelden.com/

This is the lavishly designed official web site of the lavishly designed book Electronic Plastic (a beautiful full-color volume with illustrations of handheld games of the golden age). The book itself can be ordered from Amazon UK (follow the links on the page).

http://www.gameandwatch.com/

If you like Nintendo's line of Game and Watch handhelds, you need to see this site. Featuring not only pictures of each handheld but reviews, instructions, and screenshots of the LCD action in easy-to-view format, browsing this site is as addictive and fun as the games themselves.

http://madrigal.retrogames.com/

There is some extraordinary retro game hacking going on here. The site's author makes scans of his handheld games, and then programs a perfect simulator in Borland Delphi 4.0, using the graphics and sound from the original games. The fidelity is amazing; it's like having the machine embedded in your monitor. Even better, there's a tutorial for those who want to try making their own simulations.

Popular Handhelds for Collectors

So your interest is piqued, but you've seen the massive photo galleries at the web sites just mentioned and you're not sure where to begin. Well, how about thinking back on your childhood and what, if any, handhelds you might rediscover a fond nostalgic attachment to. If that doesn't work, read this section.

Mattel Classic Football. Okay, it wasn't called "Classic" when it was first released, but you've probably seen this handheld, revitalized for the modern-day retro-happy market, on shelves in Wal-Mart. It proved single-handedly the theory of suspension of disbelief by creating a football game out of nothing more than a few horizontal lines of red LED lights. You controlled a dot running to the right and tried to dodge the dots coming from the left. If you reached the end, touchdown!

Of course, they could have turned the dots on their side and it could have been called Avoid the Bricks, or turned it upside down and called it Sink or Swim. It's just a few lights. But the football branding paid off and other sports handhelds followed, such as Basketball (which Mattel has also re-released).

Coleco tabletop games. It's hard for me not to love Coleco; I'm from Connecticut just like them, and of course they made my favorite golden-age system, the Colecovision [Hack #36]. They also made incredible tabletop games based on popular arcade licenses like Donkey Kong, Pac-Man, and Frogger.

Not only are they superb display items, shaped like foot-tall, miniature arcade machines with replicas of the cabinet art found on the originals— they play pretty good, too! They use multicolored LED displays to create bright, detailed (for a handheld game!) displays with solid gameplay. Unfortunately, the fact that they were considered to be toys, not electronic equipment, meant that they got banged around a lot back in the day. So it's rare to find them in mint condition (or at all!).

Nintendo Game and Watch. If you want to combine your love of handhelds with your love of Nintendo, this series can be a rewarding hobby. The tiny pieces of hardware (about the length and width of a credit card, though ten times as thick) held some big games, many of which were based on Nintendo's arcade and home successes like Mario Bros. and The Legend of Zelda.

Unfortunately, since these are so coveted, collecting them can be expensive. Some of the more common games, though, can be had without dropping a lot of cash. The Game and Watch specialty web site linked earlier in this hack features selling and trading forums for collectors to hook up and make deals.

Buy Your Own Arcade Hardware

Know the hardware to buy when it comes to playing arcade games.

Having your own, personal arcade machine is a very, very cool thing, and there are several ways you can go about making this a reality. Of course, there are plenty of intricacies to deal with—for example, what's the JAMMA standard? Should you buy a large American cabinet at auction or hold out for a sweet sitdown Japanese mini-cabinet? Even if you're not interested in the rather titanic task of building an arcade cabinet from scratch, there's still plenty to learn about buying, understanding, and customizing your own arcade hardware.

Arcade Cabinet Hardware Basics

If you're starting from scratch and know absolutely nothing about arcade machine hardware, think of the arcade machine as a big games console and the games as cartridges. Simply open your cabinet, plug in the cartridge (the circuit board containing the game), and turn the cabinet on to play that game. You don't need any detailed electrical knowledge at all.

However, the console/cartridge analogy doesn't quite hold water, because there's no built-in CPU in the arcade machine itself; the arcade game circuit board is a self-contained computer that has all the gaming hardware needed to play that game. Obviously, this makes arcade games potentially expensive propositions. Imagine buying a whole new PlayStation 2 every time you want to play a new game! Fortunately, because arcade operators very quickly switch games, there's a flood of older titles that nobody except collectors want, so second-hand prices for arcade boards are relatively reasonable.

Although there was a mess of conflicting standards early in the life of the arcade machine, the Japanese Amusement Manufacturer Association, or JAMMA, introduced a standard in the mid-'80s that most games have since followed. If you have a JAMMA cabinet you can easily swap Final Fight for Bad Dudes Vs. Dragon Ninja, because they both connect to your cabinet using the same pin-based connector.

However, there are custom variants of the JAMMA standard. Some recent games, usually with custom controllers or cabinets, don't adhere to JAMMA at all. You can still go a long way by buying a JAMMA cabinet, though. Browse the Killer List Of Videogames (*http://www.klov.com/index.php*) to see the percentage that support JAMMA to see what we mean.

If you're really a classic game fan, you have to accept that Pac-Man won't easily play in the same cabinet as Q-Bert, since both use non-standard, non-

JAMMA connectors. If your classic games have fairly standard controls, you may be able to find JAMMA adaptors for each of them in places such as the Multigame.com web site (*http://www.multigame.com/KITS.HTM*), but it's really not straightforward. Worse yet, Pac-Man cartridges rarely exist outside of Pac-Man cabinets and it's the artwork of classic cabinets that makes them particularly good-looking. You may be best off buying specific old arcade titles as separate machines, then buying a generic JAMMA cabinet for everything else.

The other alternative for running those classic arcade titles is to run the MAME emulator through JAMMA. See the PC2JAMMA project (*http://www.mameworld.net/pc2jamma/*) for more information. Heck, you could skip the JAMMA step altogether and make a fake arcade machine. That's not the real thing, of course, though it's workable. It's also ethically and legally dubious unless you own the original boards or run homebrew [Hack #24] or legal ROMs from places such as StarROMs [Hack #25].

Finding a JAMMA Arcade Cabinet

You've made the momentous decision to somehow buy a JAMMA cabinet. What are your options, and how much will it cost you? Here's a rundown.

Buying used American JAMMA cabinets. If you're looking for a JAMMA cabinet originally constructed in the States—the larger, stand-up, heavy arcade cabinets, generally made of wood, that you'll see in your local game room or bar—then you have a few choices. Go on eBay, find a live auction, or talk to your local arcade operator.

Since eBay has a Location / International option in its advanced search which will find items local to you, you can search for arcade cabinets in your area. Be aware that shipping cabinets can be as or more expensive than the cabinet itself—even brief freight trips to you, the lucky buyer, can cost over $300. If you can manage it, try to buy a cabinet that you can pick up yourself.

You may need to do some detective work to see if the cabinet in that perfect eBay auction supports JAMMA, because many cabinets that include games won't have the phrase "JAMMA compatible" in their auction listings, even though they actually are. Search for information on the game currently working in the cabinet with KLOV (*http://www.klov.com/index.php*).

Make a note of the button configuration, too. The basic JAMMA setup supports two players with three buttons per player as well as a Start button. If the cabinet you're bidding on has fewer buttons, you may have trouble playing standard JAMMA games without modifying your control panel.

As for auctions, SuperAuctions (*http://www.superauctions.com/*) are probably the most famous regular arcade game auctioneers in America. They hold multiple yearly auctions from the West Coast to the East Coast. Prices range from a hundred to over a thousand dollars, depending on the size and quality of the cabinet and the ferocity of the bidding.

Cabinet Auction Fever

If you're at an auction, remember that buying a generic JAMMA cabinet with a poor-quality game already installed in it can be much cheaper than shelling out more cash for a similar cabinet with a particularly well-known game in it.

For example, we were at a Bay Area auction where a JAMMA cabinet with the X-Men fighting game in it sold for over $600, whereas basic old JAMMA cabinets with early '90s titles in them went for $100 or so. You can buy the X-Men cartridge for under a hundred dollars on eBay, so what are you really paying for?

However, in this case, the cheaper cabinet wouldn't have the Capcom fighting game harness with the extra buttons needed to play 6-button Capcom games.

Finally, it might be worth going into your local (perhaps slightly rundown) arcade to see if they have any old cabinets they might sell cheaply. Unfortunately, given the upkeep of a lot of these establishments, you may not find a perfectly preserved artifact, but it's better than nothing.

Buying used Japanese JAMMA cabinets. Although the mid- and late-'90s Japanese arcade cabinets that made their way to the States have the same basic design and no region lockouts, they have quite a different style and form factor from American cabinets. To start with, they're generally made of metal and are much shorter, so players sit, not stand, at them. They also have larger monitors—at least 25 inches diagonally—and have generic, good-looking decals on the sides, which should suit almost any game you put in them. If you can deal with sitting down to play and sometimes being uncomfortably close to your fellow player when dueling in 2-player combat due to the smaller size, then Japanese cabinets are the stylish, cool-looking choice for the JAMMA acolyte in a hurry. Remember, you can play American games in Japanese cabinets and vice versa.

Finding Japanese cabinets is a little trickier than old American cabinets, though. The vast majority of these cabinets enter the U.S. via container ships steaming into Los Angeles right now. You'll always find at least one seller on eBay selling generic Japanese JAMMA cabinets. Prices start at around $250 for 25-inch monitor models and can reach $700 or more for deluxe 29-inch versions. These cabinets are actually branded around specific arcade game manufacturers, but will work for all JAMMA titles.

Some common Japanese cabinet brands turning up in the States include the Sega Aero City and Astro City, the quirky but excellent-looking Taito Egret, and a variety of SNK Candy cabinets that come ready with the extra JAMMA connections to play Neo Geo games. Most of these cabinets sell without any included games, incidentally. Unlike the majority of U.S. arcade cabinets, which started life with a specific game inside them, the Japanese cabinets are completely generic by design.

The biggest problem with buying Japanese cabinets is probably location, location, location. Unless you live close to Los Angeles, you'll probably spend $300 to $500 just to ship the cabinet to your house.

The problem is similar to that of buying non-local American cabinets, which means that the relatively competitive pricing on these Japanese-imported cabinets becomes uncompetitive pretty quickly. Many collectors think the extra shipping is still worth it to pick up the good-looking, versatile Japanese cabinet styles, though.

Building your own JAMMA cabinet. Cabinet building is an extremely complex topic all on its own, admirably covered in another O'Reilly title, *Hardware Hacking Projects for Geeks*, which you should check out at your leisure. Suffice to say that many cabinet-building projects don't include JAMMA connections, but are set up for the player to simply put a PC and a normal computer monitor into the cabinet and pretend like it's a real arcade machine. We call cheating on that, but your mileage, naturally, may vary.

Anyhow, if you want to build a cabinet and then build JAMMA connections into it, the ArcadeRestoration.com site has a good explanation of how to go from an empty cabinet to a JAMMA cabinet (*http://www. arcaderestoration.com/index.asp?OPT=3&DATA=63&CBT=24*). This page explains the full, if complex wiring set-up you'll need.

Safety is really important, even if you're just buying an already-constructed videogame cabinet, so bear in mind that you shouldn't interfere with the innards of the machine while it's turned on. Make sure the machine is properly electrically grounded (many Japanese machines are not, using two-pronged plugs only), and especially avoid the back of the monitor, even when the machine is off.

In most arcade machines, if you have the keys to open the cabinet and are dumb enough to wiggle your hands into the dangerous parts around the back of the monitor, you're in trouble: there's enough voltage up there to kill you.

Be careful, and by all means touch the adjustment knobs often situated around the back of the arcade monitor, but try not to expire in the name of playing arcade-perfect Street Fighter II.

—Simon Carless

HACK #13 Find the Holy Grails
Collect the hardest of hard-to-find golden age retro games.

It all starts out so cheaply. You buy an old Atari 2600 and a stack of games at a yard sale for a few bucks, or maybe you just dig your old setup out of the attic. Bit by the collecting bug, but still keeping your financial priorities intact, you hunt down bargains and start to build up a relatively inexpensive collection.

But before long you can't find any games that aren't already checked off on your master list. You're starting to pay some eBay prices you swore you'd never plunk down for some old pieces of plastic and silicon. You're ever so close to completing your collection; you just need a few more games. You're ready to start paying out the big bucks and find the last few super-rare items you need—the "Holy Grails," as they say.

Or maybe you've just got a whole bunch of crap in the basement and want to know if any of it's worth the big bucks so you can sell it on eBay to hapless collectors. In either case, you'll find this hack beneficial. I'll tell you about some of the rarest classic video game stuff, how it got so rare in the first place, and why collectors prize them.

I've heard dumb-luck stories of people getting some of the items in this hack for *a quarter*. That's twenty-five American cents. Folks, this isn't going to happen to you. If you want these goodies, you'll have to be ready to pay up. The best way to do it is to keep an eye on online auction site *www.eBay.com*.

Search the completed auctions for your game of choice to get an idea of how much they usually sell for [Hack #1].

Also, all of these items had some form of public release; that is to say there are no prototypes listed here. If you were alive when these were produced, you had some chance of getting one.

Golden-Age Grails

When the U.S. video game market crashed in 1983, it crashed under the weight of too much product. There were far more video games, systems, and accessories on the market than consumers wanted, all produced because of what turned out to be an overly optimistic prognostication of the industry's future.

That is to say that there were actually some excellent video games produced during this time, but when the companies went out of business, only the small quantities that they'd produced up until then ever trickled out to retail. Lots of inventory was destroyed. And some devices were only test-marketed in certain regions before a nationwide launch that never happened.

Chase the Chuckwagon. And some, like Chase the Chuckwagon for the Atari 2600, weren't produced in huge quantities to begin with. When Atari video games were all the rage, makers of other consumer products rode the wave with giveaways of special 2600-compatible games that shilled their products. If kids sent in box tops they could get a Kool-Aid Man game, a Tooth Protectors game from Johnson & Johnson, and this: Chase the Chuckwagon, from the then-popular brand of dog food.

Sending in proof-of-purchase labels from the bags would get you an Atari 2600 game, produced especially for the giveaway by publisher Spectravision, in which you, as the dog from the famous Chuck Wagon commercials, chased the titular horse-drawn vehicle. Since it was only given away as a promotional item, it is rare today. Loose cartridges can cost in the $100-$125 range.

Quadrun. Chase the Chuckwagon was produced by a relatively obscure publisher as a promotional giveaway, while Quadrun was produced by Atari themselves. Which is by far the more valuable title? Contrary to what you might think, it's Quadrun. Atari only produced 10,000 of them, and distributed them by mail order only to Atari Club members. Why? The web site

AtariAge has an amusing story about it (*http://www.atariage.com/software_
page.html?SoftwareLabelID=381*):

> According to programmer Steve Woita, the game was play-tested by a group
> of young girls. Not surprisingly, they did not like the game and found it too
> difficult, so Atari decided not to heavily distribute the game.

Quadrun sells for upwards of $350 loose. Interestingly enough, another one
of Steve Woita's games—Waterworld for the Virtual Boy—is one of the
rarer titles on that system, though not anywhere near $350...

Keyboard Component. When they released their video game system Intellivision [Hack #35] in 1980, Mattel promised consumers that a keyboard attachment that would turn the Intellivision into a full-fledged home computer
was coming soon. This turned out to not exactly be true. In fact, the Keyboard Component was delayed and delayed for years, though Mattel continued to promise that it would be out "soon."

But, the Keyboard Component did actually make it out. Sort of. It was test-
marketed in certain areas of the United States, so it did in fact feature a retail
release. It is incredibly rare today, so much so that the Digital Press Collector's Guide refuses to even put a price on it.

A different add-on was later released for the system, called the ECS Computer Module. This is not easy to find, but should not be mistaken for the
Keyboard Component, which is truly a Holy Grail.

3D Imager. The vector-graphics-based Vectrex video game system [Hack #10]
was doomed before it was even released, going almost straight to bargain
bins. No small wonder that the 3D Imager, a pair of motorized glasses that
let players see games in pseudo-3D, is so difficult to find.

Even worse, a separate disk of colored acetate is required for each of the
three games that worked with the accessory (3D Crazy Coaster, 3D Minestorm, and 3D Narrow Escape). Add all that up, and a 3D Imager in complete condition can go for around $500. Another rare Vectrex accessory is
the Light Pen, which let users draw on the screen. But it sells for upwards of
$100 these days.

Post-NES Grails

The U.S. video game market hasn't crashed since Nintendo revitalized it in
1985, and Chase the Chuckwagon-style promotions haven't been too popular (probably due to video game production costs going so high that releasing a game as a promo only would be folly). So how are Grails produced in
the post-Nintendo era? Read on to find out...

Stadium Events. In Japan, as Nintendo's Famicom game system was taking off, a licensee company called Bandai created an innovative and fun new accessory for the system called the Family Trainer. It was a soft pad that players laid on the ground and jumped around on to make the onscreen characters run and jump. When Nintendo brought the Famicom to America as the Nintendo Entertainment System, Bandai released the pad as the Family Fun Fitness system, bundling it with a game they called Stadium Events.

Nintendo—always looking for ways to assure parents that their products were healthy and nothing like those old Atari games of yore—licensed the pad and game from Bandai, redesigning and releasing it as the Power Pad. Bandai's versions were taken off the market; both the game and the pad fetch about $100 each today. Meanwhile, Nintendo's version of Stadium Events, called World Class Track Meet, might be worth about one hundred *cents*.

Nintendo World Championships 1990. This cartridge is the true Holy Grail of NES collectors, at least if you're limiting yourself to officially licensed, Nintendo-produced merchandise. During the heyday of the NES, when Nintendo held "world championships" (which were limited to the United States and maybe Canada, just like the World Series), they produced a special cartridge for the contest.

It was a mix of Super Mario Bros., Rad Racer, and Tetris; players had to complete certain goals in the first two games then play Tetris until time expired. 90 finalists in the contest won their very own competition cartridge to take home. Another 26 of the carts were given away by the magazine Nintendo Power. These 26 were gold-painted (the original 90 were gray), making them the rarest of the rare.

Super Star Fox Weekend. When the Super Nintendo was king, Nintendo decided to hold another competition. This time, it was on a much grander scale but more accessible to the average gamer who wanted to have a go. Rather than trekking down to the convention centers where the Nintendo World Championships were held, all you had to do was go to your local game store that weekend in 1993.

At participating stores, you could play one level of the new 3D shooter Star Fox. If you got past a certain high score, you'd get a Star Fox T-shirt. If not, you got a consolation prize—in my case, it was an awesome Star Fox "floater" pen that I still think is better than any old T-shirt! After the contest was over, Nintendo sold the cartridges through mail order to Nintendo Power subscribers. A similar cartridge was produced for a Donkey Kong Country competition, and then later sold in the same catalog. Only about 2000 of each exist today, and sell for hundreds of dollars each.

Find Classic Games for Cheap

Save lots of money in your quest for retro gaming goodness.

Retro game collecting is fun, but it can get pretty expensive. That's especially the case now that "traditional" sources for game buys—flea markets, thrift stores, and game stores—are starting to dry up. Sometimes it seems like eBay is the only option. And sometimes this is true. But that shouldn't keep you from going out on a summer Saturday and hitting the garage sale circuit. You can't make finds if you're not out there looking!

But just being out there isn't enough. If you want to get the best deals you've got to strategize. Yes, you can buy retro games and save money, whether on eBay or in real life. And with the strategies in this hack—which I am presenting to you at great personal risk—you may very well emerge with a trunk full of games and a wallet still reasonably full of cash.

eBay and Other Online Shopping

You might think that your only option for buying retro games online is the auction site eBay (*http://www.ebay.com*), but that's not true. In fact, there are plenty of other options. They don't offer the same sort of protection that buying on eBay will get you—but you can recoup that risk in better deals. For more specific information, as well as general eBay buying tips, check out [Hack #1].

One important thing to keep in mind is that when you're buying online, you are buying from a potentially global marketplace. Some games that are obscenely rare in this country are very easy to find elsewhere. For example, although the Sega Saturn game Panzer Dragoon Saga saw an extremely limited print run in the States, it is common in Japan, where it goes by the name of Azel: Panzer Dragoon RPG. Sure, if you want the game to be in English, you'll have to pony up for the more expensive U.S. version, but if you're just interested in checking out what all the fuss is about...

Which brings me to another point—research alternate names and spellings for the game you're trying to track down. When you're searching eBay auctions, try to think of alternate ways of phrasing what you're looking for. If you're looking for a new-style NES deck [Hack #5] and search for "toploader NES," you're using a term only popular with collectors. Thus, you're searching for auctions run by collectors, and they're going to know what their stuff is worth. You want to find a seller that has a great item with a poor description, so that you're one of the only people bidding.

Garage Sales, Flea Markets, and Thrift Stores

Time was you couldn't swing a dead cat in a thrift store without knocking over a mint, boxed Vectrex. Okay, maybe it was never that great, but church basements were gold mines a decade ago. Now you're lucky if you find a few things after a full weekend of going to garage sales. But there are strategies you can use to maximize your deal-finding potential...and to negotiate with the seller once you've found something you can't live without.

 Making a spectacular find can sometimes seem like divine providence. According to a certain sect of collectors online, it is, though it does not come from the God of Abraham. No, it comes from Bira Bira, the God of Classic Video Game Collecting. Check out his homepage (with some "big find" stories sure to inspire envy and rage, but also hope) at *http://birabira.chaosmagic.com/*.

Before the sale. Before you venture out to the yard/garage/tag sale, flea market, or thrift store, here are a few things you can do to get the most out of your day.

Plan your day out

You could just drive around and look for garage sale signs (and see plenty of them), but if you buy the newspaper on Friday morning, you'll be able to look through the classified ads and find what sales are happening and where. Even better, you'll be able to see what sort of things they're selling! If you see one listing "video games," well, obviously that might be first on your list. But "toys," "old computer stuff," and "electronics" might also be winners.

Go alone or with a similarly goal-oriented partner

If you go tagging (by which I mean "visit tag sales," not "write your name in graffiti") with a friend, you are flirting with disaster unless he or she understands that there is to be no dawdling at sales that turn out to be total duds. If you're alone, you can speed through the sales, but if you're burdened down with a compulsively lackadaisical browser, you might as well not even go out. If you can't avoid it, you might want to seek out a flea market, and then split up so you can browse at lightning speed.

Bring lots of $1 bills and change

Change is a little less important, because you'll be doing most of your purchasing in dollar increments. But I can't stress those singles enough. You'll see why in the next section.

At the sale. Once you get there, here are a few things you can do to increase your chances of finding a holy grail (and getting a good deal on it).

Arrive early
> Don't pester people before their advertised start time; if the tag sale starts at 9:00 and you're there at 8:00 while they're still setting up, it's considered rude. But neither should you head out for the day at 1 PM. By that time, you've missed everything.

Ask, ask, ask
> If you're at someone's house, and you don't see any video games, *ask*! Many people might just have decided not to bother dragging the games out of the attic or basement. "You wouldn't happen to have any old video games around, would you?" can work wonders. And even if you see old video games out on the lawn...ask if they have any more!

The marked price is a suggestion; you're supposed to bargain
> Talk them down! If it's marked $10, offer $5 and see where it goes from there. Maybe you'll get $7. (Warning: don't attempt this when the seller is under eleven years old. You'll look like a jerk.)

Have the appropriate amount of singles in your hand
> One of the most aggravating things about selling at a garage sale or flea market is having to make change, especially when you don't have enough singles to do so. Ease their burden by having the appropriate amount ready in your hand. It's harder to get somebody to take $5 for a $10 item when you're brandishing a $20.

If they have many different things that you want, make an offer for the lot
> But don't say, "Will you take [amount] for all this?" The first thing you should do is ask, "What would you want for all this?" They might give you a lower price than you were about to say, just happy to get rid of so much "junk" in one fell swoop!

Finally, there's one really awful tip that I'm keeping out of the main list. I've never seen it work, and in fact it might just make you look ridiculous. However, if you feel like you've established a rapport with the seller, pick up an item and say, "Would [amount] *be too much to offer* for this?"

Note that almost any answer to this question is in your favor. Of course, if you're not really good at this, you'll just end up embarrassing yourself. You might experiment with this at a flea market far from home.

Playing Neo-Retro Games
Hacks 15–19

Retro is in, baby! Old is new! Then is now! There's a legion of twentysome-things out there who are just beginning to feel the regressive pangs of nostalgia for their lost childhood, and you know what that means—it's time to make some money off it! I'm referring not simply to O'Reilly Media and myself here. Video game companies are starting to realize the value of their back catalogs, and we're getting the benefits.

Or are we? For every collection of retro games that's full of quality titles on the cheap for your PlayStation 2, there's another that's buggy, unfun, and overpriced. For every all-in-one joystick controller that packs in perfect emulated versions of classic games for a low price on the shelves of Wal-Mart, there's one made of shoddy materials and filled with crappy software.

Retro games might be budget titles, but that doesn't mean you can't get ripped off. This chapter shows you how to separate the wheat from the chaff when it comes to newly-marketed retro games. You'll even learn how to play a stack of retro-styled games for free. That's a deal you can't beat.

Play Retro Games in All-in-One Joysticks
HACK #15
Plug-and-play classic titles with ease. You don't even need a game console!

What's the easiest way to play retro games right now? Emulation requires more computer knowledge than most people have, and retro collections for modern game systems [Hack #16] require you to purchase hundreds of dollars worth of hardware before you can play them.

There is a solution for the rest of us, and it's more than likely that you've already seen them around. Standalone plug-and-play joysticks going by names like TV Games and Arcade Legends have been all over toy and electronics stores for the past few years. These devices run off of AA batteries and plug directly into your television set, containing a handful of games and a joystick all in one compact piece of hardware. You can't add in any more games, but since most of them retail for between $20 and $25, that's not such a big deal.

But not all is perfect. Retro gaming hackers have found that some of the games differ substantially from the classic versions. In this hack, I'll give you some general information on the value and quality of each device, supplemented (where possible) by my own hands-on impressions.

> In shopping malls across the United States, especially around Christmastime, it's not at all uncommon to see kiosks spring up in the middle of the mall selling all-in-one gaming joysticks that play classic Nintendo games like Super Mario Bros. These often go by the name "Power Player" and are shaped like Nintendo 64 joypads. These are bootleg, unauthorized devices. At the time of this writing, Nintendo has not officially released any such device.

Jakks Pacific

The leader of the all-in-one games revolution has some excellent products to its name from a variety of popular publishers.

Atari Classics 10 in 1 TV Games. This is the device that kicked off the TV Games boom a few years back (see Figure 2-1). Packing ten Atari 2600 classic titles into a joystick nearly the exact shape and size as the 2600 joysticks everyone remembers, it was a smash hit product for Christmas 2002. It includes the games Adventure, Asteroids, Breakout, Centipede, Circus Atari, Gravitar, Missile Command, Pong, Real Sports Volleyball, and Yars Revenge.

The games are mostly accurate, but not entirely. One of the biggest goof-ups is that the famous "Easter Egg" in the game Adventure, in which you used to be able to find designer Warren Robinette's name, now only leads to a screen that reads "TEXT." Another complaint is that a full three of these games—Breakout, Pong, and Circus Atari—were originally designed for the paddle controller, and don't work well at all with the joystick.

Atari Paddle Controller with 13 TV Games. Addressing many of the issues with the 10 in 1 controller, Jakks released this paddle controller (Figure 2-2) around two years later. The Atari 2600 system originally shipped with a pair of these controllers. The quality of the games in this version is said to be much better than the previous model, although I have only played the Pong game included (and it was pretty good).

Figure 2-1. Atari Classics 10 in 1

In all, it contains seven new 2600 games—Warlords, Super Breakout, Demons to Diamonds, Night Driver, Casino, Canyon Bomber, Steeple-chase, and Street Racer. It also contains the three 2600 games that use the paddle that were also included in the joystick version—Pong, Circus Atari, and Breakout. And rounding out the package are the original arcade versions of Warlords and Pong.

Be aware that a two-player version, with two paddle controllers, is available for $10 more than the single-player model.

Atari Flashback 2. Released as this book went to press, the Atari Flashback 2 console contains 40 classic games, including several homebrew games and prototypes. It's a huge improvement over the original Flashback console, which was hobbled by uncomfortable controllers that resembled those of the Atari 7800 [Hack #37] and some bad game conversions. The Flashback 2,

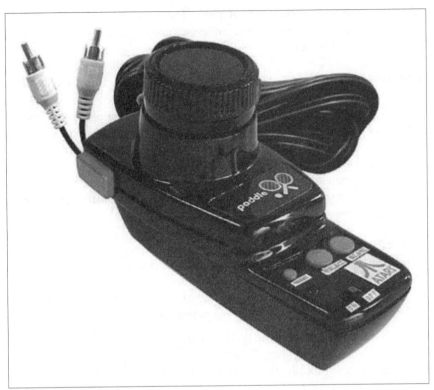

Figure 2-2. Atari Paddle Controller 13 in 1

on the other hand, features a form factor modeled after the original woodgrain style Atari 2600 [Hack #3], and captures the feel of a real Atari by using classic-styled joysticks—you can even use these joysticks with an older 2600 console! Highlights include some sequels to previously released titles such as Yars' Return, Return to Haunted House, Combat 2, and Adventure 2. The hard-to-find-in-cart-form Quadrun (complete with voice support), is also included, as are Secret Quest and Off the Wall. If you want to play the classics, they're here too—Pong, Asteroids, Centipede, Millipede, Breakout, Missile Command, and Combat are as good as ever. You'll need your own paddles to play some of these games, but it's worth digging them out: there are additional paddle games "hidden" in the unit. If you get stuck and can't find them, check out this AtariAge forum: *http://www.atariage.com/forums/ index.php?showtopic=75350.*

Still need another reason to drop $29.99 on this system? Here it is: the console is hack-friendly, so you can add a cartridge slot to the Flashback 2. All you have to do is solder a ribbon cable to the motherboard and add the slot. The connections are clearly labeled on the motherboard, and it doesn't take an expert technician to do it right. The process will void your warranty, however. See *http://www.atarimuseum.com/fb2hacks/* for illustrated instructions, and enjoy!

Activision 10 in 1 TV Games. Many of the best Atari 2600 games were actually made not by Atari but by a publisher called Activision. Luckily, they've licensed some of their classics to Jakks Pacific as well, and you can find an Activision version of the joysticks in stores now. It contains ten games: Pitfall, Atlantis, River Raid, Spider Fighter, Crackpots, Freeway, Tennis, Boxing, Ice Hockey, and Grand Prix. The joystick model is based on some of the third-party joysticks that were released for the 2600 back in the day; it is much more comfortable and features a fire button on the top of the stick for extra ease of use.

Namco: Pac-Man. Namco's Pac-Man controller (Figure 2-3) is the first TV Games joystick that made me stand up and take notice. I was never much of an Atari player, but the idea of having an inexpensive, attractive-looking joystick that played five Namco games—Pac-Man, Dig Dug, Galaxian, Rally-X, and Bosconian—was enough to get me pretty excited.

I wasn't disappointed with the final product—the retro-styled menu screen shown in Figure 2-4 was particularly cool—but I did find that the versions of the games were hardly arcade-perfect. Indeed, it seems they were reprogrammed from scratch. The Pac-Man patterns **[Hack #81]** that allow you to evade the ghosts in the original arcade versions simply don't work, and you'll notice other changes made to the rest of the games.

And although I love the snazzy yellow-topped joystick, it's very hard to hit the diagonal inputs. This isn't really a problem with four of the five games, but it makes Bosconian basically unplayable. If this is a problem for you, you might check out the pocket version of this device that Jakks recently released. The joystick is replaced with an eight-way directional thumbpad and the entire device fits into a much smaller form factor.

Namco II: Ms. Pac-Man. Following up the success of the first Namco games joystick, Jakks released a sequel featuring Ms. Pac-Man, Galaga, Xevious, Pole Position, and Mappy. The pros and cons of the first Pac-Man joystick apply here as well. The reason it gets its own section is because by the time you read this, Jakks will have released a wireless version of the controller, as shown in Figure 2-5. Plug the included wireless base into your TV set and you can carry the joystick anywhere you want. It seems as if they are only releasing the Ms. Pac-Man stick as a wireless product, but as a bonus it

Figure 2-3. Pac-Man all-in-one joystick

Figure 2-4. The boot menu screen for Pac-Man

includes a full seven games—the five just mentioned, as well as Bosconian and New Rally-X. It will retail for about $40.

Figure 2-5. The wireless Ms. Pac-Man controller

They're not as retro as other joysticks, but Jakks has also released controllers that play Mortal Kombat and the 1995 versions of Electronic Arts' Madden Football and NHL Hockey. I haven't had the chance to test either, but the Mortal Kombat game is apparently based on the lackluster Genesis version of the game, and the sports package doesn't contain any player names due to licensing issues.

Building on the success of the TV Games joysticks with the younger market, Jakks has released several entries in the series that feature original, simple games aimed directly at the pre-K set. Amazon.com reviews have been relatively kind to the Spongebob Squarepants, Spider-Man, and Disney games among others. These aren't retro games *per se*, but they bring back the simplicity and broad appeal of the old days.

Majesco

Not to be outdone, jack-of-all-trades gaming publisher Majesco has part-nered with Konami to release standalone versions of that company's classic franchises.

Konami Arcade Advanced. Much like the controllers listed earlier—and even though its name is Arcade Advanced—this joystick doesn't actually contain the original arcade games. The hacker community's best guess is that (like many of the other products mentioned in this hack), what is inside this joy-stick is a miniature Nintendo Entertainment System clone that plays NES ports of the games.

If this sounds fine to you, Konami Arcade Advanced is a good addition to your plug-and-play collection. The most popular game on the device is Frog-ger, but the rest—Rush N' Attack, Gyruss, Scramble, Yie Ar Kung Fu, and Time Pilot—are classics in their own right.

This controller takes its name from a Game Boy Advance title also released by Majesco that features the same six Konami games. At the time of this writing it can be pur-chased new from Amazon.com for $11.95.

Frogger TV Arcade. I'm scratching my head as to why this even exists. It's a standalone joystick, shown in Figure 2-6, that only includes one game—the exact same version of Frogger included in the Konami Arcade Advanced joy-stick. Both models cost exactly the same amount of money. So...why would you buy this one? The mind boggles.

There's one more entry so far in the TV Arcade series, called Golden Nugget Casino. It's not a retro game, although I'm sure it's enjoyed a bit of success due to the current Texas Hold 'Em craze...

Radica

You might not have heard of the company, but Radica has partnered with some strong licensors to bring classic arcade and home games to the plug-and-play format.

Arcade Legends: Space Invaders. Much like the Namco joysticks—although Arcade Legends: Space Invaders is named after the most recognizable game included in the package—it actually contains five: Space Invaders, Lunar Rescue, Colony 7, Qix, and Phoenix. And much like the Majesco joysticks,

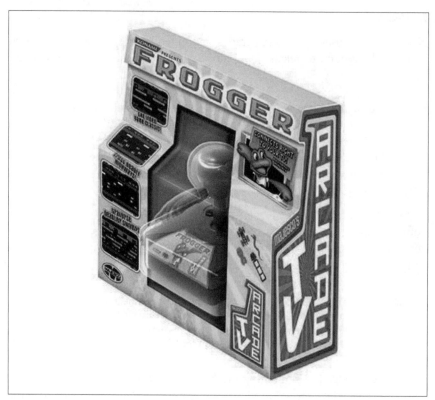

Figure 2-6. Frogger—yes, just Frogger

although it includes the word *Arcade* right there on the box, these are most likely NES ports.

Sigh. Well, for my money Qix is still the most playable, innovative, addictive, and damn hard of the games on the device. By drawing boxes with a cursor, you have to wall off a certain percentage of the screen without touching the Qix, an evil bastard represented by flashing strings of light.

This, like Radica's other games (listed next), originally retailed for a wallet-breaking $34.99, but prices have since come down at most discount retailers and toy stores.

Sega Genesis series. At last—here's a retro game control pad (see Figure 2-7), that couldn't *possibly* contain a miniature NES clone inside. Though the company has since left the hardware business, there was a time when the Sega Genesis console was at the top of the United States' video game business. Speeding into gamers' homes on the back of Sonic the Hedgehog, the Genesis was the most popular system of its day (much to the chagrin of Nintendo).

Figure 2-7. The Sega Genesis Arcade Legends joystick, version 1

And now you can relive those classic games with three separate plug-and-play control pads. Since the controllers themselves are perfect replicas of the originals, the actual hardware can't fit inside. So the controllers are attached to a tiny box that looks sort of like a miniature Genesis, which then attaches to the TV.

The first version of the controller includes Sonic the Hedgehog (naturally), Altered Beast (the original pack-in game for the console until the blue blur bumped the beast out), Kid Chameleon, Flicky, Golden Axe, and Dr. Robotnik's Mean Bean Machine (a Sonic-branded version of the popular puzzler Puyo Puyo). True classics all.

The follow-up edition included Sonic the Hedgehog 2 (of course), Columns, Ecco the Dolphin, The Ooze, Alex Kidd in the Enchanted Castle, and Gain Ground. Perhaps these classics aren't as well-remembered as the first joystick's selection, but it's hard to argue with the first three, at least.

Finally, the latest addition to the series features the Genesis port of Street Fighter II: Special Champion Edition. It was never the best version of Street Fighter (that honor belonged to the versions for the Super Nintendo), but the six-button Genesis control pad that was released alongside it was quite nice (and inspired the amazing Sega Saturn pad design).

This $39.99 package includes two six-button controllers in the original design and two games inside the mini-Genesis box: SFII: SCE and Ghouls N' Ghosts, another Capcom classic that Sega ported to the Genesis back in the day.

Other Sticks of Note

Computer hackers will appreciate the Commodore 64 30-in-1 plug-and-play device, not only for the wealth of classic software included but because you can hack a Commodore keyboard and floppy drive into the unit [Hack #57].

There's one other major retro-games joystick on the market today, though I'm sad to say it merits but a footnote. The Intellivision joysticks, released in 25-game and 10-game versions, were almost universally panned by those who love the originals. They just don't play anything like them, with poor control and sloppy emulation.

Hopefully, if the plug-and-play gaming market continues to grow, we'll see a better and more accurate Intellivision device hit the shelves one day. For now, I'd recommend the console game Intellivision Lives [Hack #16].

HACK #16 Play Retro Games on Current Consoles

Sift through the many classic collections on PS2, Xbox, and GameCube.

Playing retro games with inexpensive plug-and-play hardware [Hack #15] is quite convenient if you don't already own any video game systems. But what if you do? What if you're used to using your Wavebird, Dual Shock 2, or Controller S for all your gameplay, and want a retro game solution that will work with your system(s) of choice?

Well, there are quite a few game publishers willing to accommodate you. Now that retro fever has taken hold, you can buy collections of classic games, emulated or reprogrammed to play on modern-day gaming systems. Although they typically retail for a budget price of $19.99, the quality of the packages can vary. In this hack, I'll give you the rundown on all the major classic game collections on the shelves, and some preliminary information on upcoming releases that will hopefully be out by the time you get this book.

Publisher-Based Collections

The compilations listed next feature a variety of games from a single publisher; sometimes encompassing all the games that a classic publisher ever released on a single system—and then some!

Midway Arcade Treasures. The original Midway Arcade Treasures was one of the first retro collections to hit stores. As its name so aptly implies, it contains emulated versions of Midway's classic arcade hits. There are currently two volumes in stores, with another on the way this year. They are available for PS2, GameCube, and Xbox.

The first volume includes the oldest of the old classics. Highlights include Spy Hunter, Defender, Joust, Paperboy, Smash TV, Robotron 2084, Sinistar, Marble Madness, Satan's Hollow, etc. All in all, 24 games are on the disc. (Not included are arcade games that Midway distributed in the United States, but no longer holds the rights to, like Pac-Man and Space Invaders. Pac-Man can be found in Namco Museum, listed later in this hack.)

The second volume, Midway Arcade Treasures 2, features some more recent classics: Mortal Kombat II and 3, Gauntlet II, NARC, Total Carnage, Pit Fighter, Xenophobe, etc. There are 20 games in total. Both volumes include a wealth of bonus content like developer interviews, making-of video segments, and art galleries.

I recommend you buy either the GameCube or Xbox versions of the games. All three are virtually identical, but since the GameCube and Xbox have four controller ports each, you can play the three- and four-player games like Rampage, Gauntlet, and Rampart without having to buy extra hardware. (Rampage just isn't Rampage unless you've got three giant monsters!)

Atari Anthology. Interestingly enough, the most famous of retro game publishers was the last to the party with their compilation. They certainly packed quite a bit of content inside, though. Atari Anthology features 18 classic Atari arcade games and a whopping 67 Atari 2600 games. It is available for PS2 and Xbox.

The arcade games are ones you'll all remember: Battlezone, Asteroids, Centipede, Tempest, Super Breakout... even Pong. The games play identically to the originals (although at first it can be a pain in the butt to use a joystick for Tempest and Centipede instead of a spinner or trackball). The games are all bordered by artwork that imitates the design of the arcade machines, but I found this to be rather poorly implemented, because the playable area of the screen shrinks and it's hard to pick out details.

The Atari 2600 titles here might not include the ones you remember best, mostly because many of the most memorable titles were either licensed games (and the license has long expired) or created by Activision (who have their own anthology available, described later). So you won't find Pac-Man, Raiders of the Lost Ark, or Space Invaders on this disc.

The games you do find range from the truly classic (Yar's Revenge, Adventure, Demons to Diamonds) to the I-wish-I-could-forget-them (3D Tic Tac Toe, Atari Video Cube, Atari Math Gran Prix, Video Checkers). Well, at least Quadrun is here (the original game sells for about $400 now).

The disc also includes some great extra features. There's a large art gallery in which you can view box art, manuals, and artwork for every game in the collection. My favorites are the extra gameplay modes, especially Hot Seat. In this mode, you begin by playing the game you've selected. But after a minute or so, you're switched to another game, then another. If you pick the arcade version of Crystal Castles, for example, you'll be switching back and forth between it, the home version of Crystal Castles, and the shooting game Outlaw. As the games go on the intervals get shorter, and you're challenged to essentially keep track of your place in three games at once!

Atari Retro on the Go

Depending on your portable system of choice, there may be a classic Atari collection for your mobile lifestyle. Atari Retro (*http://www.mobilewizardry. com/multi-platform/atariretro/index.php*) is a software package available for Palm, Pocket PC, and Nokia Series 60 Smartphones that includes seven games on a single MMC card.

Also available is Retro Atari Classics for the Nintendo DS system, which features versions of ten different Atari games. These are not emulated; they are entirely reprogrammed and redesigned to take advantage of the DS' dual-screen, touch-enabled hardware. You can slide the Breakout paddle with your finger, for example. It also includes "remix" versions of all the games, which feature graphic updates by popular graffiti artists.

You'll also find many of the titles described in this hack for the Nintendo Gameboy Advance, including Activision Anthology and collections from Midway and Namco.

Intellivision Lives! This collection is unique in that it was created by some of the original programmers who developed the library of games for the Intellivision. (For more about these guys, who are called the Blue Sky Rangers, see [Hack #35].) Over 60 of the games that Mattel created for the Intellivision are in this package.

Since the games are split up by category, it can be a little difficult to find the game you're looking for. In fact, the manual doesn't even list them all. So to find out all the games in the collection, you have to visit each "machine" in a virtual arcade that serves as the game's hub screen.

Some of the classics to be had include Astrosmash (a space shooter made *much* easier by using the PS2's controller instead of the Intellivision's original painful design), the strategy game Utopia, and of course Baseball (this used to be called MLB Baseball, but like the rest of Intellivision's stellar sports lineup, the licenses have long run out).

Those who remember the Intellivision might be wondering how the system's controller—which featured a numeric keypad that was used heavily in many games—is emulated. Pressing the Select button brings up an image of the classic controller on the TV screen, pasted over the game display. You can then use the analog stick to move a cursor around and push the buttons. This is a limited, but understandable, solution.

Bonus features include historical information, a handful of previously unreleased games, and interviews with the Blue Sky Rangers. You can even view classic Intellivision TV commercials.

Activision Anthology. This was one of the very first retro collections to hit shelves—and still one of the best. It helps, of course, that Activision's Atari 2600 titles were some of the best software on the system (and based on original ideas, thus the company still owns the rights to publish them). But what really makes Activision Anthology worth a purchase is the amount of polish that went into its design.

First things first. There are 45 classic games on this PlayStation 2 disc, all from the 2600. If you owned one, or even if you didn't, you know about or have played Activision's games: Pitfall, Freeway, Ice Hockey, Kaboom, River Raid, Stampede... any of this ringing a bell? There are a few previously unreleased games here as well, and the emulation on everything is fantastic.

That's just scratching the surface. One of the best touches to Activision Anthology is the photorealistic 1980's vintage gaming setup that serves as the main menu. The game cartridges are accessible from a classic spinning organizer, and a stereo off to the side of the TV set plays a classic 80's soundtrack, featuring brilliant songs like "We're Not Gonna Take It," "Tainted Love," "Take on Me," and "Safety Dance."

Adding this soundtrack to the mix makes the games even more fun, and a variety of unlockable extras—including new video modes that map the game display onto rotating cubes or trippy patterns—are available for scoring high on every game. Even Activision's 2600 version of the Data East/Capcom shooter Commando is on here—wonder how they arranged that?

A version of Activision Anthology for the Game Boy Advance was released to rave reviews, not only for the accuracy of the emulation but because Activision included in the package many games from the Atari 2600 homebrew development community [Hack #75].

Namco Museum. Namco Museum titles, featuring the company's classic games like Pac-Man and Dig Dug, have been released for a number of different systems, including the PSone and Dreamcast [Hack #17], but the package currently on shelves is available for the Xbox and PlayStation 2.

In comparison to the packages listed so far, Namco Museum's game list is paltry. The classics available when you boot the game number only seven: Pac-Man, Ms. Pac-Man, Galaga, Galaxian, Dig Dug, Pole Position, and Pole Position II. If you score over 25,000 points on the two Pac games, you'll unlock two more: Pac-Mania and Pac-Attack.

The games are reprogrammed rather than emulated, which means that you might find them to be slightly different than the arcade games you remember or just completely wrong. For example, if you know any Pac-Man tricks [Hack #81] you might be disappointed to find that they don't work at all in the Namco Museum version.

The rest of the collection is filled out with what Namco dubs "Arrangement" versions of the games. These are similar to the classic games, but with 3D graphics and some new gameplay elements. In Pac-Man Arrangement, there is a new ghost named "Kinky" (not even kidding you), and panels on the floor let you dash at high speed, knocking out ghosts in your path. Unfortunately, some of the arranged games feel unfinished—there are no sound effects to be heard in Pac-Man Arrangement, for example, just music.

> Namco has released a Museum collection for the Sony PSP handheld. It features many more classic games (seventeen instead of seven), head-to-head play over WiFi, and Arrangement versions that are much better and well-suited to the portable hardware.

NES Classic Series. Leave it to Nintendo to do things differently. Rather than releasing multiple Nintendo Entertainment System titles in one console package, they split the games up into single budget-priced releases for the Game Boy Advance system. Currently available for $19.99 each (although you can find most of them cheaper now) are Super Mario Bros., The Legend of Zelda, Ice Climber, Excitebike, Donkey Kong, Xevious, Bomberman, Pac-Man, Metroid, Castlevania, Dr. Mario, and Zelda II: The Adventure of Link.

The emulation is decent, considering that the games had to be compressed to fit onto the GBA's smaller, differently proportioned screen. At twenty bucks each, buying a complete collection might be a bit expensive, but it's not difficult to imagine people dropping the cash for one or two special favorites.

That said, some of these releases are pretty much rip-offs, since you can find many of these games hidden within others [Hack #19]. For example, if you buy the game Metroid: Zero Mission for the GBA and complete the main game (which is tons of fun and not especially taxing) you'll unlock the same version of Metroid that sells for $19.99 on its own. And it's tough to justify an entire Hamilton for NES Pac-Man when the Namco Museum and Pac-Man Collection games for GBA include the same game plus a few more.

There are more than double the number of classic games available on the Game Boy Advance in Japan than in the United States. If you want to pick up some Famicom Mini titles, as they are called, check out "Collect Classic Handhelds" [Hack #11].

Single-Series Collections

The second category of neo-retro game releases focus not on a single publisher's lineup, but on collecting all (or most of) the installments of a particular series. These can be a boon to collectors, especially as the price of the originals continues to escalate.

The Legend of Zelda Collector's Edition. This was only made available as a promotional giveaway, although there were quite a few ways to get it. You could subscribe to Nintendo Power magazine, register some other Nintendo games on the company's web site, or buy a GameCube and get it included for free. The promotions are all over, but many discs routinely go up for sale on eBay or in the used bins at outlets like EB Games and Gamestop.

The disc includes the two Legend of Zelda games for NES as well as the two N64 installments of the series (Ocarina of Time and Majora's Mask), all emulated to run on the GameCube hardware. The only emulation glitch comes in Majora's Mask; at times the sound will skip. This is a minor flaw though, especially for a collection that was essentially given away for free.

Sonic Mega Collection. Originally a GameCube exclusive, an updated version of this collection is now available for the PlayStation 2 and Xbox. It is just what you might think it is—a compilation of the 16-bit adventures of Sonic the Hedgehog. The only games represented are the Genesis installments of the series, which means that Knuckles Chaotix for the 32X or Sonic CD for the Sega CD are sadly not present.

Bonus games depend on which version you buy. The GameCube only features Sega platformers Flicky and Ristar as unlockable secrets, but the PS2 and Xbox games feature those two plus well-regarded Genesis hits Comix Zone and The Ooze.

Mega Man Anniversary Collection. Another blue-clad hero gets his own multi-platform collection? It's true. Capcom has collected the ten games in the main Mega Man series, which were originally released on the NES, SNES, and in arcades, and put them all together for GameCube, PS2, and most recently the Xbox. You may wish to avoid the GameCube version, as the jump and fire buttons are reversed from the original NES layout, which has caused many players no end of frustration.

Classics to Come

And the hits keep on coming. Flush from the success of Mega Man Anniversary Collection, Capcom has announced that an arcade collection for consoles is on the way. As mentioned earlier, Midway Arcade Treasures 3 will be out this year, featuring some more recent racing titles. And a collection of classic Taito games is planned for release in Europe, though no Stateside release has been announced.

No, the retro game craze won't be over until the last remaining publisher has finally put out a collection of its arcade classics... and by that time, the next generation of console hardware will be available, so they'll probably start re-releasing the oldies all over again. What a great racket!

HACK #17 Play Retro Games on Older Systems

Mess around with older attempts at classic collections.

How retro are you? So retro you don't even have a PlayStation 2 or Xbox? Possibly. But I bet you've at least got a PSone or a Nintendo 64 around somewhere.

("But," you explain, "it was on sale, and isn't it retro nowadays? Hell, it came out in 1994...")

Okay, okay, I get it. You're retro. But you've got to admit, those classic game compilations [Hack #16] look pretty sweet, huh? Come on, I see you staring. You might want to know that there are a few retro game collections for older systems, too. Some are well done, but some are total ripoffs. In this hack, I'll help you separate the golden oldies from the just plain outdated.

A few of the games discussed in this section are available only in Japan. To learn how to get your hands on these games, read "Buy Retro Games from Japan" [Hack #9].

Classic Arcade Game Collections

Home versions of arcade games were always inferior to their coin-op counterparts. That was just something we had to deal with back then. Not in today's age of high-powered hardware, right? Yes and no. While some of the collections shown next are perfect, others have some problems. Read before you buy!

Namco Museum. You can find Namco Museum collections, which feature a sampling of the company's classic arcade games, on most contemporary systems from the Xbox to the PSP. But the series started on the PlayStation, which is where the most complete array of titles can still be found. All in all, Namco released a full six volumes of Namco Museum for the PSone—though only five of them were brought to the United States. They were released between 1996 and 1997.

There are more than a few reasons why you might want to buy the PSone versions of the games. They're presented in much more attractive packaging—each volume bearing one letter of the Namco logo, rather than a jumbled collection of screenshots like the later versions. And the games are accurately emulated from the arcade versions; you can adjust the "machine" settings and change the games around just like an arcade operator would. Later editions do not include this feature.

Here's a list of what games are included in each collection.

Namco Museum Volume 1
> Pac-Man, Pole Position, Rally-X, Galaga, Bosconian, Toy Pop

Namco Museum Volume 2
> Mappy, Xevious, Super Pac-Man, Gaplus, Grobda, Dragon Buster

Namco Museum Volume 3
> The Tower of Druaga, Ms. Pac-Man, Galaxian, Phozon, Pole Position 2, Dig Dug

Namco Museum Volume 4
> Pac-Land, Ordyne, Assault, The Return of Ishtar, The Genji and the Heike Clans

Namco Museum Volume 5
> Pac-Mania, Baraduke, Dragon Spirit, The Legend of Valkyrie, Metro-Cross

Namco Museum Encore (Japan-only release)
> Rolling Thunder, SkyKid, Dragon Sabre, King & Balloon, Motos, Rompers, Wonder Momo

There is a single Namco Museum title for the Nintendo 64 called, appropriately enough, Namco Museum 64. It features the games Pac-Man, Ms. Pac-Man, Galaxian, Galaga, Dig Dug, and Pole Position.

Atari Collections. During the 1990s the rights to Atari's games bounced back and forth like the dot in Pong, before coming to a permanent stop at French publisher Infogrames (who now call themselves Atari). In the meantime, several collections of Atari arcade classics were released, often of dubious quality. Some of the titles you may still find in bargain bins include:

Arcade's Greatest Hits: The Atari Collection, Vol. 1 and Vol. 2 (Midway, PlayStation, 1996/1997)

The first volume of this collection contains emulated versions of six golden-age Atari arcade games: Asteroids, Battlezone, Centipede, Super Breakout, Missile Command, and Tempest. The second contains some Atari titles—Crystal Castles and Millipede—mixed with some classic Midway games: Paperboy, Roadblasters, Marble Madness, and Gauntlet. The first was well-received, but Midway seems to have dropped the ball with the second volume—its emulation isn't accurate, and the video is poor. Much like...

Atari Anniversary Edition (Atari, Sega Dreamcast, 2001)

This collection of twelve of Atari's most well-known arcade titles was universally panned. The critical drubbing mostly centered on the terrible visuals, which looked markedly worse than the arcade originals, and the fact that the Dreamcast's painful controller design wasn't up to the task. Games included are Asteroids, Asteroids Deluxe, Battlezone, Centipede, Crystal Castles, Gravitar, Millipede, Missile Command, Pong, Super Breakout, Tempest, and Warlords.

The other collection in this series is Williams Arcade's Greatest Hits, which features six titles originally released under the Williams name: Defender, Stargate, Robotron: 2084, Joust, Sinistar, and Bubbles.

Capcom Generation. Arcade giant Capcom produced an arcade anthology series much like Namco Museum on the PSone and Sega Saturn. The Capcom Generation games were for the most part released only in Japan, with one exception: Capcom Generation 5 for the PSone was released in the United States as Street Fighter Collection 2.

The collections are excellent, if a bit light on content at only three games each. The games were organized by series:

Capcom Generation 1
  1942, 1943, 1943 Kai

Capcom Generation 2
  Ghouls 'N Ghosts, Ghosts 'N Goblins, Super Ghouls 'N Ghosts

Capcom Generation 3
  Vulgus, Son Son, Higemaru, Exed Eyes

Capcom Generation 4
  Commando, Mercs, Gun.Smoke

Capcom Generation 5
  Street Fighter II, SFII Champion Edition, SFII Turbo

Konami Antiques: MSX Collection. Jumping on the PSone retro release bandwagon, Konami released its Konami Antiques collection, featuring the large selection of games that the publisher released for the MSX computer in Japan, on PSone and Sega Saturn. Bizarrely, the PSone collection is split up over three volumes that were sold seperately, whereas the one-disc Saturn version of the game contains all thirty titles listed.

In general, these are not exceptional games. They're only really relevant to Japanese gamers with lots of nostalgia for the old MSX software they used to play. If you gag when you look at the blocky graphics of Atari 2600 games, these probably aren't for you. You will certainly recognize a few of the titles in the list, though, because the arcade and/or Nintendo Entertainment System versions of them were released in the United States. (The "Hyper Sports" games, for example, were released as the very popular Track and Field series here.)

Konami Antiques MSX Collection Vol. 1
  Konami Boxing, Konami Ping-Pong, Mopiranger, Arctic Adventure, Yie Ar Kung Fu, Road Fighter, Sky Jaguar, Gradius, Ambition of Gofer

Konami Antiques MSX Collection Vol. 2
  Konami Golf, Konami Billiards, Athletic Land, Magical Tree, Super Cobra, Twin Bee, Gradius 2, Hyper Sports 3, Knightmare, Yie Ar Kung Fu 2

Konami Antiques MSX Collection Vol. 3
  Konami Tennis, Konami Soccer, Konami Rally, Pippols, King's Valley, Time Pilot, Parodius, Comic Bakery, Penguin Adventure, Salamander

Classic Home Game Collections

Arcade games are all well and good, but my collection of retro console games is getting too unwieldy to bring along with me every time I move. Thank goodness for the following collections!

Activision Classics. Released on the PSone in 1998, this collection of games that Activision released on the Atari 2600 system certainly didn't lack for content. It included thirty of the publisher's classic titles: Atlantis, Barnstorming, Boxing, Chopper Command, Cosmic Commuter, Crackpots, Dolphin, Dragster, Enduro, Fishing Derby, Freeway, Frostbite, Grand Prix, Hero, Ice Hockey, Kaboom!, Keystone Kapers, Laser Blast, Megamania, Pitfall, Plaque Attack, River Raid, River Raid 2, Sea Quest, Skiing, Sky Jinks, Spider Fighter, Stampede, Starmaster, and Tennis.

Unfortunately, the emulation just isn't as good (and the package not as impressive) as Activision Anthology on the PS2.

Intellivision Classics. Another Activision PSone release, another thirty games, but this time they're straight from the Intellivision console. Included on this disc are Armor Battle, Astrosmash, Auto Racing, Baseball, Basketball, Boxing, Checkers, Chess, Football, Frog Bog, Golf, Hockey, Hover Force, Las Vegas Poker and Blackjack, Night Stalker, Pinball, Sea Battle, Shark! Shark!, Sharp Shot, Skiing, Snafu, Soccer, Space Armada, Space Battle, Space Hawk, Spiker! Super Pro Volleyball, Stadium Mud Buggies, Star Strike, Sub Hunt, and Tennis.

> Although this Intellivision collection is considered to be pretty good, there are much better ways to get your INTV fix [Hack #35].

Play Contemporary Classics
HACK #18
Find and play new games that feel old.

Retro gaming isn't just about playing old games. That is to say, what separates classic video games from contemporary titles isn't just their age. Game design as a whole has changed radically since the days of 2D shooters and point-and-click adventures, and to find new examples of those types of games on modern consoles is quite rare.

Luckily, there are quite a few game designers committed to the idea of creating new games using the design sense of a past age. What's more, quite a few of them are available for free. In this hack, I'll tell you about some web sites you can visit to download and play games that offer entirely new gameplay experiences. In large part, these aren't remakes or throwbacks to old classics, but original designs. Imagine it as an alternate reality where 3D never took off, but game design continued on.

 Many (though not all) of the games described in this section are playable right in your web browser, using plug-in software such as Java or Flash. Be aware that while the sites described here are free of spyware, annoying pop-up windows, and other such bothersome things, there are quite a few sites offering free web-based gaming that will assault your computer with all sorts of unwanted things. Use your best judgment.

PopCap Games

One of the most successful web-based gaming sites, PopCap Games (*http://www.popcap.com*), has nurtured some original, simple designs to the heights of success. You've probably heard of one or two of its more famous offerings. Bejeweled is a puzzle game in which you match up gems of like colors, and Bookworm (shown in Figure 2-8) challenges you to make words out of a random screen full of Scrabble-style lettered tiles. But the site also offers about two dozen other games in a variety of genres, all featuring simple gameplay that anyone can get into.

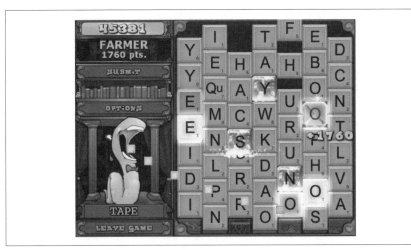

Figure 2-8. Bookworm, an addictive and educational word game playable at PopCap Games

Every game is designed to be played right in your web browser (you'll have to download a free, safe Java runtime applet). If you're tired of playing online, PopCap offers free downloadable standalone versions of each game. If you want to upgrade to the super deluxe editions, you can buy them either as a download or shipped to you on CD. The site even offers versions of many of the games that will play on your PDA, whether Palm or Windows Mobile (Pocket PC).

Newgrounds

On the opposite end of the web-based gaming spectrum is Newgrounds (*http://www.newgrounds.com*). PopCap Games offers a concise selection of polished, professional, complete games. Newgrounds, on the other hand, is open to any budding Flash programmer who wishes to inflict his or her designs on the world. Thus, it can be a bit difficult to separate the wheat from the chaff, as it were. (Not to mention that the chaff, and some of the wheat even, can be pretty violent and/or pornographic.)

Newgrounds is becoming well-known these days for being the birthplace of the beautifully designed retro-throwback shooter Alien Hominid. This side-scrolling, hand-animated adventure is reminiscent of arcade classics like Metal Slug and Contra, but with a cartoon design and comic sensibilities. You can buy the full version of the game (shown in Figure 2-9) on the Play-Station 2 and GameCube, but you can still play the incredibly popular Flash prototype in the Games section of Newgrounds.

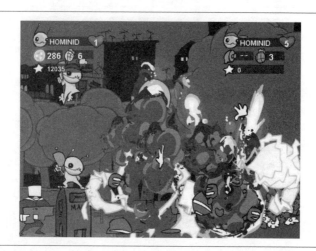

Figure 2-9. The console version of Alien Hominid

Other highlighted games on the site's gaming portal include Soulmech: Shinobu, a hack-and-slash ninja action game; Pimp's Quest, an adventure game with shooting and puzzles all centered around the difficult life of an inner-city pimp; Trapped, a dungeon puzzle game with simple graphics that belie its clever design; and League Bowling, a Flash remake of a popular arcade bowling title. This, of course, is only scratching the surface of the many, varied submissions on Newgrounds. Be aware that most games aren't nearly as fully realized as Alien Hominid, though.

Orisinal

Orisinal (*http://www.orisinal.com*) is a page full of Flash games by artist and web designer Ferry Halim, who has designed Flash animation and games for such clients as Cartoon Network, SciFi Network, and Lifetime. What makes Orisinal so popular and fun is that not only are the games frequently based on original and clever designs, but the art design, music, and animation are all exceptionally beautiful.

One of the most popular titles is Pocketful of Stars (*http://www.ferryhalim. com/orisinal/g2/stars.htm*). I won't spoil the secret of its gameplay; it's something you have to experience for yourself. I also really enjoy the music and design of Cats (*http://www.ferryhalim.com/orisinal/g3/cats.htm*). Each game offers online high score tables, so you can compare yourself against the rest of the Internet.

Homestar Runner

Though Homestar Runner (*http://www.homestarrunner.com*) became an underground success based primarily on the strength of its hilarious and constantly updated Flash-based cartoon shorts starring an array of original characters, the site also boasts some fun and surprisingly detailed Flash games based on the characters.

Mark and Matt Chapman, the brothers who animate and voice nearly everything on the site, are old-school Nintendo fans who constantly drop references to classic gaming in their work. So it's not surprising that their games are all at once parodies and loving tributes to that era, complete with nostalgic opening sequences and throwback graphic styles. Some of the best are:

Population: Tire
Bounce a tire in the air and keep it up as long as you can for a high score. While it's up there, different targets will randomly appear that you can hit for point bonuses.

Peasant's Quest
A parody of/tribute to King's Quest, this lengthy adventure game pokes fun at the parser-based graphic adventures of yore, while being quite adept in the puzzles itself.

Stinko Man

NES players will appreciate the classic graphic effects and intentionally bad translation work (both on display in Figure 2-10) in this Mega Man-styled side-scrolling platform shooter.

Figure 2-10. Stinko Man, hero of badly transrated adventure

Trogdor!

A classic knight-fights-dragon story, as told from the point of view of the dragon. Stomp villagers and burninate their huts, but don't get sworded!

Point-and-Click Adventures

Hey, remember point-and-click adventures like King's Quest and Maniac Mansion? Wish that old genre hadn't shriveled up and died circa 1997? Well, as it turns out, it didn't! Fans of adventure games, people just like you, are churning out new ones every day using the incredible PC software Adventure Game Studio [Hack #80].

But what if you don't want to make one, and would just like to play more 2D adventures with compelling stories and brain-destroying puzzles? If that sounds like you, head on over to the Games page on the project's official web site (*http://www.bigbluecup.com/games.php*) to check out a vast array of titles created with the software. You don't need to download the AGS editor to play them; they're all standalone files. Browse through the AGS Awards section to see the games that have been honored for their achievements. Some of the more popular titles are:

The Adventures of Fatman

Once offered for sale as a commercial product (yes, you can do that with your AGS creations), Fatman is now freely downloadable. The comic adventures of an overweight superhero saving his city from the evil and hazardous Toxicman.

Apprentice

Actually a trilogy of titles starring lovable magician's apprentice Mortimer "Pibs" Pibsworth. Each installment is rather short, but put them all together and you've got a lengthy experience.

King's Quest I VGA

A graphically enhanced (oh boy, is it enhanced) accurate remake of the game that started the genre. In addition to the graphics, shown in all their glory in Figure 2-11, the remakes also feature optional downloads for full sound and voice acting. Also available is a similarly gussied-up remake of King's Quest II.

Figure 2-11. King's Quest I VGA

Hacking the Hack

If you're wondering whether anybody's taken up the challenge of making new games that run not on the PC but on retro video game consoles, there are indeed other hacks—in this very book you are holding!—that cover such things. Check out "Create Your Own Atari 2600 Homebrew Games" **[Hack #75]** and "Put Your Homebrews on Cartridges" **[Hack #78]** for more on newly minted games for older hardware.

 H A C K **#19** ## Find and Play Hidden Classics

Discover bonus retro titles hidden in contemporary titles.

You might have retro games in your home and not even know it! For quite a while now, software publishers have been sneaking ports or emulated versions of classic games into their modern titles. While the list in this hack is nowhere near exhaustive, read on to find out what retro treasures might be tucked away in the games sitting innocently on your shelf.

Animal Crossing

In Nintendo's innovative life-simulation game, you start a new life in a woodland town filled with animal neighbors. As you while away the hours in Animal Crossing you can collect furniture and other things to fill your in-game house with—including NES consoles that play emulated versions of about twenty different games. And if you have a Game Boy Advance and the appropriate link cable, you can download the games to your GBA and play them until you shut the system's power off.

A memory card included with new copies of Animal Crossing will start you off with two random, common NES games. You're supposed to find the rest of them by playing the game and waiting for special events in town, trading with friends, and/or buying packs of Animal Crossing e-Reader cards,* hoping to find rare games. But if you want to skip all that, you can use the following passwords to unlock every common game except *Tennis* and *Pinball*. To use these passwords, talk to Tom Nook in the town's general store and select the "Say Code" option:

> *Balloon Fight*: CbDahLBdaDh98d 9ub8ExzZKwu7Zl
> *Baseball*: 1n5%N%8JUjE5fj 1EcGr4%ync5eUp
> *Clu Clu Land*: Crm%h4BNRyu98d 9uu8exzZKwu7Zl
> *Clu Clu Land D*: Y#PpfrxSOAMLSG B7H3K5xBho5YSY
> *Donkey Kong Junior Math*: bA5PC%8JUjE5fj 1jcGr4%ync5EUp
> *Donkey Kong*: 2n5@N%8JUjE5fj 1jcGr4%ync5EUp
> *Excitebike*: 3%Q4fhMTRByAY3 O5yYAK9zNHxLd7
> *Golf*: Crm%h4BNRbu98d 9un8exzZKwo7Zl
> *Wario's Woods*: bA5PC%8JUjE5fj 1EcGr4%ync5eup

As of this writing, there is another game that takes little effort to snag. To get *Soccer*, go to the official Animal Crossing web page at *http://www.animal-crossing.com/news.jsp* and click the banner with the talking pelicans. You'll be taken to a special Flash-based page where you will be able to enter your name and town information from Animal Crossing to receive a unique code for Soccer. Enter the code using the same methods as the others. (Other games that were previously released in this manner include *Donkey Kong Jr.* and *Donkey Kong 3*, but the pages are no longer available on the site and no universal passcodes have been found for either.)

That leaves five games: *Ice Climber, Punch-Out, Super Mario Bros., The Legend of Zelda,* and *Mario Bros.* The only legitimate way to unlock these is to buy packs of Animal Crossing e-Reader cards and cross your fingers that

---

* And an e-Reader attachment, a Game Boy Advance system, and the cable that connects that whole setup to your GameCube.

you'll come across cards bearing passwords for the games, or beg a friend to send you theirs (fat chance!). But if you own the Action Replay cheat device for GameCube, there are codes on the disc that will let you unlock these rare games in your copy of Animal Crossing. If you don't want to drop forty dollars on the Action Replay just for this trick, you can hunt down a standalone disc called "Ultimate Codes for Animal Crossing" that retails for about $10 and will let you unlock every NES classic in the game. You can buy the disc direct from the manufacturer at *http://us.codejunkies.com*.

> Animal Crossing was released in the United Kingdom in late 2004, over two years after the U.S. release. Thus, the official UK web site for the game (*http://www.nintendo-europe.com/ microsite/animalcrossing/enGB/*) is still being updated. At the time of this writing, players from all Western countries could visit the site to get a code for the game *Donkey Kong 3*. Unfortunately, there is no telling what games, if any, will be available by the time you read these words.

Metroid

You can buy a near-perfect version of the classic NES title Metroid for $19.99 as part of the NES Classics series on the Game Boy Advance **[Hack #16]**. But why would you want to when you can get an identical version of the game included as a free bonus with Metroid: Zero Mission for the GBA? Simply complete the main game (which is a real treat in the first place) to unlock it.

A version of Metroid is also included on the Metroid Prime disc for GameCube, but you'll need some extra equipment to coax it out of its hiding place. Specifically, you'll have to buy and complete Metroid Fusion for the GBA (again, quite a fun experience!), then use a GBA-GameCube link cable (sold separately) to connect your GBA to the Cube. Prime will detect your completed Fusion save file, and unlock Metroid, which you can access from the game's main menu even after you unplug the GBA. Of course, since this version of the game is inferior to the original (with fuzzy anti-aliased graphics and a reversed control scheme that maps shooting to the A button and jumping to B), you may not want to bother after all.

Star Wars Rogue Squadron III: Rebel Strike

Gamers who preordered Rebel Strike, a GameCube-exclusive mission-based shooter that draws on the most intense battle sequences from the first three Star Wars films, received quite a nice bonus—a GameCube disc with a demo of the game and an emulated version of the classic Star Wars arcade game, complete with Tempest-style color vector graphics.

An even better surprise awaited once Rebel Strike was finally released—not only was the original Star Wars arcade game unlockable, but its two arcade-only sequels as well. To unlock all three games, enter the Passcode screen from the Options menu and enter "RTJPFC!G / TIMEWARP" for Star Wars, "!H!F?HXS / KOOLSTUF" for The Empire Strikes Back, and "!?ATH!RD GAME?YES" for Return of the Jedi.

Donkey Kong 64

Back before Microsoft acquired them, British developer Rare was all lovey-dovey with Nintendo. Among Rare's voluminous Nintendo 64 output was Donkey Kong 64, the first and only fully 3D platform game starring the legendary monkey. Since the title was equal parts Nintendo and Rare, it seems only fitting that both companies' first big hits be represented as Easter Eggs.

Thus, players will find not only the original arcade Donkey Kong but also Rare's classic Spectrum action game JetPac tucked away in DK64. They aren't exactly hidden, though—you're required to find both games and then achieve a certain score in order to complete the main adventure.

Donkey Kong
In the Frantic Factory level, you'll be able to buy the special technique "Gorilla Grab" from Cranky Kong. Once you have it, you'll be able to pull the lever next to the Donkey Kong arcade machine and activate it. Complete the game twice to unlock it in DK64's main menu.

JetPac
You'll see the JetPac machine every time you visit Cranky's laboratories. But the old monkey won't let you play it until you bring him 15 banana medals. Once you get them, score 5000 points in JetPac and you'll unlock it from DK64's main menu.

Star Fox Assault

Like Donkey Kong 64, Star Fox Assault is the fruit of a team-up between Nintendo and an outside developer—Namco in this case. Though none of the previous Star Fox titles are unlockable (a shame, as they were both better than this GameCube installment!), the design team at Namco tucked away three of the company's classic arcade shooters in the game as rewards for good performance.

Unfortunately, for some reason the American version of the game only includes one of the bonus titles—Xevious, which is unlocked by collecting silver medals for each of the game's ten stages. You'll have to buy the Japanese version of the game if you want to play Battle City (collect all ten bronze medals) or Star Luster (collect all fifty S-Flags).

Pitfall!

Of the many amazing titles that Activision, the video game console world's first independent software publisher, released during the heyday of the Atari 2600, David Crane's masterpiece Pitfall! is easily the most popular and perhaps the best. This seminal platform game put the player into the shoes of Pitfall Harry as he collected treasure in a jungle filled with perilous dangers.

Given the original title's near-timeless place in popular culture, Activision has attempted to revive it on modern consoles numerous times. From Super Pitfall on the NES to Pitfall: The Lost Expedition on the Xbox, Pitfall Harry has starred on nearly every major console (although occupying a far less central role). And the original Pitfall! games are hidden in a few of them.

If you still have the Super NES version of Pitfall: The Mayan Adventure, you can play the original game by pressing the A button six times, followed by the Select and Start buttons, at the Game Start screen. In the PC version of the game, typing the phrase "letsdothetimewarp" at any time during gameplay will have the same result.

In the PSone title Pitfall 3D: Beyond The Jungle, go to the Password screen and enter "CRANESBABY" to play the classic game. Unique to this version are some secret Easter Eggs—try pressing the L1 and L2 buttons simultaneously during gameplay for infinite lives, or hit the Triangle and R1 buttons simultaneously when one of the dreaded crocodiles is on screen for a secret message.

And in Pitfall: The Lost Expedition for PlayStation 2, GameCube, and Xbox, you can unlock versions of Pitfall! and Pitfall 2: The Lost Caverns. In the PS2 version, hold the L1 and R1 buttons while on the title screen, then push Circle, Circle, Left, Right, Circle, Square, X, Up, Circle to unlock the first game. To unlock the sequel, hold L1 and R1, then push Left, Right, Left, Right, Triangle, Triangle, Triangle. (The codes for the Xbox and GameCube versions of the game differ slightly. To find them, go to *http://www.gamefaqs.com/search/index.html?game=pitfall* and click on the Code hyperlink next to the appropriate version of the game.)

Mortal Kombat Deception

Well, it's not exactly hidden, but to promote its latest entry in the Mortal Kombat fighting game series, Midway removed the original Mortal Kombat from Midway Arcade Treasures 2 [Hack #16] and placed it on a separate bonus disc included in the Kollector's Edition of Mortal Kombat: Deception for the PlayStation 2 and Xbox. Bad news for Arcade Treasures fans (especially GameCube owners), but good news for Deception buyers.

## CHAPTER THREE

Playing Arcade Games on Your Computer

Hacks 20–32

Unless you're a competitive Dance Dance Revolution player, the importance of the video arcade in the modern-day gaming diet has dwindled to nearly nothing in recent years. This would come as a shock to someone who was cryogenically frozen in 1982 and reawakened just last week.*

For a long time, arcade games *were* retro gaming. Sure, you could technically play a version of Pac-Man on the Atari 2600, but that's not how the yellow dot-muncher found world fame. Arcades were packed full of bodies because they offered the definitive gaming experience in every category from graphics to play control.

But now that most of the arcades have closed down, how can you get your retro arcade fix? I suppose you could start buying up old arcade machines, but your basement would get filled up pretty fast. Here's an idea: MAME, the Multiple Arcade Machine Emulator.

An emulator is a software program that, in layman's terms, tricks one piece of hardware (your computer) into acting like another piece of hardware (an Asteroids machine). In this chapter, you'll learn the ins and outs of MAME: installing the software, finding the ROM files that contain the games you want to play, and tweaking everything until it runs just the way you want it to.

HACK #20 Play Arcade Games Under Windows

Play classic arcade games on that most popular of operating systems.

Although the art of running the Multiple Arcade Machine Emulator (MAME) on Macintosh [Hack #21] and Linux [Hack #22] is discussed later in this

---

* No, I'm *not* talking about Hiroshi Yamauchi.

chapter, this hack deals solely with the ubiquitous Windows operating systems.

MAME was originally written as a DOS program, and the official Windows build still uses the classic DOS command line prompt. The first section of this hack teaches you how to use the Windows command line version; if you are running a DOS machine, most of the tips will apply to you as well.

If you'd prefer to have a graphical user interface (GUI)—that is, a program that looks and feels like every other application you use in Windows—there are a few different options. You can get an all-in-one program like MAME32, or use what is known as a *frontend*, which works with the command line version of MAME but removes the hassle of having to type commands manually. I'll discuss both later in this hack.

MAME

Since the MAME emulator is freely distributed, you can find it on many different emulation enthusiast web sites across the Internet. I recommend you download the latest version (0.96, as of this writing) from the official project home page at *http://www.mame.net/downmain.html*. The first two files on the download page are the Windows command-line versions of MAME. If you have a Pentium Pro processor you will want to get the optimized version, usually called `mameVERSION_i686.zip` (*mame096b_i686.zip* as of this writing). Otherwise, download the first file, `mameVERSION.zip` (*mame096b. zip* as of this writing).

> The DOS versions of MAME are not available on the official site. You can find them at the MAME page of emulation portal Zophar's Domain (*http://www.zophar.net/mame.html*). The current version as of this writing is 0.97.

The emulator will be in Zip archive format, which means you'll need to open it with a program like WinZip (*http://www.winzip.com*), Info-Zip (*http://www. info-zip.org*), or the Windows Explorer (Windows XP and later). Extract all the files in the archive to a new directory on your computer (I suggest that you create a directory called *mame* under your existing *Program Files* directory.) The extraction process will automatically create a number of sub-directories underneath the directory you specify.

Starting a game. You could run MAME right now, but why bother when you have no ROM files—images of the classic arcade games—to use with it? Let's grab some first. Other hacks in this volume will tell you how, so check out [Hack #24] and [Hack #25] for more information on where to get them, and [Hack #26] to find out how to install them.

But if you've already found some ROMs by using a web search utility such as Google (*http://www.google.com*) and don't need me to tell you where to find them, you'll want to know that you should simply save the Zip archive that they come in to the *roms* directory that was automatically created for you under your MAME directory.

Alright, well, let's pretend that you've just downloaded *gridlee.zip*, a freely distributed ROM available from the official MAME home page. To run it, you'll first need to open the Command Prompt window. Do this by opening your Start menu, clicking Programs, and then locating the Command Prompt (it may be located under the Accessories menu). The Command Prompt's icon is a tiny black box that says C:\. You'll get something like Figure 3-1.

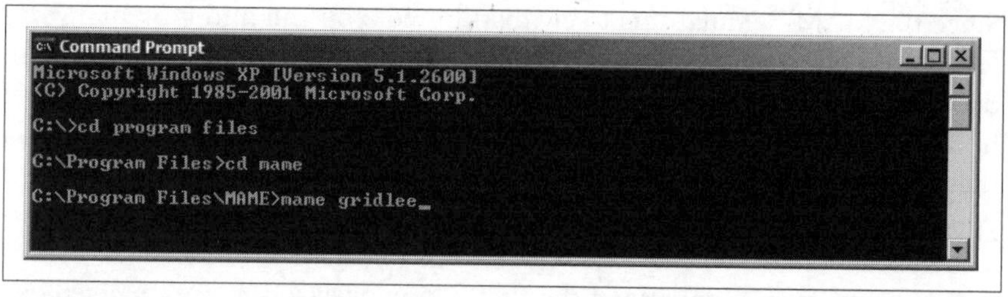

Figure 3-1. Running MAME, using the Command Prompt window in Windows XP

As you are probably able to make out by reading the figure, the Command Prompt will start you out in the root directory of your main hard drive, or *C:*. From here, you'll type three lines, pressing Enter after each one. Note that I'm assuming you followed my advice as to what folder to place the MAME files in. If you named your MAME folder something creative, or put it in a directory other than your Program Files folder, you'll need to substitute the names of the directories when you use the *cd* (i.e., change directory) command.

```
C:\>cd "program files"
C:\Program Files>cd mame
C:\Program Files\MAME>mame gridlee
```

This will run MAME and start up the game Gridlee. Any other ROMs you have downloaded can be run by replacing *gridlee* with the name of the Zip archive that you saved to your *roms* directory.

More command-line options. Typing gridlee after the name of the *mame* program is what is known as a *command-line option*. There are many different such options you can include on your command line when you run MAME, which can be entered in any order. (As long as you type *mame* first, of course!) In general, you'll only need to use these if you're having a problem running MAME with the default settings. Table 3-1 shows a few of them.

Table 3-1. MAME command-line options

Command-line option	Effect
-joy	Allows for joystick input (default is keyboard).
-volume n	Sets the volume level where n is between -32 and 0. The default is 0.
-autoframeskip	If your game is running too slowly, use this command to automatically skip some animation frames and speed it up.
-resolution *XxY*	Sets the display resolution to whatever you want. For example:
	-resolution 640x480
-scanlines	Adds in faked "scan lines" to more accurately simulate the experience of ancient arcade raster-scan monitors.

So, for example, typing

```
C:\Program Files\MAME>mame gridlee -joy -volume -1
```

would result in loading the game Gridlee, using a joystick, with the volume turned down a bit. If you get sick of typing in these options every time you run MAME, you can edit a file called *mame.ini* (*mame.cfg* if you're using the DOS version). For more information on how to edit the file, and to see the rest of the command-line options, check out the Win32 Setup page at EasyEmu (*http://www.mameworld.net/easyemu/*).

Playing in MAME. If MAME boots up successfully, you'll first see the imposing screen in Figure 3-2.

Figure 3-2. The copyright warning screen for Gridlee

Since you are indeed legally entitled to play Gridlee, go ahead and hit the O, then the K key. (If you're using a joystick to play and don't have a keyboard handy, you should be able to enter your assent by wiggling the joystick from left to right a few times.) You'll then see the title screen of the game you're playing.

Okay, so how do you start playing? The first thing you should do before playing a new game is to hit the Tab key on your keyboard, which will bring up MAME's menu, shown in Figure 3-3.

Figure 3-3. MAME's internal menu, running over the Gridlee title screen

Use the arrow keys and the Enter button to navigate it. Select "Input (this game)" to view and change the button assignments for Gridlee. While you're in there, take note of not only the keys used to move and fire, but also the keys for "Insert Coin" and "1P Start." Since MAME accurately emulates the arcade machine, you'll have to make the program think that you've inserted a coin before it will let you play! If you've selected the -joy option, you'll be able to reassign joystick buttons in this menu.

MAME32

I think it's safe to assume that some of you out there, having just read that entire section on command-line options and DOS prompts, are utterly confused and afraid of MAME. And that's fair. If I hadn't grown up inside of a C:\ prompt (see the hacks in Chapter 7 for more on DOS), I'd have no idea how to run MAME either.

But have no fear, for there is a solution for the rest of us. There is an officially recognized GUI-based version of MAME for Windows, called MAME32. You can download it from the official MAME page at *http://www.mame.net/downports.html*. Install it in much the same way as you installed MAME—unzip everything to a new directory, then run the *mame32* executable file.

When you load it up, you'll see a screen resembling Figure 3-4. You'll notice that on the left-hand side of the window is an organized list of pretty much every ROM known to MAME. No, you didn't just magically download every arcade game ever made. You'll have to click on the Available tab (with a teal icon next to it) to see your own personal ROM list.

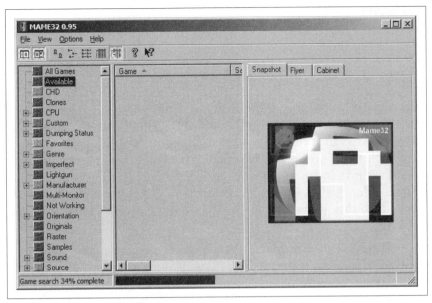

Figure 3-4. MAME32, building a ROM list

You can use the Options menu to change most of the things that you'd otherwise have to use command-line prompts to mess around with. You can change settings for every game, or alter the settings for specific games one by one (if, for example, you want Gridlee to run in a different resolution than Robby Roto). But there is one thing to be aware of... MAME32 can do funny things to your screen resolution.

> When I ran a game in MAME32, it automatically altered my monitor's resolution to fit the game screen. But when I was done, and exited the game, not only did the screen resolution not revert back to my original settings, I wasn't able to manually change it back! This necessitated a reboot, which thankfully solved the problem. I've been told this was an isolated problem that most users will probably not experience; I don't think I'll be using MAME32 again, however.

If that warning scared you, you might want to try AdvanceMAME (*http://advancemame.sourceforge.net/*), another GUI-enabled version of MAME that is available for DOS, Windows, Mac OS X, and GNU/Linux. Or, if you are already happy with your MAME command-line installation but would like the experience to be a little smoother, you might try installing a MAME frontend.

MAME Frontends

A *frontend* is a program that does not contain the MAME emulator, but will automatically launch the command-line version for you. Use the frontend to select your preferred settings, then select your ROM from a list and the frontend will run the program automatically with all the settings you selected.

One popular frontend is AdvanceMENU, created by the team behind AdvanceMAME. You install it by extracting the Zip file into the same directory as MAME, then running the *advmenu.exe* file. One word of warning: I wasn't able to get AdvanceMAME running because it was incompatible with my video card. This is a known issue and the official help documentation offered little assistance beyond "try using the DOS version." Of course, when I tried that, it told me that the DOS version wouldn't run under Windows XP.

So I decided to try EasyMame (*http://www.mameworld.net/easymame/*), a frontend popular among many MAME users for its simplicity and small file size (about 2 megabytes). You'll want to install EasyMame into the same directory as MAME, then run the *EasyMame.exe* file. Hit the F5 key or click Setup, then click Initialize Roms to build a list of the available ROMs on your computer (see Figure 3-5).

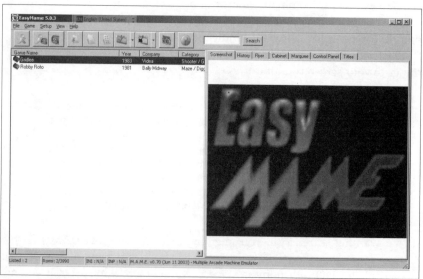

Figure 3-5. EasyMame, after initializing the list of ROMs

If you press Ctrl-O or click File and select Default MAME Options, you'll be able to manually adjust everything that would otherwise require you to input a command-line option. This will change the settings for every game.

If you want to individually adjust options from game to game, right-click on the game's title in the left hand menu, then select Game Options.

If you're using a special MAME joystick like the HotRod, X-Arcade, or Slik-Stik [Hack #27], you can control the EasyMame menu using the stick. Click Setup, then Preferences, then click the tab corresponding to the joystick you own. Check the box and you'll be using your stick of choice to control Easy-Mame. View the handy visual aid in the window (see Figure 3-6) to see what button performs what function.

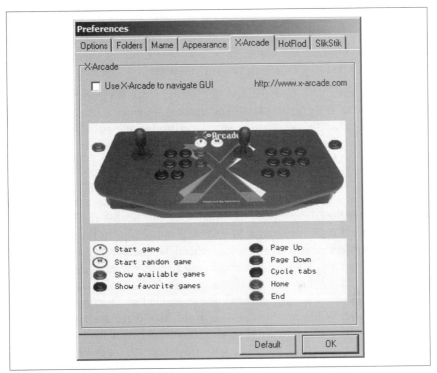

Figure 3-6. Controlling EasyMame with the X-Arcade joystick

 ## HACK #21 Run Arcade Games on a Mac

Play classic arcade games using MacMAME.

Yeah, you've heard it all before. "But Jimmy, you can't play videogames on your computer. You have a Mac." You can hear the venom in their voice as they say it like you've caught some foreign disease. However, this blanket statement and your friends are dead wrong. While general support from major companies might be lacking, there are many classic arcade games and homebrews available to you. If you have a Mac, and the ability to read past this sentence, you're well on your way to learning how to use your computer to play classic arcade games.

Before you even think about firing up your engines and diving headfirst into the world of MAME, ROMs, and reliving those days you spent in the pizzeria plunking fistfuls of quarters into the Pac-Man machine, you need to do a couple of things. First off, you're going to need to get an emulator. This is the program that allows you to play MAME ROMs. For Macs, the best and one of the only options is MacMAME, available for download from their web site at *http://www.macmame.org/*. From the main page just click on downloads, and then check to see you're downloading the most recent version. Also, if you want to get started right as you're reading this, it's good to make sure you have a fast connection and some time, as MacMAME is 10 MB and up, depending on which version you want.

Also, MacMAME isn't updated too frequently, since support for over two thousand games is firmly in place. The updates only come out as often as a real fix is needed to deal with overall performance issues. So don't be alarmed if you see that the last version of the software came out sometime in 2004. The MacMAME team will still be hard at work making sure the emulator can play as many games as possible.

Something that's also really great about MacMAME is the fact that it's available in a variety of languages other than English. So for those nonnative speakers of the English language, MacMAME is available in French and Italian on the project web site, and an unofficial Japanese version available at *http://www.zophar.net/*. Also, those wanting to use alternate displays, such as TVs and Fixed Frequency Monitors will get more mileage out of Advanced MAME, which is available for download at *http://advancemame. sourceforge.net/*. While the file size is only 12 MB, there are no binary versions available for Mac OS X, so if you're not confident in your ability to compile a large program yourself, you are better off sticking with Mac-MAME.

Compiling the program really isn't a daunting task, but for the rest of the instructions in this part of the book, I'll be explaining how to do things with MacMAME. It's much more of a ready-to-run application than Advanced MAME. This isn't to say one is better than the others, but those who are just getting into playing MAME games on their Mac would be more at ease with MacMAME. However, more detailed instructions about using Advanced MAME, as well as the compatibility with certain ROMs and how to use certain features are better covered at the project's web site.

After you download MacMAME, your web browser should automatically mount its disk image. Next, drag and drop MacMAME to your /*Applications* folder as shown in Figure 3-7.

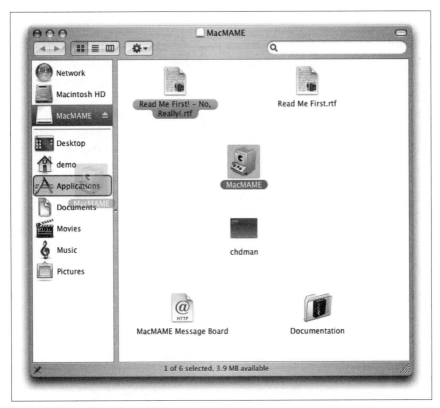

Figure 3-7. Installing MacMAME

 Hey, wait, didn't you read the *Read Me First* file that was on the MacMAME disk image? It's important. If you didn't read it, you wouldn't know that since version 0.87 MacMAME looks for ROMs and other files in a *MacMAME* folder in your *Documents* folder. If you don't have one, MacMAME is a nice emulator and wants to make a good impression on you, so it will create the folder the first time its run.

From here, you'll need to drop your ROMs into the ROMs subdirectory inside the *MacMAME* folder in your *Documents* folder. Now you're all ready to fire up MacMAME and get started with your playing. All the ROMs will be on the left-hand side, and all you need to do is select one (that's not flagged as corrupted!) and click play to get your game on. However, you should tweak some settings before jumping right in to the fray. Yes, I know, you're so close, but there are a few things you can change to improve your experience, and that's worth waiting an extra minute or so. Click the Options button to configure MacMAME.

Configuring MacMAME

One thing you'll want to check is whether you're using OpenGL or software rendering, which will affect the overall graphics quality. On the right-hand side of the MacMAME Options window, there is a drop-down menu to select between the two; OpenGL will look better in most cases. Also, you can configure a few more options if you're using OpenGL, such as syncing, smoothing, and overlays. If you're having problems with the speed of the program though, you might want to turn off the OpenGL support. However, speed versus rendering is more of a personal choice. Figure 3-8 shows the MacMAME Options window.

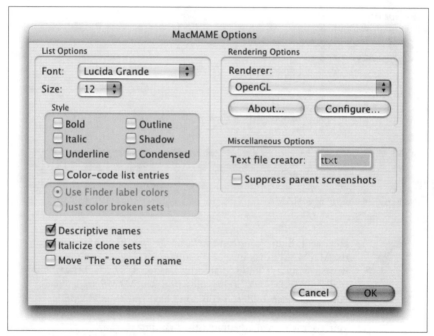

Figure 3-8. Configuring MacMAME

Close the Options window and go back to the MacMAME main window. There are a couple of default options you'll want to check to make sure you're getting the fastest performance possible out of your MacMAME emulation. In the Misc tab, you're going to need to enable Automatic Frameskip-ping. Also, while you're there you should make sure that Generate Debug Log is off, since it's not going to serve any use to the average user. Both of these options should be configured correctly by default, but it's good to double check to make sure you're getting the best performance possible from your Mac.

Running MacMAME

To load a game, double-click a game from the list on the left (see Figure 3-9). From there on, the MAME user interface will resemble the Windows version [Hack #20] (type OK to confirm you have the rights to run the game, press Tab to bring up the configuration menu). To play a game, press 5 to simulate plunking in a quarter for player one. If you're going to be playing with some friends, they'll need to hit 6, 7, or 8 respectively. Then you hit the player one start button, 1, (2, 3, and 4 for players two through four) and you're ready to go! Now, if you feel like changing the keyboard configuration, when you're playing just press Tab and you'll bring up MacMAME's configuration menu. Figure 3-10 shows MacMAME running Gridlee [Hack #24].

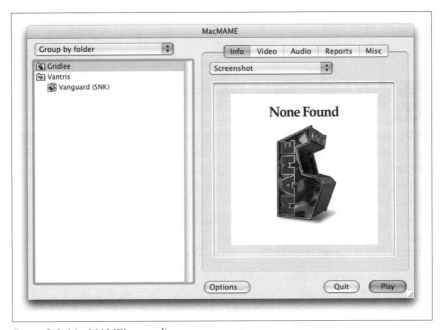

Figure 3-9. MacMAME's game list

There you have it. With all the information in this hack, you're now more than qualified to begin playing MAME ROMs on your computer. Now you

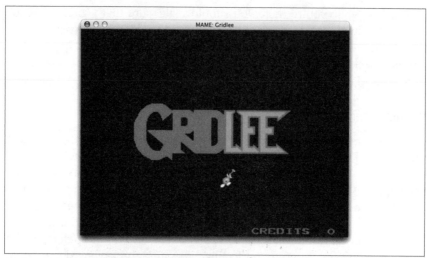

Figure 3-10. Gridlee, running under MacMAME

know how to use your Mac to shut up all those friends who say you can't play games on your computer. Playing MAME ROMs on your Mac really is just about as simple as installing every other game on your Mac. All five of them.

—Daniel Dormer

HACK #22 Play Arcade Games Under Linux

Play classic arcade games on your favorite open source OS.

Home gaming consoles might be fine for some people, but if you are reading this hack, you are probably one of those old-school arcade wizards that we used to congregate around in smoky pizza joints, hoping for the honor of holding your tokens, as you obliterated the previous high scores on Spy Hunter or Dig-Dug or Sinistar (or maybe you're one of the congregants, hoping to improve your skills so you can finally take on that wizard). You might even be the sort who dreams of filling your den with original arcade cabinets, bringing up your children in the Way of Pac-Man.

This hack is for you. I show you how to emulate a startling variety of arcade hardware on the Linux/Unix platform. In the Unix world, there are two ports of MAME, the Multiple Arcade Machine Emulator, worth worrying about: AdvanceMAME (*http://advancemame.sourceforge.net/*), a Linux port of MAME; and Xmame (*http://x.mame.net/*), an X11 port of MAME.

Xmame

I start with Xmame, which is a port of the MAME program to Unix. It can use native X11R6, SVGAlib, ggi, XF86-DGA, OpenGL, or SDL display drivers. The fact that Xmame supports pretty much every combination of libraries, hardware, and ROMs out there is a definite win for the serious emulation fan on the Unix platform. To build and install Xmame, follow the instructions for your Linux distribution or flavor of Unix.

Gentoo Linux. To install Xmame under Gentoo Linux:

1. Become *root*.

2. `emerge xmame`

Other Linux distributions/Unix flavours. To install Xmame under other Linux or Unix distributions, check your installation media or online package repositories to see if it's already available. You should also check the Xmame project's home page (*http://x.mame.net/*) to see if a binary version is available. If not, you can install it from source:

1. Visit the Xmame project's home page, click on the Download link in the menu on the left side of the page, and save the latest Xmame source tarball to your */tmp* directory (remove any older versions of the Xmame source tarball you may have lying around first). Then, run the following commands:

   ```
   $ cd /tmp
   $ tar xvjf xmame-*.tar.bz2
   $ rm xmame-*.tar.bz2
   $ cd xmame-*
   ```

2. Edit the *Makefile* in your favorite editor. If you are building Xmame on an x86 (i.e., Intel-compatible) box running Linux, just scroll down until you reach the "Input Devices" section, and skip to the next step. If you are running on different hardware:

   a. Scroll down to the "Architecture; choose your CPU (only one!!)" section and comment out the

      ```
      MY_CPU = i386
      ```

      line by inserting a hash character in front of it, so the line reads:

      ```
      #MY_CPU = i386
      ```

   b. Now, find the line that describes your processor type (e.g., if you are building on a Sparc machine, the `# MY_CPU = risc` line), and uncomment it by deleting the hash and any whitespace before the `MY_CPU` bit. Follow the same steps if you are using an OS other than Linux, which is the default. Simply comment out the `ARCH = linux` line and uncomment the line that describes your OS (for example, if your Sparc box is running Solaris, uncomment the # ARCH = solaris line).

3. Scroll down to the "Input Devices" section, and uncomment any lines that relate to features you want to enable, by removing the hash character and any leading whitespace. You almost certainly want to uncomment JOY_STANDARD = 1, if you are planning to use a joystick with Xmame. I would also recommend uncommenting JOY_SDL = 1, as I find that SDL joystick support works best for me.

4. Scroll down to the "Sound Devices" section, and uncomment lines for features you want to enable. I recommend uncommenting SOUND_ALSA = 1, SOUND_SDL = 1, and SOUND_WAVEOUT = 1. If you are a KDE user, you will probably want to uncomment the two lines pertaining to ARTS. And of course if you are unfortunate enough to have to use ESD, uncomment the SOUND_ESOUND = 1 line as well.

5. Save the *Makefile* and exit your editor.

6. Next, run the following commands (you need to run the second command as *root* or use *sudo*):

```
$ make
# make install
```

You have just built Xmame using the X11 graphics drivers. If you would like to build versions of Xmame for another display driver, simply run make DISPLAY_METHOD=*METHOD* (such as make DISPLAY_METHOD=SDL for SDL). Then run make install as *root*. (The available values for DISPLAY_METHOD are SDL, svgalib, ggi, svgafx, openstep, and photon2.)

If you survived this long and arduous process, you will have Xmame installed. To run it, open a terminal as a normal user and run something like this:

```
$ xmame.SDL -jt 7 -rp rom_dir -s 2 rom_name
```

Here is an explanation of each option:

xmame.SDL

This is the SDL version of Xmame (the one I compiled with the make DISPLAY_METHOD=SDL incantation). SDL, or Simple Directmedia Layer, is a cross-platform multimedia library used by many popular games and emulators. You can find out more about it at *http://www.libsdl.org*. I am using SDL because it handles video better for my laptop's video hardware than any of the other display methods.

-jt 7

This switch instructs Xmame to use the SDL joystick drivers.

-rp *rom_dir*

This switch tells Xmame where to find your ROM files (make sure to replace *rom_dir* with the actual directory in which your MAME ROMs reside **[Hack #26]**.

-s 2

This switch causes the display to be scaled by a factor of two in both the X and Y directions.

rom_name

This is the name of the ROM that you want to run; note that MAME, unlike most other emulators, does not expect a filename here. Instead, use the name of the game (e.g., robby or rotox for "Robby Roto"). If you cannot guess the proper name, search for your game in MAME's official games list (*http://www.mame.net/gamelist.html*).

Figure 3-11 shows an example of me running the excellent public domain MAME ROM Gridlee **[Hack #24]**. Here is the appropriate incantation:

Figure 3-11. Gridlee running on Xmame

```
$ xmame.SDL -jt 7 -rp /data/roms/mame/ -s 2 gridlee
```

Once in the game, press the 5 key on your keyboard to insert a credit (you may do this as many times as you like—feel free to dock yourself a quarter or a *hyaku-en* coin every time, if you want a more realistic arcade experience). When you are sufficiently loaded up with credits, press the 1 key to start the game!

Xmame has tons more command-line options and the ability to store said options in both site-wide and user-specific configuration files. Check out the Xmame man page for more details.

GXMame

Like almost all command-line emulators, Xmame and a graphical frontend are two great tastes that taste great together. And of all the graphical frontends for Xmame that exist in the Unix world, GXMame seems to me the tastiest. So let us not delay even a fraction of a moment, but instead install this treat:

Gentoo Linux. To install GXMame under Gentoo Linux:

1. Become *root*.

2. Run the command: `emerge gxmame`

Other Linux distributions / Unix flavors. To install GXMame under other Linux or Unix distributions, check your installation media or online package repositories to see if it's already available. You should also check the project home page (*http://gxmame.sourceforge.net/*) to see if a binary version is available. If not, you can install it from source:

1. Visit the GXMame project's download page (*http://gxmame.sourceforge.net/downloads.php*) and save the latest source tarball to your */tmp* directory (remove any older versions of the source tarball you happen to have laying around first). Then, run these commands:

   ```
   $ cd /tmp
   $ tar xvzf gxmame-*.tar.gz
   $ rm  gxmame-*.tar.gz
   $ cd  gxmame-*
   $ ./configure -enable-joystick
   ```

2. Next, run the following commands (you need to run the second one as *root* or use *sudo*):

   ```
   $ make
   # make install
   ```

Once GXMame is installed, simply open a shell under X11 as a normal user and run:

```
$ gxmame &
```

You will be immediately warned that GXMame could not recognize the gamelist version, and asked if you want to rebuild it—this is expected. Click the Yes button and let GXMame do its thing for a few moments. You will then be presented with the main screen, which displays the very impressive list of all of the games that Xmame can play, helpfully categorized for you. The first order of business, as in any frontend, is to do a little configuration.

Configure the path to Xmame. Click on the Option menu, and then select Directories... in the Xmame Executables section of the GXMame directories tab. You need to add all of the various Xmame versions (e.g., *xmame.SDL*). In the bottom of this tab, you may need to change the base Xmame data directory from */usr/lib/games/xmame* to wherever your distribution installed Xmame. For Gentoo users, this is */usr/share/games/xmame*. If you need to, change */usr/lib/games/xmame* to the correct path for all of the paths: Flyers, Cabinets, Marquees, Title screenshots, and Icons.

Configure the ROMs directory. Now, click on the XMame basic paths tab and add your MAME ROMs directory to the Roms Paths list (you will probably also want to remove the default, as it is unlikely that you want to keep any ROMs in */usr/lib/games/xmame/roms*). In the Samples Paths list and the Art-work Path text box, you may need to change */usr/lib/games/xmame* to the correct directory, as in the preceding section. Click on Xmame's Additional Paths tab and change all of the directories, if necessary. Click on the User Resources tab and verify that all of the paths are correct—they should be, since the defaults match my Xmame install. Now, click OK to close the directory configuration dialogue.

Set gameplay options. Click the Option menu again, then Executable, then select the executable that you plan to use (e.g., *xmame.SDL*). Now, click on the Option menu and select Default Option, which will open the Default Properties dialogue to the Display tab. Flip through the tabs, making any changes that you like. Make sure to change the DSP Plugin option on the Sound tab to Alsa Sound System DSP plug-in if you use ALSA instead of OSS.

Also, change Joystick type on the Controllers tab from No joystick to the proper type of joystick driver (again, I recommend the SDL joystick driver), and check any of the applicable boxes to the right (interestingly enough, even though I have a PlayStation DualShock 2 controller, if I check USB PS Game Pads, my controller will not work!). When everything is to your lik-ing, click OK to save your preferences.

Play a game. You may mess about with the other items in the Option menu if you like, but when you are done, you're ready to actually launch a game! Click the View menu, then Refresh (or hit the F5 key on your keyboard), to re-scan your ROMs directory(s)—you will need to do this every time you add or change a ROM path. Now, click on the Available folder in the left pane. The right pane should now display some games as shown in Figure 3-12! To start a game, simply double-click its name (you can also enable the "Allow game selection by a Joystick" option by selecting the Option menu, then clicking Startup Option).

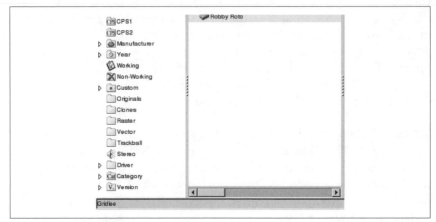

Figure 3-12. Selecting games in GXMame

Once in the game, it behaves exactly as if you had started Xmame from the command-line: use 5 to insert credits, 1 to start playing.

AdvanceMAME

If Xmame is not your thing, why not give AdvanceMAME a shot? To build and install it, follow the instructions for your Linux distribution/Unix flavor:

Gentoo. To install AdvanceMAME under Gentoo, perform the following steps:

1. Become *root*.
2. Run the command: `emerge advancemame`

Other Linux distributions and Unix flavors. Check your distribution's package repository as well as the AdvanceMAME project download page (*http:// advancemame.sourceforge.net/download.html*) for a binary version. If one is not available, use the following instructions to install it from source:

1. Download a source tarball from the AdvanceMAME project download page and save it to your */tmp* directory. Be sure to remove any older versions of the source tarball, and then run these commands:

   ```
   $ cd /tmp
   $ tar xvzf advancemame-*.tar.gz
   ```

```
$ rm advancemame-*.tar.gz
$ cd advancemame*/
$ ./configure
```

2. Next, run these commands to compile and install AdvanceMAME. You need to run the second command as *root*:

```
$ make
# make install
```

If you are building from source, note that AdvanceMAME's configure script should do a good job of auto-detecting which features to turn on or off, but it if does not get things right, run:

```
$ ./configure --help
```

This will list all of the features that the configure script can control. The generic pattern is this: to turn on a feature called "foo", use the --enable-foo switch; to turn it off, use the --disable-foo switch. For example, to configure AdvanceMAME with ALSA (the Advanced Linux Sound Architecture), the expat XML parser, and SDL, but without OSS (the Open Sound System, which is "the old way" to do sound in Linux), you would run:

```
$ ./configure --enable-alsa --enable-expat --enable-sdl –disable-oss
```

Then proceed with the rest of the build and installation process as described earlier in this section. Once you have AdvanceMAME installed, you will need to run it once with no command-line options so that it will create a configuration file:

```
$ advmame
Creating a standard configuration file...
Configuration file `/home/jmglov/.advance/advmame.rc' created with all the
default options.

The default rom search path is
`/home/jmglov/.advance/rom:/usr/share/games/advance/rom'. You can change it
using the `dir_rom' option in the configuration file.
```

The first order of business is editing the *~/.advance/advmame.rc* configuration file and changing the dir_rom option to reflect the actual location of your MAME ROMs directory **[Hack #26]**.

Now, you should be able to fire up AdvanceMAME simply by running:

```
$ advmame rom_name
```

Replace *rom_name* with the name of the game that you want to play. AdvanceMAME is so helpful that if you get the name wrong, it will give you a few possible matches! Here is an example of me firing up Gridlee:

```
$ advmame gridle
Game "gridle" isn't supported.

Similar names are:
gridlee Gridlee
ridleofp Riddle of Pythagoras (Japan)
3stooges The Three Stooges In Brides Is Brides
gseeker Grid Seeker: Project Stormhammer (World)
gseekerj Grid Seeker: Project Stormhammer (Japan)
gseekeru Grid Seeker: Project Stormhammer (US)
gprider GP Rider (set 2, FD1094 317-0163)
gprider1 GP Rider (set 1, US, FD1094 317-0162)
gtmr Great 1000 Miles Rally
gtmre Great 1000 Miles Rally (Evolution Model)
gtmrusa Great 1000 Miles Rally (USA)
gtmr2u Great 1000 Miles Rally 2 USA (95/05/18)
$ advmame gridlee
AdvanceMAME - Copyright (C) 1999-2003 by Andrea Mazzoleni
MAME - Copyright (C) 1997-2003 by Nicola Salmoria and the MAME Team
```

Once the game starts, just as in Xmame, the 5 key inserts a credit, and the 1 key starts the game. AdvanceMAME has a welcome twist, however: an on-screen menu! To activate it, hit the Tab key on your keyboard. You can now configure pretty much any aspect of the emulator! A good starting point is the "Input (general)" menu shown in Figure 3-13, where you can view the default controls for players 1-8, and change things you do not like!

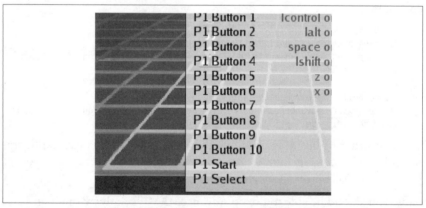

Figure 3-13. Messing with control settings in AdvanceMAME

The menus are quite useful, and configuration changes made in-game will be written to your resource configuration file right away!

——*Josh Glover*

Run MAME on the Xbox

HACK #23

Turn your Xbox into a virtual arcade.

Microsoft's Xbox is both the most powerful and the most flexible game console on the market. In addition to playing off-the-shelf Xbox games, it can serve as a jukebox, a region-free DVD player, a media center, and an arcade machine. That last bit of magic is done by way of emulators such as MAME, the Multiple Arcade Machine Emulator. To run arcade games on the Xbox you will need the Xbox version of MAME, MAMEoX.

Getting MAMEoX

MAMEoX could be called a grey market product. The source code is completely original, and therefore legal to distribute. But the compiled binary—the program that runs on your system—is not, because an official Xbox Development Kit is required to create it.

Developers with the kits are not supposed to distribute programs over the Internet, so you won't find MAMEoX on any web site. However, there are plenty of retro game aficionados working in the business who will often anonymously upload the newest, compiled version of MAMEoX to an FTP server where anyone can download it. Try a Google search.

It is also worth noting that MAMEoX *requires* a modified (or "modded") Xbox with a replacement dashboard installed, such as Avalaunch or Evolution-X. If you do not have a modded Xbox with a custom dashboard, running MAMEoX from the hard drive will be impossible. The nuts and bolts of how to mod your Xbox escape the scope of this hack, but there is a vast Internet community dedicated to the subject. The following books also have a great deal of information on modding an Xbox:

> *The Black Art of Xbox Mods*, by Jonathan Harbour (SAMS, 2005)
> *Game Console Hacking*, by Joe Grand (Syngress, 2004)
> *Hacking the Xbox*, by Andrew "Bunnie" Huang (No Starch Press, 2003)

Installing MAMEoX on your Xbox

First, you will need to install an IRC client on your computer, so you can access the channels that will allow you to download the proper software. If you are using Windows the easiest program to use is mIRC, which can be found at *http://www.mirc.com*. mIRC is free for the first 30 days; after the trial you are strongly encouraged to register (although the program will not stop functioning).

1. Install mIRC.

2. Choose a Nickname to use on IRC.

3. Connect to the channel #*xbins*.

4. Type **/msg xbins !list** in the main channel window to send an access request to the FTP server. You will get back a private message listing the FTP address, as well as a username and password.

5. You *must* leave mIRC open. Do *not* close any windows.

6. Start up your favorite FTP program and connect to the Xbins FTP server.

7. Change to the following directory: *XBOX\apps\emulators\arcade\ MAMEoX*.

8. Download the latest Zip archive for MAMEoX. Once you have downloaded the file you can close the FTP connection.

9. On your local machine, unzip the MAMEoX archive into its own folder.

Now that you've downloaded MAMEoX, you need to FTP it over to your Xbox:

1. Connect to your Xbox via FTP and move the MAMEoX folder over to the Xbox.

2. Once it is fully copied over, close your FTP program and reboot the Xbox.

3. Launch MAMEoX on the Xbox to check that it's been installed properly.

4. If you can see the title screen (shown in Figure 3-14), then everything is working.

Figure 3-14. The MAMEoX title screen

Copying the ROM files onto your Xbox

While MAMEoX emulates arcade hardware, that hardware can't do anything without software found in the form of ROM files. While most MAME ROMs are protected under copyright law, some public domain and freeware MAME ROMs [Hack #24] are available on the Web. Once you have some ROM files, installing them in MAMEoX is incredibly simple:

1. Connect to your Xbox via FTP.

2. Navigate to the MAMEoX program folder and look for a *roms* subfolder.

3. Copy your ROM files into the *roms* folder. It is usually best if you keep the ROM files stored in a single Zip file for each game. This will make them easier to manage as MAMEoX can load an entire ROM set from a single Zip file.

4. Once the ROM files have been copied over, force MAMEoX to scan for updated ROMs.

5. Your newly installed games should appear in the MAMEoX main menu, as shown in Figure 3-15.

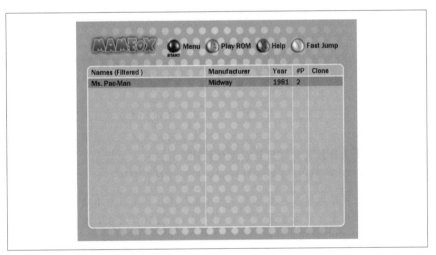

Figure 3-15. The MAMEoX ROM list screen

Playing the Games

Playing a game is arguably the easiest (and most enjoyable) part of the process! Once you have all your ROM files loaded onto your Xbox, playing a particular game is as simple as starting MAMEoX and then choosing the game from the ROM list. After you have selected the game it will automatically load up and be ready to play.

> Since all the games you will be playing in MAMEoX are arcade games, you cannot simply "Press Start" the way you would with a home console game. Instead you must first press the Xbox's Back button a few times to drop a few "virtual quarters" into the machine. If you ever run low on credits, just tap the Back button to drop in more quarters.
>
> Although MAMEoX is capable of emulating more than 3,000 different games, not all of them will run at full speed on the Xbox—the older the game, the better the chance of it running properly. While it is not a hard and fast rule, most games older than Mortal Kombat II will run at full speed while games newer than Mortal Kombat II will often have sound problems or suffer from slowdown.

Emulating Other Systems

Now that you've got an arcade game packed inside your Xbox, you might want to start looking for other systems to emulate. There are dozens of emulators for the Xbox including Nintendo, Super Nintendo, Genesis, Atari, Commodore 64, Game Boy Advance, NeoGeo Pocket, and more. Each of these emulators can be downloaded from the same type of web sites that carry MAMEoX, and all of them are installed in a similar manner. Now that you have MAMEoX up and running, installing the rest of the emulators should be a piece of cake.

—*Adam Pavlacka*

HACK
#24

Find Legal, Free MAME ROMs

Keep your classic gaming on the up-and-up and on the cheap.

I'll level with you here: this ain't gonna be the longest hack in the book. There's not much in the way of homebrew MAME development, and for good reason—strictly speaking, there is no such platform as "MAME." Since the program is by definition a collection of emulators that run specific arcade games, it's not exactly an attractive environment to developers. Plus, by and large, people aren't downloading MAME to play games that were never out in the arcade in the first place. However, there are indeed a few MAME homebrews and even arcade titles that have entered the realm of freeware. So let's check 'em out.

Freeware Arcade ROMs

In general, publishers want to hold onto the rights to their classic properties, mostly so that when the time comes they can re-release them as part of a retro game compilation [Hack #16]. But in a few cases, the rights holders have given their permission for the games to be freely distributed. ROMs for the following three arcade games are available at the miscellaneous downloads section on mame.net (*http://www.mame.net/downmisc.html*).

Gridlee

A charming action game in which the player, controlling a beaker-shaped alien, must run around on a grid collecting balls while avoiding enemies and electricity-charged grid squares, Gridlee was planned for a 1982 arcade release but never saw the light of day. Designed by Howard Delman, a former Atari engineer who developed the vector-graphics display used in such classic titles as Lunar Lander and Asteroids, it was originally planned for release by the company Videa, which Delman started with former Atari colleagues Ed Rotberg and Roger Hector. The three have since authorized the game's free distribution.

If you're simply interested in checking out Gridlee without going through the trouble of setting up MAME, there is a standalone Gridlee emulator and ROM download available at *http://www.aarongiles.com/gridlee/*.

Robby Roto

Created by Gorf designer Jay Fenton, Robby Roto actually did make it into arcades, courtesy of Bally/Midway. The reason you don't find this interesting combination of Dig Dug and Pac-Man in either of the Midway Arcade Treasures compilations [Hack #16] is because of a clause in Fenton's contract—after the game went out of print, the rights reverted back to him. In 1999, he authorized the free distribution of the ROM.

In the years since leaving Midway, Jay Fenton has identified as transgender, changing his name to Jamie Faye Fenton. A 1999 Next Generation Online interview with Fenton said that the number of male-to-female transgender individuals in game design was in the double digits. Read the interview and more at *http://members.tgforum.com/jamie/*.

Poly Play

In Soviet Russia, game plays you! Now we know the real reason East Germans were scrambling to get over the Berlin Wall—they were trying to get away from what was apparently the only arcade game developed in Communist Eastern Europe, Poly Play. True to its name, Poly Play is a collection of different imitations of popular games developed by capitalist pigdog swine; inferior takes on Pac-Man and Carnival join four other games as depressingly dreary as the country that spawned them. Since the company (and the government that propped it up) no longer exist, the ROM can be downloaded with little fear of reprisal.

> Immediately after Ronald Reagan ripped off his shirt (exposing his massive biceps) and took sledgehammer in hand to smash down the Wall, most of the thousand or so Poly Play machines that had been manufactured were destroyed. About three survive, making it one of the rarest arcade games in existence. More at *http://www.bbc.co.uk/wiltshire/features/polyplay.shtml*.

Homebrew MAME ROMs

Despite what I said earlier in the hack, some homebrew authors have indeed shouldered the responsibility of writing original (or semi-original) games that run on the various systems emulated by MAME. Most of these can be found at PDRoms (*http://www.pdroms.de*).

Mine Sweeper
A version of the classic puzzle game programmed to run on Sega arcade hardware. Specifically, it uses the hardware from the in-house "test game" Dottori Kun (*http://www.klov.com/game_detail.php?letter=D&game_id=7614*) to produce a simple, monochromatic experience.

Neo no Panepon
Another variation of another classic puzzle game, Neo no Panepon mimics the gameplay of the classic Nintendo-developed puzzler Panel de Pon (known as Tetris Attack or Pokémon Puzzle League in its U.S. incarnations) developed for the Neo Geo. It will also run in standalone Neo Geo emulators like NeoRAGE.

NeoPong
Yep—it's the classic video tennis game with a snazzy Neo Geo-styled facelift. Like Neo no Panepon, it will run in standalone NG emulators as well as under MAME.

Vantris
Wait, another take on a ubiquitous puzzle game for SNK arcade hardware? Yes, but this time it's not the Neo Geo—it's a popular falling-blocks puzzler designed for SNK's 1981-vintage Vanguard arcade hardware. The source code is available at author Norbert Kehrer's web site (*http://web.utanet.at/nkehrer/vantris.html*).

Various Tech Demonstrations

A few tech demos—non-interactive screens full of colorful text displays that do little more than demonstrate that the hacker in question is indeed able to get a small program up and running on obscure hardware—are available at PDRoms and elsewhere.

> All games for the Neo Geo system share a common BIOS ROM that was embedded in the hardware and contained information that each game used. This ROM, with the name *neogeo.zip*, must be in your *\mame\roms* directory for any Neo Geo game to run. Since it is a copyrighted file, neither I nor the official MAME site can offer it for download.

HACK #25 Buy Legal MAME ROMs

Put some money into the pockets of classic game publishers.

Let's face it—as fun as Gridlee [Hack #24] may be, what you really want to do with MAME is play the arcade games you remember from your misspent youth (or, depending on your age, satisfy your curiosity about what us geezers used to think was high-tech). You want the real thing, but if possible you'd prefer to do it without running afoul of copyright law. In that case you'll want to visit StarROMs, Inc. (*http://www.starroms.com*), which at the time of this writing lets you legally download twenty-seven different Atari arcade titles.

> There are a few different web sites and online auction sellers who sell CD-ROMs or DVD-ROMs containing every ROM known to work in MAME. Bear in mind that these are not in any way official products.

The web site claims that the games cost "as low as $2 each," but there is a catch. You don't purchase the games directly—instead, you buy packages of "download credits" which are then redeemed for games. The current price structure is 40 credits for $9.95, 100 credits for $19.95, 200 credits for $34.95, 400 credits for $59.95, and 800 credits for $99.00, the latter representing a 50% savings over the base price.

Games cost between 8 and 24 credits each. Do the math and you'll find that an 8-credit game purchased from the pack of 800 credits does indeed effectively cost $2. (Of course, you should bear in mind that if you purchased every ROM on the site as of this writing, it would cost a total of 452 credits.)

Sounds a bit like the tokens used in lieu of quarters at many arcades these days, doesn't it? And of course it has the same effect: since you have to buy a bundle of credits, you're sure to end up spending more money in the long run. There is a bit of good news in all this: you get 15 free credits for signing up. Of course, this means you won't be able to download the good stuff (e.g., Asteroids or Tempest), for free since they cost over 15 credits, but here are the ROMs from which you can select one effectively for free:

8 credits
> Atari Baseball, Atari Football, Atari Soccer

10 credits
> Avalanche

12 credits
> Lunar Lander, Qwak, Red Baron, Super Breakout

14 credits
> Black Widow, Cloak and Dagger, Cloud 9

Listed next are the ROMs that, one way or another, you will have to pay money for. I recommend visiting the informational page on each, then calculating how many ROMs you want to buy before signing up for a package of credits (and remember that you have those 15 free ones coming to you—rather than downloading a free game you don't want, it may be better to put those towards the purchase of a more expensive ROM you know you'll get more enjoyment out of).

16 credits
> Battlezone, Crystal Castles, Gravitar, Liberator, Monte Carlo, Peter Packrat, Quantum, Space Duel, Warlords

20 credits
> Major Havoc

22 credits
> Tempest

24 credits
> Asteroids, Asteroids Deluxe, Centipede, Millipede, Missile Command

Phew! Now, what to do with these other 363 credits?

Capcom Coin-Op Classics

StarROMs' 800-credit pricing deal actually makes this next item seem like a downright bargain. Since 1999, HanaHo Games, Inc. has been selling its deluxe PC joystick called the HotRod (*http://www.hanaho.com/products/HotRodJoystick/*). This beautiful and gigantic piece of machinery mimics a classic two-player Street Fighter six-button arcade controller setup, and doesn't even require a joystick port. Instead, you plug it in your PS/2 keyboard slot, then plug your keyboard into the stick. The buttons on the HotRod will then mimic the default MAME keyboard inputs.

The controller costs $99.95 plus shipping, but to sweeten the deal it includes a disc called Capcom Coin-Op Classics, featuring sixteen of Capcom's best-loved arcade titles. Included on the disc are 1941, Block Block, Commando, Exed Eyes, Ghouls 'n Ghosts, Magic Sword, Mercs, Section Z, Side Arms, Son Son, Street Fighter II Hyper Fighting (a.k.a. Street Fighter II Turbo), Strider, U.N. Squadron, and Varth.

There is, of course, one caveat: Capcom fans thinking of purchasing this stick just to play their favorite games may want to know that the company has announced that it will bring a collection of its classic arcade games to game consoles [Hack #16] in 2005.

 Advertisements for a competing arcade-style PC joystick, the X-Arcade [Hack #27], effectively promise that buying its product will let you play thousands of arcade games. A page on the product web site, after some legal caveats, then links to other sites where you can buy DVD-ROMs full of MAME software or download ROMs individually. Although the page states that the makers of X-Arcade are currently "coordinating an effort to provide access to thousands of arcade classic games," as of this writing, the ROMs on the sites linked to are not being sold legally.

 ## HACK #26 Care for Your ROMs

Manage ROM sets, learn to use alternative ROMs, and more.

If you prick your ROMs, do they not bleed? Well, no. But ROMs are still precious things, and you must take good care of them. Now that you've set up MAME and have started to piece together a game collection, you'll want to know how to download, store, and organize your ROM files. There are a few external utilities you can use for this task, but knowing a bit about MAME's internal workings is important as well.

Downloading ROMs

When you download MAME ROMs [Hack #24], you will probably notice that they are in Zip file format. The Zip archive format is used to compress many files into one small file for easy transfer, and usually in a case like this you will want to download an external utility like WinZip or Info-Zip (on Mac OS X and Windows XP, you can just double-click the files to open them) to extract the files from the archive. In fact, the odds are great that you didn't need me to tell you what a Zip file is, and you're just about to open up the file...

Stop! Contrary to everything you know, you're not going to open this *.zip* file. Instead, save the file to your hard drive, in the *mame\roms* directory. Do not rename the file—it must remain as-is for MAME to recognize it. MAME will automatically open and read the ROM files, and your *roms* directory will remain neat and uncluttered.

When the ROM Doesn't Work

Most of the time, the preceding two paragraphs are enough to get you playing nearly any ROM you happen to come across. But when MAME spits back an error message, it could be because you've failed to properly manage your ROMs. Don't beat yourself up over it; just learn from your mistakes.

Parent/Child ROMs: I Think I'm a Clone Now. If MAME says that it can't run the ROM because some required files are missing, first ask yourself whether you're trying to run a clone ROM without its parent set. In an effort to maximize your free hard drive space, MAME designates certain ROMs as *clones* of others. In some cases, the generally accepted definition of a clone is: a knockoff of a popular game made by an unscrupulous third party.

Hangly Ghosts, for example, was a clone of Pac-Man that you could see here and there during the game's run at the top of worldwide pop culture. (The unfortunate name comes, of course, from the Japanese confusion of the letters L and R.) Since it shares so much in common with Pac-Man, MAME's authors so cleverly thought, why force someone to download complete sets of both Pac-Man *and* Hangly Ghosts?

Thus, when you download Hangly Ghosts you are only downloading the parts of the ROM that are different. When you run the game, MAME will automagically pluck out the parts of Pac-Man that are needed, put it all together, and you'll be chomping bootleg ghosts 'till the wee morning hours.

"Chris," you might say to me if we were on a first-name basis, "this is all well and good, but when I try to run regular ol' Pac-Man I get the same errors." Well, remember how I told you that in *some* cases a clone ROM was a knockoff arcade game? In many other cases, a legitimate game is the *child* and another game is the *parent*. Usually, the game that comes first chronologically is the parent. And in the case of Pac-Man, the game that came first was Puck-Man, the original Japanese version of the game. So in fact, you need Puck-Man before you can run the U.S. version, Pac-Man, in MAME.

Is this getting confusing? Are you wondering how you're supposed to keep all this straight? You're not alone. Luckily, MAME provides a built-in function to assess all this. When you run MAME from the command prompt [Hack #20], you can use the option -listclones to generate a list of ROM names and the game of which each is a clone. If you want a complete list, type:

```
mame -listclones >clones.txt
```

This will generate a text file in your *mame* directory called *clones.txt* that contains a complete list. (You'll want to save this information to a file because otherwise, the names of the games will scroll off your screen before you can read them all.) However, if you simply want to see the information relevant to a specific game, then type:

```
mame -listclones pacman
```

This will show you, in the command prompt window (Figure 3-16), a list of games in which the parent or child is named "pacman." An asterisk may be used to denote a variable search string: mame -listclones pac* will show a list of all games and clones whose names begin with the three letters pac.

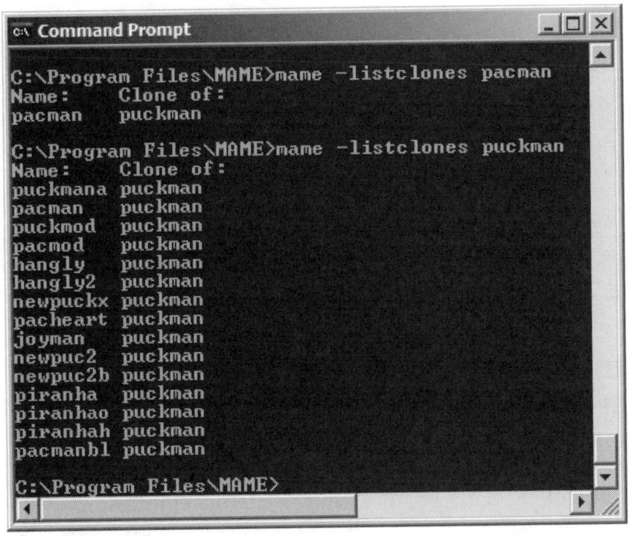

Figure 3-16. The -listclones command at work

When it still doesn't work: verifying ROMs. If you've run the -listclones command and your game isn't showing up, you might have an outdated, incomplete, or non-working ROM file. ROMs are updated occasionally as

MAME itself is updated. If, for example, a ROM that formerly used samples to generate sound [Hack #28] now features properly working emulation, some new files may be added to the ROM.

Fortunately, MAME also provides a built-in function that will examine the integrity of one or all of your ROMs. The command is -verifyroms, so at the command prompt, typing:

```
mame puckman -verifyroms
```

will check *puckman.zip* to be sure it is ready to roll. If not, you'll have to obtain the ROM again. If you wish to check all your ROMs at once and have the results output to a text file (in this case, one called *verify.txt*), type:

```
mame -verifyroms >verify.txt
```

Do it for me: CLRMamePro. If all the instructions concerning command prompt inputs and ROM verification has done nothing more than confuse and frighten you, you might be best served by an automatic ROM manager like CLRMamePro. This external, Windows-only program, which can be downloaded from its official web site at *http://www.clrmame.com/*, does all of the following automatically:

- Identify missing ROM files.
- Find and rename incorrectly named ROMs.
- Resize ROMs that are too large.
- Find and remove unnecessary files.

A complete tutorial for CLRMamePro can be found at *http://www. mameworld.net/easyemu/*. Be aware that since the program deletes, renames, and shuffles the files on your PC, you should back up anything you cannot bear to lose. That said, many MAME users swear by the software.

HACK #27 Buy or Make Classic MAME Controllers

Get the full retro experience from classic control boxes.

Tired of playing classic arcade games under MAME using only your keyboard or a tiny game pad? Want a controller that mimics the original arcade experience—but don't want to shell out the cash and living-room space required for a six-foot-tall arcade cabinet [Hack #30]? If this sounds like you, what you need is a standalone MAME controller that hooks up to your PC. This hack will explore how to buy prefabricated controllers as well as a few tips on how to create, then build, your own custom design.

Buy a Classic MAME Controller

By far the easiest option (at least for those of us not particularly technically inclined) is to buy one of the pre-made MAME controllers offered by a few different manufacturers. Although they may look virtually identical, you'll want to know some details about the devices before you decide which one to purchase.

HotRod. A manufacturer called HanaHo Games offers this joystick (*http://www.hanaho.com/products/HotRodJoystick/*). The large casing features two full sets of real arcade-style eight-way joysticks and buttons. Each side features eight buttons: a start button up above, six arranged in the standard two-by-three style used by most Street Fighter type fighting games, as well as an extra button on the lower left, which allows you to play the four-button Neo Geo games by using the bottom row only. Two buttons on the sides of the unit function as flipper controls for pinball-style games.

What sets it apart from the X-Arcade is that the HotRod connects to your PS/2 standard keyboard input. If you are using a PS/2 keyboard, you don't have to unplug it to connect the HotRod, as a jack on the HotRod's included PS/2 cable lets you hook up both at once. The price is $99.99, which includes a disc of classic Capcom arcade games [Hack #25].

X-Arcade. The X-Arcade (*http://www.x-arcade.com*) is identical in many respects to the HotRod, but differs in some significant ways. It is available in both single- and dual-player versions, which retail for $99.99 and $149.99 respectively. The joystick setups are nearly identical, but the X-Arcade features an extra button on each side.

What truly sets the device apart, however, are the various adapters available for it that allow you to use the X-Arcade not only with the PC but also the Dreamcast, Xbox, PlayStation 2, and GameCube consoles by using adapters that cost $19.99 each. (One adapter of your choice is included when you buy either model of the joystick.)

USB adapters that let you connect the X-Arcade to the Mac (or PC, if you'd rather not use your keyboard port) are available for $29.99, or free by adding the "Mac Kit" joystick bundle into your shopping cart if using the X-Arcade home page to buy the controller. If you'd rather see one in a brick-and-mortar retailer, the sticks are available at Fry's Electronics and J&R Computer World stores.

SlikStik. If you want an even more detailed arcade joystick setup with options like trackballs, dual joysticks for both players, or even spinners for games like Tempest—and aren't afraid of shelling out the big bucks to get exactly what you want—the company SlikStik (*http://www.slikstik.com*) might be worth checking out. The controllers are pricey—a two-player "Fighter" joystick with a layout similar to the X-Arcade's runs about $240, and the trackball-enhanced "Classic" model a whopping $479.95—but you can customize your order on the web site in practically any way you can imagine, changing the button colors, layouts, and other options. They even offer a four-player setup. And if you're interested in building your own controller, you can order the same arcade-quality parts they use to build their machines. And speaking of which...

Make a Classic MAME Controller

Buying a MAME controller is certainly an easy way to have an arcade-quality control setup at your fingertips, but what if you want a cheaper solution? Or, for that matter, a custom setup that puts the joystick and buttons right where you want them? Homemade MAME controllers are surprisingly simple and inexpensive to make, and can greatly improve your MAME gaming experience!

> Many different step-by-step tutorials written by hackers who have made their own custom MAME controller designs can be pored over at *www.arcadecontrols.com*.

Planning your controller layout. Planning is the most important step. Is your controller going to support one player, or two? Are you going to set it on your desk or on your lap? Is your favorite game Pac-Man (a game that uses a 4-way joystick and no buttons) or Mortal Kombat 3 (which requires an 8-way joystick and six buttons per player)? There's no reason why you can't design a controller that will work with both, but it'll never work out if you don't plan ahead! If you're a computer geek, pull up your favorite illustration program and keep moving circles around until you like what you see. If you're more the hands-on type, try cutting some circles out of paper and moving them around until you like the way it feels. I've seen many controllers completely assembled out of cardboard before a single piece of wood was ever cut. Don't forget while laying out your buttons that for MAME, you may want to include player start buttons and coin-up buttons.

Once you have a general idea of the size and layout of your controller, it's time to get some wood and start cutting! The type of wood you choose depends on the look you want and how you plan on finishing the controller. I've used both 1/2" and 3/4" wood and had good results. If you want to save yourself a ton of frustration, pick up a couple of extra drill bits at your local hardware store. Arcade buttons need a 1 1/8" hole, while joysticks generally require a 1 1/4" hole.

 Arcade quality joysticks, buttons, and other necessary parts can be purchased from Happ Controls (*www.happcontrols.com*).

Wiring your buttons. Now comes the less-fun part. You've got to get all those buttons and joysticks talking to your computer. If you want to go the quick and easy route, pick up an encoder such as the I-PAC (*http://www.ultimarc.com/ipac1.html*). All the wires from your joysticks and buttons will hook directly to the encoder, which then connects to your PC. Most encoders ship pre-configured for MAME, so once your wiring is done you're ready to go. Most of the new encoders have USB connections, which will allow you to easily disconnect your controller when not in use. These encoders are generally available for under $40. Figure 3-17 shows these components wired up.

Figure 3-17. The I-PAC, all wired up

But if the ultimate goal of your controller is to keep prices down, you may want to make your own encoder by hacking a keyboard. This involves soldering a wire from each button on your new controller to a contact point on a disassembled computer keyboard. It's inexpensive, but it takes a lot of time, patience, and frustration to get it just right.

Additionally, many keyboard hacks experience what's known as "ghosting" and/or "blocking". The next time you're at your computer, open up a text editor and, using your entire hand, press down as many keys as you can at the same time. Chances are you won't see more than three or four letters appear. Keyboards weren't designed to take in a lot of input all at once – and if that's the heart of your MAME controller, neither will it. Also keep in mind that if you use a PS/2 keyboard, that means you'll be unplugging your normal keyboard in order to use your controller.

If you plan on making a MAME controller for only one player, a better option would be to hack an existing PC joystick—Microsoft Sidewinder and Gravis Gamepad seem to be popular donors. The idea is the same as a keyboard hack: open the joystick and solder your wires directly to the contacts on the joystick's circuit board. Most of these controllers are USB, which is convenient.

Finish Him! Once you've got your controller assembled, it's time to decorate it! The only limit here is your imagination. The simplest solutions involve simply painting your controller. I've also seen the tops of controllers wrapped in $1 sheets of contact paper that turned out looking really nice. Slightly fancier controllers may end up covered in Formica. Even fancier ones may end up with graphics printed on top of them, covered by a layer of Plexiglas. Many MAME controllers end up with T-molding around their edges, just like their arcade-dwelling big brothers. Like I said, the sky's the limit here.

Even starting from scratch, you can build a really nice looking MAME controller for $50-$100, depending on the number of controls and the finish you decide on. With just a little bit of elbow grease, you can build yourself a one of a kind controller and save yourself some money in the process.

—Rob O'Hara and Chris Kohler

HACK #28 Add Sound to Your MAME Experience
Use WAV samples to replicate the original arcade sounds.

One day not too long ago, you were thinking of Q*bert. You closed your eyes and suddenly you were back in front of the machine that used to stand in the lobby of your local pizza parlor. You put in a quarter, slammed the machine to get it to drop in, and the game started up with the familiar fan-fare. You weren't just seeing the game with your mind's eye, you were *hearing* it, too. The "bwip," like a drip of water, as Q*bert bounces down the pyramid. The "oooooowwww" as he falls off the edge. And of course, the infamous "@!#?@!" when Q*bert was stomped by a Coily.

With these sounds playing a nostalgic symphony in your brain, you boot up Q*bert in MAME. But something's wrong. Some of the sound is gone. The familiar fanfare is there, and so is the "bwip." But the good stuff, the scream and the cursing? To heck with this emulation stuff, you think. They've missed the best parts! But before you email the MAME creators (subject line: "@!#?@!"), ask yourself: did you download the Q*bert samples?

Whither Samples?

In the early days of arcade games, designers used some interesting means to produce sound effects. The eponymous "pong" that sounded when a ball bounced off the paddle in that seminal arcade hit was jury-rigged by designer Al Alcorn to be produced from parts that were already built into the machine's design.

> ...I've seen articles written about how intelligently the sound was done and how appropriate the sound was. The truth is, I was running out of parts on the board... Since I had the wire wrapped on the scope, I poked around the sync generator to find an appropriate frequency or a tone. So those sounds were done in half a day. They were the sounds already in the machine.
>
> From *The Ultimate History of Video Games* by Steven L. Kent (Prima, 2001) p. 42

Pong, being entirely constructed from electronic hardware, contains no ROM code and therefore cannot be emulated in MAME. But even some games for which the graphic and gameplay data was coded on chips in ROM format, the sound effects were done using analog electronics. Furthermore, the coders of MAME have not yet been able to accurately emulate some sound chips. In the case of Q*bert, the mock curse words were randomly generated using a speech synthesizer chip that has not been emulated.

Fortunately, there is a solution. Owners of the original arcade games have meticulously recorded the individual missing sound effects, in WAV file for-mat, and the writers of the emulation code have included support for these files. In a remarkable display of foresight, some games that have been dumped and emulated have been coded to accept samples even if record-ings of the arcade sounds are not yet available, in the hopes that one day an owner of the original machine will record the sounds.

Finding Samples

Though ROMs dumped from arcade games, being of dubious legality, are not provided on any official MAME site, samples are. A page at the official MAME site, *http://www.mame.net/downsamples.html* is updated regularly with the latest officially supported sample set—all the samples you need for your game collection to be complete. Samples currently exist and are required for approximately sixty games including Donkey Kong, Space Invaders, and Zaxxon.

If sound hardware is properly emulated in the future, the samples will be removed from the official list (recent examples of this include Punch-Out!!, Phoenix, and Track and Field). Samples are also occasionally updated to better reflect the true sound of the arcade machine. If you would like to hear some of these obsolete samples (or if you are running an older version of MAME and need them), an archive of outdated versions is available at Twisty's MAME Samples Collection (*http://www.mameworld.net/samples/*).

Installing Samples

Like installing ROMs, it couldn't be easier. Samples are provided in Zip archive file format, which you do not need to extract. Simply save the *.zip* file, as is, in the *samples* directory under your MAME directory. Do not change the filename, or MAME will be unable to find the samples.

> The latest version of MacMAME [Hack #21] requires that you store samples in the *Sound Samples* folder under the *~/ Documents/MacMAME/* directory.

Twisty's archive, mentioned earlier, even contains some alternate fan-created sample sets that make your games sound rather different than you remember. Want to add synthesized speech into Galaga? Done. Just remember to back up your old sample file first so you can change the sounds back to normal later.

You might have noticed that samples add quite a bit of heft to the file size of the game—whereas the Q*bert ROM only takes up 64K, the samples are over two megabytes. There is a silver lining here: the same set of samples will suffice for all variations of a game. So if you're a Space Invaders fanatic and have not only the original game, but also the knockoffs like Space Laser, Space King II, and Space Intruders, the same Zip file of samples will be loaded up for each game. You don't have to rename or duplicate the archive.

Before I leave off, I'd like to mention that the attentive reader will have worked out one more disadvantage of samples. The Q*bert curses you so fondly remember were *randomly generated* by the speech synthesizer, regardless of the stories from kids at the pizza parlor who *swore* they heard the little guy say a real dirty word. Though the sample pack does contain an assortment of different randomly generated phrases, it is thus not entirely arcade-perfect. (Though one of the samples really does sound like he's saying "oh s—t." I swear!)

Add Cabinet Art to MAME

Gussy up your gameplay with classic arcade artwork.

So you've decked out your MAME setup with original arcade game sounds [Hack #28] and even got hooked up with a classic arcade-style controller [Hack #27]. But something's still telling you that your MAME experience isn't quite complete. Something's still missing.

Your peripheral vision is giving you different cues than you remember. You're not supposed to be looking at the grey sides of your monitor. Or the empty black unused space on the sides of the screen. Or that cheesecake photo calendar from ten years ago. No! You're supposed to see the arcade cabinet art bordering your screen. And didn't the original Asteroids Deluxe machine have a cool holographic background, or was that just your imagination?

Well, don't fret, because MAME's crew of dedicated supporters have a solution. You can download artwork files that feature reproduction of the arcade cabinet art, overlays, and backdrops for a more fulfilling and realistic gameplay session.

How to Use Artwork

Though ROMs dumped from arcade games, being of dubious legality, are not provided on any official MAME site, artwork is. A page at the official MAME site, *http://www.mame.net/downart.html* is updated regularly with the latest officially supported artwork sets. MAME only started supporting artwork with version 6.1, so be sure you've upgraded.

Artwork has been created for nearly 140 different titles so far, although they vary in quality. The list of downloadable artwork is split up into three categories: games with overlays or backdrop graphics and bezels, games with only high-quality bezels (artwork placed around the monitor), and games with low-quality bezels. (Note that the definition of *high-quality* here is subjective; some of the artwork in the high-quality section is pixilated and blurry.)

Like downloading ROMs **[Hack #26]**, downloading artwork is quite simple. Artwork files are provided in Zip archive file format, which you do not need to extract. Simply save the *.zip* file, as is, in the *artwork* directory under your MAME directory. Do not change the filename, or MAME will be unable to find the artwork.

> If you're using the latest version of MacMAME **[Hack #21]**, you must store all your artwork in the *Cabinet Art* folder under the *~/Documents/MacMAME/* directory.

Let's look at how artwork can change what MAME looks like. Figure 3-18 shows us what Asteroids Deluxe looks like running under MAME with no artwork installed.

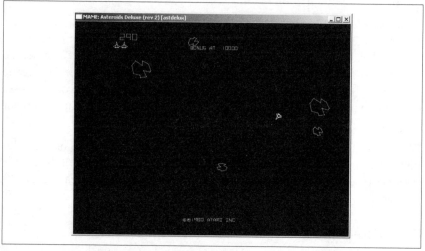

Figure 3-18. Asteroids Deluxe, no backdrop or bezels

Not bad, but not the best it can be. Install the *astdelux.zip* artwork pack, however, and start the game up to see something like Figure 3-19.

Holy cats! Now that's the Asteroids Deluxe I remember! (By the way, the backdrop is not really holographic—just a couple pieces of printed Plexiglas that are reflected onto the screen image.)

How to Not Use Artwork

You may have noticed something about the art-enabled Asteroids Deluxe screen. Namely that the gameplay area has shrunken. Well, yeah. Where did you think the bezels would go? You might be able to forgive this (especially

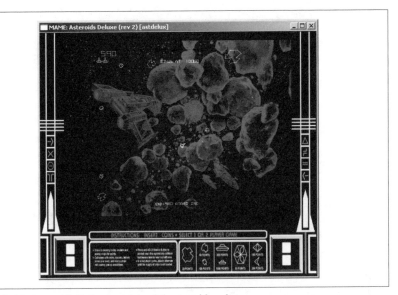

Figure 3-19. Asteroids Deluxe with backdrop and bezels

if you have a giant monitor), but if you find that having bezels turned on is starting to impede your play, you can remove them.

And you can do it without deleting the Zip file and losing your backdrop art. For example, in the PC command line version of MAME **[Hack #20]**, enter -nobezel on the command line after you type the name of the game you want to play. For example, typing c:\mame\mame astdelux -nobezel will result in the game looking like the screen shown in Figure 3-20.

How to Make Artwork

"Hey, [insert game here] is missing the cabinet artwork!"

So make some! If you have access to game art that's not yet supported, or think you can get a higher-quality scan or photograph of artwork that you think is really ugly to look at, I'm sure the good folks at MAME would love to hear from you. Instructions for how to make bezels, and the appropriate email addresses to send them to, are located at the artwork page on mame. net (*http://www.mame.net/downart.html*).

Artcade (*http://www.macmame.net/artcade/*) used to be the primary repository of MAME artwork, but stopped updating in 2002 after mame.net began hosting all the files. The reason I point you to it now is because it features tutorials for budding bezel captors, complete with photographs and explanations of how certain machines were photographed to replicate the original lighting and feel.

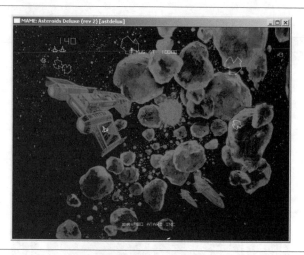

Figure 3-20. Asteroids Deluxe with backdrop… but no bezel

Build a MAME Cabinet

HACK
#30   Craft your own stand-up MAME cabinet for realistic arcade play.

More and more accurate as every new iteration of MAME is, the popular arcade machine emulator will always have one insurmountable design flaw: no matter how perfectly it emulates arcade machines, it does so on something that isn't an arcade machine. No matter how authentic a video game may look and play on your computer, it will never feel like the real thing.

If you truly want to feed your thirst for nostalgia and experience these games the way they were originally intended, you're going to have to build yourself a MAME cabinet: an arcade cabinet with a dedicated MAME computer running inside. A well-built MAME cabinet can be indistinguishable from a "real" arcade game when done right—plus it has the advantage of being able to play thousands of different arcade games instead of being dedicated to playing only one!

Planning Your Personal Cabinet

Building a MAME cabinet isn't particularly hard, but it can become both expensive and disastrous in a hurry if you don't do some simple planning before you start building. One of the most important decisions you can make is determining what general era and type of games you plan on playing the most. This will help you make several specific decisions about your cabinet later, such as the control panel layout, minimum computer specs, and even monitor orientation (horizontal versus vertical). I have seen

MAME cabinets dedicated to playing a small handful of classics, and I've seen cabinets configured to play literally thousands of different games. That's the beauty of building your own cabinet; it's all about designing and creating the machine you want to own!

The first thing you'll need is the cabinet structure itself. There are two solutions to this problem, the easier of which is to find an older, dead arcade game and convert it into your MAME machine. Dead or dying arcade games can often be found for $50 or less and can be easily modified to meet most people's needs. If you're unable to find a donor machine and are handy with power tools, you may opt to simply build your own cabinet using plans and measurements freely available on the Internet (or by simply winging it). Building your own cabinet offers a lot more leeway and freedom when it comes to the shape and design of your cabinet, but of course it will require more advanced woodworking skills to pull off.

A fully fleshed-out plan for building an arcade cabinet can be found in the book *Hardware Hacking Projects For Geeks* (O'Reilly).

Filling Your Cabinet

Once you have your cabinet, it's time to find a computer to mount inside of it. As a general rule, the newer the games are you want to play, the faster your computer will need to be. A 400 MHz PC with two gigabytes of hard drive space powered my first MAME cabinet. It was perfect for playing the classics like Pac-Man and Donkey Kong, but for more recent games you'll need a bit more power. Playing newer games requires a faster processor, more RAM, and more hard drive space. You may also want to add a network card and/or a CD/DVD drive to simplify adding new games and software to your cabinet. Another consideration is the operating system you're going to run. Although anything from DOS to Linux to Windows XP can be used, slimmer operating systems like DOS and Linux typically run better on lower-end computers. Although I've never built one personally, there are plenty of MAME cabinets out there powered by Macintosh computers as well.

While you're installing and configuring your MAME PC, be sure to check out some of the frontends available for MAME [Hack #20]. *Frontends* are graphical user interfaces (GUIs) that simplify choosing and running the game of your choice. Remember, in your MAME cabinet you're not going to have quick access to your mouse or keyboard, so using a frontend is an essential part of navigating through MAME. The simplest frontends allow users to pick a game from a menu and play it. More advanced frontends will display screen shots and marquees, play MP3s during the menu, and even let you sort your games into different groups. Almost all the frontends available for MAME are free, so try several out and find which one works best for your cabinet. In an ideal situation, a MAME cabinet will boot directly into its frontend and be able to shut the machine down when MAME is closed.

When it comes to monitors for MAME cabinets there are three choices, each of which has its own benefits and shortcomings. One option is to simply use a computer monitor. It's the easiest of the three options since you can connect it directly to your PC and no major computer configuration is need. Unfortunately, computer monitors provide the least arcade-like experience due to their clarity (computer monitors have a much higher resolution than arcade monitors). Another fact to consider is most arcade cabinets had 19" or 25" monitors in them, so a 15" computer monitor sitting in your cabinet is going to look rather anticlimactic.

A second option, if you're lucky enough to have one lying around, is to use a real arcade monitor. While this is clearly the most authentic-looking solution, you're going to need a special video card to connect it to, and possibly more parts to get it to work (not to mention that all monitors contain lethal doses of electricity in them—this may not be the project on which you wish to discover that). If you still want to try this, software capable of video-trickery, such as VGA2TV drivers or ArcadeOS (*http://www.mameworld.net/ pc2jamma/frontend.html*) can be used for routing PC video output to a standard low-resolution arcade monitor.

The third option (and a great middle ground) involves using a television set. This provides a picture quality similar to actual arcade monitors, and hooking up a newer television to a computer is a breeze especially when using a newer video card with s-video or composite video outputs! Bear in mind that the video output generated by the TV Out on most modern video cards won't be as pretty as an arcade monitor's display, due to the interlacing that video cards use when generating NTSC signals.

Another detail to begin considering is whether you want to mount your monitor horizontally or vertically. Most classic games from 1983 and before (like the aforementioned Pac-Man and Donkey Kong) used vertically-mounted monitors. The majority of games after that date moved to horizontally mounted monitors. If you mount your monitor horizontally (e.g., by simply setting a television set on a shelf), you can still play vertical games; however, a lot of empty black space will appear on either side of the game. Likewise, horizontal games can be played on a vertically mounted screen, with black bars appearing at the top and bottom of the picture (kind of like the black bars that appear when watching a letterboxed DVD on a standard

4:3 ratio television). Again, it's all about forethought, deciding what type of games you're going to be playing the most, and building the cabinet that fits your needs. If in doubt, go horizontal; it's easier.

Controlling Your Cabinet

One of the most fun parts of building your own MAME cabinet is designing your control panel. What and where you decide to install is completely up to you, but this is one part of your cabinet that should receive a lot of attention and planning, as a poorly designed control panel can ruin your entire project. Even the simplest MAME control panels will need a joystick, a "player one" start button, and one or more player buttons. Most control panels contain (at least) two joysticks and three or four buttons per player (in addition to the player one and player two start buttons). Trackballs, spinners and even steering wheels can be added if you so desire.

I have seen control panels that support four players with six buttons per player, four start buttons, a pause button, a spinner, a trackball, and a four-way joystick (for playing the classics) all on one control panel. Not only was it even less aesthetically pleasing than it sounds, but also it was three-feet wide! One alternative to having such a busy control panel is creating interchangeable control panels (one for regular games, one for driving games, etc.) that can easily snap in and out. Again, it's all up to your own personal needs and tastes.

 You can purchase arcade-quality joysticks, buttons, and other necessary parts from Happ Controls (*www.happcontrols.com*).

Eventually you're going to need to wire all those controls up to your computer. Most modern arcade controls connect to small leaf switches with metal connectors for connecting wires. Each leaf switch will use two wires (a hot and a ground). Wiring up the ground wires is easy; they can all be wired together in one big loop, with the last switch being wired to a ground point. Each hot wire from your control panel is eventually going to be connected to something. That "something" can either be a keyboard or an encoder [Hack #27].

Hacking keyboards is for people who are on a tight budget, like to experiment and tinker with projects, and have more time than money to spend. Keyboard hacking involves connecting the wires from your controls to a keyboard's contacts by using solder. The keyboard control panel is then connected to the PC inside your MAME cabinet. When a button is pressed on your control panel, the signal is sent along the wire to your hacked keyboard, which then sends the key press to your computer, and eventually to MAME. Hacking a keyboard is a time-consuming, intricate, and often frustrating experience, but it is cheap.

The alternative (and usually preferred) method is to purchase an encoder. These handy devices are small circuit boards with pre-made connectors on them for your wire inputs. The backsides of these encoders have either a PS/2 or USB connection that is used to connect the encoder to your MAME computer. Ultimarc's I-PAC encoder (*http://www.ultimarc.com/ipac1.html*) runs $39, but the advantage is that by using an encoder you can hook your control panel up in minutes versus hours or days of soldering on a hacked keyboard. Encoders are well worth the investment.

Once you have your frame, computer, monitor, and control panel, it's time to assemble your MAME cabinet! If you purchased a previously used arcade cabinet, now's the time to gut all the old parts out and clean it up. If the cabinet needs any repair work (Bondo does wonders) or painting, now's the time to do it, before any electronics have been installed. Once the woodwork is done, it's time to mount your monitor. If using a computer monitor or television, you can either remove the chassis from the plastic housing and mount it directly to your cabinet, or you can simply build a shelf inside your cabinet for your monitor to sit on top of. If you do end up using a shelf, make sure your monitor is secured into place with a few 2×4s and metal brackets. You really don't want that large television falling out of the back of your cabinet the first time you try to move it. Regardless of how you mount your monitor, you'll also need a bezel to block out the edges around the front of the tube. Poster board works really well for this. It's cheap, easy to work with, and looks great when mounted behind Plexiglas.

Next you'll want to attach your control panel, secure any loose wires, and mount your PC into place. For cooling reasons, I've always preferred mounting my computer components directly to the wood inside (without using the case); others often simply place the computer (tower and all) inside their cabinet. It's just a matter of personal preference.

Once the big stuff is done, it's time for the details. PC speakers can be connected to your MAME computer and hidden behind the cabinet's original speaker grills. Custom marquees and sideart for your cabinet can either be downloaded or custom made, printed out and mounted to your cabinet to make your MAME machine really stand out. Likewise, your control panel and bezel can also be customized with printouts and custom artwork as well. Again, the only limit here is your own imagination. You can make your MAME cabinet as subdued or as wild as you like! Figure 3-21 shows my finished arcade cabinet.

Figure 3-21. Rob's finished arcade cabinet

When you're all finished, you should end up with something that resembles an original arcade cabinet, configured and ready to play all of your favorite classic videogames at a moment's notice! It's amazing how different the experience of playing games is when you're standing in front of an actual arcade cabinet. And the best news of all is that if you wire up the coin slots on the front of your cabinet, you can start making the money you invested into your cabinet back from your friends, one quarter at a time!

—*Rob O'Hara*

HACK #31 Make a Self-Booting MAME Disc

Play MAME on any computer you discover in your travels.

Playing your favorite arcade games using MAME at home is a lot of fun, but what happens when you're forced to leave the house? (Hey, it happens.) If your friends and relatives are tired of you reconfiguring their computers and installing MAME every time you visit, or your boss has your workstation locked down so you can't install any new software, what you need is a boot-able MAME CD.

Bootable MAME CDs allow you to boot computers from a CD directly into MAME. An operating system (usually a flavor of Linux), MAME, and all your game ROMs are contained directly on the disc, so the computer's hard drive is never even accessed.

AdvanceCD

The best and most complete solution is a package called AdvanceCD, named so because it also includes the emulator, AdvanceMAME, and the frontend AdvanceMENU. Getting AdvanceCD to work could not be sim-pler. First, users need to download the installation files from the official AdvanceCD web site (*http://advancemame.sourceforge.net*).

Once the files have been downloaded and unzipped, users can copy their MAME ROMs [Hack #26] of choice to the proper directory. The custom Linux kernel used in AdvanceCD takes up around 20 MB of space, so that will leave you approximately 680 MB of room for your games on a standard 80 minute CD-R. If that's not enough space for you, AdvanceCD also supports DVD-Rs and USB devices!

Once you've copied over the ROMs you wish to include on your image, all you need to do is run the included utilities to create a bootable CD image (both Linux scripts and DOS batch files are included to create the bootable ISO). Once the ISO has been created, it can be burned with the CD burning software of your choice.

Included in the CD image are hundreds of video and audio drivers. What makes AdvanceCD work so well is that for most computers no setup or cus-tomization is needed. Assuming the target machine has anything resembling standard hardware, AdvanceCD is able to automatically detect what video card and sound card you have installed and load the appropriate drivers. AdvanceCD worked on all my machines at home (including everything from a Dell laptop to an eMachine desktop machine).

Although AdvanceCD has worked for me on every machine I've tried, you may run into a situation where it doesn't work for you. In that case, you may wish to make your own boot CD instead. If you're planning on making a Linux-based MAME boot CD, the source code for AdvanceCD is available for download via the author's web site.

If DOS is more your style, a DOS-based MAME boot CD can be created as well. To create a DOS-based MAME bootable CD, you'll need to brush up on your old *config.sys* and *autoexec.bat* editing skills. Unfortunately MS-

DOS predates the idea of plug-and-play and is a bit pickier than Linux when it comes to hardware. To get a DOS-based bootable MAME CD to work, you're going to need to track down DOS drivers for your CD-Rom drive and soundcard (assuming they exist). You'll also need a USB driver if you plan on using a USB game controller. Getting a DOS-based bootable CD working on your own computer is definitely possible, but the end result will be a lot less portable than using the Linux-based AdvanceCD solution.

Uses for Your New MAME CD

There are many practical uses for Bootable MAME CDs. As mentioned earlier, they come in handy when visiting a friend's house (or stuck at the parents' house over the holidays) and want to play MAME without installing any software on their machine. The same thing goes for the office; Bootable MAME CDs allow you to spend the afternoon gaming away on company time without ever touching your own hard drive, leaving no trace of your time-wasting activities behind.

Another use for these CDs is they can allow you to benchmark a computer "out in the wild." If you're looking for an older computer to use in a MAME cabinet, you can take your Bootable CD with you and pop it into the machine you're looking at to make sure the games you want to play will play at full speed and that all the hardware is recognized. A word of warning, however: when people see how much fun you're having playing MAME on their old computer, they may not wish to sell it as quickly!

—*Rob O'Hara*

HACK #32   Play MAME Anywhere

Use LaserMAME to project vector arcade games onto any surface.

If you've ever seen a professional laser light show, you know what a thrill it is to watch such vivid, colorful light patters projected onto enormous screens (or the sides of buildings, or any flat surface). And it's a safe bet that somewhere in the audience, there were more than a few people thinking, "You know, it would be awesome if this were a video game."

Well, if you have LaserMAME—and about five thousand dollars—it can be.

LaserMAME, or more appropriately, the LaserMAME Vector Engine, is a program that works with MAME and a laser projection setup to display arcade games that use vector graphics on any surface. Created by Rob Mudryk and Matt Polak, the project's official web site is *http://games.lasers.org*.

Unfortunately, the site hasn't been updated in about five years, and there's a large notice on the Downloads page that says "NO MORE COMING SOON!" So if you're itching to replicate this hack, you'll have to dig around a few different web sites to find the info you need. In this hack, I'll explain a bit more about LaserMAME and what equipment is required to pull it off.

 Note that this hack is written by a total amateur. The most complicated thing I ever did with a laser was shine a tiny keychain laser on a wall to get the dog to jump at it. It worked, and for the record it was way more fun than Lunar Lander.

Why Only Vector Games?

In the early days of the video arcade, most games used raster-scan monitors whose video display was similar (identical, in some cases) to the home television sets of the time. But some used vector displays. Put simply, these could only display graphics made up of solid, straight lines, but the lines were much sharper and brighter. Popular games of the time that used vector displays include Asteroids, Lunar Lander, and Tempest.

The projectors that run laser light shows do something very similar to vector monitors, since their displays, too, are made up entirely of thin, solid lines of color. Only because of this commonality of design does Laser-MAME make sense. This doesn't mean, however, that it was a simple hack. The electron beam that powers vector displays can change direction almost instantaneously, but the mechanical apparatus inside laser projectors isn't nearly as fast. So the LaserMAME authors had to do quite a bit of coding to get everything to work right, hence the need for the LaserMAME Vector Engine in addition to the MAME software.

What You'll Need

You'll need the LaserMAME software. The version developed by Mudryk and Polak is no longer available on the web page, although you can download "teaser" frames of the display output that you can run on a laser projector (if you just happen to have one lying around, I mean).

Fortunately, a new home has sprung up in its stead: The open source Laser-Mame project is now online at *http://www.nightlase.com.au/lasermame/*. There, you can download the LaserMAME patches. You'll need to download the MAME source code and a few other files as well, then go through a complicated how-to setup process to mash them all together into a working LaserMAME-enabled program. But that's a walk in the park compared to what you do next.

Before you can go on with this hack, you'll need a lot of money. The Laser-MAME site states that if you want the cheapest possible setup—a mono-chrome display with a laser just powerful enough to display well on a moderately-sized white wall in a dark room—you'll be paying about four to five thousand dollars. For full-color output that can power a display on a giant screen or the side of a building, you're looking at between twenty and thirty thousand.

Where's all that money going? Here's a list of equipment you'll need. No, I didn't write this off the top of my head—you should definitely check out, like I did, the Laser Show Resource Guide at *http://www.pangolin.com/resguide00.htm.* Included in the guide are links to companies that sell all the products you need.

A laser

Duh. If you're going for the cheapest possible LaserMAME setup, your best bet is a low-powered helium-neon (or HeNe) laser. These are red in color, start at about $200, and display well in smaller areas, like your house. (The author of the open-source version of LaserMAME is using a 5mw HeNe in his sample pictures, for example: *http://www.nightlase. com.au/lasermame/images/27012004_1.jpg.*)

If you want the full-color setup, the original LaserMAME creators used a 29 mw HeNe for their red color and a 130mw Argon (which displays in blue and green, thus completing the range of colors needed for Tempest, et al). This will cost you considerably more.

A laser projector

This is the hardware that focuses the raw, destructive energy of your new laser beam and makes it do useful things. Laser projectors are actually made up of a few different parts: you need scanners, amplifiers, and possibly a blanking device. In general, you should be able to buy a complete projector that includes all of these things already assembled from the companies listed in the pangolin.com Resource Guide.

Scanners control two tiny (3 x 5 mm) mirrors that redirect the laser beam. You need two: one for X axis movement, one for Y. For the accurate projection that MAME demands, you'll want to use what are called *closed-loop galvanometer scanners,* a.k.a. *galvo scanners,* a.k.a. *position-detecting scanners.* Both LaserMAME crews use Cambridge Technologies (*http://www.camtech.com*) 6800GP scanners, which cost about $495 each.

Galvo scanners require matching amplifiers that, true to their name, amplify the signal coming from the computer program generating the graphics (in this case, LaserMAME). Cambridge Technologies offers matching amplifiers for their 6800GP scanners for $295.

Finally, for the most accurate picture possible, you may want a blanking device. This optional device turns off the laser's beam when it is moving on areas of the screen where you don't want lines drawn. Without it, you'll see ghostly images on the screen muddying up your game of Asteroids (as seen in the images on the open source LaserMame page, taken without a blanker). There are many different types of blanking systems, so you'll want to check with your scanner provider.

A projector controller board for your PC

You're going to need to send commands to that projector somehow. Pangolin—the outfit that wrote the helpful Laser Show Resource Guide, don't you remember—produces the one used by both LaserMAME teams, called the QM2000 (*http://www.pangolin.com/LD2000/qm2000board.htm*). The board is sold only with Pangolin's Lasershow Designer 2000 software; the basic version is $1995.

A MAME joystick

This is the easy part. Read [Hack #27] for more on this less-than-taxing job, and how to save some money doing it.

A blank wall near your computer

You might have to move the couch.

Now that you've got everything you need (plus a couple more mortgages on the house), just toss it all into a box, shake it up, and magically a LaserMAME system should fall right out. Actually, you're probably in for a long session (or ten) of assembly, configuration, and testing. Nobody ever said this was going to be easy!

Hacking the Hack

As an aside, the LaserMAME page—last updated, let's remember, in the year 2000—ruminates on the possibility of using the technology to output MAME graphics to a traditional vector monitor. In the intervening years, a company called Zektor actually pulled it off, designing VectorMAME (*http://www.zektor.com/zvg/zvg_vmame.htm*) to work with a vector graphics PC display card crafted by the company.

Unfortunately, the web site seems to have fallen into near-total disrepair. The download links are no longer active (and mirrors of the software are nowhere to be found), and most of the other links on the page just lead to 404's. But in an ironic and tantalizing twist, the links to the picture pages still work, showing you the results they achieved. They even hooked up the whole thing to a Vectrex monitor! Now *that's* a retro gaming hack.

## CHAPTER FOUR

Playing Classic Console Games

Hacks 33–52

Perhaps the most popular emulator software is MAME, the Multiple Arcade Machine Emulator, which was discussed in depth in the previous chapter. But retro gaming isn't just about arcade games, and neither is emulation. In this chapter, you'll discover how to use emulation to play classic home console games.

No matter what your operating system—DOS or Windows, Mac OS X or Linux—you'll find hacks in this chapter that let you turn your computer into practically any retro console you can imagine, from the Nintendo Entertainment System to the Atari 2600 and more.

But that's not all—hacks in this chapter will also tell you how to turn your Xbox controller into a USB game pad or play homebrewed Game Boy Advance games on your actual GBA hardware.

Emulate the Earliest Game Systems

Bring the Odyssey, Adventurevision, and more back to life on your PC.

I'm starting this chapter off with a few dinosaurs. Odds are you never had one of these machines, and you might never even have known that there *were* video game systems before Pong and the Atari 2600. It's unlikely now that you'll ever find a Magnavox Odyssey game system in the wild (although you might want to try hunting one down **[Hack #2]**).

So if you'd like to get a sense of what some of the very first video game systems played like, without breaking the bank buying one or going through the hassle of hooking it up to your modern television set, you might want to try some of the emulators that have been written to mimic the systems. In this hack, I look at how to use your PC to emulate the Odyssey, Entex Adventurevision, and RCA Studio II hardware.

Odyssey

Another hack in Chapter 1 will tell you a bit more about the history of the Odyssey [Hack #2]. There is indeed an emulator that will let you see what the very first video game system looked like on a TV screen. It's called ODYEMU, and its official home page is *http://www.pong-story.com/odyemu. htm.*

> The Pong-story web site, where the ODYEMU page is hosted, is an excellent resource center for all things pertaining to the origin of video games, from the legal battles surrounding Magnavox and Atari to the great debate over who really invented video games.

Unlike practically every other console emulator in existence, you don't need to download any additional software to fully enjoy ODYEMU. Every game program that was released for the system is included in the download on the home page. After you unzip the archive to a new directory, you're ready to start playing.

Since ODYEMU is written for DOS, you'll need to run it from the command prompt; non-Windows users can use DOSBox [Hack #68] (some Windows users will get more mileage out of DOSBox [Hack #69] than they will the command prompt). From the Start menu, choose Programs → Accessories → Command Prompt. Use the *cd* command to move to the directory in which you placed the ODYEMU files; for example, if you put them in the directory *\Program Files\earlyemulators\ody* on your *C:* drive, then type

```
cd c:\"Program Files"\earlyemulators\ody\
```

and hit Enter. Once you're in the directory, type `dir` and hit Enter to see a list of the games available.

Everything with the file extension *.MO1* is an Odyssey game cartridge; you can run a cartridge with the command ODYEMU ***FILENAME***.MO1. Be aware that only a few of the cartridges actually work, and that updates are not forthcoming (the last update to ODYEMU was in 1998). This is because the Odyssey shipped with many different accessories that the games are unplayable without.

You can still play the very first game of video tennis, though, on *CART1. MO1* or *TENNIS.MO1*. The colored background in the latter (see Figure 4-1) is a replication of the colored acetate overlays that shipped with the Odyssey; you could place them on top of your television screen to have backgrounds and color in your games. How high-tech is that?

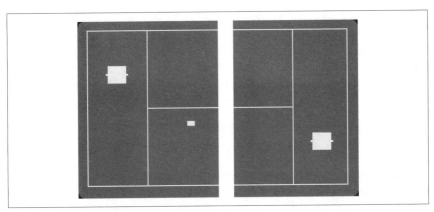

Figure 4-1. Odyssey tennis, better than it ever looked on the Odyssey

Adventurevision (…really?)

The Adventurevision was and is an interesting little piece of hardware. Released in 1982 by a company called Entex, it was one of the first portable game systems. Shaped roughly like a miniature arcade game that sat on a table or shelf, it featured its own screen made up of a matrix of red LED lights. (Ten years later, Nintendo would try something similar with the Virtual Boy, but we don't talk about that.)

Unfortunately for collectors of video game obscurities, the Adventurevision didn't last long on the market, released as it was just before the great 1983 market crash. There were only four games released for it: Defender, Space Force, Super Cobra, and Turtles. Games and system are all extremely rare and pricey. But if you want to check out what it was like, there is indeed an Adventurevision emulator out there.

Specifically, Adventurevision is one of the systems emulated in that great Multi-Emulator Super System, a.k.a. MESS. MESS functions much like MAME (the Multiple Arcade Machine Emulator, covered in depth in Chapter 3), except that it emulates console systems instead of arcade hardware. You can get it from the official home page at *http://www.mess.org*. Much like MAME, there are command-line (DOS-style) and GUI (Windows-style) versions of MESS; I recommend the GUI version for its ease of use.

Open the MESS Zip file and extract its contents to a new directory on your hard drive. The *messgui.exe* file that you see is what you'll want to run to start MESS, but before you do that you'll need to download the Adventurevision BIOS ROM (software required by MESS before it can emulate the system) and one or more games. You can find the BIOS, as well as the system's entire extensive (cough) library at *http://adventurevision.com/tech.html*.

This gets a bit tricky, so pay close attention. Don't unzip the BIOS ROM—simply save it to the *bios* directory that was automatically created when you extracted the MESS archive. But *do* extract the ROM file from its Zip archive. You'll see a *software* directory under your main MESS folder. Within that directory, create a new folder called *advision*. Then extract the contents of the Zip files to that folder.

If you think you've got all this straightened out, run *messgui.exe*. You'll soon see something like Figure 4-2.

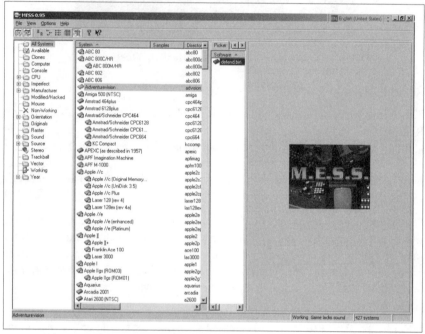

Figure 4-2. A total MESS

Before you start playing, you might want to check out the options menu. It is very similar to (you guessed it) MAME's. One important option you might want to turn on is the ability to run the game in a window rather than blown up to the size of your monitor. Looking at what is supposed to be a small screen full of tiny red dots can be a bit unplayable when it's a giant screen full of enormous red dots.

Click Options, then Default Game Properties, then the Display tab. Uncheck the "Start out maximized" box, then check "Run in a window." (If you want to apply this setting to the Adventurevision only, leaving all other emulators at full screen, just right click on the Adventurevision line in the middle window, then follow the same instructions.)

Having set that option (or left it at the default eye-bending setting, if you so chose), let's play. If you've got the BIOS ROM in the right place and a game ROM all unzipped and ready to go, you should have no problem from here. Starting from the leftmost window and working your way to the right, click "All Systems," click "Adventurevision," then double-click "defend.bin" (or whatever game you installed).

After proceeding through some introductory screens you'll see the game boot up, similar to what's shown in Figure 4-3. Enjoy!

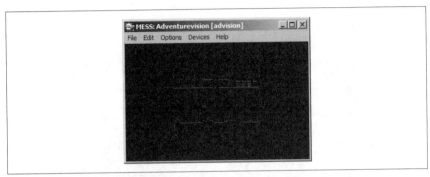

Figure 4-3. Defender on the Adventurevision

MESS emulates many classic video game systems, but what a lot of people use it for is emulating old personal computers. See "Emulate Other Classic Computers" [Hack #59] to make an even bigger MESS.

RCA Studio II (...not that you would want to)

Here's a system responsible for more than a few teary Christmas mornings. Not tears of joy, of course—tears of anger, frustration, and deep sorrow that Santa had brought an RCA Studio II setup instead of an Atari 2600. Featuring ugly, blocky black-and-white graphics, a dreary lineup of software, and—worst of all—number pads in place of joysticks, the Studio II might be the worst video game system ever created.

And some brave soul wrote not only an emulator, but *actual homebrew software* for the thing.

How could I not mention this act of self-abuse, performed as it was in pursuit of the emulation hacker ideal? If you want to check out STEM, as the emulator is called, you can download it from designer Paul Robson's home page at *http://www.classicgaming.com/studio2/*. While you're there, you can grab ROM files of five of the games the system ran, plus three homebrew titles all created by Robson.

If you're running Windows, you'll want to download WinSTEM. There are two DOS versions of the emulator, one written in C and the other in Assembler. The Assembler version features a debug option in case you want to try your hand at developing Studio II titles. A wealth of technical manuals and information is also available on the site.

Unzip WinSTEM and any ROM files into the same directory, then run *winstem.exe*. Click File, then Open to load up the game (see Figure 4-4), and have fun (or not)!

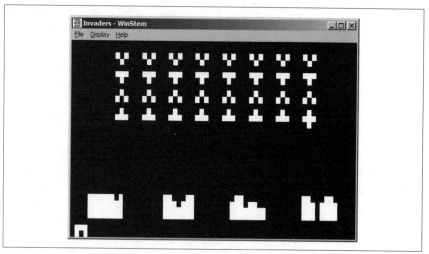

Figure 4-4. WinStem playing a Space Invaders homebrew clone

HACK #34 Emulate the Atari 2600

Bring Stella back to life using only your computer.

It's no stretch to imagine that the very reason you bought this book was to read this very hack. Even those of us who were born after the Atari 2600 (or Video Computer System, if you're a purist) know what it is and what it signified for the video game industry. (And if you don't, you can go read up on its history [Hack #3].)

In addition to buying a classic system and games, there are many other ways you can get your old-school Atari fix these days. You can buy an all-in-one device that plugs into your TV [Hack #15] or buy a collection of classic games for your PlayStation 2 or Xbox hardware [Hack #16].

And you can also use programs called emulators that run the classic games on your home PC. Even better, these programs let you run homebrew software that today's programmers have developed for the old hardware, sometimes squeezing out unbelievable results!

Atari 2600 Emulators

In this hack, I'll walk you through installing two of the more popular Atari 2600 emulators, then get you started on finding some freely distributed games to use with them.

Stella. Named after the original code name for the VCS project (which itself was named after Atari engineer Joe DeCuir's bicycle), Stella is one of the oldest 2600 emulators. It was originally programmed for Linux [Hack #43], but has since been ported to many different operating systems. For purposes of this hack, I'll discuss the Windows version. You can get it from the project's official home page (*http://stella.sourceforge.net/*), but it's easier to just grab the file from the emulation portal Zophar's Domain (*http://www.zophar.net/ a2600.html*).

If you open the Zip file using WinZip or Windows XP's built-in Zip support (it opens right in Windows Explorer), you'll probably notice that all the files in the archive already have a directory path attached to them. So just extract everything to your Program Files folder, and a new folder with the name shown in the righthand column in WinZip will be created. You'll want to run *StellaX.exe*, which is the version that has a handy graphical user interface.

But before you run the program, you'll want to grab some ROM files so you'll have games to play. Later in the hack, I'll show you where to get them. For now, let's just pretend you've downloaded some ROMs, extracted the files using WinZip or another unzip program, and dumped the contents into the *roms* directory under the main *Stella* folder. Run StellaX and you'll see something akin to Figure 4-5. (You may have to click the Reload button.)

Note that everything you've got in the *roms* folder—not just the ROM files—is displayed. You'll have to figure out which ones are the ROMs; this is made easier by the fact that ROMs are not displayed with file extensions like *.WAV* or *.ZIP*, and also probably have Manufacturer and/or Rarity data displayed alongside them.

Double-click on DUP Space Invaders (Ron Corcoran), for example, and Stella will start up in a separate window, as shown in Figure 4-6. As with most Windows programs, you can hit Alt-Enter to run the game in full-screen mode. The file *stella.html* in your *docs* directory will explain which keyboard buttons do what, but if you want to look at (and reassign) keyboard commands while running the game, hit Tab to bring up the menu, then hit Enter to use Event Remapping.

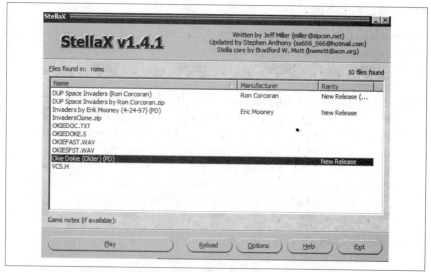

Figure 4-5. StellaX, displaying the messy contents of my roms\ directory

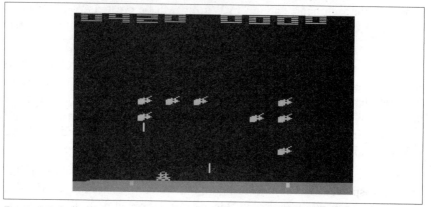

Figure 4-6. Stella. I'm not going to make the obvious Tennessee Williams reference

PC Atari. Stella might not be your bag, baby, for a few reasons. First off, although StellaX is a nice GUI, it's not fully integrated into the emulator. It just runs the command-line version of the program, and so when you're adjusting settings, you have to do it in the clunky DOS-style Event Remapping mode. And you'll have two programs open at once while you're playing the game. If you'd rather have an emulator that looks and works more like the Windows programs you're used to, you might try PC Atari, available from the same Atari 2600 page at Zophar's Domain referenced earlier in this hack.

When you run PC Atari, you'll see a screen like Figure 4-7. Ordinarily, you'd want to hit File, then Open to open up a ROM file. But regardless of the directory you extracted it to, PC Atari's default settings are to search for ROMS in the directory *c:\emu\2600\roms*. The odds are likely that this isn't the exact directory structure of your hard drive, so you'll want to change that setting. Click File → Preferences to access this setting, as shown in Figure 4-8.

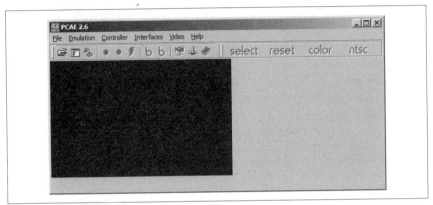

Figure 4-7. PC Atari's startup screen, with no games loaded

Click on the yellow folder icon next to the Games drop-down box, and you'll be able to select the folder where your ROMs reside. Now click OK and you'll be thrown back to the main PC Atari screen. Click Open to bring up a list of the ROMs in your folder. Double-click the name of the ROM you want to open, and you'll again be thrown back to the main screen. Now click Emulation → Start, and the game will launch.

The default controller setup has the first player joystick mapped to the number pad and the second player joystick on the arrow keys; you can change all keyboard assignments by clicking Interfaces → Configure (though you must stop the emulation before you can change this or most other menu options).

Finding Freely Distributed 2600 ROMs

I got the ROMs pictured earlier in this hack from PD ROMs (*http://www.pdroms.de*), a web site that collects hundreds of public domain ROM files for a variety of different systems and boasts over thirty different 2600 games and tech demos. But there are other places to get homebrew 2600 ROMs.

One such place is from the company Atari Age (*http://www.atariage.com*). Their web site hosts a veritable treasure trove of information on all things Atari, and their store (*http://www.atariage.com/store/index.php*) sells all

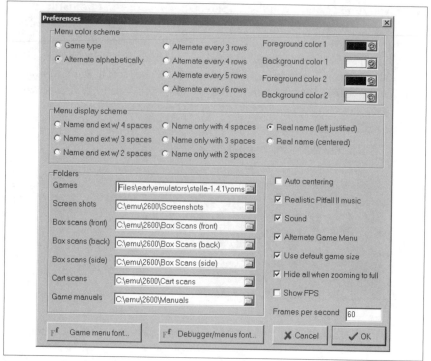

Figure 4-8. PC Atari's Options screen

manner of Atari stuff, including homebrew cartridges (with professional labels, manuals, and packaging). If you click on the Homebrew section in the store, you'll see a list of homebrew games that Atari Age sells.

If you click on the name of a game that interests you and then scroll nearly all the way down its listing page, you'll see a link that says "For more information, please visit this product's webpage." Click the word *webpage* and you'll be sent to a page where usually you can download the game's ROM file.

Packrat Video Games (*http://www.packratvg.com*) also offers a few Atari 2600 homebrews on cartridge, but doesn't list the ROMs for download. If you really want to find them, try searching Google for the program author's name and the name of the game. You'll probably turn up the author's personal web page.

Emulate the Intellivision

HACK #35

Turn your PC into an intelligent television.

If any golden-age hardware gave the Atari 2600 a run for its money, it was Mattel's Intellivision console. The system's higher-powered capabilities let it create what were at the time exceptionally detailed graphics, resulting in some very impressive sports games. Comparing Mattel's baseball title to Atari's was like comparing prime rib to roadkill meatloaf. But Atari still had the exclusive rights to hit arcade titles like Pac-Man and Space Invaders, which Mattel couldn't match.

But the Intellivision was so appealing that Mattel had a major hit on their hands, and the in-house design teams cranked out titles by the dozen. The Intellivision was able to keep chugging along until 1990, but finally was not able to stand up against the onslaught of Nintendo. In 1997, original Intellivision game designers Keith Robinson and Steve Roney bought the rights to the system and game library and immediately set about repackaging the games for a new generation of players. They teamed up with other former Mattel employees, reviving the team name that they'd taken in 1981: the Blue Sky Rangers.

Intellivision Lives!

If you want to emulate Intellivision titles on your PC, there's an easy and conscience-soothing solution. Head over to Robinson and co.'s web site, *http://www.intellivisionlives.com*. There, you can purchase Intellivision Lives! and Intellivision Rocks!, two collections of emulated games that run on the PC and Mac. The first contains most of the games that Mattel made, and the second contains the nearly complete libraries of third-party Intellivision developers Imagic and Activision. Both discs include all sorts of bonus materials from art galleries to histories to video interviews.

If you're not willing to put down $29.99 sight unseen, the web site also offers not one, not two, but *three* free downloadable Intellipacks that let you play a handful of games each. And they're not just any ol' games, either. The first Intellipack contains three of the most highly rated Intellivision games—Astrosmash, Skiing, and Utopia. The second contains Night Stalker, Space Spartans, and the previously unreleased game Deep Pockets: Super Pro Pool and Billiards. And the third contains B-17 Bomber, Beauty and the Beast, and Shark! Shark! You can grab them at *http://www.intellivisionlives.com/download.shtml*.

Each pack is available in a self-extracting file, but the PC version doesn't allow you to choose the directory the files are extracted to. Instead, as soon as you run it, a directory called *Intellipack N folder*, where *N* is the number of the Intellipack, is created underneath the directory where the *.exe* file was placed.

Therefore, don't open the file using Internet Explorer, or the files will be extracted to some *Temporary Internet Files* subdirectory and you'll never find them. Instead, save it to a directory one level higher than you want the Intellipack files to go (if you want, you can just put it on your Desktop and move the resultant directory later), then run the *.exe* file.

An easy-to-read PDF file is included with the emulator that explains how to use it and the full instructions for each game, including an author bio.

Think about it—the original creators of the games bought the rights, then released perfect emulated versions for free. Now *that's* a great retro gaming hack.

If you'd rather play Intellivision on your television, the Blue Sky Rangers have you covered. Check out their site to find out how to get plug-and-play Intellivision game systems [Hack #15] or Intellivision Lives! for PlayStation 2 and Xbox [Hack #16].

Bliss

But, what if you want to do some underground emulation? Play Intellivision homebrew games? Find that old copy of Donkey Kong that the Blue Sky Rangers will never, ever get the rights to release? (But why would you want to play it, anyway?)

Alright, maybe just for comedy value. Well, if that's your thing, there is indeed an independent, multiplatform Intellivision emulator out there, called Bliss. It had lain dormant for years since its last update in 2001, but a new Windows version was just released in April 2005. You can get it at *http://bliss.kylesblog.com*. (If you want older versions, or versions for different operating systems, you can find them at the emulation portal Zophar's Domain: *http://www.zophar.net*. Beware of popup windows, however.)

Bliss won't run without the Intellivision system's BIOS ROMs, however, and for copyright reasons they can't be packaged together with the emulator. You'll have to figure out some other way of getting them. Apparently they are included on the Intellivision Lives! disks (though not in the free Intellipacks). The filenames are *exec.bin* and *grom.bin*.

Once you find them, just save them into the directory into which you installed Bliss. (Bliss uses a standard Windows installer, so you'll be able to customize the directory name easily when you run it.) Unzip and save any ROMs you download into the same directory, and run Bliss. If it crashes when you try to load a ROM, you probably don't have DirectX 9.0c installed, so you'll need to install that before you can use it.

Nostalgia

If this sounds like far too much work for you, you should probably check out Nostalgia, a recently released and very cleverly designed emulator. You can get it from the developer's web site (*http://www.shiny-technologies.com*) as well as Zophar's Domain (*http://www.zophar.net*). It comes packaged with everything you'll need to run it; the *exec.bin* and *grom.bin* files have been replaced with fan-created versions. This means they're legal to distribute, but some games might not run properly. You can replace them with the originals if you obtain them. Install and run Nostalgia and you'll get the exciting menu screen in Figure 4-9.

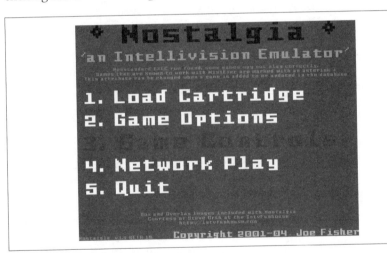

Figure 4-9. The Nostalgia menu screen

Nostalgia also comes packaged with a selection of freeware and public domain ROM files. Click on Load Cartridge and you'll get a menu screen that lists the ROMs available (if you download more, put them inside the *nostalgia/roms* directory that was created when you installed the emulator and they'll automatically show up in this menu). Try choosing 4Tris, which should be the first ROM in the list, to play a surprisingly complete Intellivision version of the popular falling block puzzle, shown in Figure 4-10.

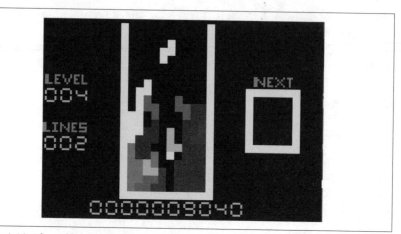

Figure 4-10. The public domain ROM 4Tris, running on Nostalgia (much like my writing career)

HACK #36   Emulate the Colecovision

Get back in touch with a surprisingly powerful classic system.

I'll admit to being not the biggest fan of retro systems older than myself. It's not as if I don't see the fun in the Atari 2600 or Intellivision, and it's certainly not as if I haven't spent quite a bit of time playing both systems. But I have this theory that we can only truly go back and enjoy the retro games that we played when they were new.

That said, I never had a Colecovision console when it was new. And I don't predate it by that many years—I was born in 1980; it was born in 1982. But for someone who came of age during the Nintendo era, the Colecovision experience hits close to home. The graphic quality is close to the early days of the NES, and it even shares some of the same games.

If you will permit me the comparison, the Colecovision was the Sega Dreamcast of its time. It featured graphic power above and beyond anything else on the market. It was the only system that could faithfully recreate the graphics and gameplay of the games that were hot in arcades. It had a smallish but high-quality library of software that garnered it diehard fans. And it was doomed to an early grave (though for different reasons).

In this hack, I'll explain how to emulate the Colecovision hardware using software available for your DOS/Windows PC. If all this talk has gotten you interested in buying the classic Colecovision hardware, it is entirely possible for you to do so [Hack #4].

Children of ColEm

Read the documentation for most Colecovision emulators and you'll find that many of them are ports or updates of Marat Fayzullin's ColEm, which he wrote for the Unix platform in the early nineties. Fayzullin's original web page (*http://fms.komkon.org/ColEm/*) is still up, but many of the links are broken. The download of the Unix version should still work, however.

I can still remember running the DOS port of ColEm way back in the day (I think I discovered it just as the Nintendo 64 was coming out, so it would have been the summer of 1996). Soon enough after that, Colecovision emulation was pretty much perfected, and development of most of the emulators slowed to a halt.

The newest dedicated Colecovision emulator is ADAMEm (*http://www. komkon.org/~dekogel/adamem.html*), which was last updated in 1999. As its name implies, it emulates not only the Colecovision but the ADAM computer as well. The ADAM was Coleco's attempt at breaking into the growing personal computer market. It was built around the Colecovision hardware and was a colossal failure. But it did feature souped-up versions of Colecovision hits like Donkey Kong, with better graphics and more levels.

If you want to emulate the ADAM, then either try out ADAMEm or MESS, the Multi Emulator Super System [Hack #59]. ADAMEm might also be your emulator of choice if you are running an older computer under DOS—and in that case, you might want to also check out the discontinued ColEm-DOS, available at Zophar's Domain (*http://www.zophar.net/coleco.html*). (ColEmDOS also includes the unique option of letting you log the sound from your game directly to a MIDI file; perfect for aspiring avant-garde musicians!)

Virtual Colecovision

If you're running Windows 95, NT, 2000, XP, or something of that nature, you'll almost definitely want to use Virtual Colecovision (*http://www. classicgaming.com/vcoleco/*). Last updated in 1997—and formerly known as ColEm97—it is generally considered to be the Windows emulator of choice for the console.

When you visit the official web site's Download page, be sure to download the first file in the list, which is the version for Windows 95 and above. Ports of the emulator for Java and Windows 3.1 are also available here, so be sure not to confuse the Windows versions. (If you're running a DOS computer and using Windows 3.1, you'll probably just want to get one of the DOS emulators, because the 3.1 port is in a permanently incomplete and discontinued state, lacking joystick and sound emulation).

To install the program, simply unzip the files to a new directory. Run the *VColeco.exe* file and you'll be up and running in no time flat. The first time you run the program, the first thing you'll have to deal with is a window like the one in Figure 4-11.

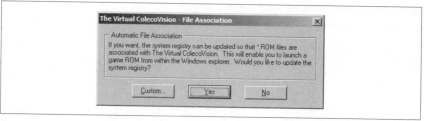

Figure 4-11. *Virtual Colecovision's automatic file association feature*

If you click Yes in this window, all files ending with the extension .*ROM* will attempt to open in Virtual ColecoVision if you double-click on the filename in Windows Explorer. This could be extremely convenient or extremely annoying for you. Don't do this if you've already assigned files with the ROM extension to open in a different emulator. (For example, games for the Atari 7800 console commonly use the same extension.)

After you're safely over that crucial life hurdle, you'll be in Virtual ColecoVision. It couldn't be easier to start up—just click File, then Run, then pick out a ROM. The freely distributed game Cosmo Fighter 2 (see Figure 4-12) is included in the zip file you downloaded, so start with that one! Web sites like *http://www.pdroms.de* feature other public domain and freeware ROM files that will run on Colecovision emulators; although the homebrew scene is not as lively as the one for the Atari 2600, there are some solid, playable titles out there.

Figure 4-12. *Virtual Colecovision running Cosmo Fighter 2*

If you have a reasonably fast computer, you'll find that Virtual Colecovision should run well in its standard windowed mode. But when you attempt to run it in either Double Size mode or Full Screen (click Emulation → Display to change modes), you might find that it runs too slowly; the music will skip and the animation will be choppy. If you don't really care about the sound, you can usually speed things up by turning it off in the Emulation menu.

Alternately, you can usually speed things up by adjusting the "Frame Skip" settings from the default. Raise the frameskip value to speed the game up. Conveniently, Virtual Colecovision lets you make separate adjustments to the frameskip option depending on whether you are in windowed or full-screen mode. This is helpful since the speed your machine can crank out will often differ depending on your display mode.

A Bit About blueMSX

Before I close, I'd like to point out that you do have one more option for emulating the Colecovision on PC. The emulator blueMSX (*http://www.bluemsx.com*), which true to its name is primarily concerned with emulating the MSX personal computers, features Colecovision support. This is because the original MSX wasn't that different a piece of hardware than the Colecovision; in fact, ColEm originally started as a scaled-down version of an MSX emulator.

The upside to installing blueMSX is, of course, that you'll be able to play all sorts of MSX games as well, if you can find the ROMs online. It never caught on in the US, but was huge in Japan. In fact, it was one of the main competitors to Nintendo's Famicom (NES) hardware there, and a few games were released for both systems at first, including such Famicom mainstays as Castlevania and Final Fantasy.

The downside is that the program is much larger than other Colecovision emulators and requires a fast machine to run properly (they recommend at least a Pentium III or equivalent). But it does have a very nice user interface—check it out running homebrew Coleco game Star Fortress in Figure 4-13.

Windows users aren't the only ones who can enjoy the Colecovision. Of course, you can run the DOS version of ColEmDOS on nearly any platform using an emulator [Hack #70]. However, there are Colecovision emulators for Linux and Mac OS X as well. For Linux and Unix, you can use ColEm. For Mac OS X, check out Mugrat (*http://www.bannister.org/software/mugrat.htm*) or ColEm.

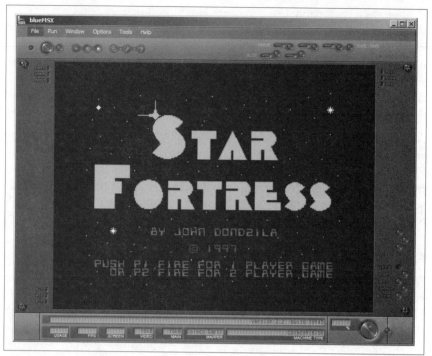

Figure 4-13. blueMSX running the Colecovision game Star Fortress

Emulate the Atari 7800

Bring a woefully ignored console back from the dead.

The poor thing never had a chance. Originally designed as the true successor to the incredibly successful 2600 VCS [Hack #34], the Atari 7800 fell victim to all sorts of internal power struggles and botched management decisions. First, while the 7800 was still in development, Atari hacked its existing line of computer hardware, turning it into the quick-fix Atari 5200, to fend off the Colecovision in 1982.

Two years later, as the system that was supposed to be the next big thing was about to be released, Atari execs decided they didn't want to be in the video games business anymore, and put the manufactured 7800 systems and games into storage. Only after Nintendo revitalized the video game market did Atari ship the 7800 in 1986. But they immediately followed it with the XE Game System, an incompatible console that played the same games as the company's line of computers.

Thus bookended by competing hardware from the same company, the 7800 died an ignominious death. But in its short life span it amassed some software support that illustrates just how powerful a system it was (especially for 1984 tech, mind you!). It was even backwards compatible with the 2600 library. The only real problem with the system was its awful standard controller. Atari missed the D-pad revolution ushered in by Nintendo and Sega, sticking the 7800 with a pair of joystick controllers so antithetical to every principle of ergonomics that they could have been designed by the Marquis de Sade.

Which is an excellent reason to play 7800 games via an emulator, using your own preferred PC joystick.controllers:joystick: for Atari 7800;

Since I brought it up, I might mention that Atari *did* release a standard joypad for the system, but only outside the US—read more about it in an Atari Times piece titled "The Europeans Were Lucky" (*http://www.ataritimes.com/7800/features/7800pad.html*).

Do the MESS-Around

If you already use and love the Multi Emulator Super System (MESS; *http://www.mess.com*), then you already have a 7800 emulator. Since it's unlikely that you'll do that much 7800 emulation (you can burn through the entire game library in a couple of days), this might be your best choice.

You can learn more about MESS basics, including where to get it and where to set it up, in the Adventurevision section of [Hack #33]. In fact, since the setup process is identical for both systems, you can just read that section and think *7800* in your brain whenever you see the word *Adventurevision*. (For the rest of this section, I am assuming that you are running the Windows-based GUI version of MESS, but you can easily adjust these instructions for Mac OS X and Linux.)

After you install MESS, but before you can play any games, you'll need to download a ROM image of the 7800's internal BIOS. This file is usually named *7800.rom*, and is often found as a zipped archive called *7800rom.zip* or *a7800.zip*. Games won't run without it, but since it is a copyright-protected piece of software, it is not included with the emulators. You'll have to find it on your own.

Once you do, save the Zip file, without extracting it, to the *bios* directory that was automatically created when you installed MESS. When you save it, you might have to rename it to *a7800.zip* since this is the filename that MESS searches for when you try to run the 7800 emulator. If the file isn't zipped, is named anything else, or isn't in the *mess\bios* directory, you won't be able to run the emulator. If everything is set up correctly, you'll be able to see the Atari 7800 listed in the Available tab when you start up MESS.

MESS is a little picky about BIOS files. Before it runs the emulator, it verifies the BIOS ROM to make sure it is correct. The *7800.rom* file that I found didn't agree with MESS, and so even though I had everything set up correctly, MESS refused to put Atari 7800 in the Available category. I had to scroll down and click the Console tab to find the Atari 7800 button. When I attempted to run it, it gave me a warning that the BIOS ROM may be bad, but the game ran perfectly.

Click on "Atari 7800," and a list of ROMs that you downloaded will appear in the rightmost window. If nothing appears, check to make sure that you unzipped the ROMs and placed them into the directory *mess\software\ a7800* (which you may have to create yourself). Also make sure that you have, in fact, downloaded some ROMs. If you haven't but want to, you might try skipping ahead to "The Atari 7800 Homebrew Scene," a tasteful little number that appears later in this hack.

On the other hand, if you've already got a directory full of 7800 ROMs on your PC but don't want to copy them over, you can add additional directories that MESS will automatically check upon startup. Right-click on Atari 7800 in the middle window of the GUI, then click Properties. Click the Software tab, click Insert, and choose the directory in which you keep your ROM collection.

If you are successful at either of these things, a list of games should appear in the rightmost MESS window when you click on the Atari 7800 tab. Actually, MESS will list everything that appears in the directories it searches, and the working game files will be marked with a little computer-chip icon to the left of the filename. Double-click on one of them and you should be playing within seconds. A happy game of Space War is shown in Figure 4-14.

Standalone 7800 Emulators

If MESS is too messy for your tastes, and you're looking for an emulator that is strictly for the 7800, you have a couple of options. One is called ProSystem Emulator (*https://home.comcast.net/%7Egscottstanton/*) and the other is EMU7800 (*http://emu7800.sourceforge.net/*). Of the two, ProSystem Emulator seems to be the most complete and compatible. The EMU7800 page has a brief list of incompatible games and other glitches.

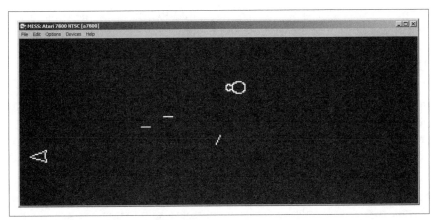

Figure 4-14. Space War for the 7800, running in MESS

 EMU7800 also requires the Microsoft .NET runtime environment to function, so if you don't have it installed and
would rather skip the lengthy download and installation process, you might just use ProSystem Emulator instead.

There are a few advantages to going with a standalone, system-specific emulator: the file size of the program is smaller, installation is easier, and the
menu system is not cluttered with options only necessary for other hardware. Another advantage specific to the Atari 7800 is that you can disable
the use of the BIOS, a feature that the latest version of MESS (.095, as of this
writing) lacks. The BIOS in the 7800 console was apparently only used to
display a flashy Atari logo every time the system was turned on. If you disable it, the only consequence is that the logo will not display before each
game.

In ProSystem Emulator, you can turn off the BIOS ROM by clicking
Options, Emulation, Bios, then clicking Disable. The next time you pull
down the menu you should see no checkmark next to the Bios button. If you
want to enable it, you'll have to find the *7800.rom* file in the dialog box that
pops up, then click Enable with the filename selected.

In EMU7800, enter the program's internal Control Panel (not to be confused with Windows' Control Panel!), click the Settings tab, then check the
"Skip BIOS" checkbox.

Otherwise, there are not many secret tricks you'll need to worry about. If
you're running EMU7800 and are trying to load ROMs, be aware that the
Open dialog box will look for files that end in the extension *.bin* by
default—in other words, Atari 2600 game ROMs (which the emulator also

supports natively). To search for Atari 7800 ROMs, click the drop-down box on the bottom of the window and pick the *.a78* extension.

The Atari 7800 Homebrew Scene

There isn't much of one. The development tools for the platform only appeared a few years ago; and there's not a whole lot of extra 7800 nostalgia floating around out there anyway. But if you check out the Downloads section of the excellent site Atari 7800.com (*http://www.atari7800.com*), you'll find the two titles that have been released thus far: Space War and Senso DX.

Space War is a conversion of the seminal computer game of the same name. It is for two players only; each player controls a ship that moves just like the one from Asteroids: up to thrust, left and right to rotate. Players must avoid the gravity of the shining sun in the middle of the screen and fire on each other. (Oh—and it doesn't work. Shots have no effect and the sun doesn't kill you.) And Senso DX is a version of the electronic match-the patterns game Simon.

There is also hope for more games. The web site Static Gamer has announced an Atari 7800 homebrew development contest. The winner of the contest will have their game published by AtariAge (*http://www.atariage. com*) and sold in cartridge format on the web site, so there should be enough incentive for some decent entries.

AtariAge has also announced that Ken Siders (who created Atari 5200, eight-bit, and 7800 versions of a Burgertime-like game named Beef Drop) will bring the classic arcade game Q*bert to the 7800. So with any luck, you'll have much more to play on the 7800—whether emulated or on the actual console—by the time you read this.

HACK #38 Emulate the Nintendo Entertainment System on a PC

Find the NES emulator that works best for you.

For some people, Nintendo Entertainment System emulation *is* emulation. It's the only console they've ever emulated; it's the only console they will ever emulate. Sure, they probably know that you can emulate other systems. They might have even messed around with an Atari 2600 emulator once or twice, just to see if it really worked. But that was probably only for a few minutes. NES emulators can suck up hours, days, weeks.[*]

[*] In fact, my "research" for this section took me way longer than I'd planned for.

The numbers bear this theory out. While you're lucky to find one working emulator for certain classic game systems, the NES page at the emulation portal Zophar's Domain (*http://www.zophar.net/nes.html*) lists a whopping 77 different programs that run NES games on your home computer!

Thus, the challenge of getting started with NES emulation is not finding the programs—it's figuring out which one you should download. In this hack, I'll take a look at four emulators that are both popular and fully-featured. Between these four, you should be able to find something that fits your needs.

The how-to segments of this hack will concentrate on the Windows versions of the emulators. Some of them also have DOS versions. In general, if you check Zophar's Domain you can get a good idea of what DOS emulators are out there.

I suggest that you use the web site PD Roms (*http://www. pdroms.de*) to find NES-compatible games that are freely distributed or in the public domain, such as the ones shown in the illustrations accompanying this hack.

RockNES

RockNES (*http://rocknes.kinox.org/*) has been my emulator of choice for a while. It has that rare combination of being both full-featured and fast— games will run at full speed in a large (800 x 600) window with perfect sound on my three-year-old laptop, something that no other emulator on this list has accomplished. Installation is quick and painless—just download the Zip file, extract the files to a new directory, and then run *rocknesx. exe*. In Figure 4-15, you can see the emulator running the homebrew game Hot Seat Harry.

Even better, its GUI builds a ROM list for you that you can click and scroll through rather than having to click File → Open and then scroll through folders every time you want to load a new game. You can add as many directories as you want to the automatic search feature by clicking Options → Folders, and then the Add button. Then, on the main GUI window, you need only click View, Refresh Game List and RockNES will search the folders you named for ROMs (which can be in the .*nes* format or zipped), building a handy list.

The reason that RockNES works so efficiently is because it adjusts the frame rate automatically based on your system's performance. The program's

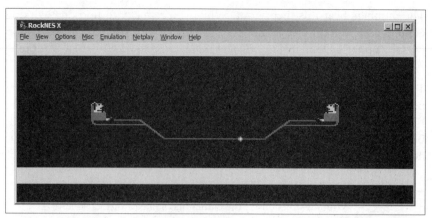

Figure 4-15. Hot Seat Harry in RockNES

readme file suggests that you should expect the following frame rates in 800x600 windowed resolution and full 32-bit color:

- Pentium 233 CPU, Trident video card: 60 fps (emulation), 35 fps (video)
- Pentium II 300MHz CPU, TNT2 video card: 60 fps (emulation), 60 fps (video)
- Pentium III 1GHz CPU, Trident video card: 60 fps (emulation), 10-30 fps (video)
- Athlon 1.2GHz CPU, Sis6326 video card: 60 fps (emulation), 40 fps (video)
- Athlon 1.2GHz CPU, GeForce3 video card: 60 fps (emulation), 60 fps (video)

Though it's not likely, you may experience some sound issues—the audio might "pop" or stutter. If that's the case, you'll want to adjust the sound buffer. It's set at a default of 66 milliseconds. If you're having problems, raise this value by clicking Options → Audio Setup, and then moving the sliding bar to the right (towards "Safe"). You can also adjust the Audio Priority by clicking Options → Advanced—just be aware that this can have an adverse effect on your frame rate.

FCE Ultra

FCE Ultra (*http://fceultra.sourceforge.net/*) is an open source project that has been ported to many other operating systems, including Linux **[Hack #40]**. It doesn't feature an elaborate GUI; in fact, when you first unzip it and run the *fceu.exe* file, all you'll see is a tiny black window. But it's a window to fun! Just look at FCE Ultra in Figure 4-16.

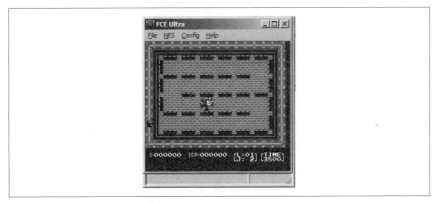

Figure 4-16. FCE Ultra running Bomb Sweeper

Since it doesn't feature RockNES' automatic frame-skipping routines, odds are that it will run slowly on your machine if the window size is anything over the standard 320x240. One thing you can do to increase the display size while speeding up emulation (which applies to all the emulators in this hack) is to display in Full Screen mode by hitting Alt-Enter. Note that if you put the emulator into Full Screen mode before you load up a ROM, you won't be able to do anything since you can't access the GUI in Full Screen.

FCE Ultra's claim to fame, besides a generally high level of compatibility and stability, is that it can emulate many different quirky controllers that were released for the Famicom and NES. You can switch to these by clicking Config → Input and then selecting Famicom Expansion Port on the bottom drop-down box. FCE Ultra supports:

Zapper (light gun)
Power Pad, sides A and B
Arkanoid Paddle
Hyper Shot (light gun)
Four Score or NES Satellite (4 player adapters)
Family Keyboard
Hyper Shot pads
Mahjongg controller
Oekaki Kids drawing tablet
Quiz King buzzers
Family Trainer, sides A and B
Barcode World (barcode scanner)
Top Rider (handlebar controller for motorbike games)

Sure, using your mouse as a Zapper gun might make Duck Hunt way too easy, but admit it: as a kid, you just put your gun up against the glass of the television screen and fired at point-blank range, too.

NEStopia

The promised land of NES emulation? For some, perhaps. When you boot it up, NEStopia (*http://sourceforge.net/projects/nestopia/*) looks very much like FCE Ultra—a small black window (see Figure 4-17). Mess around and you'll see lots of the same options you'll remember from the other NES emulators we've visited today. In the Options → Timing window you can select the Auto Frame Skip option, which should clear up any speed problems you experience.

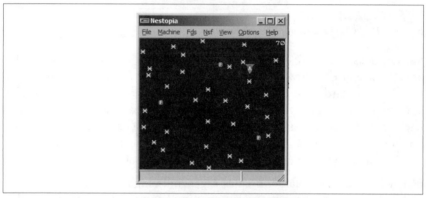

Figure 4-17. NEStopia running the homebrew game Galaxy Patrol

You can also turn on and off the NES' different sound channels in the Sound options menu, just in case you want to hear different parts of your favorite tunes separately. And in the Preferences menu you can easily use checkboxes to turn file associations on and off, which means that when you double-click on a supported file in Windows Explorer it will open automatically in NEStopia. This is not really preferable if you don't want NEStopia to be your one and only emulator, nor if all your ROMs are in zipped format.

Hit Alt+L and you will bring up the optional Launcher, which is a very useful tool indeed. This provides functionality similar to RockNES, allowing you to search specific directories for ROM files, either in *.nes* format or zipped. Choose Options → Paths, and click Add to name as many directories as you want.

But wait, there's more! Once you've got directories in there, you can check or uncheck them, causing NEStopia to search and skip them, respectively, all without permanently deleting them from the list. There's even a check-box that will let you eliminate duplicate files from the master list that is generated. As you can see, when combined with some judicious directory organizing on your part, the Launcher can make your emulation experience an easy one.

NSF: NES Sound Format

If you're following along at home, you've probably noticed that NEStopia also supports a file format called NSF. Short for NES Sound Format, NSF files are basically like NES-format ROM files, but only contain audio data. Among aficionados of video game music, listening to original sound tracks in NSF format has become quite preferable to MP3 and the like, since it faithfully reproduces the actual sounds of the NES while taking up only a miniscule amount of disk space.

What's more, though the NES homebrewing scene has yet to produce much in the way of full-featured gaming experiences, there is a vibrant community making music in NSF format. The web site 2A03 (*http://www.2a03.org*) features over twelve hundred different original NSF-format songs as of this writing as well as all the software you'll need to play them—there are standalone players as well as plugins that allow the popular WinAmp digital music player to handle NSF.

Downloading actual game soundtracks in NSF format is legally questionable, although publishers do not seem to be pursuing web sites that offer the files. The legendary NES web site |tsr's NES Archive offers a selection of NSF files for some popular games (*http://www.atarihq.com/tsr/nsf/nsf.html*).

Nessie

And now for something completely different. The NES emulator Nessie (*http://nessie.emubase.de/*) takes a very different approach to emulator design. Specifically, the author has taken pains to simplify the entire process, from downloading to running. Nessie is distributed as a single executable file that is not even zipped, so all you need to do is save it anywhere you wish, and then run it. If you want Nessie to support zipped ROMs, you have to save the file *unzip.dll*—also available on the project's web site—to the same directory as Nessie.

Inside, things are even simpler. Click on Options → Preferences; where most emulators would feature screens full of options, Nessie only presents you with the tiny menu shown in Figure 4-18.

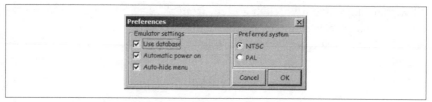

Figure 4-18. Nessie's basic Preferences menu

If you leave the settings at default, Nessie will use its built-in database to determine the names of ROMs automatically, power the "system" on as soon as you load a ROM, and hide the menu when you are playing a game.

But this small Preferences screen belies some of the very cool things that Nessie can do. Like most emulators, it can save your game at any point and let you resume it right where you left off. But Nessie doesn't stop there. When you save a game, you can enter one line to describe the save (perhaps a description of where you left off, or even just the date and time). And when you select Load Game, you'll be able to scroll through those descriptions, and each of them will feature a screenshot of the game from where you left off, as shown in Figure 4-19.

Figure 4-19. Nessie's Load Game menu

The tradeoff here is that, unlike most emulators, you can't instantly save and load games by just tapping a single button; you have to navigate through the menus each time. But you might find that the helpful screenshots and descriptions are more suited to your playing style (especially if you're not saving and loading every time you screw up, cheater).

Oh, and as you might have guessed, there's one more tradeoff with Nessie: you can't manually adjust any of the video or sound options. What this means is that if Nessie doesn't run well on your computer as soon as you boot it up, it's almost definitely never going to run well. But if it does work perfectly, you might really want to stick with it. Either way, with the many different emulators in this hack—and the seventy-three other NES emulators out there—you're bound to find something that works.

> If you're running a very old DOS machine—a 486, for example—you might find that what works is the tastefully named emulator NESticle (*http://bloodlust.zophar.net/NESticle/nes.html*). It's been discontinued for over half a decade now, but then again, so has your old 486.

Run NES Emulators on the Mac
Make the switch without losing your Nintendo homebrews.

Ah, the bastion of classic gaming for generation Y—the Nintendo Entertainment System. The eight-bit era had a profound impact on the videogame industry, and many people late at night, after downing that second glass of store brand whiskey and half of a leftover burger in the fridge, want to relive the so called "glory days" of gaming. Sure, it'd be simple if it was on their PC. But you're a hipster with a Powerbook and a massive collection of CDs from indie bands. It's not that easy. Don't worry, as this section of the book will walk you through just exactly how you go about playing those NES classics on your Mac.

Before you even worry about stock piling ROMs for the hours upon hours you've freed to relive your youth, you're going to need an emulator. This is the program that allows you to play the ROMs on your Mac. Now, there are a variety of options, and there are a couple really top-notch programs available. Here's a list of the NES emulators for the Mac:

RockNES
> Available at *http://www.bannister.org/software/rocknes.htm*, this is the premier emulator for NES games on a Mac. The problem is that it isn't entirely universal. Users with older computers are going to experience some slowdown due to cycle-exact emulation, and the creator recommends at least 1Ghz for proper performance. Testing this program with a 867Mhz G4, I found his statements to be true, as it was choppy at best. When I tested it on a 1.8Ghz G5 processor, I had a much smoother experience.

> For those who like the feel of RockNES, there are older versions not supported by the creator available on the net. *http://www.johnl.org/* is

home to an older version of RockNES that will work on systems with less than a 1Ghz processor.

Also, RockNES supports the Famicom Disk System, along with providing excellent sound support. If you have a new Mac, this is really the emulator you want to be using. Though, if you're interested in having USB gamepad support, bilinear filtering, full screen mode, and aspect ratio correction, you'll need to download the available Emulation Enhancer shareware at *http://www.bannister.org/software/ee.htm*. This software isn't free and will run you $25. However, Richard Bannister has ported a lot of emulators to Mac OS X, and you only need to purchase Emulation Enhancer once to bring its features to all his emulators.

Nestopia

Also available at *http://www.bannister.org/software/nestopia.htm*, this program offers a little more of a buffer in terms of processor speed and is widely accepted as the most compatible of Mac emulators. In addition to having cycle-exact emulation, Nestopia supports 143 mappers (which correspond to different chips used in NES cartridges) and five more sound chips. It's extremely robust, and even if you have above an 800Mhz G4 you'll get fairly nice emulation with only a couple of hiccups. Nestopia can also use the Emulation Enhancer software to add more features and functionality to this already impressive program.

iNes

For all those who believe OS X is the devil and OS9 is God's gift to mankind, iNes is definitely the program of choice. It's an extremely well rounded program, offering a high compatibility rate with both NES ROMs and FDS titles. The one downside is the fact that this emulator doesn't have the best sound output. Other than that, iNes is a fine emulator.

macFC

While it's not going to be the main choice for many, this emulator is important because it's a Japanese version. As such, those who want to play those Famicom Disk System games without a hitch should look into using this emulator (if you know Japanese). Available for download at *http://macfc.at.infoseek.co.jp/*

These are really your best bets in terms of compatibility, system requirements, amount of mappers, and sound quality. While there are other emulators out there, such FCEUltra and FakeNES, users not experienced with compiling programs themselves will find using the aforementioned programs much easier. Also, RockNES and Nestopia really do everything you need or would want in an emulation program. They've also been updated in the past year, meaning if there are glitches, bugs, and a lack of support, they're more likely to be fixed in programs like Nestopia and RockNES.

Of course, there are many of you who want to do more than just play games. You want to put that noodle to work on your own NES game. Those looking to do just that, or just want to mod someone else's NES ROM will be dismayed to find there is only one real program for doing this called TileEater. Available at *http://www.emulation.net/nintendo*, this program only runs in OS 9, so those working on OS X will need to make sure they have the classic software installed to emulate the older operating system. Being the only such program available for any version of the Mac operating system, beggars really can't be choosers in this case.

Emulation Enhancer, which I mentioned earlier, is one of the many add-ons that you might want to consider to improve the quality of this nostalgic enterprise you've embarked on and allow you to use an actual gamepad instead of a keyboard. It's shareware, so you can download and test this utility before you buy it ($25). It also offers screen filtering, full screen mode, and the developer, Richard Bannister, is also working on network play as well.

For those who want to organize their ROMs, Bannister also provides a utility called RomOrganizer, available at *http://www.bannister.org/software/ romorga.htm*. The program is shareware, reminding you of this fact after every 20 ROM files examined and processed, but allows you to get a really good idea of what it's all about before you buy. The great thing about this program is that it will be great for looking at the embedded info in the ROM file for not just NES ROMs, but for 22 other systems. That's right, RomOrganizer supports 23 systems, making it a must have for Mac users in general, not just those who want to play NES ROMs.

With the information in this hack, you should be more than ready to try your hand at running some NES ROMs on your Mac. It might not seem as easy as it was on the PC, which has a multitude of emulators and editing programs, but just remember that even after you make the switch, it's not really that hard at all to rejoin the world of NES emulation. You're got the essentials, you've got the knowledge, and you've got the ROMs—why now, friend, you're playing with power.

—Daniel Dormer

HACK
#40   Run NES Emulators Under Linux

Combine your love of Nintendo homebrews with your love of open source.

If you are reading this book, the odds are fairly good that you remember late nights in front of the television, gripping an ergonomically abusive NES controller in your hand, hoping against hope that the 127th time is the charm as you just try to slide underneath the fire-breathing Bowser and save that eternal damsel in distress, Princess Toadstool. Or maybe you remember checking your mailbox twice an hour for the latest edition of Nintendo Power magazine, certain that it would contain the necessary codes to allow you to finally finish Teenage Mutant Ninja Turtles II: The Arcade Game.

The purpose of this hack is to let you transport yourself back in time to the 1980's, but you will not need a specially modified DeLorean; no, your trusty Linux box will serve in its stead (flux capacitor purely optional). I will take you through the process of installing, configuring, and using the best NES emulators available on the Unix platform. To determine which NES emulators were "the best," I started with the Unix-only TuxNES, then consulted Emulator Zone's NES Emulators page (*http://www.emulator-zone.com/doc. php/nes/*), which is nice enough to display average ratings, on the good old 10-star scale, culled from hundreds or thousands of votes from emulator fans just like you. So here they are, in order of popularity.

FCE Ultra

FCE Ultra (*http://fceultra.sourceforge.net/*) began its life as a DOS-only freeware program, but was subsequently open sourced and ported to Windows, and then to Unix. It stands as one of the best NES emulators now, though its Sourceforge page seems a bit bare.

Gentoo. To install FCE Ultra under Gentoo Linux, follow these steps:

1. Become the root user.
2. Run the command: `ACCEPT_KEYWORDS='~x86' emerge fceultra`

Other Linux/Unix distributions. To install FCE Ultra under other Linux or Unix distributions, first check your installation media or online package repositories to see if it's already available. You should also check the project's home page to see if a binary version is available. If not, you can install it from source, but you may need to install SDL (*http://www.libsdl.org/*) and OpenGL drivers first. At the time of this writing, the best place to get the FCE Ultra source code is from Gentoo (*http://distfiles.gentoo.org/distfiles*).

Look for a file called *fceu-VERSION.src.tar.bz2* (for example *fceu-0.98.12. src.tar.bz2*).

1. Download the FCE Ultra source distribution into */tmp* (be sure to remove any older versions of the file you have kicking around), and extract, configure, and compile FCE Ultra:

```
$ cd /tmp
$ tar xvjf fceu-*tar.bz2
$ rm fceu-*tar.bz2
$ cd fceu
$ ./configure && make
```

2. Next, become root using *su* or *sudo*, and install it:

```
# make install
```

FCE Ultra does not come with a fancy GUI like some of the other emulators, so if the command line is no friend of yours, you may want to install a generic emulator frontend such as Game Launcher (*http://www.dribin.org/ dave/game_launcher/*). I will demonstrate the harder path (which seems fouler but feels fairer?) of invoking FCE Ultra from the command line.

Open a terminal window (no need to become root here) and change to your NES ROM directory. The first step is to configure your input devices [Hack #52]:

```
$ fceu -inputcfg gamepad1 SolarWars.NES
```

You must specify a ROM, as for some strange reason FCE Ultra will not let you just configure your controller without running a game. If you wish to configure other controllers as well, simply add an -inputcfg *<device_name>* switch to the command line for each. Valid options for *<device_name>* are: "gamepad1", "gamepad2", "gamepad3", "gamepad4", "powerpad1", and "powerpad2". If you don't want to play the game after configuring your controllers, simply press the Escape key to exit FCE Ultra.

To play a game, run the command:

```
fceu {<option>} <rom_name>
```

Some of the more popular *<option>*s are:

-pal
    emulate a PAL NES

-sound
    enable sound

-soundrate
    sound playback rate, in Hz

-inputcfg
    configure an input device

-opengl
> enable OpenGL

-doublebuf
> enable double-buffering

-xscale
> scale display by this factor in the X direction

-yscale
> scale display by this factor in the Y direction

-xres
> horizontal resolution, in fullscreen mode

-yres
> vertical resolution, in fullscreen mode

-fs
> enable fullscreen mode

For example, to run BombSweeper with OpenGL disabled (what can I say, OpenGL *crawls* on my laptop when using the Xfree86 built-in driver), sound enabled, and scaling the display by a factor of two in both the X and Y directions, run:

```
fceu -opengl 0 -sound 1 -xscale 2 -yscale 2 BombSweeper.new
```

Or maybe you want to run BoxBoy with OpenGL, in fullscreen mode (640x480), double-buffered, with sound:

```
fceu -doublebuf 1 -fs 1 -opengl 1 -sound 1 \
  -xres 640 -yres 480 BOXBOY.NES
```

There do not appear to be any graphical frontends available for FCE Ultra on the Unix platform, so this may be a great opportunity for the Perl/Tk- or Tcl/Tk-savvy reader to whip one up and open source it. A chap from the Gentoo Forums has made a start of it in Perl/Tk (*http://forums.gentoo.org/viewtopic-t-269497-highlight-fceultra.html*).

FakeNES

FakeNES is an open source NES emulator written in C, as opposed to FCE Ultra, which makes heavy use of assembler. This makes FakeNES a bit more portable, as evidenced by the fact that it runs on *everything*: Windows 9x/2000/Me/XP, 32-bit DOS, Linux, FreeBSD, QNX, BeOS, and Mac OS X.

Gentoo. To install FakeNES under Gentoo:

1. Become the root user
2. Run the command: `ACCEPT_KEYWORDS='~x86' emerge fakenes`

Other Linux distributions / flavors of Unix. To install FakeNES under other Linux/Unix distributions, first check your installation media or package repository for a binary package. If one is not available, visit the FakeNES project's SourceForge files page (*http://sourceforge.net/project/showfiles. php?group_id=39844*) and save the latest source tarball (*fakenes-0.3.1.tar.gz*, as of this writing) to your */tmp* directory, and follow the instructions in the FCE Ultra section shown earlier in this hack.

Once FakeNES is installed, change to your NES ROMs directory and start it up by running:

```
fakenes <rom_name>
```

FakeNES has a minimalist GUI that is toggled by pressing the Escape key. Press Escape now to show the menu bar, then access the Options menu and select Video, then Resolution. Set a decent resolution, like 640x480, which forces FakeNES into fullscreen mode. Now, select from the Options → Audio → Mixing. Set Speed to 11025 HZ, and Quality to Low. Now, access Options → Audio → Effects and de-select any effects that may be enabled. Set Options → Audio → Filters to None.

Now, click on the Options menu and select Input. If you have a joystick (see [Hack #52] and [Hack #51]), select Stick/Pad 1 and click on the Start button under the Set Buttons header. FakeNES may not say anything, but it is waiting for you to press a button on your joystick/gamepad to map to the NES controller's Start button. Do so, and then follow suit for the Select, A, and B buttons. Now, close the Input window, then hit Escape to hide the FakeNES GUI, shown in Figure 4-20. Now what are you waiting for? Start playing!

TuxNES

TuxNES (*http://tuxnes.sourceforge.net/*) was developed as a Unix-only NES emulator, based on the public-domain NEStra (covered later). It is released under the GNU General Public License (GPL), and works under Linux, FreeBSD, and NetBSD on the i386 (i.e., Intel-compatible) platform. It is a nifty little emulator, and has a nifty little graphical frontend, GTuxNES (*http://www.scottweber.com/projects/gtuxnes/*), which we will install alongside it.

To install TuxNES under Gentoo Linux, become *root* and use the command `emerge tuxnes gtuxnes`. On other Linux/Unix distributions, you should check to see if a binary package is available on your installation media or your distribution's package repository. If not, visit the TuxNES project's download page (*http://tuxnes.sourceforge.net/download.php*) and save the latest source tarball to your */tmp* directory. Now, visit the GTuxNES project's home page (*http://www.scottweber.com/projects/gtuxnes/*) and

Figure 4-20. Changing the controller input in FakeNES

save the source tarball (it is under the Download heading) to your */tmp* directory. Then, compile and install both TuxNES and GTuxNES using the same procedure shown in the FCE Ultra section earlier in this hack.

To start GTuxNES, simply open a terminal as a normal user and run:

```
gtuxnes &
```

Before playing any games, you should set your preferences. Use the Browse button in the General tab to select a ROM, and then switch to the Sound tab. Select 8-bit Mu-Law as the sample format, and 11025 Hz as the sampling rate. Now click on the Video tab and check the Enlarge option, entering 2 into the text box to its right. Click on the Input tab and select the Enable Joystick 1 option (its default value, */dev/js0, should be fine)*. Finally, click on the Run button at the bottom of the window to launch TuxNES. Both programs are shown in Figure 4-21.

One great thing about GTuxNES is that it makes it very easy to try out different options to get an especially uncooperative ROM to run. And GTux-NES spews the TuxNES command line that it is using to standard error, so you can snag it and put it in a shell script so that you can easily launch those troublesome ROMs in the future without having to remember how the phases of the moon converged with your TuxNES options.

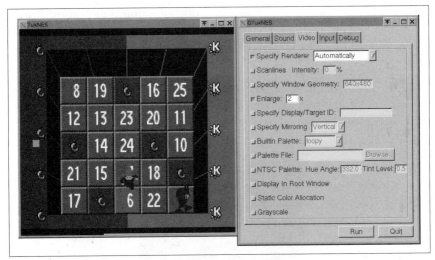

Figure 4-21. Messing with video options under TuxNES

InfoNES

InfoNES is an emulator from the Land of the Rising Sun, where the *keitai denwa* (mobile phone) rules all. It is not surprising at all to read the following description on the InfoNES project's home page (*http://www.geocities.co.jp/SiliconValley/5604/infones/*).

InfoNES is an open source NES emulator that runs on Win32, x86/Linux, PS2/Linux, WinCE(H/PC, P/PC, P/PC2002, l'genda, BE-300, BE-500), GBA(Game Boy Advance), GP32(GamePark 32), Zaurus/Linux, N-Gage(Nokia s60), OSASK, Pekoe, and PlayStation2. If you plan to create a NES emulator for embedded devices (i.e., Palm, Nokia 7650, SmartPhone 2002, etc.), InfoNES is one of the best choices.

To install TuxNES under Gentoo Linux, become *root* and use the command `emerge infones`. On other Linux/Unix distributions, you should check to see if a binary package is available on your installation media or in your distribution's package repository. If not, go to the InfoNES project's home page (*http://www.geocities.co.jp/SiliconValley/5604/infones/*), scroll down to the "What's new?" section, and save the latest source tarball corresponding to your platform and OS (such as x86/Linux) to your */tmp* directory. Then, compile and install it using the same procedure shown in the FCE Ultra section earlier in this hack.

To use InfoNES (shown in Figure 4-22), open a terminal as a normal user, change to your NES ROMs directory, and run:

```
InfoNES <rom_name>
```

The keys are mapped as follows: the arrow keys are the d-pad, the S key is Start, the X key is the A button, and the Z key is the B button. The I key pops up an information window, the V key pops up a version window, and the Q key quits.

Figure 4-22. Playing a homebrew Matrix game under InfoNES

NEStra

As I said, TuxNES grew out of the NEStra codebase, which has not been updated since mid-December, 1999. Still, NEStra is a dependable, if unremarkable emulator, and you may do well to have it around.

To install NEStra under Gentoo Linux, become *root* and use the command emerge nestra. On other Linux/Unix distributions, you should check to see if a binary package is available on your installation media or in your distribution's package repository. If not, go to the NEStra project's home page (*http://nestra.linuxgames.com/*) and save the source tarball to your */tmp* directory. Then compile and install it using the same procedure shown in the FCE Ultra section earlier in this hack.

NEStra is a no-frills emulator (which is a polite way of saying it does not do much), so it is both easy to use and *blazingly fast!* To run it, open a terminal as a normal user, change to your NES *ROMs* directory, and run:

```
nestra <rom_name>
```

The arrow keys map to the d-pad on the NES controller, the Enter key maps to Start, the space bar maps to the A button, and the X and Y keys map to the B button. The Escape key exits, as you may have suspected. Enjoy! Figure 4-23 shows NEStra playing the Solar Wars homebrew.

Figure 4-23. Navigate outer space at blazing speeds with NEStra

—*Josh Glover*

HACK #41 Emulate 16-Bit Systems in Windows

Relive the 16-bit wars all over again on your home computer.

Some of us might find it hard to believe that the three great 16-bit systems— the venerable Super Nintendo, the epochal Sega Genesis, and the hardcore favorite TurboGrafx-16—actually fall into the realm of retro gaming. For those of you still in denial, consider this: children born when the SNES was released are entering high school this year.

I'll pause for a moment so we can all weep for our lost, fleeting youth.

Better now? Hard as it is to process, the great 16-bitters, hardware from an age when the number of bits your system's CPU could process was the end-all-be-all of fanboy arguments, are now old relics. But there's an upside to all this—whereas 16-bit emulation was merely a gleam in a hacker's eye a decade ago, it's now routine. High-quality emulators exist for the SNES, Genesis, and other 16-bit systems, and in this hack I'll cover the best of them.

You can find public domain ROM files for each of the systems covered here at sites like PD Roms (*http://www.pdroms.de*). To find TurboGrafx games, be sure to check under the PC Engine heading (the name of the system in Japan).

Super Nintendo Entertainment System (SNES)

It took quite a while before a SNES emulator was released that could emulate all of the machine's various hardware modes and add-on functions, like the Mode 7 that let the system scale and rotate sprites in hardware, or the Super FX chip that allowed for rudimentary 3D games like Star Fox. Two major programs have competed with each other for years: ZSNES (*http://www.zsnes.com*) and Snes9X (*http://www.snes9x.com*).

Since ZSNES seems to be the most popular and most fully-featured emulator, I'll go into further detail on it here. To download it, click on the Files link on the web page, then click the topmost link that reads "Binary" in the Windows column. As of this writing, the latest version is 1.42. You'll note that there are also DOS and Linux [Hack #43] versions available from the same page.

You'll have to choose a mirror site from which to download. Just select the site that's closest to you geographically, and if for some reason that link doesn't work, try another. Unzip the files into a new directory on your PC, then run the *zsnesw.exe* file to start things up. After you run it, you might see a black square appear in the middle of your display, and you won't be able to click anything or even move the cursor around. If this happens to you, just hit Alt+Enter to force ZSNES into fullscreen mode, and within a few seconds you should see something like Figure 4-24.

Helpfully, the Game menu will drop down automatically for you. Go ahead and click Load to open any ROM files you've downloaded. For convenience, you can save ROMs in zipped format; ZSNES will automatically recognize and extract them when you choose Load. For extra convenience, save your games to the same directory where you put the ZSNES program; otherwise you'll have to use the (slightly confusing) menu to navigate to the directory you put them in. Figure 4-25 shows ZNES running a public domain ROM.

When you load a ROM it will run automatically and the menu will disappear; to get it back, press Esc at any time. The game will pause automatically while you have the menu up. If you're a little confused as to the keyboard layout—and why wouldn't you be? The SNES had eight buttons on its controller—click the Config menu and then select Input #1.

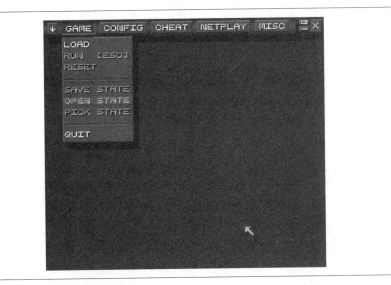

Figure 4-24. ZSNES main menu

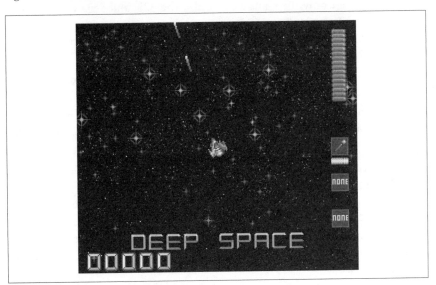

Figure 4-25. ZSNES running the public domain ROM Astrohawk

Notice that ZSNES uses the same settings for both keyboard and joystick—that is, if you want to use a joystick, you have to override the keyboard button settings. If this is what you desire (or if you just want to choose a different keyboard arrangement), click the Set Keys button. You'll be prompted to enter the mapping for each button in turn—at the prompts, hit the appropriate keyboard key or joystick button. If you're using a USB joystick,

ZSNES should recognize it, but only if it was plugged in before you started the program.

You'll notice that the ZSNES GUI is rather old school. You can't change that, but you can mess around with the colors and other graphics to tune it to your own sense of aesthetics. Click Misc → Gui Opns to mess around with the look of the GUI. Try adding the "Burning Effect" or "Snow Effect" and see what happens to the formerly drab menu screen!

Sega Genesis

Part of the beauty of emulators is that we need no longer engage in the petty "system wars" that tore us apart in middle school. Everyone can have a virtual copy of every system, so let's not fight about which one is the best.* Although there are about twenty different Sega Genesis emulators listed on emulation portal Zophar's Domain (*http://www.zophar.net/genesis.html*), there are two clear leaders: Gens (*http://www.gens.ws*) and Kega (*http://kega. eidolons-inn.net/*).

Both support not only the Genesis, but also the 32X and Sega CD add-ons. If you use them to play Sega CD games, you can use your original CDs—which is probably preferable to setting up that whole clunky machine again if you want to get in a quick game of Final Fight CD!

Also, both emulators have upgraded and expanded versions available that add in Sega Master System and Game Gear emulation. They're called Gens Plus and Kega Fusion, respectively. Of course, the emulation for these systems is still in the beta stage, and there are already better SMS/GG emulators out there [Hack #48].

As it turns out, the GUIs for Gens and Kega are not that different. For simplicity's sake, I'll assume you're going to try out the standard version of Gens, but many of these tips will suffice for Kega and Kega Fusion. Note that Genesis ROMs will run in the emulator as-is: just download the zipped file to whatever directory is most convenient for you, then after you download and run Gens, click File → Load ROM to open it up. Figure 4-26 shows Gens in action.

If you want to configure your button setup, click Option, then Joypads. Clicking the topmost drop-down box that reads "3 Buttons" by default will let you select what Genesis pad you want to emulate—the classic three-button or the awesome six-button. If you want to play a four-player game, you

---

* The SNES is, anyway.

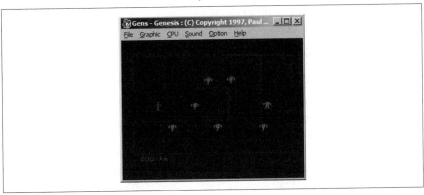

Figure 4-26. Gens running a homebrew version of a popular arcade shooter

must emulate the Team Player four-player adapter by connecting it to one of the virtual controller ports—to do so, click the drop-down box that says "pad" by default.

One other important menu you'll want to be able to use, especially if you want to play Sega CD or 32X games, is the Bios/Misc Files configuration under the Option menu. Here, you can show Gens where the BIOS files for the Sega CD and 32X are located on your computer. These are required to run the games, but aren't distributed with the emulators themselves due to copyright issues. As of this writing, you can find them at the Kega homepage. Make sure to unzip them when you save them to your computer—Gens and Kega will both recognize zipped ROMs, but not zipped BIOS files.

...And the Rest

If you didn't have a SNES or a Genesis back in the day, perhaps you were one of the hardcore (or very unlucky) few who owned a TurboGrafx-16. (Hey, I'm not saying it didn't have its share of quality titles, but you might have missed out on a lot.) Much like the Sega Genesis, the TurboGrafx-16 also had a CD-ROM add-on. So, although there are many different emulators that will run ROM files from the standard HuCard game chips that shipped with the system, if you want full functionality from your emulator you'll want one of the three that will run CD games.

Those emulators are YAME (*http://www.zophar.net/yame.html*), Hu-Go (*http://www.zeograd.com/*), and Magic Engine (*http://www.magicengine.com/*). Magic Engine is considered to be the best PC Engine emulator out there, but the quality comes at a price. Literally. You can download a preview version of Magic Engine for free, but the full software must be purchased from the official web page for $19. The demo version will play all games, but automatically shuts itself off after five minutes. You could, of course, abuse the save and restore functions if you don't mind shutting the program down every four minutes and fifty-nine seconds. If you *do* mind, then you might check out Hu-Go or YAME—the latter is said to be more stable, but is a Japanese-language program.

And finally, there's that overpriced, overpowered wonder, the Neo Geo. Since the infamous (but not especially popular) console was based on arcade hardware, the most convenient way to emulate Neo Geo games would be through MAME [Hack #20]. If you're only interested in the Neo Geo, and not other arcade games, then you might check out the sampling of Neo Geo-specific emulators at Zophar's Domain (*http://www.zophar.net/neo-geo.html*). Either way, you'll be able to find homebrew Neo Geo games [Hack #24].

Emulate Other Classic Systems on the Mac

Play classic games from even more popular consoles on your Macintosh.

If you get a taste of emulation on your Mac [Hack #39] [Hack #21], it won't be long before you're ready to find some more systems you can play around with. You won't be disappointed—the Mac has plenty of emulators available that cover all the popular systems: the Super Nintendo, Atari 2600, Vectrex, and more.

As you're accumulating a collection of emulators for your Mac, one name will keep coming up over and over: Richard Bannister (*http://bannister.org/ software/emu.htm*), who has written or ported over two dozen free emulators for Mac OS X. In addition to his emulators, Richard offers two shareware applications: Emulation Enhancer and ROM Organizer, both of which are shareware. Emulation Enhancer works with many of Richard's emulators, and brings full-screen support, network multiplayer, and USB gamepad/joystick support to his emulators. ROM Organizer helps you keep track of your ROMs, using the ROM images themselves to extract identifying information from the ROM.

Super Nintendo Entertainment System (SNES)

The hugely popular SNES brought some incredible games into living rooms around the world. With an emulator and a copy of the games you want to play, get ready to delight in this 16-bits, 3.58 MHz, and 192 KB of glorious gaming gear.

There are two major ports of SNES9x [Hack #41] that you should check out on the Mac. You can find the official port at the SNES9x home page (*http://www. snes9x.com*). SNES9x Custom HQ (*http://chrisballinger.info/public/snes9x*) is an unofficial variant of SNES9x that uses different algorithms for rendering the display, and boasts fast performance even on low-end computers. You ought to give both of them a try.

Both variants of SNES9x are free and open source, and you can download a disk image containing the ready-to-run application, or grab the source code if you feel like tinkering. To run SNES9x, put the application in its own folder somewhere—avoid the temptation to drop it into the */Applications* directory, because SNES9x will create several subdirectories wherever you put it, including: *Cheats*, *IPSs* (used to patch a ROM, often used for user-created translations of import games), and *SRAMs* (for saved game snapshots).

SNES9x will let you record (Option → Record Movie) a movie of your game (you'll need to pause the game with Emulation → Pause to make that menu available). After you play video back to completion with Option → Play Movie, SNES9x restores the state of the game so you can pick up where you left off at the end of the recording. If you want to create a QuickTime movie, pause the game and then select Option → Export to QuickTime Movie. So start recording, and get ready to show off your retro gaming skillz or create some really wild retro-machinima.

Nintendo Game Boy

Nintendo's Game Boy and Game Boy Advance (GBA) brought handheld gaming into the mainstream. Despite an unlighted grayscale screen, the original Game Boy was hugely successful, and gamers are still enjoying its vast library of games through the Game Boy Advance's backwards compatibility.

For Game Boy Advance emulation, Boycott Advance (*http://www.bannister. org/software*) and VisualBoyAdvance (*http://software.emuscene.com/view. php?softid=158*) provide excellent performance and compatibility. Visual-BoyAdvance will emulate Game Boy and Game Boy Color games as well.

If you're just going to be running Game Boy or Game Boy Color games, you may as well run a dedicated emulator, since a Game Boy Advance emulator will make your Mac work quite a bit harder. KiGB (*http://www.bannister. org/software/kigb.htm*) offers excellent Game Boy and Game Boy Color emulation on the Mac. Figure 4-27 shows KiGB in action.

KiGB has a feature whose value may not be immediately apparent: the ability to record audio. If you haven't caught on to the "chiptunes" trend, it's time to do so. Amateur and professional musicians alike are turning to retro games for samples, beats, and more. In fact, Beck released an online album of chiptunes called "GameBoy Variations (Hell Yes Remix)." Some musicians are remixing sounds from videogames, others are writing their own

Figure 4-27. A Game Boy Color classic that never was

homebrew applications to make the music. All the intrepid Mac musician needs is KiGB's audio recording feature, a composition application like GarageBand, and it's time to rock and roll retro style.

Atari 2600

For Atari 2600 emulation, there is one choice: the cross-platform Stella (*http://stella.sourceforge.net*). Although you could grab the X11 version [Hack #43] and compile it, you can download a disk image file and install. Stella likes to live in its own directory, so if you do install it in */Applications*, be sure to create a subdirectory for it there, and be sure to include everything that you found on the Stella disk image—there are a few essential files that should remain in the same directory as the Stella executable, such as *stella. pro* (not to mention the documentation you'll want to keep handy). Stella isn't particular about where you keep your ROMS. As soon as you start it up, it will prompt you to choose a ROM. Figure 4-28 shows Stella in action.

Other Systems

There are many more systems you can emulate on your Mac. Here are a few that you might enjoy:

SMSPlus

> (*http://www.bannister.org/software/sms.htm*) is a Sega Master System and Game Gear emulator.

Handy

> (*http://bannister.org/software/handy.htm*) is an emulator for the Atari Lynx handheld system.

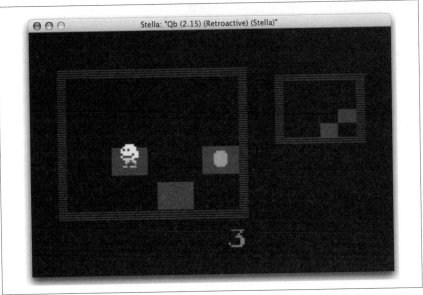

Figure 4-28. Stella for Mac OS X running the very addictive QB

fMSX

(*http://bannister.org/software/fmsx.htm*) is a port of Marat Fayzullin's original fMSX to the Mac.

VecX

(*http://www.bannister.org/software/vecx.htm*) is a Vectrex emulator. You can delight in the fact that the copyright holders of the original Vectrex ROMs allow them to be distributed freely (see *http://www.classicgaming. com/vectrex/emu.htm* or search for "vectrex roms").

For more Mac emulators, check out Richard Bannister's site (*http://www. bannister.org*).

—Brian Jepson

HACK #43 Emulate Other Classic Systems in Linux

Emulate some of the most popular gaming consoles of yore.

So, the emulation bug has bitten you harder than you imagined, and you're not satisfied with merely running the arcade machine emulator MAME [Hack #22] or the Nintendo Entertainment System [Hack #40]? Then read on to find out about emulators for many different retro consoles that will run on your Linux box, including the Super NES, Atari 2600, Sega Genesis, and more.

Super Nintendo Entertainment System (SNES)

The venerable Super NES was one of the most popular console systems to ever hit the United States. But even the huge number of games that were available here pales in comparison to the number of games published in the motherland: Japan. With an emulator, and maybe a Japanese dictionary—or see "Play Japanese Games Without Speaking Japanese" in *Gaming Hacks* (O'Reilly), you may be able to explore a vast new sampling of SNES games! So let's get down to it.

ZSNES (*http://www.zsnes.com*) is widely considered to be the best Super NES emulator available on the Linux platform. To install it, follow the steps listed next for your distribution.

Debian. Use *su* or *sudo* to run the following command as *root*:

```
# apt-get install zsnes
```

Gentoo. Use *su* or *sudo* to run the following command as *root*:

```
# emerge zsnes
```

Other Unix/Linux distributions. Visit the ZSNES home page (*http://www.zsnes. com*) and click on the Files link in the menu at the top of the page. Save the Linux source file for the latest version to your */tmp* directory. Then:

1. Extract, configure, and compile the source code:
   ```
   $ cd /tmp
   $ tar xvzf zsnes*src.tar.gz
   $ rm  zsnes*src.tar.gz
   $ cd zsnes*/src
   $ ./configure && make
   ```
2. Use *su* (or *sudo*) to install ZSNES as the root user:
   ```
   # make install
   ```

Once you have obtained some ROMs, starting ZSNES is as easy as typing zsnes at the command line. ZSNES's nifty little GUI will be displayed automatically when you start it. The first thing you will want to do is configure things for your particular setup. Start by clicking on the CONFIG menu and then INPUT #1. This will bring up the INPUT DEVICE configuration screen. In the DEVICE box, select KEYB/JOYSTICK, then click on the SET KEYS button. (You did read [Hack #52], and maybe [Hack #51] as well, right?) ZSNES will now prompt you to hit the key or joystick button that will be used for each button on the SNES controller that is being emulated. Follow the steps as prompted, then click on the X in the title bar of the INPUT DEVICE window (shown in Figure 4-29) to close it.

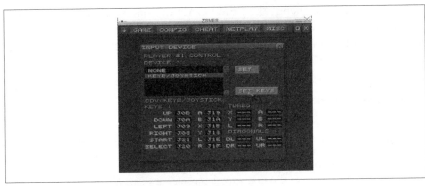

Figure 4-29. The Input Device menu in ZSNES

You will probably also want to change the video settings, so click on the CONFIG menu again and select VIDEO. Take a look at all of the resolutions listed in the VIDEO MODES box. The left column, as you probably guessed, is the resolution. The middle column is the rendering engine ("R" means the default engine, "DR" is the direct rendering system, and "OGL" is OpenGL). The right column indicates whether ZSNES will run in a window or in full-screen mode. You will probably want to select the highest resolution that your video card can handle, and most people prefer fullscreen mode to get that sprawled-in-front-of-the-television-at-3-AM-trying-to-beat-that-damned-Bowser feel. To change video modes, click on the mode of your choosing, then click on the SET button. You will be prompted to press any key, the video mode will be switched, and then you will be prompted to press any key again to make the change permanent.

Don't worry if your screen goes all crazy due to an unsupported resolution—just don't touch the keyboard for ten seconds, and your previous resolution should be restored. Note that running the X Window System (i.e., XFree86 or X.org) at color depths greater than 16-bit forces ZSNES to scale back to 16-bit color in software, thus degrading performance. If you know that you are running at a higher color depth, and know how to change it, you should probably do so. When you are satisfied with the video mode, click on the "X" in the title bar of the VIDEO CONFIG window to close it.

Now, click on the CONFIG menu again and select SOUND. You will probably want to select both ENABLE SOUND and STEREO SOUND by clicking on the checkbox to the left of each option. When you are satisfied with the sound settings, click on the "X" in the title bar of the SOUND CONFIG window to close it.

Feel free to poke about in the CONFIG and MISC menus for a bit. When you are done, load a ROM and play it!

Click on the GAME menu, then the LOAD option. You will be presented with a file browser window. Use it to browse into your SNES ROMs directory, select the ROM that you want to play, and then click the LOAD button.

If everything is groovy, the game should start. Congratulations, you now have yourself a working SNES emulator!

> If you don't want to log out of your current desktop, you could also start up a separate X11 instance at the desired color depth. Switch to another virtual console (for example, to switch to the first virtual console, use Ctrl-Alt-F1), log in if necessary, and use *startx* to launch a new X11 session):
>
>   startx -- :1 -depth 16
>
> The -- option passes all the subsequent commands to the X server itself (:1 specifies the second display, -depth 16 specifies 16-bit color depth. After you've started the second server, you will be able to switch back to your first X11 session with Ctrl-Alt-F7, and to your second one with Ctrl-Alt-F8.

If for some strange reason you do not like ZSNES, here are some other SNES emulators worth trying:

Snes9X
 (*http://www.snes9x.com/*)

GooSNES
 (*http://bard.sytes.net/goosnes/*), a GTK+ front-end for Snes9X

For more Nintendo emulation on the Unix platform, take a look at:

BoyCott Advance
 (*http://boycottadvance.emuunlim.com/*), a Game Boy Advance emulator

Virtual Game Boy Advance (VGBA)
 (*http://fms.komkon.org/VGBA/*), a Game Boy Advance emulator

Gcube
 (*http://gcube.exemu.net/*), a Gamecube emulator

Mupen64
 (*http://mupen64.emulation64.com/*), an N64 emulator

Nintendo Game Boy

With all this talk of Nintendo emulation, did you think I had forgotten about the original Game Boy? Not bloody likely, as this old-school classic is also *the best-selling video game system of all time!* And it ain't even close, people: the latest figures that I have seen (which are from March 2004) esti-mate that the Game Boy series has sold 160 million units (with the GBA only accounting for around of 20 million of those)!

So, without further ado, let's build and install VisualBoyAdvance (*http://vba.ngemu.com/*), the most popular GBA emulator for the Unix platform.

Gentoo Linux. Gentoo Linux users should become *root* and run the com-mand emerge `visualboyadvance`.

Other Linux distributions. If you're using another distribution of Linux (or other Unix variant), check your installation media or online package reposi-tories to see if there is a binary build of VisualBoyAdvance available. Other-wise, visit the VisualBoyAdvance project's Sourceforge files page (*http://sourceforge.net/project/showfiles.php?group_id=63889*) and download the latest source tarball (*VisualBoyAdvance-src-1.7.2.tar.gz*, as of this writing).

Proceed as for ZSNES (i.e., uncompress the tarball, change into the result-ing directory, and do the `./configure && make && make install` dance).

Once VisualBoyAdvance is installed, open a terminal as a normal user, change to your Game Boy ROMs directory, and type (replace *TETRIS.GBC* with the name of a Game Boy or Game Boy advance ROM that you have):

```
VisualBoyAdvance -3 TETRIS.GBC
```

Figure 4-30 shows VisualBoyAdvance in action.

Figure 4-30. A freeware version of the ubiquitous falling-blocks puzzle running in VisualBoyAdvance

Make sure to check out PD ROMS (*http://pdroms.de/*), as there are public domain, freeware, and/or open-source clones of most of the Game Boy clas-sics that you grew up with!

As a full-featured emulator, the command-line options to VisualBoyAdvance are myriad. Thus, you may wish to employ a graphical frontend. Here are three that exist for Unix:

GnomeBoyAdvance
   (*http://developer.berlios.de/projects/gnomeboyadvance/*)

KvisualBoyAdvance
   (*http://www.gentoo-portage.com/games-emulation/kvisualboyadvance*)

QTVBA
   Frontend for VisualBoyAdvance (*http://www.apex.net.au/~twalker/qtvba/*).

Several other Game Boy emulators exist for Linux:

Gngb
   (*http://m.peponas.free.fr/gngb/*), a Game Boy Color emulator

gnuboy
   (*http://gnuboy.unix-fu.org/*), a Game Boy Color emulator

KiGB
   (*http://kigb.emuunlim.com/*), a Game Boy / Game Boy Color emulator

BoyCott-Advance-SDL
   (*http://sdlemu.ngemu.com/basdl.php*), an SDL port of the BoyCott-Advance (*http://boycottadvance.emuunlim.com/*) Game Boy Advance emulator

And if you like Game Boy emulators, you might also enjoy emulating other hand-held systems:

NeoPocott
   (*http://neopocott.emuunlim.com/*), a Neo Geo Pocket emulator

Handy
   (*http://homepage.ntlworld.com/dystopia/*), an Atari Lynx emulator

MEKA
   (*http://www.smspower.org/meka/*), an emulator for, amongst other things, Sega Game Gear (more on MEKA in the Sega Genesis section of this hack)

Atari 2600

Ah, the Atari 2600. Whenever talk turns to classic consoles, this lovely beast is bound to come up. Luckily, there is a wonderful emulator for the Unix platform, called Stella, that will allow us all to relive our glory days. To install it, follow the steps listed for your distribution.

Gentoo. If you're a Gentoo user, become *root* and run the command emerge stella.

Other Linux distributions. If you're using another distribution of Linux (or other Unix variant), check your installation media or online package repositories to see if there is a binary build of Stella available. Otherwise, visit the Stella project's home page (*http://stella.sourceforge.net*) and click on the "Stable Releases" link under the "Downloads" heading on the left side of the page. Then:

1. Save the source *.tar.gz* file for the latest version to your */tmp* directory.

2. Extract and compile Stella:

```
$ cd /tmp
$ tar xvzf stella-*-src.tar.gz
$ cd stella-*/src/build/
$ make linux
```

3. (or, to build the OpenGL version: use make linux-gl)

4. Next, become the root user with *su* (or prefix each command with *sudo*), and install Stella and its associated files:

```
# cp stella /usr/bin/
# cp ../emucore/stella.pro /etc/
# mkdir -p /usr/share/docs/stella
# cp -r ../../docs/ ../../*.txt /usr/share/docs/stella/
```

After you have built and installed Stella, open a terminal as a normal user, change to your Atari 2600 ROMs directory **[Hack #26]**, and fire up the emulator:

```
stella -video soft -sound 1 -zoom 2 -grabmouse 0 seantsc.bin
```

I am using the -grabmouse 0 option to turn off mouse grabbing, because I use the keyboard to control Stella—it works about how you would expect: the arrow keys emulate the joystick, and the space bar emulates the fire button. The -video soft option instructs Stella to use software video rendering. If you built Stella with OpenGL support, try -video gl to use your graphics hardware to its utmost (which is *very* important when emulating that graphical powerhouse, the Atari 2600!). Figure 4-31 shows Stella in action.

If Stella cannot quench your thirst for Atari emulation, check out some of the following projects:

Atari 800
> (*http://atari800.sourceforge.net/*), an Atari 800, 800XL, 130XE, and 5200 emulator for Unix, Amiga, MS-DOS, Atari TT/Falcon, SDL, and WinCE

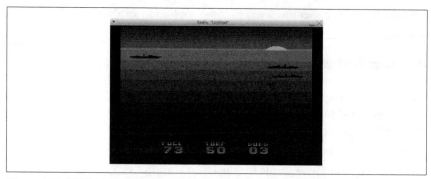

Figure 4-31. STELLAAAAAAAAAAAAAAAAAA!

Hatari

    (*http://hatari.sourceforge.net/*) and STonX (*http://stonx.sourceforge.net/*), Atari ST emulators for the various flavors of Unix (Mac OS X being one of them!)

Atari Running on Any Machine (ARAnyM)

    (*http://aranym.sourceforge.net/*), a virtual machine for running Atari ST/ TT/Falcon operating systems and TOS/GEM applications

EmuTOS

    (*http://emutos.sourceforge.net/en/index.htm*), a singleuser singletasking operating system for 32-bit Atari computer emulators, like ARAnyM, STonX, or Hatari

Handy

    (*http://handy.sourceforge.net/*), an Atari Lynx emulator

Virtual Jaguar

    (*http://www.icculus.org/virtualjaguar/*), an Atari Jaguar emulator

Sega Genesis/MegaDrive

Many readers of this book probably remember the sheer exhilaration that we all felt when we saw Sonic the Hedgehog for the first time. The raw speed that the Sega Genesis console displayed was courtesy of nothing more than a 7.1 MHz Motorola 68000 processor—of the same sort you might have seen if you cracked open your early Apple Macintosh or Commodore Amiga (if you were lucky enough to own one of those beauties). As such, emulating a Genesis at full speed should not be too much to ask of a modern PC. Let's install Gens, the best Genesis emulator available (which conveniently runs on Unix, the best OS available), and see what it can do.

Gentoo. Gentoo users need to become *root* and then run the command emerge gens.

Other Linux distributions. If you're using another Unix or Linux distribution, check your installation media and online package repositories for a binary build of Gens. Otherwise, visit the Gens project's Sourceforge downloads page (*http://sourceforge.net/project/showfiles.php?group_id=73619*) and download the most recent tarball under the "Gens Source Code / Gens WIP linux" heading (as of this writing, it was named *gens-rc3.tar.gz*). Save the file to your */tmp* directory.

Make sure you have GTK+ version 2.4 or greater installed, then proceed as for ZSNES (i.e., uncompress the tarball, change into the resulting directory, and do the ./configure && make && make install dance).

Once Gens is installed, using it is as easy as using ZSNES—just change to your Genesis ROMs directory and launch Gens:

```
gens &
```

This will pop up a display window and the Gens title bar. The first step is to click on the Option menu and select Joypads. (Make sure to check out [Hack #52] and [Hack #51] if you have a Saturn controller lying around.) If you are going to be using a gamepad with only a few buttons (e.g., four), you should probably change the drop-down box next to Player 1 from 6 buttons to 3 buttons. In any case, click on the A icon to the right of the drop-down box to configure your gamepad. Gens will prompt you to press a key (see Figure 4-32) to map to each Genesis controller button.

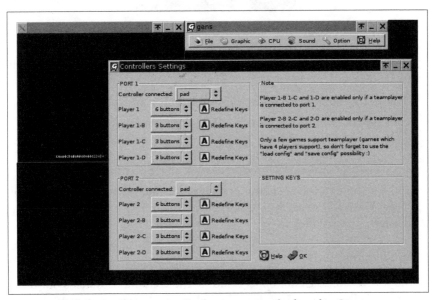

Figure 4-32. Mapping Genesis controller buttons to your keyboard in Gens

After setting up your gamepad and clicking on the OK button to save your configuration, you will probably also want to visit the Graphic menu and select a new Rendermode (I like Double, which simply makes the display window twice as large). You may also want to run Gens in fullscreen mode, in which case there is an option in the Graphic menu, or you can just press Alt+Return at any time to toggle fullscreen mode on or off. Now, click on the File menu and select Open ROM. This will bring up a very strange browser window, which you should use to navigate to your Genesis ROMs directory. Double-clicking on Filesystem in the left pane will allow you to browse in the right pane, and once you have found your Genesis ROMs directory, highlight it and click on the Add button, which will add the directory to the left pane. Now, double-click your ROMs directory in the left pane, select a ROM file in the right pane, and click the OK button to start the game! Figure 4-33 shows Gens in action.

Figure 4-33. Monk and Monkeys running under Gens

If you do not like Gens, here are some other Genesis emulators that run on Linux (and other Unixes, too!):

- Generator (*http://www.squish.net/generator/*)
- DGen-SDL (*http://www.pknet.com/~joe/dgen-sdl.html*)

For more Sega emulation goodness, check out:

- Yabuse (*http://yabause.sourceforge.net/*), a Sega Saturn emulator
- MEKA (*http://www.smspower.org/meka/*), a multi-machine emulator for Sega Master System, Sega Game Gear, and a few other, slightly more esoteric, Sega platforms

Other Systems

As the serious console connoisseur knows, there are more systems out there than I have talked about in this hack, and some of them are worth playing. There are also emulators for newer systems that will require some serious horsepower and a good 3D graphics card to run. So reach, if you will, into this emulator grab bag:

- DAPHNE (*http://www.daphne-emu.com/*), a multiple-machine arcade laserdisc emulator
- FBZX (*http://www.rastersoft.com/fbzx.html*), a Sinclair Spectrum emulator (yes, I know, the Spectrum is not really a video game system, but this was too cool to leave out of this hack!)
- Hu-Go (*http://www.zeograd.com/parse.php?src=hugof&path=0,1,*) a PC Engine emulator
- openMSX (*http://openmsx.sourceforge.net/*), "the MSX emulator that aims for perfection" (their tagline is brilliant—I guess the other MSX emulators out there aim only for mediocrity!)
- ePSXe (*http://www.epsxe.com/*), a PlayStation emulator
- Pcsx (*http://www.pcsx.net/*), a PlayStation emulator
- pcsx2 (*http://www.pcsx2.net/*), a PlayStation 2 emulator

—*Josh Glover*

Emulate the Game Boy on Your PC

Make the classic portable not so portable.

Although Nintendo has been producing home video game consoles since the 1970s, soon after the introduction of its portable Game Boy system in 1989, gaming on the go has become the company's main moneymaker. The latest in the line, the Game Boy Advance SP, can play every Game Boy game going all the way back to the original black-and-white cartridges. So there's still quite a bit of nostalgia, even at Nintendo, for the classics.

In fact, the Game Boy (GB) evokes such heartfelt feelings in its fans that there are a tremendous number of homebrew games and tech demos available at public domain ROM sites like *http://www.pdroms.de*—over 300 for the original GB and 700 for the Game Boy Advance! If you'd like to play these games quickly and easily, you'll need to use a Game Boy emulator for your personal computer. And with the right equipment and software, you can even play them on a real Game Boy Advance [Hack #47].

Emulating the Game Boy and Game Boy Color

When selecting an emulator, you'll want to make sure that it can emulate all three iterations of the first Game Boy hardware—Game Boy, Super Game Boy, and Game Boy Color. The Super Game Boy was an add-on to the Super Nintendo Entertainment System that let users play GB games on the system, and certain GB games were programmed with Super Game Boy-specific color palettes and extra features such as backgrounds and hidden games.

Although a staggering amount of Game Boy emulators have been developed and are listed on emulation portals such as Zophar's Domain (*http://www. zophar.net*), I recommend you stick with an emulator called BGB. It does all of the above, can use the Game Genie cheat add-on, and it runs pretty much any ROM you can throw at it. You can read more about BGB and download the emulator at *http://bgb.bircd.org/*. There are a couple of other emulators that Linux **[Hack #43]** and Mac OS X **[Hack #42]** users should check out.

Setting up BGB. You'll have to unzip the BGB archive into a new directory, but if the ROMs that you download are zipped, you can leave them that way. Run the BGB program, then right-click inside the window to bring up a menu. Click Load ROM and you'll be able to open the ROMs you have saved (see Figure 4-34).

Figure 4-34. BGB running a homebrew combat game

If you want to explore one of BGB's more advanced features, you might try playing the games online. If you and your friends all have a ROM that allows for multi-player support, you can play it online. You'll need each others' IP addresses. One player will host the game (select the Link option from the main menu, then select connect), and others will join in (select Link, then listen). At the appropriate prompts you'll put in the IP addresses as requested.

If you want to configure your controller or display settings, you can enter the robust Options menu by right-clicking and selecting Options. Most of the stuff in here is better left untouched unless you know what you're doing, and it's likely you'll never need most of it anyway. You might try messing with the display scheme. The original Game Boy games can only display four colors, but you can pick which colors those are. Select the GB Colors option. Once there, you can use the sliders to tweak the colors some more if you wish. Five pre-set palettes are available by using the Scheme drop-down box, and you can add your own.

Select the Graphics tab and you can enable Super Game Boy borders for games that support them, like Donkey Kong and Space Invaders. Also in this tab, you can resize the game play window. Note that if you pick Full Screen Stretched, you'll lose the Super Game Boy backgrounds, but the gameplay area will fill up your monitor, making for a very different experience indeed!

Another useful option is the ability to save your position at any time during gameplay. It's a quick and painless process. Right click, then look for the seventh option down, State, and click Quick Save. To load, first boot up the ROM and click Quick Load.

Emulating the Game Boy Advance

Nintendo's Game Boy Advance is one of the most popular game consoles in the history of the industry, so is it any doubt that a thriving emulation and homebrew community exists for the console? Over 700 homebrew Game Boy Advance games and demos are available at the public domain ROMs site *http://www.pdroms.de*.

Although there are many different GBA emulators for Windows, I'll narrow the field down to two excellent choices: BoycottAdvance (*http://boycottadvance.emuunlim.com/*), which doesn't really require anything other than Windows to get started, and VisualBoyAdvance (http://vba.ngemu. com/). Neither has been updated all that recently, but both seem to fully support any new software. Of the two, Boycott seems to be a bit more stable, is a notch easier to use, and it even comes with a free game. That's not a bad place to start.

Deeper into Boycott. Download and unzip the Boycott archive, and everything should be ready to go. The game Pongfighter v1.2 will be automatically placed into the ROM subfolder. You'll need at least a Pentium III to really run things smoothly, though you should be able to choke decent performance out of a fast Pentium II. Having the latest version of Direct X will help a bit, too.

If you have a joystick hooked up to your system, head into the Options menu and set that up first. The drop-down menus are a little inconvenient if your joystick's buttons are not labeled, but you should be able to set it up correctly with some trial and error.

It's much easier to get a keyboard set up, but not easier to play a game using one. You can configure the keys any which way you want, although you'll probably find that the default settings are acceptable. For certain games, having the auto-fire option turned on can be easier on the thumbs.

Let's play a game of Pongfighter to get things moving. Click File → Load ROM, and you'll arrive at the default ROM folder. There you should see the game's file, still zipped. (The emulator also supports ROMs archived in *.rar* format.) Double-click it to play a GBA version of the classic Pong, augmented with a musical theme from the game Street Fighter II. (Can you guess what character's music it is?)

If games aren't running fast enough for you, there are some options you can toy around with. As is the case with most emulators, skipping frames of animation (done by raising the Frameskip value) can speed things up. You can usually get away with setting it to just 1 or 2, and not lose very much of the detail in the process. You can also resize the window. The smaller the window, the less graphic data there is to process, and the faster the emulation.

A feature unique to Boycott is the ability to adjust accuracy versus speed on a sliding scale. Taking accuracy will make things run smoother, but sacrifice speed. Obviously, speed will try and make things run faster but the game will look "choppier" when it animates. It's a personal choice depending on what you feel is more important. If you're unsure of whether or not the game is running properly (some games look choppy even on the GBA hardware, of course), you can check the frame rate with Show FPS. If it's over or at 60, you're not losing any speed and the game's probably just not very well-programmed. Finally, turning off sound emulation with Sound Enable will lessen the load on the PC, although you might feel that playing a game without the music and sound effects isn't exactly a worthwhile experience.

If you find a game isn't working right and you're sure it's not your PC, check the History file under Help. There will be a list of games that are known to not work correctly with that version of the emulator. Downloading the last revision as of this writing, version 0.2.8, should remedy all problems.

GBA on Mac OS X and Linux. There are Mac OS X ports [Hack #42] available of both Boycott Advance and VisualBoyAdvance. Boycott Advance requires major horsepower under the hood (at least a G4) to get things running smoothly. If you want to add full features to Boycott Advance, you'll need to get the emulator enhancer available at *http://www.bannister.org/software/ee. htm*. This shareware program enables joystick support, fullscreen gameplay, and more. VisualBoyAdvance has a few nice bonuses, including the ability to play Game Boy and Game Boy Color games (which it does quite well).

There is also no need for an enhancer, and it doesn't have the massive hardware requirements either.

There is no shortage of emulators available for Linux users [Hack #43], either.

—*Matt Paprocki*

Play Games on a Smartphone or PDA
Get your retro gaming fix in the palm of your hand.

From game watches to programmable calculators, people have always found ways to play video games on the sly. The steady advance of technology has served to increase the sophistication of these covert gaming efforts. The latest generations of smartphones and PDAs are capable of running console emulators, granting users the ability to run thousands of classic games from the Atari, NES, and SNES eras. Now, tech-savvy office workers can play classic console games wherever they happen to be. Not at work, of course.

The Emulation Scene on Handhelds

While the novelty factor of running console games on a handheld is a reward in and of itself, emulating games on a handheld (whether PDA or Smartphone) can be an iffy prospect. Typically, the longer a handheld's operating system has been able to support emulators, the more likely you'll find software for it.

The development community for handhelds is not as large as desktop platforms, so most of the emulators are not nearly as developed, robust, or intuitive as their cousins on other operating systems. Even finding the programs can be difficult, as some are hosted on personal pages that come and go. With some persistence and a decent search engine though, these programs can usually be found somewhere. There are a growing number of repositories for handheld emulators. Here are a few:

Palm
> Although it hadn't been updated in over a year at the time of writing, PalmEmu (*http://www.palmemu.com/*) has a good list of emulators for Palm-powered handhelds. Zophar's Domain also keeps a list at *http://www.zophar.net/palmos/palmos.phtml*. Tapwave Zodiac users should also check out Alternative Handheld Emulation, described later in the Symbian section.

Pocket PC
> Pocket PC Freeware maintains a list of free emulators at *http://www.freewareppc.com/utilities/utilities_emulators.shtml*. You can also find a list at *http://www.zophar.net/ppc/ppc.phtml*.

If you're one of the lucky folks with a Pocket PC that's too fast for your emulator, you can slow your CPU down with a CPU speed application such as Pocket Hack Master (available at both *http://www.pocketgear. com* and *http://www.handango.com*).

Microsoft Smartphone

Being the youngest of this bunch, the Microsoft Smartphone operating system doesn't have quite as many emulators for it. However, it's a great platform for gaming, and you can find a list of free emulators at *http:// freeware.msmobiles.com*; we'll also discuss a few of them in this hack.

Symbian

Alternative Handheld Emulation (*http://ngage.dcemu.co.uk/*) keeps track of emulators for Symbian devices (UIQ, used primarily by Sony Ericsson and Series 60, used primarily by Nokia), but also includes emulators for the Tapwave Zodiac (a game-enhanced Palm-powered device). In the gaming world, Nokia's N-Gage is perhaps the best known Symbian device, but the smartphones from Nokia and Sony Ericsson are powered by Symbian. Many other manufacturers make Symbian devices, including Panasonic, LG, Samsung, Sendo, Lenovo, and Siemens. For the best gaming experience, you'll want a Nokia N-Gage or a newer phone. When in doubt, check the system requirements of the emulator you want to play.

 You may find yourself visiting some dark corners of the Internet trying to find some of these programs. It's important to remember to scan what you download for viruses before you run it or put it on your cell phone. Many a piece of malicious software has been disguised as entertainment software. If in doubt, don't run it.

Even after you've gotten an emulator downloaded and running on your phone, the gaming experience is hardly ideal. The processors in many handhelds are barely adequate for emulation and the handheld itself does not make a comfortable gaming machine. Poor control response, limited support for diagonal movement, and cramped button layout can make reflex-based games a chore (however, gaming systems such as the Tapwave Zodiac and Nokia N-Gage can be a joy to use). Even RPGs and other turn-based games may be unplayable due to the limited resolution of most handheld screens, reducing onscreen text to an unreadable mash. That being said, if you're still not daunted by the challenges of console emulation on a handheld, then read on. The most you'll give up is the time it takes to download and play the game. If you don't like it, you can always delete it! If you do like it, you've succeeded in moving the retro experience into the palm of your hand.

Installing Emulators and ROMs

When installing applications (e.g., an emulator) and ROMs, you have two choices: the handheld device's internal storage or a removable storage card (e.g., MMC or SD). To install an application into internal storage, you must have the media card inserted when you run the installer. However, most handhelds use their internal storage space as both RAM and disk, so you should conserve internal storage as much as possible by using a storage card.

Using a memory card gives you plenty of room to store ROMs and, whenever possible, you should install the emulators themselves to the storage card (the installers for Palm, Pocket PC, Smartphone, and Symbian allow you to choose where to install software). Since some programs have trouble running from a storage card, you should check the documentation for your emulator to make sure it will work OK. Most newer Palms, Pocket PCs, Microsoft Smartphones, and Symbian smartphones have support for MMC and SD storage cards—and with prices around $15 for a 128 MB card (see *http://www.dealram.com*), you can't go wrong.

Let's look at the installation options for some common handheld OSes:

Symbian

Symbian installers (*.SIS*) files are typically beamed over to the phone using Bluetooth or Infrared, but they may also be downloaded using the built-in web browser on some phones, and are sometimes delivered as Over-the-Air (OTA) messages. When you run a Symbian installer on a phone with a memory card, you'll be prompted to choose between the internal memory ("Ph. mem") or the storage card ("M. card").

Pocket PC and Smartphone

To install an application on a Pocket PC or Smartphone, you will usually run an executable (*.EXE*) on a Windows machine that has an ActiveSync partnership with the handheld. After you run the installer, you'll be asked whether you want to install the software using the default application installation directory. You should say no, and then select Storage Card from the Destination Media dialog. Click OK and installation will continue.

Palm

To install an application to the storage device, install it as you normally would—it will go to internal memory. Then, tap the Home button to go to the Launcher, tap the menu button, and choose Copy. When the Copy dialog appears, make sure Copy From: is set to "Handheld," and To: is set to your storage card. Select the application you want to copy, and tap Copy.

Once you are sure you can run the application from storage memory correctly, return to the Launcher, and delete the application from the handheld: tap the menu button, choose Delete, and the Delete dialog will appear. Make sure Delete From: is set to "Handheld," choose the application, and tap Delete. Once you've moved an application to the storage card, you'll need to select the storage card from the Launcher's categories menu (the upper right menu) to find the application.

To install ROMs to the storage card, your best bet is to use a card reader on your desktop computer and place the ROMs in the location specified in the following sections (but double-check the documentation for the emulator you are using, since things often change). Although the synchronization utilities (Palm Desktop, Microsoft ActiveSync, and Nokia PC Suite) provide file transfer utilities, a card reader is cheap, fast, and easy.

Atari 2600

There are a few emulators for the Atari 2600 that can be used to run ROMs of classic and homebrew games [Hack #34]. At the time of this writing, the only Atari 2600 emulator available for Palm and Nokia Series 60 devices is Mobile Wizardry's Atari Retro [Hack #16], which also supports Pocket PC (all on one cross-platform MMC card). Unfortunately, you cannot add your own ROMs to this emulator; it is limited to the seven games that it ships with.

Microsoft Smartphone. SmartVCS is a 2600 emulator for the Microsoft Smartphone. At the time of this writing, it could be found at the following locations:

> http://msmobiles.com/ catalog/i.php/345.html
> http://www.fox-ts.nildram.co.uk/SmartVCS/

Installing SmartVCS is as simple as copying the file using ActiveSync to your Smartphone along with any ROMs you intend to play. You'll need to configure ActiveSync as per the instructions that came with your phone.

To launch SmartVCS on your phone, use File Explorer (if your SmartPhone doesn't have this essential utility, check out SmartExplorer at *http://www.binarys.com/smartexplorer_en.asp*) to browse to the directory where you put *smartvcs.exe*, usually *Storage* or *StorageCard*, and execute it. You can then load any Atari 2600 ROMs in the same directory as *smartvcs.exe* by using the Open command under the File menu. Once a ROM is loaded and running, you can use the phone's directional pad as a joystick and the 4 key as the Fire button. Pressing 1 allows you to start/restart a game and pressing 2 stops emulation and returns you to the SmartVCS menu screen.

Microsoft Pocket PC. PocketVCS is a free Atari 2600 emulator with great performance. You can find more information at *http://pocketvcs.emuunlim.com/* and download it at *http://www.clickgamer.com/pocketpc.htm?category=emulators*.

Unlike SmartVCS, PocketVCS is distributed as an installer that puts PocketVCS in the right place, and even creates a Start Menu shortcut for you. To install it, run the installer on a PC that has a partnership with your Pocket PC, and let ActiveSync install PocketVCS on your Pocket PC. Figure 4-35 shows PocketVCS in action.

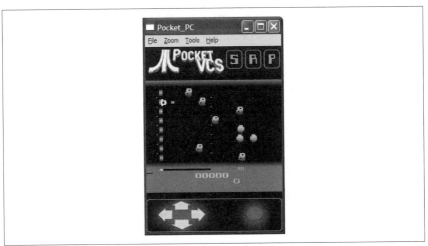

Figure 4-35. Oystron running on PocketVCS

Performance. Both SmartVCS and PocketVCS allow you to configure various settings to optimize the appearance and performance of Atari ROMs. In particular, disabling sound and increasing frame skipping can improve the execution speed of lagging ROMs. Skipping a high number of frames may cause some objects, such as the explosions in Missile Command, to not appear because they happen to only be displayed during the skipped frames. Note that setting the frame skip to 0 frames may cause some versions of SmartVCS to crash.

Game Boy

GNUBoy, as the name implies, is a Nintendo Game Boy emulator that was produced under the GNU General Public License and has been ported to multiple operating systems, including the Windows Compact Edition line of OSes used in PocketPCs and Smartphones.

Microsoft Smartphone and Pocket PC. The various permutations of GNUBoy can be hard to find at times, but the MS Smartphone version can, at the time of this writing, be found at *http://www.surrealservices.dsl.pipex.com/gnuboy. html*, and the Pocket PC version was available at *http://gnuboyce.cjb.net*. GNUBoy CE can load standard Game Boy (GB) and Game Boy Color (GBC) ROMs, but not Game Boy Advance (GBA) ROMs. Another option for Pocket PC users is the shareware MorphGear (*http://fms.komkon.org/ MorphGear/*), Aaron Oneal's framework for running emulators based on Marat Fayzullin's emulators.

These emulators are distributed as Windows-based installers that copy the applications onto your phone or Pocket PC. Instead of copying the downloaded file, *gnuboySetup.exe*, directly to your phone, you run the installer on your PC while your phone is connected via ActiveSync. Once installation is complete, you should be able to launch the emulator from the Start or Programs menu on your phone.

When you launch GNUBoy CE, it presents a list of ROMS that it finds in the same directory as *gnuboy.exe*. By default, the GNUBoy CE directory is either *Storage\Program Files\Games\gnuboy* or *Storage Card\Program Files\ Games\gnuboy*. MorphGear will load ROMS found in *My Documents*, a subdirectory of *My Documents*, or a subdirectory of your storage card.

On the Samsung i600, we found GNUBoy CE to be prone to frequent freezes. In particular, enabling sound and playing ROMs that allow you to save your game seem to cause the most problems. In the case of running savable games, GNUBoy CE seems to have trouble whenever it attempts to load or save a *state file* for the ROM. State files are used to record the state of an emulated game so it can be resumed from the same spot the next time the emulator is run—this is different from a *save file*, which lets you load a game that was saved using in-game menus. The first time a game loads, it is fine because its state file has yet to be created. Upon exiting, and on every subsequent load and exit, GnuBoy CE chokes on the state file. The way around this problem is to use File Explorer to go to the GNUBoy CE directory and delete the state file, usually named *ROM_name.000*. For example, if you were having trouble running *Final Fantasy Legend II.gb*, you would delete *Final Fantasy Legend II.000*. While this does destroy your state data, the in-game save that is recorded in *ROM_name.sav* works just fine, so you can start the game up, tell it to load your saved game, and pick up from there.

Palm. There are a few choices for Game Boy and Game Boy Color emulation on Palm-powered devices. Phoinix (*http://phoinix.sourceforge.net/*) is an open source Game Boy emulator. We found that Phoinix would not run ROMs off of the memory card unless we had installed at least one game in the Palm's internal memory. As with all other emulators, installing a ROM on a memory card is simply a matter of putting the file into the right place (in the case of Phoinix, it's *\Palm\Phoinix*). However, to install a ROM into internal memory, you need to convert it with the converter available at *http://phoinix.sourceforge.net/convert.html*.

Another choice for Palm users is the shareware GBulator (*http://www.kalemsoft.com/gbulator.html*), which emulates both the Game Boy and Game Boy Color. To install games to the memory card, place their ROMs in the *\Palm\Programs\GBulator directory*. Figure 4-36 shows a Game Boy remake of Activision's classic Atari 2600 Boxing game.

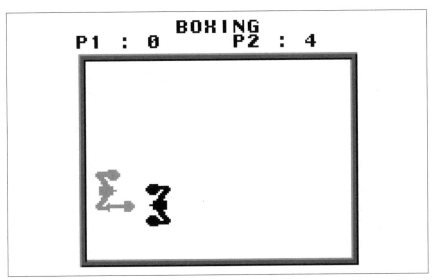

Figure 4-36. A classic Atari 2600 remake, Game Boy style

Symbian. GoBoy (*http://www.wildpalm.co.uk/GoBoy7650.html*) is a free Game Boy and Game Boy Color emulator for a number of Nokia phones. It has been ported to support UIQ devices (*http://stevesprojects.com/*), and a newer shareware version, Super GoBoy (*http://www.wildpalm.co.uk/SuperGoBoy.html*), is also available. GoBoy users can store their Game Boy and Game Boy Color ROMs in their storage card's *\GoBoy* directory.

Play NES Games

The Nintendo Entertainment System (NES) provides a home for some of the most fondly remembered titles in console gaming.

Microsoft Smartphone. SmartNES, or Smartphone NES, allows you to play your favorite NES titles anywhere using your Smartphone. SmartNES can be found, at the time of this writing, at the following sites:

> http://perso.wanadoo.fr/wawawoum/smartnes.exe
> http://msmobiles.com/catalog/i.php/347.html

Installing SmartNES is a simple process of unzipping the downloaded zip file on your PC and copying *smartnes.exe* to your phone using ActiveSync. When you run *smartnes.exe*, you will be able to load any NES ROMs that are located in the same directory on your phone as the executable via the File menu. While you are running a ROM, the Back button returns you to the SmartNES menu so you can adjust your options or load a new ROM.

In addition to the standard ROM loading and control configuration abilities, SmartNES also allows you to change the orientation at which a game is displayed on the screen. Using this feature, located under Options → Rotation, you can set either the vertical or the horizontal axis to be the longer axis. Most console games are designed for screens that are wider than they are tall, so it can be quite beneficial to rotate the image on the tall Smartphone screen 90 degrees. Setting SmartNES to 90 degree counter-clockwise rotation will give you a decent setup with your controls to the right of your screen. This configuration allows you to manipulate the directional keys with your left thumb and the other buttons with your right, like a standard controller. Note that you will have to redefine your keys to take advantage of this new orientation. That is, unless you prefer the extra challenge of moving down when you press right.

Pocket PC. There are a couple of good NES emulators for Pocket PC. At the time of this writing, PocketNester's site (*http://jetech.org/*) had been replaced with a directNIC "under construction" page, suggesting that the domain name has expired. However, there is still the lovable PocketNES (*http://pocketnes.retrogames.com/*), which is an excellent donationware NES emulator that plays well (although its sound was choppier than PocketNester's, which delivered smooth gameplay all around). You can install ROMs for both emulators in a subdirectory of your Storage Card. Fortunately, Zophar's Domain still had PocketNester available for download (*http://www.zophar.net/ppc/nes.html*) at the time of writing.

Palm. KalemSoft's shareware NesEm (*http://www.kalemsoft.com/nesem. html*) is a full-featured NES emulator. It ran a bit slowly on the admittedly older Palm Tungsten T that we tested it with, and we got best performance with sound off. NesEm supports multiplayer games over Bluetooth, and can run games right off of a storage card (put your ROMs in \NesEm).

Symbian. YewNes (*http://www.yewsoft.com/home.php*) is a shareware Series 60 NES emulator that can play a lot of games. Although the audio was a bit choppy on the Nokia 3650 we tried this on, the emulator ran quite well. Nokia N-Gage users and those with new model phones should get better performance. To install ROMs, put them in the \yewsoft\nesroms directory on your storage card.

Many Symbian users can also use vNES (*http://www.vampent.com/vnes.htm*), a shareware NES emulator that runs on a lot more phones than just Symbian-powered ones. If you have a fairly fast phone with support for Java midlets, give this one a try. vNES also comes in a Symbian-specific version, so visit the vNES site to figure out which version is best for you.

> Some combinations of programs and hardware can be rather picky about which simultaneous button presses they will accept. On the i600 we tested with, SmartNES seems unable to recognize any keys on the number pad being pressed when I'm pressing down on the directional pad, a definite handicap in shooters like Gradius. You may have to be flexible in trying to find the ideal key configuration for playing some games on your handheld.

Super Nintendo Entertainment System (SNES)

Once you get into SNES emulation on a handheld, you're starting to push the limits of current devices. To get acceptable performance, you're going to need something fairly fast. At the time of this writing, we couldn't find an SNES emulator for the Palm, but there are some out there for other devices.

Pocket PC and Microsoft Smartphone. PocketSNES is an open source Super Nintendo emulator based on the popular multi-platform SNES emulator, SNES9x. It provides surprisingly good performance and manages to keep many games running at a fairly playable pace. It's available both for the Pocket PC (*http://paqpark.nuclearfallout.net/projects/pocketsnes.php*) and the Smartphone (*http://www.surrealservices.dsl.pipex.com/pocketsnes.html*).

Unfortunately, in the Smartphone version, many features seem to be not yet or only partially implemented. In our testing, I was never able to enable sound or translucency effects. Although it lacks several features, the gameplay is quite decent. As with other emulators, it allows you to load ROMs that are in the same directory as the executable (the Pocket PC version lets you store ROMs in subdirectories off of your storage card as well as other locations). Like SmartNES, PocketSNES allows you to rotate the display in order to have a wider viewing area. In a welcome improvement over Smart-NES, PocketSNES automatically orients your directional keys with respect to the screen orientation, so pressing the key that is currently facing downward will actually move you down.

Symbian. vSun (*http://www.vampent.com/vsun.htm*) is a shareware SNES emulator for Nokia Series 60 phones. Although the Nokia 3650 we use for testing is listed as supported, we were unable to free sufficient memory to run this emulator.

Play Doom on an MS Smartphone

Whenever a new piece of hardware or operating system comes around, it's only a matter of time before someone attempts to port Doom (*http://www. itplaysdoom.com*) to it. MS Smartphone is no exception. While it's not necessarily a console game per se, Doom is a perennial classic and always worth having available right at your fingertips. There are two major versions of Doom available for MS Smartphone: DoomSPV and CellDoom. DoomSPV is the older application and provides a fairly decent Doom experience on most Smartphones, although its menu navigation leaves much to be desired. It has since been supplanted by the more feature-rich and stable CellDoom.

CellDoom can be found in several Smartphone software repositories, such as Smartphone.net. You can download it at *http://www.smartphone.net/ software_detail.asp?id=665*. You can then unzip the downloaded zip file, *CellDoom Installer.zip*, and run *Installer.exe* from your PC to install Cell-Doom on your phone.

Once CellDoom is installed, you can use it to load and play almost any Doom data file, called a *WAD*. CellDoom itself doesn't include any data files. You will need to copy the data file from a commercial release of Doom to the directory on your Smartphone where CellDoom is installed. You can also use custom WAD files or the WAD file (*doom1.wad*) from the shareware version of Doom, which is available at various locations on the Internet, such as *http://downloads.gamezone.com/demos/d36.htm*.

With CellDoom and various console emulators, you are ready to turn your handheld into a covert gaming rig. Now you never have to go anywhere without some sort of gaming readily available at all times.

—*Brian Jepson and Robert Ota Dieterich*

Play Homebrews on Your GBA

Use Flash Linkers to put Game Boy Advance ROMs onto your system.

So, let's say you've set up a Game Boy Advance emulator [Hack #44] and begun to delve into enjoying the fruits of the vibrant GBA homebrew scene. But playing these games on your PC monitor just isn't enough—isn't there some way to get them from there onto the GBA SP sitting on your desk? Yes, there is. And it's easier than you might think (albeit a little expensive).

What you need is commonly referred to as a *flash linker*. It's a small device that connects to your PC and lets you write Game Boy Advance-compatible ROMs to what is known as a *flash cart*—a blank, rewriteable cartridge that will work with your GBA. These come in many different sizes from 64 Mb all the way up to 1 GB. The average user tends to buy either a 256 Mb or 512 Mb cartridge. The average GBA game is much smaller than this, but you can write multiple games to a flash cart.

> Most vendors will report the size of flash carts in megabits (Mb). So a 128 Mb cart is actually 16 megabytes (MB).

One major advantage to playing GBA homebrews via a flash linker is that they will play perfectly. You won't have to worry about adjusting emulator settings, wondering if the homebrew you're playing is just badly programmed or if there's something wrong with your emulator. What you see is what you get on the real GBA hardware.

> Since the newly released Nintendo DS console has a GBA media port, the devices described next will all work in a Nintendo DS system. They cannot, however, be used to run Nintendo DS-specific homebrew content—only GBA programs. The flash devices will also work in the Game Boy Player attachment that connects to the Nintendo GameCube and plays GBA games on a television set.

Types of Flash Linkers and Carts

A few years ago, the most popular flash linker was called the Flash Advance Pro Linker, which was a bulky device that ran on six AA batteries and plugged into a computer's printer port. The software, FA Writer, was included on an unmarked 3.5 inch floppy disk. No manufacturer's name or information could be found on the box or manual. But the device worked flawlessly (if you didn't mind giving up your printer port to connect it, or the slow-as-molasses write speed).

Play Homebrews on Your GBA

Nowadays, the Flash Advance Pro Linker has been replaced by USB devices that are faster and smaller. Such devices include GBA X-ROM, EFA-Linker, and EZFlash Advance. They use a USB cable, which plugs into a mini-USB port on the flash cart itself, then attaches to an open USB port on your computer, eliminating the need for a large external writing device. 256 Mb and 512 Mb versions are available for around $80 and $130 each.

Other USB devices, like the EZ-Flash II, shown in Figure 4-37, do feature an external writer. Available sizes and prices are similar to the EFA-Linker. Another interesting alternative for GBA gameplay is the SuperCard, which uses standard CompactFlash memory media. Simply write the software to a CompactFlash card, insert it into the $60 SuperCard, and plug the entire apparatus into your GBA.

Figure 4-37. The EZ-Flash II flash writer and 128 megabit cart

You can write original Game Boy and Game Boy Color ROMs to a flash card, but they will not play on a Game Boy Advance unless you have a GB Bridge, which is a dongle that forces the GBA into classic Game Boy mode. More information on this device is available at *http://www.gameboy-advance. net/flash_card/gb_bridge.htm*. An alternate solution is to use a Game Boy emulator like Goomba [Hack #47].

Flash Linker Retailers

Web vendors who sell third-party Game Boy development products like flash linkers and carts tend to come and go like the wind. It's hard to tell whether a flashy looking web site is reliable or whether the owners will simply take your money and not deliver on their promises. Luckily, the diligent folks at the GBA development community *http://www.gbadev.org*, in addition to maintaining an archive of GBA homebrew projects, FAQs, and other information, have a section on their forum that features customer feedback on sites that sell flash equipment.

As of this writing, retailers with recent positive feedback on the forum include *http://www.flashlinker.net*, which sells both versions of the EFA-Linker; *http://www.jandaman.com*, which sells the EZFlash Advance and EZ-Flash II in many different sizes; and *http://www.kicker.ca*, a Canada-based site that sells the EFA-Linker and SuperCard. European homebrewers may wish to check out *http://www.totalgba.com*, which is based in the UK and sells both sizes of the EFA-Linker to all customers domestic and international.

Writing Games to your GBA

Each type of linker hardware will ship with its own software. Since much of it is developed outside of the US, the English menus will generally not be especially user-friendly. Again, the forums at *http://www.gbadev.org* will be of help should you run into any issues. Most writers will flash multiple ROMs to a cartridge at once, and automatically include a small menu program so you can switch between them when you boot up your GBA.

If for some reason you are unsatisfied with the software that shipped with your flash writer, there is a program called LittleWriter (*http://www. gameboy-advance.net/fal_soft/flash_advance_little_writer.htm*), shown in Figure 4-38, that supports many popular flash devices. Advantages to using this program include being able to delete individual ROMs without formatting the entire flash cart as well as automatic backup and rewriting of saved game data.

One common problem with flash carts is that they can become "locked" and any attempts to write software on them will fail in mid-burn. If you think this has happened to you, one solution may be to insert the cartridge into your GBA and turn it on, leaving it on for a few minutes. If this does not work, LittleWriter has a function that will attempt to repair your card—one more reason to use it.

Another possible sticking point is that, while the game ROM data that you write to your flash carts should theoretically stay there until you delete or overwrite it, sometimes your saved game progress files will erase over time. The saved game data is typically written into volatile memory that only persists while the built-in battery backup maintains a full charge. If you're planning on playing a game long-term, be sure to back up your *.sav* files from your flash cart to your hard drive.

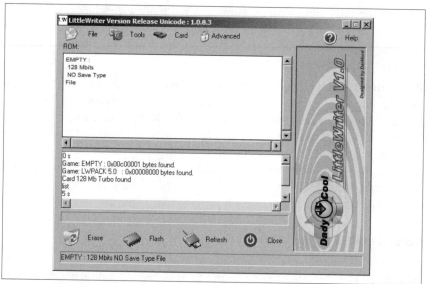

Figure 4-38. LittleWriter

Play Classic Systems on the GBA

HACK #47

Embark on retro adventures using your Game Boy Advance.

Considering that it shipped in early 2001 for under a hundred bucks, the Game Boy Advance is a pretty powerful piece of hardware. It's so powerful in fact, that you can actually use it to emulate other classic gaming consoles. And indeed, many such emulators are available online.

"But wait," you interrupt. "Why would I want to run an emulator within an emulator?" You're right: the only reason you'd want to emulate a system within another emulator is for the pure hacker spirit of seeing if it can be done. And I'm sure there are quite a few people reading this right now to whom that sounds perfectly reasonable. But there is a goal here for even the casual hacker—by using rewriteable flash cartridges [Hack #46], you can run the emulators and ROMs on your actual Game Boy Advance, Nintendo DS, or even a Nintendo GameCube equipped with a Game Boy Player attachment.

By far one of the most appealing uses of GBA emulation is to run games on the go that used to be tethered to a home system. And though you might instantly think of the Nintendo Entertainment System, there are also a wealth of other emulators for the GBA that are currently being developed. Most of these can be found at Zophar's Domain, on the page *http://www. zophar.net/consoles/gameboy.html.*

PocketNES

By far the most popular GBA emulator is PocketNES, which allows you to run classic NES games on the portable. As is the case with the rest of the emulators described in this section, the executable files that you download with PocketNES will run a Windows program that lets you create a GBA ROM from a selection of NES ROMs. A built-in menu will be included in the ROM file that the program generates. So you will only have to copy one file to your GBA flash card.

After you have unzipped the PocketNES files to a directory, you'll have to copy the NES ROMs you want to use into that same directory. Then when you run the main PocketNES executable, it will automatically generate a list of the ROMs it finds. To add ROMs to this list you will have to copy them into the PocketNES directory, then click Refresh (see Figure 4-39).

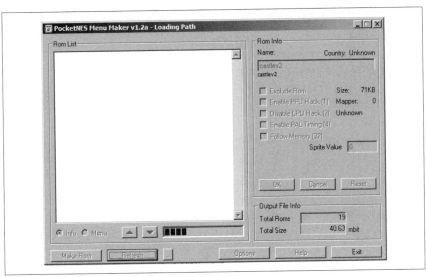

Figure 4-39. The PocketNES Menu Maker window

PocketNES allows you to individually determine how each game shows up in the menu when you play the ROM; click the Menu radio button in the lower left-hand corner of the window to edit the names. If during this process you decide that you don't want certain ROMs to be included, you can click the Exclude ROM checkbox. Note that the program keeps track, in the lower right-hand corner, of the size of the output ROM that you will create.

When you are done editing names, click the Make ROM button to generate a ROM (a *.gba* file) that can be loaded in a GBA emulator or on a flash cart in a real GBA. Note that an internal menu inside PocketNES can be used to fiddle with the video settings—you can squash the display or display it at full size (but you'll only be able to see part of the screen at once).

SNESAdvance

As the name so aptly implies, SNESAdvance will allow you to play Super Nintendo Entertainment System games on your GBA. The emulator currently has limited compatibility—at the time of this writing, only about 50 games will work. A complete compatibility listing, as well as all the files and documentation you will need to run the program, are located at the project's official home page: *http://www.snesadvance.org*.

After you install and run SNESAdvance, you'll see the screen shown in Figure 4-40.

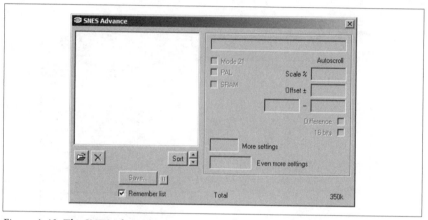

Figure 4-40. The SNESAdvance main window

Click the Open icon (the folder with an arrow above it) to select the ROMs you'd like to use. When the ROMs are loaded you will be able to select each one in the left side of the window, then alter settings for them individually. The Scale and Offset values, for example, will alter how the game's graphic display shows up on the Game Boy Advance screen. Other settings will be set automatically by the program for each specific game. Consult the documents included with the program for more information.

Once you are satisfied with your list, click the Save button and SNESAdvance will create a file, default name *SNESAdvance.gba*, that can be loaded in a GBA emulator. When you boot the file, a built-in menu will allow you to select the game. Now for the downsides: most of the introductory cinematics are messed up, there's no sound emulation, and the speed of the gameplay—although workable—is still slow.

That's what you get for playing with the leading edge of hacker tech, kids.

DrSMS

Bored with hot Nintendo-on-Nintendo action? Then try some games that nobody *ever* figured they'd see on a Game Boy system. DrSMS lets you play Sega Master System ROMs on your GBA. The downloadable archive at Zophar's Domain is simple enough, since it only contains two files: the readme file and the executable program. Run the program and you'll see the screen shown in Figure 4-41.

Figure 4-41. The DRSMS main window

Note that you can drag-and-drop ROM files into the top window or click the Add button to browse your hard drive. The bottom part of the window will constantly keep you apprised of how large your ROM file is growing; this is important if you want to preserve the space on your flash cart.

Once your window is filled with games, you'll have to type a name for the ROM you will create. Be sure to manually type in the *.gba* extension so you can keep track of it later. Then click Create GBA Rom and within seconds your ROM will be created in the directory you placed the DrSMS executable.

While playing a game (which will probably run with excellent speed and perfect sound), you can press Select to access the menu, which will let you select a new game or fuss with the settings to your heart's content.

Goomba

Named after the first enemy that shows up in Super Mario Bros., Goomba (*http://www.webpersona.com/goomba/*) is a Game Boy emulator for the Game Boy Advance. This might sound completely useless, as the Game Boy Advance already plays regular Game Boy and Game Boy Color games. But in fact, it comes in handy for two major reasons. First, it lets you run homebrew GB ROMs without using that obscure dongle known as the GB Bridge [Hack #46]. Second, and perhaps most important, it lets you play classic Game Boy games on the new Nintendo DS system, which features a GBA media port but does not include support for classic Game Boy and Game Boy Color software.

If you can use the emulators listed earlier in this hack, you'll be able to figure out Goomba.

GBAGI

The final emulator I will discuss in this section is perhaps the most interesting, and definitely my personal favorite. Brian Provinciano, the creator of the NES homebrew Grand Theftendo [Hack #84], has created an emulator that runs many of Sierra's classic PC adventure games on the GBA. The new version 2.0 allows for full text input via a virtual keyboard (the original release only allowed you to select from an automatically generated list of terms).

The project's official web page, *http://www.bripro.com/gbagi/index.php*, has the program, called GBAGI (AGI is short for Adventure Game Interpreter, the common software that Sierra used to create and distribute its games from King's Quest on), as well as extensive documentation. Source code and demo ROMs can also be downloaded from this page.

What's great about GBAGI is that if you still have your old Sierra games in the closet (or find them on eBay) you can copy the files off the original disks and use them with the emulator. You can even create your own AGI games, or edit Sierra's to your own tastes, by using a separate program called AGI Studio, available at *http://agidev.com/download/*.

GBAGI supports the following titles:

> King's Quest
> King's Quest II
> King's Quest III
> King's Quest IV
> Leisure Suit Larry
> Manhunter: New York
> Manhunter 2: San Francisco

Police Quest
Space Quest
Space Quest 2
Gold Rush!
Mixed Up Mother Goose
Disney's The Black Cauldron
Donald Duck's Playground

Donald Duck's Playground can be downloaded, for free, at designer (and Retro Gaming Hacks foreword author) Al Lowe's web site (*http://www.allowe.com/More/download. htm*). I'm sure that's not the first game you thought to play with GBAGI, but them's the breaks.

Emulate Other Classic Portables

HACK #48

Rediscover the Lynx, Game Gear, and Neo Geo Pocket Color.

Classic portables are an interesting footnote in gaming history. Not only do they let you play some of the best console games of the era in condensed form (sometimes with added levels), they offer up plenty of unique software that made them worth owning. Emulating these systems is relatively painless, requiring very little computing power and even less set up. Even better, public domain ROMs, including both games and tech demos, are available from websites like *http://www.pdroms.de*. At the time of this writing, 12 homebrew ROMs are available for the Lynx, 7 for the Game Gear, and 48 for the Neo Geo Pocket.

Atari Lynx

Originally called the Handy, the Lynx was actually created by two Amiga designers, Dave Needle and R.J. Mical. It was 1987 when the first prototype was floating around at Epyx, but it wasn't until the 1990s that Atari, looking to capitalize on the portable market created by Game Boy, bought the system and released it.

The Lynx was ahead of its time, containing far more power under the hood than not only the competition, but some of the home consoles too. It even let players use the console horizontally as well as vertically. Its rather high price (just under $200) and low battery life doomed it to failure even with the ability to link up (or "Lynx up," according to the marketing material) with up to eight players. That doesn't mean quality software isn't to be found, and the appropriately named Handy is a great emulator to run pretty much everything. It's also the only one available for PC or Mac.

Getting Handy for Windows/Mac OS. You can download Handy from the official site at *http://homepage.ntlworld.com/dystopia/*. The latest version is 0.90, and it was released back in 2002. Once you download the file, you also need to find a file called *lynxboot.img*. (Try doing a Google search for the filename.) Note that you cannot run any games without it, since it is a copy of the system BIOS. By not offering this BIOS for download, the developers of Handy avoid coming under legal fire. This BIOS image file is protected by copyright.

Once you've found it, you need to place it into the same folder you have the *Handy.exe* executable. It will automatically recognize the file the next time you start the emulator. If the system BIOS file is zipped, you'll need to extract it or it will not work. However, you should not unzip any game ROM files that you download, since they must be in zipped format for the latest Handy to recognize them. Run the file *Handy.exe* to start playing, and it will automatically bring up a menu allowing you to select a ROM file. Click on one of the zipped files to start your game (see Figure 4-42).

Figure 4-42. Handy running a homebrew Lynx paddle game

Handy fully supports joysticks and should have no trouble recognizing them if your operating system supports the joystick you're using. There are a few interesting options available to the Handy user, unique to it because of the Lynx console. First is of course the ability to mimic the console being flipped vertically. Simply click on Options to access a drop down menu and select "rotate screen" in the direction you need it to go.

The Lynx has some very pixilated graphics and Handy has a somewhat reasonable solution. You can play a game in Eagle mode, which smoothes out the graphics but also requires a bit more PC power. You can also simulate the real Lynx screen by selecting interlace mode. It's actually pretty accurate, but without the occasionally annoying blur that you got with the real thing. If you like backgrounds, the latest revision even allows you to play the console "inside" the real console. Just choose Select Background Type and pick from Lynx, Lynx II (the smaller, slimmer model released late into the console's life), or the basic screen border.

Handy for Mac OS. There's very little difference between the Mac and PC versions of Handy. They offer the same functionality and ROM selection. You need the same *lynxboot.img* to get started. Loading a ROM is exactly the same as well. The Mac version does require a little more horsepower than the PC version, and there are some speed problems with certain games that have never been fixed (this version has not been updated since 2001). In this case, the PC version is probably the better choice.

Sega's Game Gear

Sega released their portable in 1991 to counter Nintendo's Game Boy. Not only did Sega's console have a color screen, it could play all the games from the company's home system, the Sega Master System, via an adapter called the Master Gear Converter. It also let gamers turn it into a portable TV with a TV Tuner.

Unfortunately, even with a string of innovative TV advertisements, the system was doomed against the mega-popular Game Boy. A company called Majesco (now specializing in high-quality software for home consoles as well as all-in-one retro game joysticks [Hack #15]) actually picked up the rights to the portable around 1995 and re-released it at a bargain price with a few pieces of software.

Multiple choices for emulation. Unlike the Lynx, there are many options for Game Gear emulation. The vast majority emulate both the Master System and Game Gear, since the consoles are so similar. The two best are BrSMS (*http://snespad.emulationworld.com/sms.html*) and the excellent Meka (*http://www.smspower.org/meka/*). BrSMS is great for those with slow machines, as it requires little power to get going. However, Meka (MekaW in Windows) seemingly supports everything, is easy to use with a sharp GUI, and even supports Colecovision ROMs as an added bonus. Thus, we'll focus on MekaW.

Starting with MekaW. To get the most out of everything, MekaW is the way to go. It's so much easier to use thanks to the GUI. There should be some documentation included, like the *compat.txt* file, which provides complete documentation on what games will work and which games have problems. That will save you time from downloading ROMs that don't work.

MekaW will recognize both unzipped and zipped ROMs. Upon double-clicking the icon, MekaW brings up a rather self-explanatory menu screen, shown in Figure 4-43. (For a little fun before you even start playing, click "Mario is not a fat plumber" in the main drop-down menu under Options.) This is the same menu that you'll be loading ROMs from. Once you have selected to load the game, another menu should appear on your right to let you select your games. Once loaded, the game will begin playing in the small screen on the lower left.

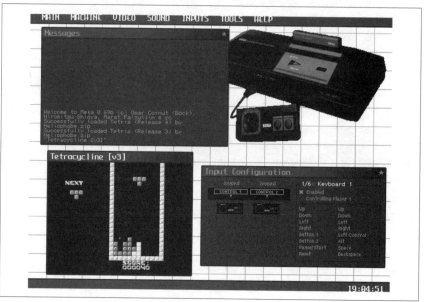

Figure 4-43. MekaW's slick main menu screen

If it's too small for you, head up to the Video toolbar and select "full screen." Other options here let you play the game interlaced (under Blitters), in a window so you can minimize the emulator if necessary, and, rather strangely, eliminate the sprites or backgrounds from the game you're playing by using the "layer" option. The toolbar option Machine contains mostly things that should switch automatically, such as NTSC and PAL controls. If you want to do it manually, that option exists for you.

Sound offers the ability to actually capture audio with the "dump" option. Simply click start and stop to capture the audio. The file will appear in the same folder as your ROMs. Inputs is not something you'll need to deal with when using this emulator for Game Gear games except for the rapid-fire option. The rest exists to mimic Master System accessories like the awkward Sports Pad.

SMS Plus for Mac. The Mac user will need to download SMS Plus at *http://www.bannister.org/software/sms.htm*. If your OS is a little older, you'll probably want to try MasterGear, which can be found at *http://www.zophar.net*. SMS Plus is the more updated of the two and falls more in line with other

Mac emulators. To get the most out of it, you need to download the Emulator Enhancer from here: *http://www.bannister.org/software/ee.htm*. It offers features like fullscreen gameplay, USB support, etc. This is a shareware piece, so there will be pop-up windows encouraging you to purchase the full software. However, the current version lets you continue using it as long as you want with no penalty. Once downloaded, it works for any supported emulators, something that makes emulation on the Mac quite easy.

To get Emulation Enhancer working, you need it in your home directory, under *Library/Application Support*. That's where the main file needs to be for the emulator to recognize it. Stick it anywhere else, and you'll be out of luck. Once it's installed, you can head into the Options menu when the emulator is loaded and see that a plethora of new options are now accessible.

SNK's Neo Geo Pocket

SNK is probably best known for their Neo Geo home console, which cost upwards of $600 when it was first released and played perfect versions of the company's popular arcade games. Nowhere near as popular, but appreciated by its fans, is the Neo Geo Pocket (NGP) portable console. The NGP, plus a Color version that was released later, got scaled-down translations of many popular Neo Geo fighting games. Very few American retailers carried it, and it died soon after the release of the Game Boy Advance.

Little choice for emulation. Many of the NGP emulators do not feature sound. NGPocket (*http://www.zophar.net/ngpocket.html*) is a decent emulator, but requires a registration fee of $5 to get sound and joystick support. But there's little reason to pay for that when NeoPop is free. You can find the latest version at their web site, *http://www.emuxhaven.net/~neopop/*. It has full support for sound, joysticks, and debugging if you wish. It does run a little slow on older hardware, so you might want to have at least a Pentium 3 to run at full speed.

Getting NeoPop running. As usual, you'll need to download and unzip the file. It should create its own ROM folder, which, of course, is where the ROMs should go. If you want them someplace else, you can open the emulator, go into the Options menu, and click on Paths. You can also select where you want save states and battery saves to go (some games have internal batteries to save progress; that's what will go into this folder automatically if you save in-game).

Loading a game is easy, much like everything else associated with this emulator. Either hit F1 or select Game from the toolbar. That should bring up a window directly to your ROMs folder. Select the game you want (zipped or unzipped, your choice) and it should start without a problem (see Figure 4-44). The *Readme.txt* file that was extracted when you unzipped the package should contain any information on games that don't work.

Figure 4-44. NeoPop running the homebrew game Invader

Probably the best feature of this emulator is the ability to link up with other players. It's fairly simple to do. Simply type your IP address (if you plan on hosting the game) into the appropriately labeled box after selecting Link-Up from the drop-down menu and then put your friend's into Remote IP (see Figure 4-45). Your friend should click Listen In to make sure the connection is there (and to make sure you've typed the addresses correctly). If it is, load up your 2-player compatible ROM and you're set!

Mac Users and NeoPocott. Mac users have only one choice here: NeoPocott 0.4.6 (*http://www.bannister.org/software/neopocott.htm*) for Mac OS 10.2+. It runs exactly like the Game Gear emulator mentioned above. Note that NeoPocott, unlike many emulators, does not feature support for zipped ROMs, so be sure to click Open when you download the file, then extract the ROM to the NeoPocott directory. Also, there is no Internet play as featured in NeoPop. If you have older hardware, you might want to check out an older version of the emulator, which will run a little faster. It is available at *http://www.arcadeathome.com/ngpc.phtml*.

—*Matt Paprocki*

Figure 4-45. NeoPop lets you link up via the magic of the Internet to play NeoGeo Pocket games versus a buddy

HACK #49 Retro-Hack the GP32

Use the Korean handheld marvel to play retro games and other bizarre amusements.

In the early years of the 21st century, a Korean company decided to try something a little different in the handheld arena. As gamers went about their business, they were scrutinized and studied, as Gamepark slowly and surely drew its plans against us. The fruit of Gamepark's loins? The GP32 handheld, a 320×240 pixel monster with a 32-bit ARM9 RISC CPU, 8-MB SDRAM, and up to 128MB of storage memory on a normal SMC smart media memory card, with data transferred from any PC using USB.

The advantages of such an open system for the GP32 are obvious in terms of homebrew content, and *Gaming Hacks*, the previous book in the hacks series that dealt with, well, gaming hacks, has a hack devoted to cool things you can do with the GP32, from running alternate operating systems to notable emulators—even overclocking it. But honestly, that book's hack just scraped the surface, especially in the retro arena—the fact is that there's much more you can do with your GP32, especially with the plethora of new software coming out for it.

So, here are some pleasant, advanced, retro-related starting points for the Korean handheld, which definitely doesn't have the firepower of new handhelds such as Sony's PSP, but has an adorably free attitude to software (you can download and run any executable you like), meaning that it will continue to be adopted for some time to come by the cult-loving, niche, and plain crazy among us.

MAME for GP32

In particular, much progress has been made in recent months on MAME for GP32. Previously thought to be a near-impossible project, perhaps due to the relative size of the MAME code-base, there are now playable versions of MAME in existence. The GP32 port author, Franxis has the latest information on this on his web page (*http://www.talfi.net/gp32_franxis/*). As of press time, the new executables were withheld until the source code could be published, but are likely to have debuted by the time you read this.

Obviously, this doesn't mean that Metal Slug or Primal Rage (both emulated in MAME) will work in this new version of GP32 MAME. In fact, due to the relatively lethargic GP32 processor (though it's a lot heartier than many other previous-gen handhelds!), those games will likely never work. But earlier custom-hardware games such as Pac-Man definitely behave well on GP32, especially if you rotate the screen ninety degrees to maximize the available height for the game's display.

In fact, talking of the little yellow dot-gobbling fellow, Franxis has also converted Pac-Man emulator MultiPac to GP32. Originally created by MAME founder Nicola Salmoria as a predecessor to the multi-arcade emulator, it's a history lesson and a good low-end example of MAME stylings. Also downloadable via Franxis' page, (*http://www.talfi.net/gp32_franxis/*), MultiPac GP32 will help you emulate other games on the same hardware, including Ms. Pac-Man, Crush Roller, and the multitude of Pac-clones.

Beats of Rage GP32

Although you may find it mentioned elsewhere, since Beats of Rage appears on multiple platforms, this strange retro-styled 2D scrolling beat-em-up takes, in its original form, much gameplay inspiration from Sega's classic Streets of Rage series, plus many sprites from SNK's even more cultish King of Fighters series.

So, at a base level, that's exactly what you get—a GP32 version that looks borderline stunning, and runs at an eminently sensible speed on the GP32, available from the official Beats of Rage page (*http://www.segaforums.com/senileteam/bor_game.php*). But the whole fun of Beats of Rage is the inordinate ease in which you can mod it to make your own version of the game— just swap the *BOR.PAK* file with the custom *.PAK* file made by the modder, and you're ready to go.

There are some particularly cool Beats of Rage mods which run great on the GP32, and I'd like to highlight the following particularly smart ones:

Kill Bill (http://jypy32.free.fr/GP32News/Games/GP32_BOR_KillBill.rar)
> A stunning, if extremely short version of Kill Bill Vol.1, with The Bride as your main player character, and any number of the Crazy 88s to fight, all the way up to O-Ren Ishii. Beautifully drawn sprites and a keen sense of carnage make this an extremely fun mod, at least for the limited amount of time it lasts.

Golden Axe: Curse Of Death-Adder (http://jypy32.free.fr/GP32News/Games/goldenaxe.zip)
> Obviously, this is use of the same engine to approximate the classic Sega sideways-scroller Golden Axe, and although it's currently billed as the Final Demo version, it's clear that creator FunkMeister Smith has done a great job of making things look authentic.

Naruto (http://www.gp32x.de/cgi-bin/cfiles.cgi?0,0,0,0,11,213)
> Based on the anime, and again decidedly unofficial, this mod is notable for the sheer insane amount of enemies it throws at you. Yes, it's likely excessive when there are literally tens of sprites on-screen, but you have to appreciate the insanity of author HungryMan.

If you're looking for more along the same lines, the excellent GP32x site has an entire file section (*http://www.gp32x.de/cgi-bin/cfiles.cgi?0,0,0,0,11*) filled with GP32-specific Beats of Rage mods, so go crazy, and see what you can dig out.

Go Super-Retro with GP81

Some people seem to think that they're quite retro enough when they, say, grab a Genesis emulator. Not acceptable. Emulator authors often have a way of gravitating to the more obscure; the appearance of GP81, a Sinclair ZX 81 emulator for the GP32 by Woogal (*http://gp32.sector808.org/gp81.php*), is a prime example of that rule.

The ZX 81, which debuted back in 1981, was a machine created by the legendary Sir Clive Sinclair, also maker of the later ZX Spectrum computer and the infamous flop that was the Sinclair C5 electric car. It has just 8k of ROM, and its infamous rubber keys on the full keyboard were a bane to many, but a good touchpoint for many relentless nostalgists. It was sold (in a slightly reconfigured versions) as the Timex Sinclair 1000 in the United States, for those wondering why they definitely haven't heard of it.

Largely big in Europe, the Z81 emulator has nonetheless been ported to GP32, and its extremely rudimentary games are an intriguing throwback to the very early days of home computers. Matt Barber's ZX 81 game charts (*http://www.honneamise.u-net.com/zx81/zx81cht.txt*) give you a good idea of the kind of titles to look for if you want to try the top ZX 81 games at the time.

Mazogs, a large sprited maze title, was a highlight for many. And the extremely influential 3D Monster Maze, which many claim is the first 3D game on a home computer, is another top tip—surprisingly suspense-filled, as you try to sneak through the maze without being eaten by the tyrannosaurus rex.

Incidentally, Woogal has created a number of other neat applications for GP32, including Lazy Reader (*http://gp32.sector808.org/lazyreader.php*), an auto-scrolling text viewing app, plus the surreal but excellent homebrew game Lacuna (*http://gp32.sector808.org/lacuna.php*), and the still in development YAFL (*http://gp32.sector808.org/yafl.php*). YAFL, of course, stands for Yet Another File Loader.

—Simon Carless

HACK #50 Retro-Hack the Dreamcast

Use your Dreamcast to relive your childhood or play homebrewed games.

Can it be a coincidence that the current explosion of emulator popularity didn't take off until a few years after the Sega Dreamcast hit the market? Sure, you could run Nintendo games on your PC for a long time, but there was something even more appealing about playing old-school console games on an actual gaming console. Though the Xbox is the modern console gamer's choice for emulation [Hack #23], the first console to be blown open by hackers was the venerable (though not especially impregnable) Sega Dreamcast.

A Brief History of DC Hacking

So, why did emulation take off along with the Dreamcast? It was all a matter of timing. There were a few emulators for consoles prior to the Dreamcast, but they usually required special equipment and were thus only popular among a few hackers. With the release of the Dreamcast, hobbyists were handed a game console that was not only incredibly powerful, but was also produced with off-the-shelf parts that were well-documented. All that was needed was a way to test the game code on an actual system.

By default, the Dreamcast would only boot software that was recorded on Sega's custom GD-ROM discs. Since Sega was the only source of those discs, booting homebrew software was a pipe dream until a creative coder discovered a back door. In 1999, an enhanced audio CD format was released in Japan called MilCD. These CDs included extra features, like photo and video files, that would be available if you inserted the CD into a computer.

It was soon discovered that the Dreamcast would attempt to boot the extra features on MilCDs. Creative hackers soon began writing CDs in the MilCD format that booted on unmodified retail Dreamcasts, replacing the MilCD data with Dreamcast code. Since these CDs could be burned to standard CD-R media, this blew the doors open for the first major homebrew scene.

Creating a Bootable Dreamcast CD

Creating your own Dreamcast CD from scratch is a rather involved process, requiring a fairly in-depth knowledge of how audio and data tracks are laid out on a disc. For most common software though, there is no need to go through the hassle of creating a custom CD image, as the major Dreamcast sites have already done the work for you. In most cases, using an emulator is as simple as downloading a single CD image file and burning it to a disc. What could be simpler?

Due to the esoteric format required for Dreamcast CDs, most of the software images on the Net are images designed for the CD duplication software DiscJuggler. They use the extension *.cdi*. The best software for the task, at least when running Windows, is a tool called Alcohol 120% (*http://www.alcohol-soft.com*). A thirty-day free trial is available for download from the site; the full version costs about $55.

When it comes to homebrew Dreamcast software, the selection is quite widespread. In fact, the hardest part can be deciding what to choose first! In the next section, I'll cover the NES emulator NesterDC and the homebrew fighting game Beats of Rage, but you can find much more software by exploring the following web sites:

- *http://www.dcemulation.com*
- *http://www.dcemu.co.uk*
- *http://www.dcevolution.net*
- *http://www.consolevision.com/dreamcast*
- *http://cagames.com*

Going Old School with NesterDC

Of all the homebrew Dreamcast software, one of the most robust programs available is NesterDC, a full-featured Nintendo emulator. Capable of running nearly every game for the classic 8-bit powerhouse, NesterDC is a true blast from the past. Here's what you'll need to do to download, burn, and run it.

Creating the NesterDC disc. Here's how to burn the CD:

1. You can download NesterDC from *http://www.dcemulation.com/dcemu-nesterdc.htm*. Choose the Disk Juggler version.

2. Once you have the file on your system you will need to extract *NesterDC7.1DJ.cdi* from the Zip file. (The actual file name may vary depending on the version of NesterDC.)

3. Start Alcohol 120% and click on Image Burning Wizard.

4. Click on Browse and navigate to the image file. Click Open and you will see the screen in Figure 4-46.

5. Click Next.

6. On the following screen, leave the settings at their default values and click Start.

7. Insert a disc and wait for the burn to finish. Because the image is very small (around 5 MB in size) it should only take a few minutes.

8. Test the disc in your Dreamcast. Simply place it in the system and turn it on. If everything worked correctly, you should see the title screen in Figure 4-47.

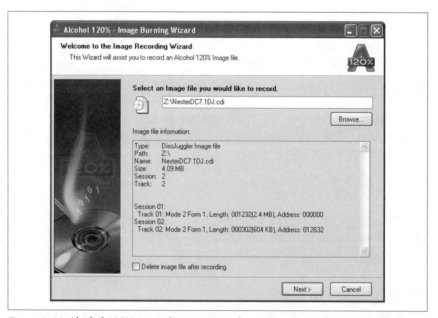

Figure 4-46. Alcohol 120% image burning wizard

Loading ROM files. You've created a functional emulator disc, but now you need the software to play on it. If you already have a Nintendo emulator for your PC [Hack #38], you can use the same ROM files. Preparing them to run

Figure 4-47. NesterDC

with NesterDC is easy; you need only burn them to a second CD-R. NesterDC has a built-in file manager that you can use to navigate a standard CD
and choose from any ROM file available on the disc.

1. Boot the NesterDC disc.

2. Once the program has loaded the main menu, you can eject the NesterDC disc and insert your CD-R containing the ROM files.

3. Press the A button to bring up the file manager.

4. Press the Y button to reach the root directory on the CD. You will see
   /cd at the top of the screen if you are in the right place.

5. Now, use the D-pad to navigate up and down and use the A button to
   choose a directory.

6. Once you have found a ROM file you wish to play, highlight it and then
   press the Start button on the Dreamcast controller.

7. After a brief pause, the game will load and you will be playing just as
   though the Dreamcast were a Nintendo. Use the D-pad for control, the
   X and A buttons for A and B and the Y button for Select.

8. When you are finished playing you can press the L, R, and Start buttons simultaneously to return to the NesterDC main menu.

If you really crave old-school style, you may want to use the classic rectangular Nintendo controllers on your Dreamcast. It takes some soldering, but it can be done! See *http://devcast. dcemulation.com/mods/madnes/nes2.php* for a fully illustrated tutorial.

Although NesterDC is a great place to start, there are many more emulators. Everything from Super Nintendo to Genesis to Neo-Geo Pocket to MAME can be downloaded and used on your Dreamcast. Check out *http:// www.dcemulation.com* for more.

Beats of Rage

Created as an homage to the Sega classic Streets of Rage, Beats of Rage is an entirely user-created game with a well-documented (and freely modifiable) side scrolling beat-em-up engine. Produced by a group known as Senile Team, Beats of Rage was the first major Dreamcast homebrew title.

You can download the full version of Beats of Rage at *http://senileteam. segaforums.com*, which also contains information on the many available modifications. In addition, there are PC and PlayStation 2 versions of the game available (although you can't play the latter without a mod chip). There's even a portable version for the GP32 handheld [Hack #49].

—*Adam Pavlacka*

H A C K
#51
Use Console Controllers on your PC
Convert practically any video game controller into a USB joystick.

So you're running some classic games on your PC, but the feel just isn't right. You're not getting the same vibe as you do playing the real thing. Maybe what you need is your old controller.

Thanks to those tireless hardware manufacturers in Hong Kong, it should be possible to use a controller from nearly any console system as a PC joystick or gamepad. For most controllers, you will need an additional piece of hardware: an adapter that lets you plug your controller into your PC's USB port. The Xbox controller, however, is already a USB device, so we can apply the hacker spirit to connecting it to a PC by making our own physical adapter!

For Windows users, this hack should proceed in a fairly plug-and-play fashion (once you have purchased or created the proper adapter so that you *can* plug, that is). Linux users will want to read "Use USB Gamepads Under Linux" [Hack #52].

Since the Xbox controller can be made into an interesting project for the handy (or not so handy, in my case!) with a soldering iron, let's tackle it first!

Xbox Controllers

As stated above, Xbox controllers are USB devices, so you will not need any fancy silicon to convert the electronics to USB. You will, however, need a physical adapter, as Microsoft made sure (for purely technical reasons not related to marketing lock-in, one presumes) that the physical plug for the controllers is not a standard USB one. Such an adapter can be procured from the usual sources like the online retailer Lik-Sang (*http://www.lik-sang.com*), but the strong of heart may have more fun rolling their own. If you decide to purchase an adapter, just plug the controller into it, plug the adapter into your USB port, and away you go! (Linux users will need to build the driver first—read on to find out how.)

Making an Xbox-to-USB physical adapter. Making a physical adapter is very much in the do-it-yourself hacker tradition, and is pretty easy, too. So grab the following items, shown in Figure 4-48, clear a work-space, and let's get started!

- Xbox breakaway cable. You can either buy one of these (any decent video game store should carry them, or try your local Blockbuster), or maybe you have a broken Xbox controller sitting around that you could cannibalize.
- USB "AB" cable. You actually only need the end that plugs into the PC's USB port, so you can probably use non-working cable. If you cannot find a cable in your pieces and parts bin, or at the local computer store's bargain bin, *http://www.newegg.com* has new AB cables for as little as $4.00.
- Wire stripper
- Electrical tape
- Soldering iron (recommended, but not strictly necessary)
- Coffee? (actually *not* recommended, for reasons that will be made clear in due time)

Assemble these materials on a clean, dry surface with plenty of elbow room.

The first step is to cut the end off of your breakaway cable. You can cut it just above or below the hard plastic bit in the middle. I cut mine above, leaving enough cord on the end that plugs into the Xbox so that I can use the end for some other project (see Figure 4-49).

Figure 4-48. The materials you'll need

Figure 4-49. The Xbox breakaway cable, cut

Now, cut the USB cable in a similar fashion as shown in Figure 4-50. Remember, you will be joining the end that plugs into the PC to your Xbox breakaway cable, so be sure to leave yourself plenty of cable so that you will be OK even if you make a mistake or two with the wire strippers.

Figure 4-50. The USB cable, about to be cut

The next step is to strip away about three centimeters (an inch or so) of the outer insulation on both the USB connector wire and the Xbox breakaway wire. The outer insulation is fairly thick, but you still need to be careful when stripping it that you do not cut any of the internal insulation on the individual wires. I found that the best technique was to use the largest gauge on my wire stripper, close it just enough to bite into the insulation, and then rotate the strippers around the wire, slowly increasing the pressure. Then the insulation can be removed with a pair of pliers. This will reveal a braided mesh of wire, which needs to be peeled back. The next layer of the onion, as it were, is some aluminum shielding. This can be peeled away with your fingers or a knife. Just discard the shielding, as it will be almost impossible to keep it, and the electrical tape that we use later will serve quite admirably in its stead. Finally, you will see the actual wires—four of them on the USB connector end, five on the Xbox end, as shown in Figure 4-51.

Figure 4-51. The actual wires

Note that the colors should match up, leaving an extra wire, hopefully colored yellow, on the Xbox end. Forget that wire (don't ask me what it is there for—I would assume extra power, but I am not sure), it does not do anything that will prevent the controller from working as a USB gamepad. Strip enough off of the internal wires on both ends to connect them (maybe a centimeter if you are soldering, probably two or a little more if you are twisting them together—see Figure 4-52).

Connect the red wire on the USB end to the red one on the Xbox end, the white to the white, the green to the green, and the black to the black, by soldering them if you have access to a soldering iron (and the know-how needed to operate it), or by simply twisting them together. This step is the main reason that you should not drink a liter of coffee while attempting this hack. My wife actually had to come to my rescue, connecting the wires with hands so steady that a surgeon would have been impressed (as my own hands were oscillating so fast that they were actually causing packet loss on my wireless network). Using either method, be careful not to break off the

Figure 4-52. The wires perform a strip show

individual strands of the wires. Once the wires are connected, wrap each one with electrical tape (don't forget the yellow wire!).

Now, wrap electrical tape liberally around all four (well, four and a half actually, counting the pesky yellow), as shown in Figure 4-53. Reconnect the outer, braided wire around the electrical tape core, then wrap more tape around the whole thing.

Figure 4-53. Wires wrapped in electrical tape

Now, detach the standard breakaway cable from your Xbox controller and attach your new USB breakaway as shown in Figure 4-54. If you are a Windows user, plug the controller into your PC. It should be detected right away, ready to serve your emulation needs. (If you are a Linux user, there is one final hurdle to overcome—again, read on and you'll learn how.)

Building the Linux kernel module. First, become *root* and change to the directory where your Linux kernel sources live and run make menuconfig. Select Device Drivers from the main menu, then select USB Support. Scroll down

Figure 4-54. The completed dongle

to the USB Input Devices section and highlight X-Box [*sic*] gamepad support. Press the M key to enable the module, and then hit the Escape key to return to the Device Drivers menu. Hit the Escape key twice more to return to the main menu and exit menuconfig. When prompted, "Do you wish to save your new kernel configuration?", press Enter to select Yes. Now run: make modules modules_install. If you see no errors, you should now have a /lib/modules/`uname -r`/kernel/drivers/usb/input/xpad.ko file. Make sure that the *usbhid* and *joydev* modules are loaded [Hack #52]. Go ahead and load the module by running the command modprobe xpad. Tail your message log: tail -f /var/log/messages, and plug your Xbox controller in. You should see something like:

```
Feb 27 13:40:48 laurana hub 1-0:1.0: state 5 ports 6 chg ffc0 evt 0008
Feb 27 13:40:48 laurana ehci_hcd 0000:00:1d.7: GetStatus port 3 status
001803 POWER sig=j  CSC CONNECT
Feb 27 13:40:48 laurana hub 1-0:1.0: port 3, status 0501, change 0001, 480
Mb/s
Feb 27 13:40:48 laurana hub 1-0:1.0: debounce: port 3: total 100ms stable
100ms status 0x501
Feb 27 13:40:48 laurana ehci_hcd 0000:00:1d.7: port 3 full speed -->
companion
Feb 27 13:40:48 laurana ehci_hcd 0000:00:1d.7: GetStatus port 3 status
003801 POWER OWNER sig=j  CONNECT
Feb 27 13:40:48 laurana hub 3-0:1.0: state 5 ports 2 chg fffc evt 0002
Feb 27 13:40:48 laurana uhci_hcd 0000:00:1d.1: port 1 portsc 0083,00
Feb 27 13:40:48 laurana hub 3-0:1.0: port 1, status 0101, change 0001, 12
Mb/s
Feb 27 13:40:48 laurana uhci_hcd 0000:00:1d.1: wakeup_hc
Feb 27 13:40:48 laurana hub 3-0:1.0: debounce: port 1: total 100ms stable
100ms status 0x101
Feb 27 13:40:48 laurana usb 3-1: new full speed USB device using uhci_hcd
and address 7
Feb 27 13:40:48 laurana usb 3-1: ep0 maxpacket = 8
Feb 27 13:40:48 laurana usb 3-1: new device strings: Mfr=0, Product=0,
SerialNumber=0
Feb 27 13:40:48 laurana usb 3-1: hotplug
Feb 27 13:40:48 laurana usb 3-1: adding 3-1:1.0 (config #1, interface 0)
Feb 27 13:40:48 laurana usb 3-1:1.0: hotplug
Feb 27 13:40:48 laurana hub 3-1:1.0: usb_probe_interface
Feb 27 13:40:48 laurana hub 3-1:1.0: usb_probe_interface - got id
```

```
Feb 27 13:40:48 laurana hub 3-1:1.0: USB hub found
Feb 27 13:40:48 laurana hub 3-1:1.0: 3 ports detected
Feb 27 13:40:48 laurana hub 3-1:1.0: compound device; port removable status:
FRR
Feb 27 13:40:48 laurana hub 3-1:1.0: individual port power switching
Feb 27 13:40:48 laurana hub 3-1:1.0: individual port over-current protection
Feb 27 13:40:48 laurana hub 3-1:1.0: power on to power good time: 100ms
Feb 27 13:40:48 laurana hub 3-1:1.0: hub controller current requirement:
64mA
Feb 27 13:40:48 laurana hub 3-1:1.0: 436mA bus power budget for children
Feb 27 13:40:48 laurana hub 3-1:1.0: enabling power on all ports
Feb 27 13:40:49 laurana hub 3-1:1.0: state 5 ports 3 chg ffff evt ffff
Feb 27 13:40:49 laurana hub 3-1:1.0: port 1, status 0101, change 0001, 12
Mb/s
Feb 27 13:40:49 laurana hub 3-1:1.0: debounce: port 1: total 100ms stable
100ms status 0x101
Feb 27 13:40:49 laurana hub 3-1:1.0: port 1 not reset yet, waiting 10ms
Feb 27 13:40:49 laurana usb 3-1.1: new full speed USB device using uhci_hcd
and address 8
Feb 27 13:40:49 laurana hub 3-1:1.0: port 1 not reset yet, waiting 10ms
Feb 27 13:40:49 laurana usb 3-1.1: new device strings: Mfr=0, Product=0,
SerialNumber=0
Feb 27 13:40:49 laurana usb 3-1.1: hotplug
Feb 27 13:40:49 laurana usb 3-1.1: adding 3-1.1:1.0 (config #1, interface 0)
Feb 27 13:40:49 laurana usb 3-1.1:1.0: hotplug
Feb 27 13:40:49 laurana xpad 3-1.1:1.0: usb_probe_interface
Feb 27 13:40:49 laurana xpad 3-1.1:1.0: usb_probe_interface - got id
Feb 27 13:40:49 laurana input: Microsoft X-Box pad (Japan) on usb-0000:00:
1d.1-1.1<7>hub 3-1:1.0: 336mA power budget left
Feb 27 13:40:49 laurana hub 3-1:1.0: port 2, status 0100, change 0000, 12
Mb/s
Feb 27 13:40:49 laurana hub 3-1:1.0: port 3, status 0100, change 0000, 12
Mb/s
Feb 27 13:40:49 laurana hub 3-1:1.0: state 5 ports 3 chg fff8 evt 0002
```

This lets you know that the kernel has detected your controller (weird that it
shows up as a hub, huh?). Hit Ctrl-C to stop tailing the log file, then run: ls
-l /dev/js0. You should see something like:

```
lr-xr-xr-x   1 root     root     9 Feb 13 16:29 /dev/js0 -> input/js0
```

Unless *ls* returns an error, you should be all ready to use your XBox controller in Linux!

PlayStation and Other Controllers

In order to use other controllers as a USB gamepad, you will need a hardware converter. These are readily available through online retailers such as
Lik-Sang, who sell all manner of SmartJoy converters for GameCube, N64,
PlayStation 2, PSone, SNES, Dreamcast, and Saturn controllers. Especially
cool is the $20 3-in-1 PC Joy Box, which accepts PSone, PS2, Dreamcast,
and Saturn controllers.

Linux users, of course, will need to deal with extra steps to get the adapters to work. Follow all of the steps in "Use USB Gamepads Under Linux" [Hack #52], plug your controller(s) into the adapter, *tail* the system message log: tail -f /var/log/messages, and plug your adapter into a USB port. You should see some notices like:

```
Feb 13 16:29:04 laurana hub 1-0:1.0: state 5 ports 6 chg ffc0 evt 0008
Feb 13 16:29:04 laurana ehci_hcd 0000:00:1d.7: GetStatus port 3 status
001403 POWER sig=k  CSC CONNECT
Feb 13 16:29:04 laurana hub 1-0:1.0: port 3, status 0501, change 0001, 480
Mb/s
Feb 13 16:29:04 laurana hub 1-0:1.0: debounce: port 3: total 100ms stable
100ms status 0x501
Feb 13 16:29:04 laurana ehci_hcd 0000:00:1d.7: port 3 low speed -->
companion
Feb 13 16:29:04 laurana uhci_hcd 0000:00:1d.1: wakeup_hc
Feb 13 16:29:04 laurana ehci_hcd 0000:00:1d.7: GetStatus port 3 status
003002 POWER OWNER sig=se0  CSC
Feb 13 16:29:05 laurana hub 3-0:1.0: state 5 ports 2 chg fffc evt 0002
Feb 13 16:29:05 laurana uhci_hcd 0000:00:1d.1: port 1 portsc 0183,00
Feb 13 16:29:05 laurana hub 3-0:1.0: port 1, status 0301, change 0001, 1.5
Mb/s
Feb 13 16:29:05 laurana hub 3-0:1.0: debounce: port 1: total 100ms stable
100ms status 0x301
Feb 13 16:29:05 laurana usb 3-1: new low speed USB device using uhci_hcd and
address 2
Feb 13 16:29:05 laurana usb 3-1: skipped 1 descriptor after interface
Feb 13 16:29:05 laurana usb 3-1: new device strings: Mfr=1, Product=2,
SerialNumber=0
Feb 13 16:29:05 laurana usb 3-1: default language 0x0409
Feb 13 16:29:05 laurana usb 3-1: Product: PSX/USB Pad
Feb 13 16:29:05 laurana usb 3-1: Manufacturer: LTS
Feb 13 16:29:05 laurana usb 3-1: hotplug
Feb 13 16:29:05 laurana usb 3-1: adding 3-1:1.0 (config #1, interface 0)
Feb 13 16:29:05 laurana usb 3-1:1.0: hotplug
Feb 13 16:29:05 laurana usbhid 3-1:1.0: usb_probe_interface
Feb 13 16:29:05 laurana usbhid 3-1:1.0: usb_probe_interface - got id
Feb 13 16:29:05 laurana input: USB HID v1.00 Joystick [LTS PSX/USB Pad] on
usb-0000:00:1d.1-1
Feb 13 16:29:05 laurana hub 3-0:1.0: state 5 ports 2 chg fffc evt 0002
```

This lets you know that the kernel has detected your joystick. Hit Ctrl-C to stop tailing the log file, then run: ls -l /dev/js0. You should see something like:

```
lr-xr-xr-x    1 root     root          9 Feb 13 16:29 /dev/js0 -> input/
js0
```

Unless *ls* returns an error, you should be ready to use your controller in Linux!

—Josh Glover

Use USB Gamepads Under Linux

#52   Replace that keyboard with a brand new joystick.

With the advent of Universal Serial Bus (USB) devices, true cross-platform plug-and-play seemed to be within the grasp of every computer user. Well, except Linux users. But don't worry—using a USB game controller under Linux isn't that difficult. (Yes, even if it's a Microsoft Sidewinder pad.)

If you do not already have a USB joystick or gamepad, they can be acquired at practically any computer store, online at Newegg (*http://www.newegg.com*), Amazon (*http://www.amazon.com*), approximately one zillion other online retailers, or even your local Radio Shack. The Gravis Gamepad Pro (USB) is a fine entry-level model that should set you back around $20. And of course, if you have a PlayStation 2, Xbox, or other video game console controller lying around, you may want to check out "Use Console Controllers on your PC" [Hack #51].

In order to use a joystick, you may need to descend into that magical realm known as the Linux kernel, as you are going to need a few kernel modules to make this all work. The first step in this process is to make sure you have the Linux kernel sources. You should refer to your distribution's documentation on compiling kernels:

Debian
> *http://www.debian.org/doc/manuals/users-guide/ch-ctsystem.en.html#s-rak*

Gentoo
> *http://www.gentoo.org/doc/en/handbook/handbook-x86.xml?part=1&chap=7*

Fedora
> *http://crab-lab.zool.ohiou.edu/Kevin/kernel-compilation-tutorial-en/index.html*
> (note that this is not an official document)

Mandrake
> *http://doc.mandrakelinux.com/MandrakeLinux/100/en/Command-Line.html/compiling-kernel-chapter.html*

Other distributions
> Check your distribution's online documentation carefully, and if you cannot find documentation for building a kernel, you should refer to the Kernel Rebuild Guide (*http://www.digitalhermit.com/linux/Kernel-Build-HOWTO.html*), which is the successor to the Kernel-HOWTO that was hosted at the Linux Documentation Project (*http://www.tldp.org*)

Now open a terminal, become *root*, and change to the directory where your kernel sources are installed (almost always /usr/src/linux). Now, start the menu-based kernel configuration process by running the command: make menuconfig.

Note that this hack assumes that you are running a Linux 2.
6.x kernel; if you are running a 2.4.x kernel, this will still
work, but the kernel configuration menus will be a bit different. If you are running a 2.2.x kernel, you should probably
upgrade to at least 2.4.x before trying this hack.

From the main menu, use the down arrow key to scroll down to Device
Drivers (see Figure 4-55) and press Enter.

```
Linux Kernel v2.6.12.1 Configuration
 +------------------ Linux Kernel Configuration ----------->.
 | Arrow keys navigate the menu.  <Enter> selects submenus --->. |
 | Highlighted letters are hotkeys.  Pressing <Y> includes, <N> excludes, |
 | <M> modularizes features.  Press <Esc><Esc> to exit, <?> for Help, </> |
 | for Search.  Legend: [*] built-in  [ ] excluded  <M> module  < > |
 +------------------------------------------------------------+
 |  |     Code maturity level options  --->                   | |
 |  |     General setup  --->                                 | |
 |  |     Loadable module support  --->                       | |
 |  |     Processor type and features  --->                   | |
 |  |     Power management options (ACPI, APM)  --->          | |
 |  |     Bus options (PCI, PCMCIA, EISA, MCA, ISA)  --->     | |
 |  |     Executable file formats  --->                       | |
 |  | Device Drivers  --->                                    | |
 |  |     File systems  --->                                  | |
 |  |     Profiling support  --->                             | |
 |  |     Kernel hacking  --->                                | |
 |  +----------v(+)----------------------------------------+  | |
 +------------------------------------------------------------+
 |         <Select>    < Exit >    < Help >                     |
 +------------------------------------------------------------+
```

Figure 4-55. Scrolling to Device Drivers

From the Device Drivers menu, select "Input device support". Scroll down
to "Joystick interface", and if you do not see a <*> or an <M> immediately to
the left, press the M key to enable it as a module (the <*> would indicate
that it is compiled into the kernel statically, which is usually not what you
want). Your screen should now look something like Figure 4-56.

Now scroll down to the "Joysticks" option and press Return to enter the
Joysticks menu. This will result in 22 more menu items being displayed
(again, as of kernel 2.6.10). Enable building each one as a module (by highlighting the option with the arrow keys and then pressing M) so that the kernel can load the appropriate module for you (don't worry about bloat—one
of the beautiful things about modules is that they can be loaded only as
needed, so building a module for hardware that you do not have is OK).
When you enable "I-Force devices," two more options will be displayed
beneath it: "I-Force USB joysticks and wheels" and "I-Force Serial joysticks
and wheels." Use the spacebar to toggle them both on (again, this will not

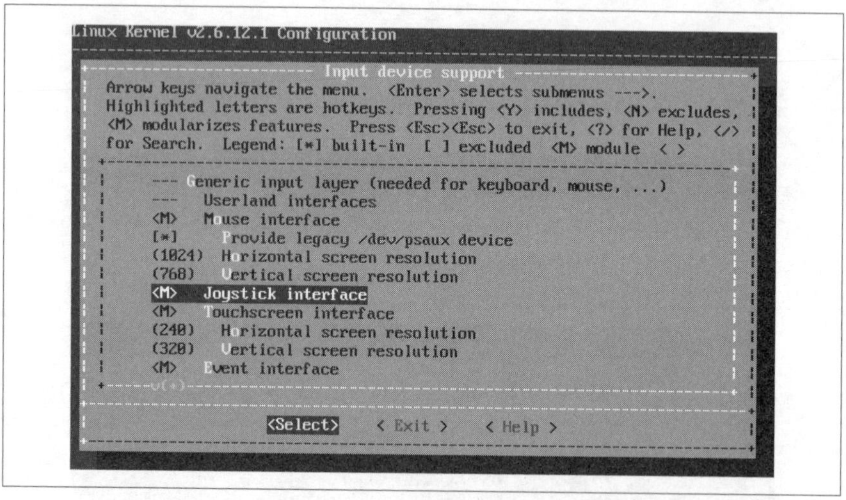

Figure 4-56. Input device support

add anything to your kernel; it is just configuring the module). Once you have finished, your screen will look something like Figure 4-57.

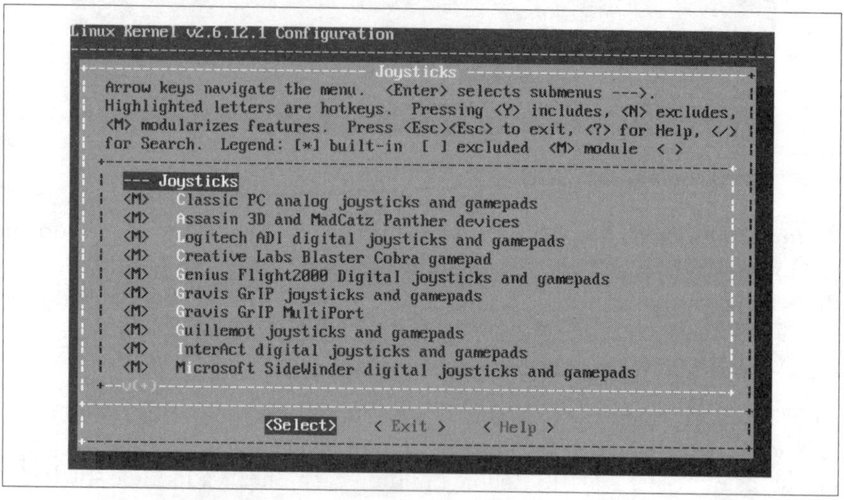

Figure 4-57. Joystick options

Finally, if you have an old-school, non-USB gamepad or joystick, hit Escape to exit the Joysticks menu and return to Input Device support, then select Hardware I/O ports and press Return. Scroll down to the "Gameport support" option and hit the M key to enable it as a module. This will expose six new options (at least, six in kernel 2.6.10, the latest version as of this writing) for supporting various types of game ports. You should enable all of them as modules.

Now, hit the Escape key to exit the Hardware I/O ports menu, and once more to return to the Device Drivers menu. Scroll down to USB Support and hit Enter. Use the M key to enable building "Support for Host-side USB" as a module. This will open up a whole new list of options, the first of which should be USB Verbose Debug Messages. I would recommend using the spacebar to turn it on, so that the USB subsystem will spew a bunch of stuff into the system's message log whenever it finds a new USB device, etc. This can be very useful in getting your devices to work, and you can always turn it off and recompile the module if you ever decide you do not need the log pollution anymore.

Under Miscellaneous USB options, use the spacebar to activate the USB device filesystem option. Under USB Host Controller Drivers, enable modules for all three HCD types—note that you should probably not enable either of the options marked as (EXPERIMENTAL) for the EHCI HCD (USB 2.0) support module. Under USB Input Devices, enable "USB Human Interface Device (full HID) support" as a module, and enable its "HID input layer support" and "/dev/hiddev raw HID device support" options. At this point, your screen should look something like Figure 4-58.

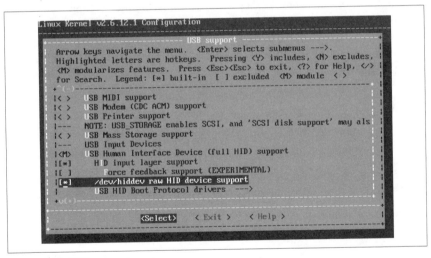

Figure 4-58. USB support menu

Now, hit Escape to return to the Device Drivers menu, then hit it again to return to the main menu. Hit the Escape key one final time to exit menuconfig. You will be asked, "Do you wish to save your new kernel configuration?" Hit Enter to select Yes. You will now be returned to the command line. To build your new modules and install them, run the command make modules modules_install. The build process will keep you informed of what it is doing.

> The build process for 2.4.x and older kernels used to display all of this great compiler spew that made you look like a real 1337 h4x0r, especially if you were sporting transparent terminal windows with green text over a black background— but that is more of a topic for *Linux Desktop Hacks*, by Jono Bacon and Nicholas Petreley (O'Reilly).

When it is finished, you will be returned to the command prompt (do not expect a message telling you that everything went fine—in the Unix world, success is usually silent).

Now, run the *lsmod* command and examine its output. If you do not see a module named *ehci_hcd* or *uhci_hcd*, you will need to load your USB host driver module now. If you have USB 2.0, you will want to run: `modprobe ehci_hcd`. Your USB 1.x controller is probably a UHCI host, so run: `modprobe uhci_hcd` (if this fails, try: `modprobe ohci_hcd`). Run *lsmod* again, and you should see whichever host driver module you just loaded and `usbcore`, somewhere in the output. Now, load the USB HID (Human Interface Device) driver module: `modprobe usbhid`. The final step is to load the generic joystick driver module: `modprobe joydev`. If you have a fancy-schmancy joystick that needs its own driver (did you notice the name of your joystick while enabling joystick modules?), use *modprobe* to load it as well (you can run `ls /lib/modules/`uname -r`/kernel/drivers/input/joystick/` to see all of the available drivers).

Now, run: `tail -f /var/log/messages` to watch your system message log file, and plug your joystick in. If your joystick is a USB device, you should see some notices **[Hack #51]**:

```
Feb 13 16:29:05 laurana usb 3-1: new low speed USB device using uhci_hcd and
address 2
Feb 13 16:29:05 laurana usb 3-1: skipped 1 descriptor after interface
Feb 13 16:29:05 laurana usb 3-1: new device strings: Mfr=1, Product=2,
SerialNumber=0
Feb 13 16:29:05 laurana usb 3-1: default language 0x0409
Feb 13 16:29:05 laurana usb 3-1: Product: PSX/USB Pad
Feb 13 16:29:05 laurana usb 3-1: Manufacturer: LTS
```

This lets you know that the kernel has detected your joystick. Hit Ctrl-C to stop tailing the log file, then run: `ls -1 /dev/js0`. You should see something like:

```
lr-xr-xr-x   1 root     root     9 Feb 13 16:29 /dev/js0 -> input/js0
```

Unless *ls* returns an error, you should be all ready to use your joystick in Linux!

—Josh Glover

Playing with Early Personal Computers
Hacks 53–62

Many people didn't have their first gaming experience in front of a game console or arcade machine. We were first introduced to video games through classic home computers. Sure, our parents and/or middle schools bought them because of their supposed educational value. But everyone just used them to play games anyway, whether it was Oregon Trail, a really bad version of Pac-Man, or who knows.

In this chapter, we'll cover all the bases. If you want to get an original classic computer, like the Apple][or Commodore 64, set up again in your living room, we'll help you out (although you're on your own if you want a lava lamp or green shag carpet). But if you'd rather emulate those old systems, running the old programs you remember on your current PC, we can help with that too.

Run the Apple][
HACK #53 Get your old system up and running again.

There are old Apple][systems, from the original Apple][to the last Apple IIgs ROM 3, lurking in attics, closets, basements, and the occasional store all over the world. I kept my old Franklin Ace 1000 (an Apple][+ clone) in my parents' attic for a decade or so, and found the hardware worked just fine when I turned it on. I've since acquired an Apple //e and two IIgs computers, and an Apple IIe card for a Macintosh LC. There's lots of Apple][stuff out there, though Apple discontinued the IIgs in 1991, and the IIe emulator card in 1993. Searching on eBay today brings up 212 items for the string "Apple II". ("Apple][doesn't work well as an eBay search string, as the][seems to get ignored.)

Apple changed its mind repeatedly about how to spell "2."
They went from][and][+ to //e and //c, then to the IIgs and
the IIe compatibility card. I've tried to keep them all straight,
but it's a strange challenge.

Making an Apple][system work requires a few key ingredients: an Apple][
(or compatible) of some kind, a disk drive that works with that computer
(unless you have a model that supports tape cassettes and have a lot of
patience), a monitor (a TV is fine), and some functioning floppy disks.
Sadly, disks can demagnetize over time, and I discovered to my sorrow that
many of my more than one hundred old disks no longer worked. The ingredients you need vary slightly by computer:

Apple][,][+, //e, Franklin Ace, or similar

All of these computers come as a box with 8 expansion slots and a video
output. Unless you want to turn them on, type for a bit, and lose everything, you'll want to have a disk controller and a floppy drive (like the
Disk II or one of its many clones) or preferably two. The disk controller, which should be installed with the power off, traditionally goes in
slot 6. Be very careful when you attach the disk drive connectors to the
controller, as shifting the connection off by one line of pins can burn
out your disk drive quickly. Figure 5-1 shows the proper alignment of
the pins and the controller connection, and Figure 5-2 shows the card in
the slot in an Apple IIe.

Figure 5-1. Connecting an Apple disk drive to the controller card

Figure 5-2. Installing the controller card

 Be very, very careful when working inside the case of the Apple II series. While installing that disk drive, I gave myself a nice deep cut to my finger while removing a port cover on the back of the machine! It's a metal case, machined for function rather than safety.

Apple //c, //c+

These computers are all-in-one units, including a built-in floppy drive with safer connectors for additional floppy drives. The //c has the more traditional 5.25" drive, while the //c+ has the more recent 3.5" drive.

Apple IIgs

The IIgs does look a lot like an Apple IIe on the inside, with slots for expansion, but it's generally a very different computer, using an ADB keyboard like old Macintoshes and a disk drive connection like the //c series. To make a IIgs work, you'll need a disk drive or two as well as an ADB keyboard and cable and possibly a mouse.

Apple IIe Compatibility Card for Macintosh LC

Apple sold these largely to convert schools from their large installed base of Apple][systems to Macintoshes. The keyboard and 3.5" floppy drive come through the Macintosh, but you can connect external floppy drives (only the A9M0107 5.25" drive and the A2M2053 3.5" drive) to the system, and also use ProDOS partitions on the Mac's hard drive. Video for this system goes to the Macintosh monitor. For more on this option, which is great if you want to play retro Mac games as well as retro Apple][games, see *http://www.mandrake.demon.co.uk/Apple/lc_card_faq.html* or *http://homepage.mac.com/vectronic/appleii/appleiiecard.html*. It only works on a select group of Macs with the LC PDS slot and the ability to run in 24-bit addressing mode, however.

The composite video output on all of the regular Apple computers (which looks like an RCA audio plug), can go directly to the composite inputs on newer TVs or VCRs, or you can use an adapter to convert them to TV channel 3 or 4, and connect through the VHF or coaxial inputs on the television. The IIgs systems also have an RGB monitor connection, but be careful about which monitor you connect. It synchronizes fine with an AppleColor RGB monitor, but won't sync at all with my Macintosh monitors, despite using the same connectors.

> While I have kept my old Franklin ACE 1000 and an Apple //e, for the most part I stick with an Apple IIgs and a Macintosh LC 475 running the //e compatibility card. Being able to connect a computer to a network, even an Apple LocalTalk network, is very useful these days. (Of course, you could find the Apple Workstation card or even the Ethernet card, but I don't have those.)

Once you have the basic parts together, you can fire up the system with a floppy in the primary disk drive and see what you get. With luck you'll see something like Figure 5-3.

If you're working with older floppies, you may find that it takes a while before finding one that's willing to boot. You can order fresh system disks from *http://store.syndicomm.com/*, in DOS 3.3, ProDOS, or OS/GS varieties. Remember, disks that won't boot may still have useful information on them. Boot up from a different floppy and look around. "Become an Apple Guru" [Hack #56] explains a variety of things you can do now that you have the hardware up and running.

Figure 5-3. An Apple IIe, running with a recent vintage television

 If resuscitating old hardware isn't exciting enough for you, you can go further into the Apple realms by building your own Apple I computer. *Apple I Replica Creation: Back to the Garage,* by Tom Owad and John Greco, includes step-by-step instructions for building, programming, and expanding the Apple][´s predecessor.

—*Simon St.Laurent*

 ### HACK #54 Trick Out Your Apple][

Buy or find the right accessories for game-playing and more on your Apple][.

The Apple][by itself is a box that lets you type in code and run it. Turning the Apple][into a game-playing console requires a few additional parts, many of which you can find on eBay or even conceivably build yourself.

The first accessory I'd strongly recommend is a floppy drive, and preferably two or more of them to avoid a lot of disk swapping in multi-disk games, like most of the role-playing games out there. For Apples prior to the Apple //c, you'll also need a disk controller card. For more recent Apples, such as the //c+ and the IIgs, you may also want a 3.5" disk drive or two. Many of the drives on the newer Apples can be daisy-chained, letting you connect a drive to the computer, another drive to that drive, and so on.

I've had some difficulties with some of my older Disk II drives not wanting to read old disks that my newer drive can read just fine. You may want to have a few spare drives around for testing in any case.

I've always been one of those strange people who prefers to play games using the keyboard, joysticks, and paddles that are available for the Apple][series. Older Apples—the][and][+, as well as some clones—have a fragile 16-pin connector inside the case. There were a number of accessories available for bringing the connector outside of the case, or for making it easy to switch between joysticks and paddles. Newer Apples, from the //e onward, use a more protected 9-pin connector. Many old IBM PC joysticks were designed to work with either PCs or Apples, so it's not that hard to find workable joysticks.

Both joysticks and paddles reported a value from 0 to 255 to the Apple, and most joysticks have trim adjustment to set the joystick's center point more precisely. Some also let you turn self-centering on and off, while others offer auto-fire options or let you reverse right and left. Joysticks (shown in Figure 5-4) have two buttons, while paddles have one button each.

Figure 5-4. A joystick for the Apple II, with trim controls, auto-fire, and reversibility

A good monitor can be a big improvement over a television set, especially for later Apples with more advanced high-resolution graphics settings. For general playing around, though, a TV set is fine, especially since today's televisions tend to be a lot larger than the tiny screens a lot of us were using for games.

Most of the games available for the Apple][series either ran on an Apple][with 48K of memory or more and DOS 3.3, aiming for the largest range of customers, or were specific to the IIgs series. There are some games that run under ProDOS as well, though DOS 3.3 was more popular for game publishers because it was a fruitful medium for the copy protection schemes that have driven gamers crazy for years. There may be cases where you want more than 64K of RAM, and the IIgs got up to 8MB of RAM, but many of the classic games are happy to run in 48K or 64K of RAM. (If you're running a IIgs, much more memory may be attractive, especially for later versions of OS/GS. You can find memory on eBay, or buy new 4MB IIgs memory cards for $49 each at *http://garberstreet.netfirms.com/RAM-4-GS.html*.)

Similarly, while it is certainly possible to attach a hard drive to later Apple][s, they aren't generally necessary for game play, and neither are 80-column cards, another common accessory. If you have vivid memories of using Visi-Calc on the Apple][or writing book after book on the system, you may want these anyway. Figure 5-5 shows the most extensively expanded Apple][system I've found locally, one which is part of the Macseum at Babbage's Basement (*http://www.lightlink.com/babbages/*), a computer recycling organization where I found many of the parts I needed to do the hacks on original hardware. Its loving owner gave it:

> 1 Megabyte of RAM
> An Apple Super Serial Card for the ImageWriter printer
> An AE Serial Pro card with a clock, used for the modem
> An Apple DuoDisk Controller card and DuoDisk 5.25" drives
> A Laser Universal Disk Controller card and an AE 3.5" drive
> An Apple SCSI card and a 52MB Apple Q Drive hard drive
> An 80-column text card
> Various enhancements to the motherboard

People are still developing new enhancements for the Apple][series. The most interesting one I've seen lately is a Compact Flash adapter card for the Apple][, which lets you use convenient Compact Flash cards like a giant hard drive. It takes up an expansion slot and requires either ProDOS or OS/GS. CiderPress software will let you write to the Compact Flash card from a PC, providing a new and convenient way to get information from the Internet to your Apple. The current list price is $105, and users report it working in computers from the][+ to the IIgs. (The //c series and the IIe card for the Mac have no expansion slots, so it's not an option for those computers.) For more information, see *http://dreher.net/?s=projects/CFforAppleII&c=projects/CFforAppleII/main.php*.

—Simon St.Laurent

Figure 5-5. An Apple //e, maxed out beyond anything that seemed possible when the Apple][first arrived

 ## Emulate the Apple][

Play old Apple games on modern hardware.

The old equipment is great, but it's difficult to lug an Apple II (or even a //c) with you when you just want to play old Apple games on your laptop. For- tunately, you have lots of options. While I can't find an Apple II emulator for a cell phone, there are emulators that run under both the Macintosh and Windows platforms and even Windows CE. The best list of emulators I've found is at *http://dmoz.org/Computers/Emulators/Apple/Apple_II/*, but in practice I tend to stick with a very few emulators. You can also find an old but interesting Apple][Emulators Resource Guide FAQ at *http://www.faqs. org/faqs/apple2/emulators-faq/part1/*.

For all of the emulators, you'll want to download some disk images before getting started. You can find lots of images at *ftp://ftp.apple.asimov.net/pub/ apple_II/images/*. You'll need to download the image (a *.DSK* file), and prob- ably decompress it. Once you have a *.DSK* file, you can use it with most emulators. For convenience, I'm going to demonstrate emulators with *ftp:// ftp.apple.asimov.net/pub/apple_II/images/masters/dos33_with_adt.dsk*, a dull but occasionally useful disk.

 Many emulators require you to provide your own images of the ROMs from the Apple computer you're emulating. You can create your own images from Apples you have around, though transferring them to a PC or Mac is inconvenient. There are downloadable ROMs available, but their legal sta- tus is uncertain.

Windows

On Windows, AppleWin is extremely convenient and free. You download it from *http://www.tomcharlesworth.pwp.blueyonder.co.uk/*, unzip it, and then double-click the *AppleWin.exe* file. When you first open AppleWin, you'll see the screen shown in Figure 5-6.

Figure 5-6. The AppleWin emulator at startup

The interface is extremely simple. The buttons along the right are the only interface beyond the Apple //e which will appear in the screen at left. The top button (or the F1 key) brings up the simple help file. The Apple logo button (or F2) restarts the emulator, rebooting the system. The next two buttons (or F3 and F4) represent the first and second disk drives. If you click them, you'll have a standard file dialog box to find the disk image you want that disk drive to contain—or, well, emulate containing. There's a button right below them (or F5), which lets you swap the disks in the two drives conveniently. The next button will switch between a partial window and fullscreen view. For this one, you definitely want to remember the keystroke—F6—so you can switch back.

The buttons below that give you access to more advanced options. The magnifying glass (F7) will let you look at the assembly language the Apple is executing when you press it. Click it again to return to the normal screen. The joystick/speaker button (F8) gives you access to configuration. AppleWin lets you adjust the type of computer (][+ or //e), the speed of the processor, the video, the sound (AppleWin emulates the Mockingbird card), serial connections, the speed of the disk drives, and a hard drive. Below the configuration button is a pair of disk activity lights and an indicator for caps lock.

When you select a disk image for drive 1 and click the run button, the emulator will boot the disk. If the boot is successful, you'll see results much like those you'd see on an Apple //e booting a real copy of that disk, as shown in Figure 5-7.

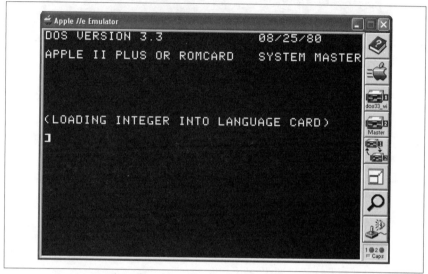

Figure 5-7. The AppleWin emulator after booting the DOS master disk

The emulated Apple is pretty much separate from the rest of your computer, but as a game-playing console, it works very nicely. The only limitation seems to be your ability to find Apple software for it. If you're feeling especially brave, source code is also available for AppleWin.

Mac OS X

Emulators are also available for the Macintosh. A good list, complete with contact information, is available at *http://emulation.net/apple2/*. As my current primary Mac is running OS X, I tend to do most of my emulation there. I've used and liked the free OSXII, but more recent versions don't run on my OS X 10.2 Mac, and the older version I downloaded won't boot. You'll need to have both an Apple][ROM and a Disk][controller ROM to use OSXII.

The other emulator I've used on OS X, Virtual][, has been my main Apple][playground for a while. It emulates the Apple][,][+, and //e. Its web site at *http://www.xs4all.nl/~gp/VirtualII/* plays a cheery "Apple][forever" song when you load it, and is worth a visit just for that if you're into that kind of thing. Virtual][has been shareware, but now comes in three versions, from free to $49. You can find details on the variations at: *http://www.xs4all.nl/ ~gp/VirtualII/VirtualIIHelp/virtual_II_help.html #EvalVersion*.

Like OSXII, you'll need to download an Apple][,][+, or //e ROM as part of your installation, but you don't need the Disk][controller ROM. When you download Virtual][, it comes as a disk image, so you can just open and copy the files to wherever you need. Add the ROM image to the directory containing the program, and you're ready to go. When you first boot Virtual][, you'll see something like Figure 5-8. You'll also hear a whirring noise, meant to sound like a Disk][waiting for a floppy disk. (The activity lights on the drive pictures also work.)

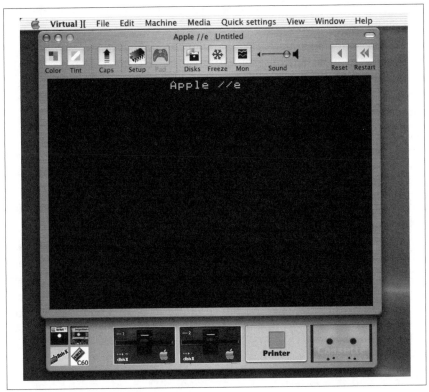

Figure 5-8. The Virtual][emulator on startup

Virtual][offers both menus and buttons for common tasks. To get the system started, you'll need to feed it a disk image. To do so, click on the floppy disk icon in the top row of the four icons at the bottom left. A standard file dialog will come up to let you find the disk image, and you can also specify the slot and drive number to use. The defaults of slot 6 and drive 1 will work fine for the initial boot. If you use the *dos33_with_adt.dsk* image, you'll hear some noise as the disk image loads and then see a screen similar to the AppleWin screen shown back in Figure 5-7.

You can boot any disk image the same way, and can change disks while you're running. Just click the disk drive you want to eject, and then select a new disk. If you want to get adventurously retro, you can even use virtual tape cassettes.

Virtual][has a lot of options, many of them exposed in the top line of buttons. You can choose between a color monitor or a monochrome one, and the tint button lets you choose what color phosphors your pseudo-monitor should have. If you're switching among programs and don't feel like using your caps lock key, the Caps button will capitalize everything you type into Virtual][.

The Setup button and the Configure option of the Machine menu let you get into the computer, changing fundamental parts. Figure 5-9 shows the options available in this area, including which computer is being emulated, what components are in which slots, the processor speed, the video refresh rate, how much memory is available, and much more.

As you can see, the Virtual][comes with plenty of cards, including a Z80 emulator that will let you run CP/M if you're that kind of diehard. You can print to text files if you like, and Virtual][will let you mount parts of your hard drive to be accessible to the Apple][as well. If you want to run the Apple][in fullscreen mode, just hit Cmd-Enter, and Cmd-Enter again to get back.

Going back to the main window in Figure 5-8, the Pad button lets you treat a USB controller as a joystick or paddles. The Disks button lets you manage a library of disks. The Freeze button pauses the emulator, so you can halt your game and come back later. (If you close the emulator and have a paid version, you can save state and return later.) The Mon shows a monitor graph of how fast the Apple][is running, and the Sound slider lets you set volume. Reset is a soft reset, like hitting the Reset button on a real machine, while Restart is the equivalent of turning the machine off and on.

Modern hardware is fast enough compared to the 1MHz 6502 that you don't have to give up much in using an emulator. Unless you need direct access to real Apple][floppy disks or hardware, emulators let you combine the best of the Apple][with the best of modern equipment.

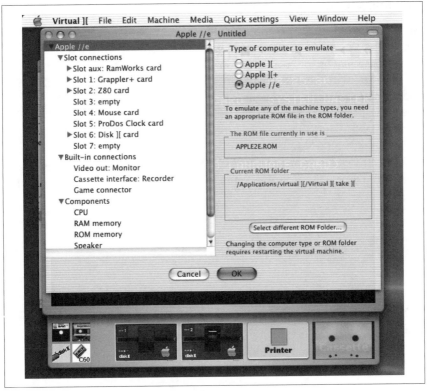

Figure 5-9. Options for the Virtual][emulator

If you'd rather emulate a IIgs, you may want to explore KEGS (*http://kegs.sourceforge.net/*), a free IIgs emulator for Mac OS X, Linux, and Windows, or Bernie][the Rescue (*http://www.bernie.gs/*), a $15 IIgs emulator for the older MacOS. Sweet 16 for Carbon, a version of Bernie built for OS X, is under development.

—Simon St.Laurent

HACK #56   Become an Apple Guru

Read the right books and sites to become an Apple][master.

A lot of people can have fun with an old Apple][or Apple][emulator just by putting disks or disk images into the emulator and booting into games. There's nothing wrong with this, but there's a lot more that you can do if you like, from looking around old disks to programming in BASIC to crafting new games in 6502 machine language.

First Steps: poking around DOS

Apple produced three versions of DOS which are still in common use. DOS 3.x was the primary version used during the Apple][through //e and //c period, supporting only 5.25" floppy disks, with DOS 3.3 becoming the effective standard after its 1980 introduction. ProDOS, which added speed and greater device independence as well as new features like support for directories, first appeared in 1983, and bifurcated into 8-bit and 16-bit versions in 1986. The 16-bit line of ProDOS evolved into OS/GS, a GUI-based environment for the Apple IIgs, which ran from 1987 to its final version, 6.0. 1, in 1992. Later versions of OS/GS also had the advantage of being able to read both DOS 3.3 and ProDOS disks, finally breaking a large compatibility barrier.

 If you encounter DOS 3.2 disks, also called 13-sector disks, you can use the MUFFIN program on the DOS 3.3 master disk to convert them to 16-sector DOS 3.3 disks.

While DOS 3.3's master disk includes a FID file utility program, and ProDOS and OS/GS come with applications that let you look around your disks in a more GUI-like environment, a basic understanding of the command line is very useful, especially if you're poking around old DOS 3.3 game disks. Once you've booted from a DOS or ProDOS disk, a few simple commands can take you a long way. The core set I recommend learning includes:

CATALOG *(or* CAT, *in ProDOS)*

> The CATALOG command shows you a list of the files on the current disk. In DOS 3.3, an asterisk will indicate locked files, a type indicator (A for Applesoft, I for Integer Basic, T for text, or B for binary) will give the type of the file, you'll see the size of the file in sectors, and then you'll see the name of the file. In ProDOS, CATALOG produces 80-column results with a lot more information, but if you're on a 40-column screen, CAT produces an abbreviated version.

BRUN *filename*

> The BRUN command lets you run binary files directly. You can also BLOAD and then call binary files, but BRUN is generally much simpler, sparing you the need for a lot of details about where to put the binary files and where to call them.

RUN *filename*

> The RUN command is familiar from BASIC, but if you add a filename to it, DOS will load the program from the floppy drive and then run it. You can also LOAD files from the floppy and then type RUN, but unless you plan to edit them, running them directly is much more convenient.

SAVE *filename*

> If you want to write your own BASIC programs, the SAVE command will let you store them to disk.

PREFIX *directoryname*

> In ProDOS and its descendants, the PREFIX command lets you see the current directory if used without a directory name, or change to the directory specified if a name is provided.

- *filename*

> In ProDOS and its descendants, you can use - to execute Applesoft, binary, text, or system files in place of RUN, BLOAD, or EXEC.

In DOS 3.3, all commands must be entered in uppercase. ProDOS and its descendants let you use lowercase for commands.

> If you want to get extra geeky, there are a few operating systems for the Apple][that I haven't mentioned, including CP/M, Apple Pascal, and a number of accelerated versions of DOS 3.3 from various vendors.

Next Steps: learning about the Apple

When I went back to my old Ace 1000, I was lucky, because I'd kept my old books, manuals, and reference cards with the computer. The Beagle Brothers Peeks, Pokes, and Pointers poster listed all kinds of internal addresses, and my Nanos Systems Corp. Reference Card for the Apple II & II Plus still provided a complete list of commands and codes. *The Creative Apple*, a collection of articles edited by Mark Pelczarski and Joe Tate in 1983, does a great job of getting me back into that early-80's "Apple][is cool" frame of mind. The critical book for getting me back up and running, though, was the *Apple II User's Guide*, written by Lon Poole with Martin McNiff and Steven Cook back in 1981.

If you don't have a huge trove of books, don't panic. There's lots and lots of information about the Apple][family available on the Web. The Apple II FAQs, available at *http://home.swbell.net/rubywand/A2FAQs2CONTENT.html*, include a tremendous amount of information about the computers, accessories, and games for the Apple][. In particular, I recommend the DOS & ProDOS section at *http://home.swbell.net/rubywand/Csa2DOSMM.html* if you need to figure out more than the basics of getting around Apple disks.

The history of the Apple][may seem arcane, but it can be critical if you're trying to figure out which pieces of hardware and software can fit together. One entertaining and detailed telling is at *http://apple2history.org/index.html*. The second half of Steven Levy's classic *Hackers: Heroes of the Computer Revolution* (Penguin, 1984) tells the story of Apple's founding as well as of the development of the gaming industry surrounding it. *The Little Kingdom: The Private Story of Apple Computer* (William Morrow, 1984), is long out of print but tells the early story in detail. Finally, for a very different perspective on the Apple][and where it led, see Andy Hertzfeld's *Revolution in the Valley* (O'Reilly, 2004), which tells a fair amount about creative Apple][use on the way to building the first Macintosh.

To see what's still happening on the Apple][platform today, I heartily recommend *http://a2central.com/*, offering the latest news updated close to daily, as well as archives of older discussions at *http://lamp.a2central.com/*. The bulletin boards there cost $35 a year, unfortunately, but include key people still working regularly on the system. The Usenet *comp.sys.apple2* newsgroup is still functioning, and if you need to read the archives, you can visit *http://groups.google.com/group/comp.sys.apple2*.

Driving the Apple

It's great to know all the Apple trivia out there, but the best feature of the Apple][series was its approachability. Want to write a program? Start typing. Want to create some hardware? Start wire-wrapping. Need to connect hardware and software? You can do that directly. By modern standards everything in the Apple][is dangerously exposed and written far too close to the hardware, but that same exposure makes it a delightful environment in which to work.

The first step in any Apple programming experience should probably be BASIC, most likely Applesoft. If you really want, Integer BASIC is an option (and has some funky features, like a GOTO that accepts variables specifying its target), or you can use the old Apple Pascal system. There were a lot of small languages published for the Apple][, including Logo, FORTRAN, and PILOT, as well as enhancements to Applesoft, like Beagle Basic. The *Apple II User's Guide* I mentioned earlier got me through learning Applesoft, but *How to Write an Apple Program* by Ed Faulk (Datamost, 1982) and David Heiserman's *Intermediate-Level Apple II Handbook* helped push me further along.

I should probably mention that I was in middle school and high school when I wrote my Apple programs, so my taste in books didn't reflect the full range of possibilities out there.

BASIC will get you started, but at some point you may well want to transition to machine language. There were lots of assemblers out there, including a mini-assembler built into some versions of the Apple ROM, but I tended to use the EDASM assembler that came with Apple's DOS Toolkit.

It's probably fair to say that I didn't know any better, and I had it, so I used it. More powerful and more popular assemblers include the TED, Merlin, and ORCA/M. I still enjoy perusing Marvin DeJong's *Apple II Assembly Language* (Blacksburg, 1982), which goes beyond the programming and takes a look at creating accessory cards as well.

There are two parts of the Apple][system that deserve special attention, as both of them reflect ingenious hardware solutions by Steve Wozniak which have befuddled many a programmer ever since. The Apple Disk Operating System did an amazing job of making the most of the limited capabilities of the Disk][drive, but there are some perhaps excessively creative angles to it. Apple's *DOS Manual* (1980) explains a lot of it, but if you feel like writing code against DOS, you'll probably want a copy of Don Worth and Peter Lechner's *Beneath Apple DOS* (1981), or the additional material in *Beneath Apple ProDOS* (1984).

Once you've (re-)learned all about the Apple][, you'll of course want to start writing some games for it. Wozniak's mapping of the high-resolution graphics memory in the Apple made great sense to the video controller but has left many programmers scratching their heads ever since. To get beyond that confusion and to learn how to handle the challenges of creating flicker-free animation using the Apple][family's limited processing power, I recommend Jeffrey Stanton's classic *Apple Graphics and Arcade Game Design* (Book Company, 1984).

Although you can't make the Apple][into a 4 GHz speed-demon with accelerated graphics, it offers a set of challenges to make you a better programmer. With any luck, and a lot of time, you'll find your own name listed on a2central.com as the proud author of a new game for old hardware.

—Simon St.Laurent

Run a Commodore 64

HACK #57

Learn what you'll need to get a real live C64 computer up and running again.

When I was in high school in the 1980s, the Commodore 64 was one of the computers to have. One friend of mine had a Commodore 64 decked out with an amazing array of music software and hardware. I'm sure my memory is exaggerating, but I swear, it looked like a huge rack of professional music equipment, and I was blown away by the sounds he was getting out of the whole package.

I was one of those Atari kids myself. I had an Atari 400 that I had upgraded to 48k (one of my few soldering projects that didn't end with me passing out from the smell of burning plastic), but I envied my C64-owning friends. Not that I wanted to give up my Atari in exchange for what they had, rather I'd have been happy with both. I finally came into a Commodore 64 a few years ago, when my stepson went off to college (he got it from his uncle) and left his behind. It still works, and many of the floppies are still in perfect shape.

There are a few ways to run a Commodore 64, and only one of them requires a real Commodore 64. I'll get to the real thing last.

Emulators and Things Suspected of Being Emulators

Of course, it's no secret that you can run a Commodore 64 emulator on all sorts of devices [Hack #58], but there are a couple of hardware options available to you, and both of them were invented by the same person. Jeri Ellsworth invented the C-One, a single board computer that is not an emulator, but a reimplementation of the original C64 hardware. Because it's based on chip technology that can be reprogrammed to its very core, the C-One is known as "the reconfigurable computer," and been extended to emulate other 8-bit computers—it's sort of like a hardware version of MESS [Hack #33]. You can find more information on the C-One at *http://c64upgra.de/c-one/*.

Jeri Ellsworth didn't stop with the C-One. Her next project was the C64 Direct-to-TV (*http://www.mammothtoys.com/products.htm*), which is a Commodore 64 with thirty built-in games, all packaged inside a joystick. Unlike many of the joystick games on the market, the C64 Direct-to-TV is expandable. You'll find solder points on the circuit board where you can connect a PS2 keyboard and a Commodore 64 floppy drive, turning the C64 Direct-to-TV into a nice little modern Commodore 64 clone. You can find more information about hacking a keyboard and floppy drive into the C64 Direct-to-TV at *http://dtvhacking.info*. The Direct-to-TV is available at *http://www.qvc.com* and some retail outlets. Figure 5-10 shows the Direct-to-TV.

Figure 5-10. There's a Commodore 64 packed into this little joystick

Set Up a Real Commodore 64

All you need to enjoy C64 retrogaming the way it was meant to be experienced is a Commodore 64, a television, and some games. If your games are on disk or cassette, you'll need a Commodore disk drive or cassette player.

If you dig your Commodore out of the attic or purchase it on eBay, you'll probably find *almost* everything you need. The power supply, Commodore, disk (or cassette) drive should be there, and hopefully you'll have a joystick, but you'll probably be missing the videogame signal splitter and the RCA cable to connect it to your Commodore.

> Ever wonder where all those video game splitters went? Are they in the same place as all those missing socks? Many of them got borrowed for use with other systems over the years. However, the fact that many of them have adhesive on them means that they are probably still glued to whichever TV you were using them with 20 years ago.

Fortunately, video game splitters are really easy to find. RadioShack Video/ Game Built-In Signal Splitter (Catalog number 15-1268) will do the trick. But don't use any old RCA cable to connect the Commodore to the splitter. Make sure you're using something with enough shielding to avoid interference. When I first set up my Commodore 64, all I had was a lightweight video cable, and the signal wasn't that great.

If you have a monitor or TV capable of taking a composite or S-Video signal, you can use the monitor port on the back of the Commodore 64 with the appropriate cable. If you don't have them, they are easy to build and require only a minimum of soldering. See *http://sta.c64.org/cables.html* for links to instructions on building various Commodore 64 cables.

Once you've got everything you need to set up your Commodore 64, plug everything in (connect the power last) and start it up. Figure 5-11 shows my family's Commodore 64 up and running.

When you first boot up your Commodore, you'll be greeted by the BASIC interpreter's "READY." prompt. Now that you've got your Commodore 64 up and running, you'll need to work with files. Whether you want to load a game or save a cool BASIC program you've written, you'll probably be working with a cassette or floppy drive.

Cassette drive
> The cassette drive uses standard audio tapes and lays down its track as a big stream of data. Cassettes usually aren't sliced up into files the way a

Figure 5-11. Still 8-bit after all these years

disk is. Most of the cassette drives you encounter on retro systems treat the tape as a forward-only stream, so there's no random access.

There's nothing keeping a programmer from storing multiple consecutive streams of data on a cassette, but in most cases, you are going to rewind the tape to the beginning, type "LOAD" on the keyboard, and wait for the C64 to ask you to "PRESS PLAY ON TAPE." You should get another prompt shortly, "FOUND PROGRAM NAME," at which point you need to press the C= key on the keyboard to load the program. Be prepared to wait ten minutes or more for the program to load.

To save a file, use the SAVE command followed by a program name (up to 16 characters) in quotes. You should rewind the cassette or position it to where you want to save the file first:

```
SAVE "PROGRAM.BAS"
```

Floppy drive

Commodore floppy drives use 5-1/4 inch floppy disks with a rudimentary file system (16-character filenames, no support for subdirectories). Most game disks are set up so that the first file on the disk is the game you want (but read the disk label for special instructions). This convention lets you use the shortcut "*" as the filename, so this command will usually load what you want (8 is the ID of the disk drive):

```
LOAD "*",8
```

You can load a specific file by typing its name in place of the *. To get a listing of files on the disk, use these commands:

```
LOAD "$",8
LIST
```

Note that LOAD will blow away any BASIC program that you have loaded, since you can only have one program loaded at a time.

To save a file, use the SAVE command:

```
SAVE "FILENAME",8
```

You can delete a file with these cryptic commands (replace *PROGRAM NAME* with your filename):

```
OPEN 1,8,15,"S0:PROGRAM NAME"
CLOSE 1
```

To format a floppy disk, these commands will do the trick:

```
OPEN 15,8,15:PRINT# 15,"N:DISKNAME,ID"
CLOSE
```

Flash memory

Floppy disks and cassettes wear out over time, and since the drives involve plenty of moving parts, they are prone to failure as well. There are a couple of products available for using flash memory as a storage medium for your Commodore 64. Even the smallest flash memory card is huge by Commodore 64 standards (where a floppy disk holds a mere 170k per side).

MMC64

The MMC64 (*http://ami.ga/*) plugs into the Commodore 64's expansion slot, and supports MMC and SDIO flash memory cards formatted as FAT16. It has an integrated filesystem browser, supports D64 disk images [Hack #58], and has an integrated SID player.

IDE64

The IDE64 (*http://www.volny.cz/dundera/*) also plugs into the Commodore 64 and 128 expansion slot, and not only supports flash memory (Compact Flash), but also supports hard drives up to 8GB as well as ATAPI CD-ROM drives.

In some cases, you may need to type RUN after a program loads. Otherwise, it should start itself. However, check the label on the tape, floppy, or look at any accompanying documentation for any specific instructions. There is a lot more you can do with your Commodore, such as writing your own BASIC programs, finding type-in programs on the Internet and in old magazines, and downloading software from the Internet [Hack #58].

—*Brian Jepson*

HACK #58 Emulate the Commodore 64

Run Commodore software on your modern-day PC.

Maybe you don't want to wait until the end of an eBay auction, or perhaps the shoggoth that shambles around your attic still hasn't left. Whatever the case, running a real Commodore 64 [Hack #57] didn't quite do it for you. No matter—you can emulate the Commodore 64, and the programs you run will be none the wiser. There are plenty of emulators that run this classic system perfectly, bringing back the classics you loved and introducing some you've never seen before. You can find emulators for just about any platform you can think of.

Windows

Windows users have plenty of Commodore 64 emulators to choose from, and many of these are listed at Zophar's Domain (*http://www.zophar.net/ c64.html*). CCS64 (*http://www.computerbrains.com/ccs64/*) is a popular and capable shareware ($30) emulator that is well-worth checking out. When you launch it for the first time, you'll probably click randomly like a wild monkey trying to find either the emulator options or a menu that lets you load a disk image—don't worry, you're just looking in the wrong place. To get to either the emulator options or to load a disk image, press F9 to enter the emulator menu. It has a delightful retro-64 feel, as shown in Figure 5-12.

Figure 5-12. CCS64's emulator menu

Frodo (*http://www.students.uni-mainz.de/bauec002/FRMain.html*) and VICE (*http://www.viceteam.org/*) are two free emulators that also work well on Windows. Although you can download the source for either and compile it yourself, you should always be able to find links to the latest Windows binary release on the web site for each emulator. These binary releases usually come in the form of a Zip file that you need to extract (with WinZip, Info-ZIP, or Windows XP's built-in Zip support) and copy to a folder somewhere on your hard drive. Although you don't get the usual Windows installer, these programs are simple to use: to run VICE, double-click on the *x64* icon. To run Frodo, double-click on the *Frodo* icon (you should only use *FrodoPC* and *FrodoSC* if Frodo, or a particular C64 application running under Frodo, malfunctions).

Linux

There are a number of Commodore 64 emulators for Linux and Unix (see *http://www.zophar.net/unix/c64.html*), but of all of them, I prefer Frodo and VICE. You may be able to find either or both of these in a package repository for your operating system (either on your installation media or online). If not, it's easy to compile and install either of these. You can download Frodo from *http://www.students.uni-mainz.de/bauec002/FRMain.html* and VICE from *http://www.viceteam.org*. Both emulators are packaged as *.tar.gz* files. Use the command tar xfz *filename* to extract the emulator's source code, change directory (*cd*) into the top-level directory that *tar* creates for you, and examine both the *README* and *INSTALL* files for instructions on compiling and installing the emulator. I suggest you install both emulators and see which one suits you best. For example, here's how I compiled and ran VICE:

1. Extract the file and *cd* to the top-level directory:

   ```
   $ tar xfz vice-1.16.tar.gz
   $ cd vice-1.16
   ```

2. Read both the *README* and *INSTALL* files (press the spacebar to proceed to the next screenfull of text, press Q to quit):

   ```
   $ less README
   $ less INSTALL
   ```

3. Run the configure and make commands as *root*. You need to prefix the configure command with ./ because the command is in the top-level directory. The *make* command is a utility that's installed on your system:

   ```
   $ ./configure
   $ make
   ```

4. Use the *sudo* command to run make install as *root* (if you don't have the *sudo* command on your machine, run *su* to become *root* first):

   ```
   $ sudo make install
   Password: ********
   ```

5. Run the *x64* program to launch the Commodore 64 emulator (see
   Figure 5-13):

   ```
   $ x64
   ```

Figure 5-13. Running VICE on a Linux system.

Mac OS X

There are a few Commodore 64 emulators for Mac OS X. Of the three I've
tried, Power64 (*http://www.infinite-loop.at/Power64/*) works best for me, if
only because it is so much more configurable than Frodo, the other native
Mac OS X C64 emulator I tried. The demo version is limited to 10-minute
sessions, and the full version is available for $25.

Frodo (*http://www.bannister.org/software/frodo.htm*) is a great port of the
excellent Frodo emulator described in the previous sections, but it was
much less configurable. For example, Power64 allows me to configure
which keyboard buttons map to the joystick, but on Frodo's Joysticks preferences, the "Configure Keyboard" option was grayed out. With the addition of Richard Bannister's Emulation Enhancer ($25; *http://bannister.org/
software/ee.htm*), you can add USB game controller support to Frodo and to
many of Richard's other emulators **[Hack #42]**.

Mac OS X supports the same X11 windowing system that's used as the
foundation of the desktop on Linux and Unix systems. X11 is an optional
install, but you can find it on your Mac OS X installation CD or DVD (look
in */System/Installation/Packages* for a file called *X11User.pkg*). X11 is not
just an afterthought add-on for rudimentary Linux/Unix compatibility. It's a
solid and fast implementation, and makes it easy to bring over X11 apps
such as VICE (*http://www.viceteam.org/*). The Mac OS X version of VICE
comes with a rudimentary Mac frontend that lets you choose which

emulator (Commodore 64, 120, Vic-20, and more) to run. Once you click the Start button, there will be a delay as X11 starts, and then you'll find VICE up and running. From there on in, VICE behaves identically to the Linux/Unix version.

Getting Software

If you're an old-school C64 user, you've probably got a nice collection of floppy disk games. But even if there isn't an unspeakable horror coming between you and the contents of your attic, Cthulhu himself might as well be guarding your old games. For even if you picked up some hardware (see *http://sta.c64.org/*) that lets you connect your Commodore 64 hard drive to your computer, there's a good chance that the disks are old enough that you'll have trouble reading them.

GameBase64 (see *http://www.gamebase64.com/mission.php*) maintains a database of screenshots, descriptions, and other information about all the games that ever graced a Commodore 64 disk drive. If you need a trip down memory lane, check out their site as well as their frontend application that lets you browse the database and launch applications from within your favorite emulator.

It's not hard to find disk images of commercial C64 games online; use your favorite search engine or P2P filesharing application, then download what you're looking for. But don't neglect the efforts of public domain, share-ware, and even modern Commodore 64 developers. You can find plenty of great games, applications, and information in the Commodore 8-Bit archive at *http://www.zimmers.net/anonftp/pub/cbm*. The *c64/games* directory is full of public domain, freeware, and shareware games. Be sure to check out the Llamasoft section for some great games from retro-gaming legend Jeff Minter. You can also find the Llamasoft titles at *http://www.llamasoft.co.uk/lc-8bit.php*. Don't let the greatness of Jeff's games keep you too occupied, though. Make sure you check out the offerings from Protovision (*http://www.protovision-online.de/*), who started writing games for the Commodore 64 in 1996. They have freeware games as well as some games that you can try in demo form.

When you download games, you'll find them in a variety of forms. A *.d64* file is a Commodore 64 disk image, and you can use the floppy drive instructions in "Run a Commodore 64" [Hack #57] to list, load, and run programs.

Files ending with *.prg* are Commodore 64 programs that need to be on a disk image or run from an emulator (such as Power64) that can run programs directly. Some files, such as the ones you download from Llamasoft, won't have an extension after you extract them from their Zip file. In this case, you can usually append *.prg* to the end of the filename. If your emulator won't load a file directly from a *.prg*, you can use a utility to create a disk image and load it just like any other *.d64* (and then you don't need that extension, but it doesn't hurt to have it).

The Vice emulator, discussed later in this hack, includes a utility called *c1541* that you can use to create a disk image and add files to it. Suppose you have a couple of Jeff Minter's Llamasoft games in your current directory. You must start *c1541* from a Command Prompt (Windows), or a terminal application (Mac OS X or Linux). Issue the following commands from within *c1541* to create a disk image (*llamas.d64*) and add a couple of games to it:

```
C1541 Version 4.00.
Copyright 1995-2003 The VICE Development Team.
C1541 is free software, covered by the GNU General Public License, and you
are welcome to change it and/or distribute copies of it under certain
conditions.
Type `show copying' to see the conditions.
There is absolutely no warranty for C1541. Type `show warranty' for details.
c1541 #8> format llamas,8 d64 llamas.d64
Unit: 0
Formatting in unit 8...
c1541 #8> write revenge.prg
Writing file `REVENGE.PRG' to unit 8.
c1541 #8> write gridrunner.prg
Writing file `GRIDRUNNER.PRG' to unit 8.
c1541 #8> exit
```

Depending on whether you are on Mac, Linux, or Windows, you'll find *c1541* in different locations. On Windows, it will be in the *WinVICE-x.xx* subdirectory (*x.xx* should be replaced with the actual version of WinVICE you are running) On the Mac, it's in the *data/bin* subdirectory of the VICE directory (defaults to */Applications/VICE*). On Linux, you'll find it in */usr/local/bin*, */usr/bin*, or wherever you installed VICE.

Once you've created the *.d64*, load it in your Commodore 64 emulator and run the game you want; for example: `LOAD "REVENGE.PRG",8,1` and then type `RUN` and press Return. Some emulators (such as Frodo) may automatically launch the first program on the disk image (you'll see the command `LOAD "*",8,1` fly by on the screen) and others (such as Power64) will prompt you to choose which program to run. Once you've got it running, read the documentation to find out which controls your emulator uses for the joystick, and start blasting!

 If you take a look at a Commodore 64 keyboard, you'll see that the " key is placed over the 2 key. So, if pressing the real double-quote key (usually Shift-') doesn't work, try Shift-2.

—Brian Jepson

Emulate Other Classic Computers

#59

Play the obscure, the bizarre, the ancient PCs.

In the early 1980s, the computer industry was very different from what it is today. Personal computers had just started to reach a price point affordable by the average consumer, and the limited technology of the time forced manufacturers to carefully select their systems' specifications. Unlike in today's more homogenized market, none of the major computer lines were compatible with one another, and each system offered specific advantages (and shortcomings) that made it unique from the rest.

These differences brought out the competitive spirit in both computer manufacturers and the fans of their systems. Owners of computers like the TI 99/4A and the Atari 800 were fiercely devoted to the systems they purchased, and would endlessly argue with their friends about whose machine was best, touting their favorite computer's abilities while conveniently ignoring its weaknesses. These bitter rivalries eventually reached Hollywood, with major celebrities like Bill Cosby and Alan Alda each trying to convince potential customers why the system they'd endorsed was better than the competition.

That was then. Now in the 21st century, the playing field has been leveled for computer manufacturers. Today's more advanced technology allows today's personal computers to have it all, and thanks to the popularity of the Windows operating system and Intel's x86 processor, there's little difference between competing systems when you get past the stylized cases and corporate logos. Despite the greatly improved technology we enjoy today, some users long for the times when choosing a personal computer really made a difference, in both the utilities you used and the games you played.

This hack will teach you how to relive those years through the power of emulation. This chapter will discuss five popular personal computers from the early 1980s, and offer helpful, easy to follow advice on how to run each system's software on your current PC. There's a special treat at the end of the chapter... I'll use emulation to bring one of the world's oldest computers back to life, and play a few games of the classic Space War, considered by many to be the world's first video game.

Finding and Installing MESS

The most convenient way to emulate computer software is to use MESS (*http://www.mess.org*), an emulator with support for many personal computers and video game systems. You can find more information on downloading and installing MESS in [Hack #33]. Depending on the computer you want to emulate, you may need additional files not included with MESS. Most personal computers from the early 1980's include a *BIOS*, a firmware utility that programs the machine on boot-up and assists it with necessary functions, such as disc drive access. You will need a BIOS file for each of the computers listed in this chapter. These files are copyrighted material so I cannot offer specific information on how to locate them. However, clever use of the search engine Google (*http://www.google.com*) should yield positive results.

Finally, to make the most of your emulation experience, you'll need software. Although the majority of commercial releases for these systems are protected under copyright law, it is entirely legal to copy, run, and redistribute public domain software for any of these machines. The best sites to find this software will be listed in the sections dedicated to each of the computers covered in this chapter.

The Atari Computer Line

The Atari line of 8-bit computers enjoyed a very long life, and it wasn't just because of its charismatic pitchman, M*A*S*H star Alan Alda. The Atari 800 and its kid brother, the Atari 400, had such advanced graphics capabilities that Atari had created two game systems (first the Atari 5200, then the lesser known XEGS) with the same hardware. The first two Atari computers also inspired a half dozen successors, with each new system in the family offering even better performance than the last.

There are several emulators available for the Atari 8-bit series of computers, including Atari++, Atari800Win Plus, and MESS32. Out of these three emulators, Atari800Win Plus is the best of the bunch. As of this writing, MESS32 only supports two Atari computers. A third, the Atari 800XL, is listed but does not yet function properly. Atari++ offers support for a wider variety of systems, but its interface is clumsy, mimicking the look and feel of the Atari computer line a bit too closely with its chunky, difficult to read font. Atari800Win Plus offers the best its competitors have to offer and a whole lot more; it's got a simple and attractive interface, along with compatibility with over a half dozen systems and countless games—although it can be a bit tricky to master its use.

Let's get started. First, you'll need to download the Atari800Win Plus emulator. You may find it either at the developer's home page (*http://cas3.zlin.vutbr.cz/~stehlik/a800.htm*) or at Zophar's Domain (*http://www.zophar.net*). Once you have located the emulator, download it, then drop it in an appropriately named folder, such as *Atari8Bit*. Double-click the file to unzip its contents into the folder you created.

Next, you'll need to find BIOS files for the computers you want to emulate. Use Google or another competant search engine to find *atariosa.rom*, *atariosb.rom*, *atarixl.rom*, and *ataribas.rom*. Atari800Win Plus also includes support for the Atari 5200 game system, so you'll want to include *atari52.rom* in your search if you'd like to play those games as well. When you have downloaded all of these files, drop them inside the *Rom* folder, which you'll find inside the folder you created for Atari800Win Plus.

Finally, no emulator is complete without games, and you'll definitely want some for Atari800Win Plus. You can find a generous supply of public domain titles at sites like *http://www.page6.org/pd_lib/pd_lib.htm* or *http://www.umich.edu/~archive/atari/8bit*. Download the files, drop them into the folder where Atari800Win Plus resides, and unzip each of them.

Now you're ready to begin. Open the Atari800Win Plus folder and click on the file named *Atari800Win*. When the Setup Wizard appears, click the Cancel button to close it. Select Atari from the menu at the top of the screen, then click on Rom Images. Click on each of the buttons on the left-hand side of the window, then open the Rom folder and choose the appropriate BIOS file for each one. For instance, for OS-B, choose *atariosb.rom*. When you're finished setting up the BIOS files, click OK.

Choose Atari → Machine Type from the menu bar, then select your preferred BIOS. Usually, XL/XE will be enough to play most Atari computer games. After you've done this, choose Atari → Settings from the menu bar, then clear the box Disable BASIC when booting Atari. Next, choose File → Autoboot Image.

After a few seconds, the file you've selected will start running. Press the F4 key to skip through the introductory screens, then press a number key to choose the program you wish to run. You may either play games with the numeric keypad (be sure the number lock is turned on!), or with a joystick if one is attached to your computer (press Alt-J to configure Atari800Win Plus for joystick support).

Coleco ADAM

The ADAM was adapted from an expansion unit for the ColecoVision game system. When Coleco realized that interest in video games was on the decline, they took the basic components of the expansion unit and integrated them into a personal computer. Sadly, due to design issues like a noisy daisy wheel printer and a slow proprietary tape drive, the ADAM was soundly thrashed by its better established competitors, leaving Coleco in a state of financial distress that ultimately claimed the company's life.

There are only a couple of working emulators for the Coleco ADAM, and neither of them run flawlessly. MESS32 is the most frequently updated and user-friendly of the two ADAM emulators, but it will only run a few games in the system's software library. For a more complete Coleco ADAM experience, you will need a second emulator, Marat Fayzullin's ADAMEM. Between the two applications you can play a substantial number of the games released for Coleco's computer.

It's easy to set up MESS32 to play Coleco ADAM games. Follow the instructions at the beginning of the chapter to download and install MESS32 on your computer. Once this is finished, download the software you wish to use with the emulator, along with the BIOS file *adam.zip*. If you're having trouble finding games, Marcel DeKogel's site (*http://www.komkon.org/ ~dekogel/classic.html*) is a good place to start. Drop the file into MESS32's *bios* folder, then create an *ADAM* folder and drop the ADAM software into it. Finally, unzip the ADAM software you've downloaded.

Once this is finished, run MESS32 by clicking on the icon labelled *messgui*. Drag the scroll bar down until you see the word ColecoAdam, and click on it once. To run games, click File at the top of the screen, then choose Open Other Software. Open the directory where the games reside, then double-click the game of your choice. The game you've chosen will appear in a white frame in the center of the screen. Double-click the game and the emulator will begin.

ADAMEM, an emulator designed for MS-DOS, is more difficult to use. Download ADAMEM from Zophar's Domain (*http://www.zophar.net*) and put the file in the folder where your ADAM games reside. Unzip the emulator, then take a copy of the BIOS file you downloaded for MESS32 and unzip it in the same directory. Then, access the Command Prompt. In more recent versions of Windows, click Start → Programs → Accessories → Command Prompt (you can also run it by clicking Start → Run, then typing cmd.exe and pressing Return).

From here, move to the directory where ADAMEM resides; for instance, if you put ADAMEM in the directory *c:\Computer Emulation\Adam*, you would type:

```
cd "\Computer Emulation\Adam"
```

Now you're ready to begin. Type in ADAMEM, then either -diska (for *.dsk* games) or -tapea (for *.ddp* games), then the name of the game you wish to play. For instance, to play the game *supercos.dsk*, type in adamem -diska supercos.dsk.

Press F9 to switch between emulating the ADAM keyboard and the joystick. Use the arrow keys as joystick directions, and the left Ctrl key and left Alt key as fire buttons. When you're finished, press the F10 key to exit ADAMEM, and type "exit" and press Enter to leave the command prompt.

> If you're having trouble getting MS-DOS programs to run in Windows, you could try emulating them using the program DOSBOX [Hack #69].

The Sinclair Computer Series

Created by British entrepeneur and tech expert Sir Clive Sinclair, the Sinclair series of personal computers were designed as a low-cost, user-friendly alternative to more robust machines like the Commodore 64 and Atari 800. These systems, especially the more advanced ZX Spectrum, sold briskly in Britain, and are still fondly remembered by the United Kingdom's most devoted computer users.

The popularity of the system in Great Britain, coupled with its limited hardware, has resulted in an explosion of Spectrum emulators for not only Windows and Macintosh computers, but for game consoles ranging from Nintendo's Game Boy Advance to Sega's discontinued Dreamcast.

Of the many Spectrum emulators available, EmuZWin offers the best balance of compatibility and ease of use. MESS32 is perhaps the most user-friendly Spectrum emulator (especially if you've already grown accustomed to its interface while using it to emulate other computers), but it lacks support for key Spectrum file formats, making it impossible to play the system's most impressive games. X128 is considered by many to be one of the best Spectrum emulators, but you're out of luck if you own a later version of Windows, like XP or 2000: it simply won't run on those operating systems.

One of the best features of EmuZWin is that it doesn't require any BIOS files. Everything you'll need to start the emulator is included. All you need to do is download the file and unzip it. You can find EmuZWin at the author's home page (*http://bonanzas.rinet.ru*) or at Zophar's Domain (*http://www.zophar.net*). Download the file, then create a folder for it. Drop EmuZWin into the folder and unzip the file.

You can use EmuZWin without any software, but where's the fun in that? You can find some fantastic demos at the ZX Demo web site (*http://www.zxdemo.org*). These flashy programs will show you what the Spectrum can do when it's pushed to its limits. Download a few of these files and drop them in the folder where EmuZWin is located, then unzip each of them.

Open the *EmuZWin* folder, and run the program by clicking on the colorful globe icon. To load software, choose File → Open in the menu bar, then double-click the file you wish to run and it will begin. Before you start playing games, you may want to customize the control to your liking. For example, to enable joystick support choose Control → Joystick On from the menu bar. You may also reassign key configurations by choosing Control → Keyboard Remapping, and then in the dialog box that appears, double-click on each of the text bars under the label PC Key, and type in the key you wish to use in the place of the one currently assigned. Click the OK button when you're finished.

TRS-80 and TRS-80 Color Computer

One of the first practical home computers, the TRS-80 was sold at Radio Shack for just $599 in the late 1970's. This low price helped get the system into peoples' homes, but its limitations and boxy construction earned it the unflattering nickname "Trash-80." After the TRS-80 had run its course, Tandy introduced the Color Computer, a smaller, more impressive home computer with a large selection of games. Tandy supported the more charitably nicknamed CoCo well into the late 1980s.

MESS32 is the best emulator for both the TRS-80 and its descendant, the Color Computer. The other emulators created for these machines were designed in DOS, making them difficult to use. In all honesty, even MESS32 doesn't offer an ideal environment for running TRS-80 and Color Computer games. You'll have to put forth some effort in order to run the software for these two systems, but ultimately, it's worth the hard work.

First, download and install MESS32 using the instructions at the beginning of the chapter. Then, locate and download the BIOS files required by MESS32. You'll need *trs80.zip*, *trs80l2.zip*, and *trs80l2a.zip* to emulate the TRS-80. The three Color Computer models require the files *coco1.zip*, *coco2.zip*, and *coco3.zip*. Once these files have been downloaded, drop them in MESS32's *bios* folder.

You will also need software to get the most out of your emulation experience. TRS-80 programs can be found, naturally, at the TRS-80 web site (*http://www.trs-80.com*). Visit the Nitros9 web site (*http://nitros9.stg.net/*) to find a cornocopia of legally distributed titles, including a demo of an astonishing first-person shooter designed for the Color Computer 3.

To run TRS-80 software, you will need a special boot file. Create a TRS-80 folder, then go to the TRS-80 web site and click Model I on the lefthand side of the screen. Scroll down to the bottom of the page, until you see the link Big 5 Software Series. This contains not only the boot file you'll need to start the software, but a bundle of impressive games. Click the link to download the file, then drag the file to the folder you created and unzip it.

Next, start MESS32 and scroll down to the entry named TRS-80 Model I (Radio Shack Level II Basic). Double-click it and the emulator will begin. In the menu bar click Devices → Floppy Disk #1 → Mount. In the resulting dialog box, double-click the boot file. Next, click Devices → Floppy Disk #2 → Mount, and then double-click the name of the software you wish to run. Next, click Options → Reset. After a brief wait, you will be presented with a menu screen. Use the arrow keys to highlight the program you wish to run, then press Enter. The program you've selected will begin.

It takes a bit more work to run Color Computer games. Much of the system's software is in a special binary format not native to MESS32. Luckily, the emulator comes with a second program, WImgTool. This utility lets you add binary files to a simulated floppy disc, making these games readily accessible by MESS32. Double-click the icon labeled *wimgtool* to launch the utility.

To create a holding file (see Figure 5-14) that will contain the software you wish to use, click File → New in the menu bar at the top of the WImgTool window. Select "CoCo DMK disk image (RS-DOS format) (.dsk)" from the drop down menu, then type in a name for the file you will create. Click the OK button. You have created a simulated floppy disk. To add files, click Image → Insert File. Double-click on the file you wish to add, then click the OK button. You may continue to add files until the simulated floppy disk is full. When you're finished, click File → Close.

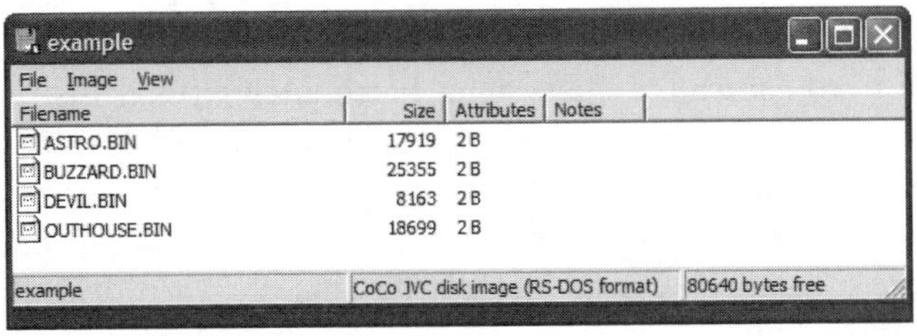

Figure 5-14. Creating a simulated floppy disk with the MESS32 utility WImgTool

Run MESS32, then scroll down to either Color Computer 2 or Color Computer 3 (NTSC) and double-click one of these entries. From the menu bar, click Devices → Floppy #0 → Mount. Highlight the file you wish to use, then click the OK button. Type DIR and press Enter to examine the files available. Type LOADM "*filename*.bin", replacing *filename* with the file you wish to load, and press Enter. Remember, the keyboard layout for the Color

Computer is slightly different than on a PC, so you will need to hold down the Shift key and press 2 to create a quotation mark. Type EXEC and press Enter to start the game.

TI 99/4A

The TI 99/4A was Texas Instruments' most popular personal computer. This capable yet inexpensive machine had a wide selection of great games that took advantage of its advanced graphics processor. Texas Instruments took advantage of the TI 99/4A's popularity with children by designing clever educational titles along with book publisher Scott Foresman. These exclusive titles made learning fun, and made the TI 99/4A very appealing to public schools.

The TI 99/4A still has a small but fiercely devoted fanbase, which inspired the creation of a handful of TI emulators. V9T9 was once the standard for TI 99/4A emulation, but it has since been abandoned by its author and hasn't been updated for nearly a decade. Classic99 is a more recent emulator, compatible with Windows. It's easy to use and includes its own set of games, but it runs slowly on older computers. Finally, there's Win994a. This isn't an emulator, but rather a simulator that requires special custom-created files in order to run software. The program is stable and runs quickly on even slower machines, but its incompatibility with standard TI 99/4A binary files makes it a hassle to use.

Currently, the best available emulator for the TI 99/4A is MESS32. After you've downloaded and installed MESS32 on your computer using the instructions at the beginning of the chapter, locate the file *ti99_4a.zip* with a Google search. Download this file, then drop it inside MESS32's *bios* folder.

Now you'll need games for the system. Fortunately, Texas Instruments has generously allowed some web sites to distribute TI 99/4A software. You'll find a handful of games included with the Classic99 emulator, which you can download from the Harmless Lion web site (*http://www.harmlesslion. com/software/Classic99*). Create a folder for this file, then drop the file into the folder and unzip it. You'll have dozens of ROMs to try, including several games.

Now, run MESS32 by opening the MESS32 folder and clicking on the icon messgui. Scroll down to the entry TI 99/4A Home Computer (US) and highlight it. From the menu bar at the top of the screen, select File → Open Other Software. Open the directory where the TI 99/4A software is located, then select the file or files you wish to run.

The TI 99/4A is different from other computers supported by MESS32 in that its games are often split into two or more files. You'll need to highlight every file in the group by holding down the Ctrl key while clicking on each file. Once you've done this, double-click the entry "TI 99/4A Home Computer (US)" and the emulator will begin. Press a key to advance past the MESS32 and TI 99/4A title screens, then select the program you wish to run by pressing the appropriate key.

PDP-1 and Space War

Back in 1961, pioneering hardware manufacturer DEC released the first personal computer designed especially for the masses. It cost nearly a hundred thousand dollars and was the size of a small room, but hey, at least most colleges and large businesses of the time could afford it! Also, this system did introduce important peripherals that have since become essential computer components, like the keyboard, printer, and monitor. The PDP-1 was also the first computer with its own video game, Space War.

There is only one emulator that can handle the incredible power of the PDP-1. Er, well, there's only one emulator that supports the PDP-1, anyway. In fact, support for the venerable computer is built right into MESS32. You won't need to download any BIOS files to run the system's software. Use the instructions at the beginning of this hack to download and install MESS32.

Although you won't need BIOS files to run PDP-1 software, you will need the software itself. In the 1960s, PDP-1 programs were written on punchcards or cylindrical drums, but today you have the convenience of downloading them from the Internet. Not much software was written for the PDP-1, and chances are you'll only be interested in one particular title, Space War. You can find it at the Computer Space Fan web site (*http://www. computerspacefan.com/SpaceWarSim.htm*). Download the file *spacewar_pdp. zip*, then create a folder for it and drop the file inside it. Finally, unzip the file to make it ready to use.

Now open the folder where MESS32 resides and click on the icon messgui to start the emulator. Scroll down to the entry PDP-1 and highlight it. Now, select Files → Open Other Software. Open the folder where *spacewar.rim* is located, and double-click on that file. *Spacewar.rim* appears in a white bar in the center of the screen. Double-click the file and the emulator will begin.

Press a key to advance past the MESS32 title screen. The screen will be split into three segments: a monochrome display on the top left, rows of switches and indicator lights on the top right, and a white paper feed on the bottom. To load Space War into the PDP-1's memory, press Ctrl-Enter. The lights on the top righthand side of the screen will flash wildly for about a minute.

Once the game is finished loading, two spaceships will appear on opposite ends of the screen as shown in Figure 5-15.

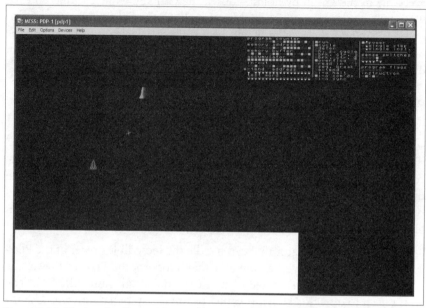

Figure 5-15. Playing the classic video game Space War with MESS32's built-in PDP-1 emulation

Space War is easy to play. Each player is given a ship, and the object of the game is to fire at the opponent's ship until it explodes. The first player uses the A,S,D,F, and Z keys to control his or her vessel, while the second player uses the arrow keys and forward slash. Both players' ships will be drawn into a shining sun at the center of the screen. Avoid the sun at all costs, as contact with it will destroy either ship.

When you're finished with the game, click on File → Exit.

Special thanks to everyone in the emulation community, especially L. Curtis Boyle from Nitros9 (*http://nitros9.stg.net/*), Ira Goldklang from TRS-80.com (*http://www.trs-80.com*), Paul Rixon from Page 6 (*http://www.page6.org*), and Rich Polivka from 99er.net (*http://www.99er.net*) for their assistance and advice.

—*Jess Ragan*

Type in Classic Computer Games

HACK #60

Dig up old classic magazines to find programs you can type in.

The type-in listing was a mainstay of specialist computer and gaming publications from the early to mid '80s. Its popularity was due to three factors: they were cheap to buy (the cost of a magazine with ten type-ins was a fraction of the price of a commercial title), they filled up space in a magazine really easily (editors could pad out half their pages with these listings, which were bought cheaply off aspiring programmers), and the inclusion of some form of BASIC on every home micro computer let everyone try their hand at being a game creator.

A type-in listing typically took the form of page after page of BASIC commands, each one on a separately numbered line. Since most versions of BASIC were the same across all formats, with some tweaking you could get (for example) Sinclair Spectrum type-ins working on a Commodore 64. Since the point of BASIC was that most commands were written in English, it was easy to see what the game was going to be like as you were typing it. Text adventures tended to spoil themselves the worst—by the time you start the game for the first time, you've already read the ending.

Type-in programs, like games of today, covered nearly every genre popular in the day: arcade clones, text adventures, sports simulations, maze explorations, and platforming quests. They were often crude, slow and full of bugs, but being able to type them in yourself and see the end result on the screen, errors included, was part of the magic. For some, it was the digital equivalent of a painting-by-numbers kit, for others it was strange voodoo. Finding bugs in other people's work and getting a stubborn type-in to work was exciting.

Being published in a monthly specialist magazine or book-sized compilation of listings was sometimes the start of a real game programming career. Jeff Minter (Tempest 2000, Unity) and Dave Perry (Earthworm Jim, Messiah) are just two names that you can find by digging through type-in listings of yesteryear.

As the genre grew and bedroom programmers started to top each other's efforts, advancements such as color graphics, sound, and even animation began to find their way into the programs. The end result of this was listings that were the size of the book you're reading now, but perseverance had its rewards. Seeing the game working on the screen after spending days typing in every line of its code is worth the eyestrain, and more satisfying than loading pre-written software.

As consoles exploded in the United States and more powerful home computers such as the Amiga took off in Europe, the type-in listing faded into obscurity. Magazines included cover tapes or discs to keep the miserly gamer interested, but you can still relive the magic of the type-in listings today.

Finding Listings

So you've decided that you have the energy to find a listing and the free time to type it in. The first thing you need to do get a listing to try out. You can either go to the original source material—classic books and magazines—or find archived or modern type-ins on the Internet.

Finding type-in listings in their original state is the preferred method of beginning a type-in project. Not only do you get the thrill of the hunt—tracking down magazines and books with listings is a tricky process—but you can come across a rare gem that nobody else has seen for over two decades. You also have the extra challenge of working on a program without the benefit of someone checking that it worked.

Magazines. The world's first computer game magazine, Computer and Video Games (C+VG; 1980-2004) featured type-in listings in every issue until 1984. C+VG is relatively easy to find, though early issues are expensive. Occasionally they would cover-mount a "Big Book of Games," featuring over 50 type-in listings (usually reprinted from previous issues).

Commodore Computing International (1984–1990)
> This was one of the few "serious" magazines about the Commodore lineup of machines, but still made room for type-in listings. About 50% of them were games, with the other being utilities that measure your biometrics or make posters, etc. One of the highlights was "celebrity" type-in listings by some of the top adventure writers of the day. The magazine is very hard to find, since it enjoyed only a small print run.

Input (1983–1985)
> This general-purpose micro-computing magazine has the distinction of having the most expensive type-in listing ever made. Editors typically paid the authors a measly page rate for their efforts, but that tradition was broken when Input commissioned commercial software house Imagine to write type-in listings for them. Only one game, a precursor to the average maze exploration title Pedro, was ever made in this deal, which was worth a reported £200,000.

Popular Computing (1977–1985)
> This one is very easy to find, though the quality of the type-ins range from the dull to the average. Focusing on simple text adventures, Space Invaders clones, and the occasional utility, the type-ins are at least short and easy to complete.

Antic (1982–1989)
> This magazine was focused on the Atari line of home computers, and it's no surprise to see type-ins take up the bulk of its content for the first few years of its life. The quality of the type-ins were a cut above the ones found in rival magazines, with some prolific authors getting a reputation after several of their games found favor with readers. The popularity of the magazine makes it an easy find for collectors.

Books. There were many books that included type-ins. Here are a few of them.

Creating Adventure Games On Your Computer (1984)
> This book by Tim Hartnell is credited as starting many a games designer on the path to making their first RPG. It's more of a "how to" book rather than a compendium of type-ins, but gives you tips and examples to work from.

100 Programs for the Commodore 64 (1985)
> John Gordon and Ian McLean's book covers all the genres and styles of the day. While the quality of the finished games is uneven, they all are at least guaranteed to work.

Basic Fun With Graphics: The Apple Computer Way (1983)
> Written by Margaret Ann Zuanich and Susan Drake Lipscomb, this book gives examples and short games to demonstrate the graphical splendor of the Apple series of home micro computers.

So now that you know what to look for, how do you get it? eBay and Amazon are great resources, as collectors and former enthusiasts are constantly clearing out their reserves to free up space. Magazines tend to appreciate in value as they get older, while books only get cheaper as the years go on (many of the books listed above are retailing on Amazon for a penny). Sites such as *http://www.old-computer-mags.co.uk/* and *http://www.vintage-computer.com/* are a good place to start finding old magazines, as well as other enthusiasts for games of bygone eras.

Second-hand book stores are usually a treasure trove for the classic gaming magazine collector, as their value is unknown in the real world. The trade off here is usually that the condition of the magazine is poor at best, but that's better then nothing.

If that doesn't work, try your local library. The bigger they are, the better the chance that they still have that elusive copy of Antic you have been searching for. While you won't be able to keep it, you can still bask in the retro-fueled glow that comes with reading it.

Online. Web sites dedicated to the lost art of the type-in have grown in popularity over recent years. They have the advantage over print in that the type-ins have usually been tried, verified, and error corrected by others, and you can even download the finished product if need be.

- *http://www.atariarchives.org* maintains an online copy of some of the more popular BASIC programming books ever made.
- *http://www.users.globalnet.co.uk/~jg27paw4/type-ins/typehome.htm* maintains several hundred type-in listings featured in popular UK Sinclair Spectrum magazines.
- *http://freespace.virgin.net/james.groom/oric/typein.htm* hosts type-in listings for the ill-fated Oric home computer. Some of them have been corrected to fix game-stopping bugs.
- *http://www.cyberroach.com/analog/default.htm* aims to archive every issue of Atari-based Analog magazine, including the type-ins.

Tips and Tricks for Typing

Missing one line or typing in the wrong DATA value can be catastrophic, rendering the game and the last few hours of your time useless. Spend a bit of time to make sure that the only errors made are by the original author or the typesetter:

Use a ruler
> It might sound stupid, but placing a small ruler underneath the line you are transcribing makes keeping track of what line you are up to much easier. This is especially true when dealing with a large stream of DATA statements, which look the same when printed together on a page.

Save early, save often (the first time this rule has been used outside of a Sierra game)
> Transcribing type-ins is painstaking work, and fatigue can set in after a few short hours hunched over the keyboard. If you don't take a break away from staring at the pixelized characters on the screen, you'll just make mistakes later. For every hour spent working on a type-in, take at least 15 minutes break. This is a good chance to save your work so far, and if you're typing it in on a real machine the saving process can take that long anyway.

Adjust to the environment

Old micro-computers weren't designed to be ergonomic like modern day keyboards. Each machine has a keyboard that is arranged different from what we are accustomed to on PCs and Macs. Take some time to get used to the differences—on a Commodore 64 The * symbol is where] is on a PC, and quotes are found by pressing Shift 2, for example. The Sinclair Spectrum uses BASIC shortcuts, so pressing P can make the word Print appear on the screen. This is useful to know if you touch type and discover afterwards that the last 30 lines are full of garbage.

Break the work up

An advantage of BASIC is that, since each line is numbered, you don't have to type-in the lines in the order they appear on the page. This is a useful tip if you're faced with the task of typing in 50 lines of nearly identical DATA statements. Break it up by typing in some DATA lines, then switching over to something more interesting. Remember to mark off the lines you have done to make sure you don't type in the same line twice (which won't wreck the program, but it's a waste of time).

Get a proofreader

This is invaluable, especially since a mistyped number can wreak havoc. Bribe a willing participant to help you with the project (promise to include their name in the credits; see "Modify the listings" later in this list) and get them to help you type it in. They can either read aloud the listings while you type (be careful they make clear the difference between similar sounding terms, such as FOR and 4, and know what an old fashioned zero looks like—it's a circle with a stroke through it) or check your work against what is on the page. Either way, a fresh set of eyes (or lips) is invaluable.

Annotate your work

Since type-in listings are already long enough, many of the original coders did not annotate their work, leaving end users to the task of figuring out what section did what. You can add new lines to the program at any point, which is a good opportunity to add annotation to help you modify the code later. Typically, the easiest way to do this would be to add a REM statement like so:

```
380 GET A$; PRINT "HELLO";A$;", I HOPE YOU ARE WELL"
381 REM THE ABOVE LINE ASSIGNED THE PLAYER'S NAME TO A$
390 PRINT "LET'S PLAY TIC-TAC-TOE"
```

Modify the listings

An advantage of basic is that it is a fairly straightforward process to change the game to your liking. You wouldn't be the first to do it, either. The brave souls who wrote new endings in a text adventure or changed a blocky Formula 1 car into a blocky space ship in a type-in listing were the predecessors of the hackers who modify Unreal Tournament and other PC games today. The simplest way of modifying the type-in (after making a backup of the original, of course) is to change the text that appears on screen. Most text is kept within PRINT statements, and written in plain English. There's no chance of breaking the program here, though the screen layout can be distorted due to the limited number of characters that can be on screen at once. Try to keep the size of the text you are changing consistent with what was there originally.

Changing graphics is slightly trickier, depending on the program. Early type-ins used character symbols (#, %, *, etc) to represent objects on the screen (e.g., an @ symbol representing Pac-Man and a period for the Pac-Pellets). These are easy to replace as soon as you find them. Later games (particularly on the Commodore 64 and Vic 20) used sprites. These are made from several lines of DATA statements, with each line containing a series of numbers ranging from 0 to 255. Each of those numbers represents one vertical line of the sprite. To find where these values are stored, you will typically need to change one of the values in the DATA lines and see if it has any effect on the sprite. If it does, you've found the right spot.

Hacking the Hack

And here's one final challenge: try changing the rules of the game. The way the game behaves is controlled by many factors, some harder to modify than others. Changing the number of lives you get is usually a matter of finding where that value is defined (usually within the first few lines of code), while changing a physics system is a complete programming job in itself. Start off by modifying base variables (usually defined in LET statements, such as LET L=5 or L=5) and see what effect they have on how the game works. At this point, you're on your way to writing your very own type-in for others to try out themselves.

—*Cameron Davis*

Find Classic Computer Games

Dig up the classics you remember using the magic of the Internet.

So you've set up your 1980's vintage personal computer or found a way to emulate it on your own PC using some of the other hacks in this chapter, but now you're wondering what you can do with it. Hmm, let's think back on all the ways you once used your thousand-dollar piece of high technology. Hmm... doing your taxes? No. Making colorful flyers? No. Spreadsheets? Hahaha! Wait a minute, I've got it... *playing games*!

Is it any coincidence that the early personal computer industry grew out of video games? Was there really that much differentiating game consoles and computers at the time? Seriously, what difference was there between the Atari 400 "computer" and the Odyssey2 "game console"? They both had membrane keyboards that are impossible to do any substantial typing with, they both used ROM cartridges as their main media, and they were both used almost entirely for playing games. One just cost a lot more and the games looked prettier.

Sure, this might be explained by the fact that game companies wanted to grow the personal computer market by leveraging the strength of their existing brands. But the cynic in me says that game companies just knew they could make more money on higher-end gaming systems if they convinced people that what they were actually buying was a high-tech learning tool that would aid their day-to-day productivity and make their kids into geniuses. Then once the sale was rung up, it was all about video games.

So you want games for your old systems. It's okay, don't deny it. In this hack, I'll show you where you can still buy classic computer games online, and where you can find some for download.

Buy Classic Computer Games

Many of the tips and tricks in the first hack of this volume [Hack #1] hold true here, so you may want to go back and read that hack if you haven't already. I'll run down some information specific to computer games here.

It's going to be much easier to find games on cartridge format due to the more permanent nature of the medium. Original copies of floppy disk or cassette tape games are much, much harder to come by.

In general, remember that old computer games included the same things that video games of the time did—the cartridge or disk itself, a cardboard box, and an instruction manual. A reputable web retailer will list what is included with the item they are selling. You'll know a really good one if they write a bit about the quality of the box (whether it's smashed up or has perfect corners or what).

Good Deal Games offers a small page of classic computer software for sale (*http://gooddealgames.com/inventory/classic_computers.html*). Games for the Commodore 64, VIC-20, Texas Instruments TI-99, and TRS-80 are on offer. Packrat Video Games (*http://www.packratvg.com*) offers games for Atari, Commodore, and TI computers on separate pages accessible from the left-side menu bar on the front page.

A lengthy list of online stores that sell Commodore 64 parts, accessories, and game software can be found on Lemon 64, a fan page devoted to the system (*http://www.lemon64.com/links/index.php?genre=12*). Note that a few of the stores are based in the United Kingdom and elsewhere around the world.

If you're at the end of your rope, there's always the old standby, online auction site eBay (*http://www.ebay.com*). Unfortunately, browsing games by category isn't really workable—eBay only features "Games" and "Vintage Games" categories where software for all systems is dumped, and even then other games are sometimes placed in categories with the old computer hardware. Instead, try searching for "apple ii game" or equivalent. (Using the old style][rarely works in searches.)

Download Classic Computer Games

If it's Apple][games you're after, Virtual Apple (*http://www.virtualapple. com*) should be your first stop. You can browse through the directory of over 1100 disk images, then play them using an emulator embedded in the site. (You'll need to be running Internet Explorer.) Alternatively, you can scroll to the bottom of each game page and download the disk images to use with your Apple emulator of choice **[Hack #55]**.

> Many sites that offer classic computer games for download mix public domain games with games that are not authorized for free distribution. In the vast majority of cases, the publishers of games for obsolete computers seem to have no interest in stopping their distribution via these sites. Use your best judgment.

A large archive of Commodore 64 games is available at the appropriately named *www.c64.com*. Similarly, games for Atari computers are available at Atari Program Exchange (*http://www.atariarchives.org/APX/*) and *www. atari8bit.org*. Both web sites state that the downloadable games listed have been authorized for free distribution by the copyright owners.

As for VIC-20 games, a brief Google search turned up the FTP site *ftp.funet.fi/pub/cbm/vic20/games/*. Which brings me to my final point: if there's a specific old piece of software you remember and want to try to dig up again, try searching for information on it. Oftentimes there will be a software download offered.

HACK #62 Emulate Classic Computers on the Dreamcast

Get some serious use out of that Dreamcast keyboard you bought on sale.

Much has been said about the quality of the Dreamcast—it's a fantastic game system, no doubt. When I was still playing Quake 2 on my PlayStation, Dreamcast players were fragging each other to bits in Quake 3. But that's not why I love my Dreamcast—fact is, it's one of the best choices for a dedicated emulation console. It plugs into my TV, is relatively small and quiet, and runs more emulators than I have time to play with.

Burning Dreamcast CDs

Burning Dreamcast CDs is very easy on Windows, but not too hairy on other platforms. If you're a Mac OS X user, check out the tutorial at *http://www.dcemulation.com/mactools.htm*. If you're on Linux, you will find help at *http://www.dcemu.co.uk/linuxburn.shtml*.

I used Selfboot on Windows to create a disk image. This program can create either a Nero (DAO or TAO) or DiscJuggler (CDI) CD image. You can download SelfBoot from either of these sites:

> *http://www.dcevolution.net/DCHelp/index.php?id=apps*
> *http://www.dcemulation.com/neededtools.htm*

When you run the SelfBoot download, it will install itself on your computer. Open the folder where it was installed, and then run *SelfBoot.exe*. You'll need to pick a top-level directory containing your emulator files, and then choose which type of image to create.

Once you have the image, you can use Alcohol 120% (*http://www.alcohol-software.com/*) or DiscJuggler (*http://www.padus.com/*) to burn a CDI, or Nero Burning ROM (*http://www.nero.com*) to burn a DAO or TAO file. "Retro-Hack the Dreamcast" [Hack #50] also has information on burning Dreamcast CDs.

> You can't simply convert the Nero or DiscJuggler image to ISO and burn it, since there are some extra bits at the beginning of the disc image that the ISO does not preserve.

Atari 8-Bit Computers

The Atari 800 was my favorite, and it was one of the first systems I played under emulation. Like perhaps many others, there are a few floppy disks out in the world, perhaps rotting (or not) in a landfill somewhere, with the BASIC games I wrote on them. And no doubt, plenty of the games I played are sitting there as well.

The Atari 800 emulator available for the Dreamcast, is a port of the Atari800 emulator [Hack #59]. You can find information on Atari800DC at any of the popular Dreamcast emulation sites [Hack #50], or at the author's (Christian Groessler) web site, *http://www.groessler.org/a800dc/index.html*.

When you download the binary version of the emulator, you'll end up with a *.tar.gz* file that you can extract with the *tar* utility, WinZip (*http://www.winzip.com/*), or a number of other utilities. This file will extract to a directory named something like *atari800dc-0.75-bin*, although the actual version number in the directory name may vary.

The first thing you need to do is check the *README.dc* file for basic instructions. This will explain what you need to do to configure the emulator. The fundamental steps you need to take are these:

1. Obtain and extract the Atari ROM files into the *atari800dc-0.75-bin* directory. When you are done, *ATARIBAS.ROM*, *ATARIOSB.ROM*, and *ATARIXL.ROM* should be sitting in the same directory as the *IP.BIN* and *atari800.scrambled* files. You can obtain these ROMS from the PC Xformer Classic emulator, which is available at *http://atari800.sourceforge.net/download.html* and *http://www.emulators.com/xformer.htm*. You don't need anything else from the Xformer Zip file, but you might want to hang onto the disk images that come with it (**.xfd*, **.atr*), since they are fun to play with.

2. Copy all your disk images into the *disks* subdirectory under *atari800dc-0.75-bin*. Copy all your cartridges into the *roms* subdirectory. If neither the *roms* nor the *disks* subdirectories exist, you can create them.

3. Rename *atari800.scrambled* to *1ST_READ.BIN*. This is the emulator itself; the Dreamcast expects the program name to be *1ST_READ.BIN*.

Now you're ready to burn a Dreamcast CD from the contents of the *atari800dc-0.75-bin* (the top-level files, such as *IP.BIN* and *1ST_READ.BIN*, must be in the root of this CD). See "Burning Dreamcast CDs" earlier in this hack for more information.

Now that you've burned your CD, it's time to see whether you've made a coaster or an Atari. Put the CD into your Dreamcast and boot it up. If all goes well, you should see a splash screen, followed by the Atari self-test screen.

Your next step is to enter the emulator menu, select a disk or cartridge, and reset the Atari. Figure 5-16 shows the familiar Atari logo running off of an old demo disk that can be found in the PC Xformer Classic distribution.

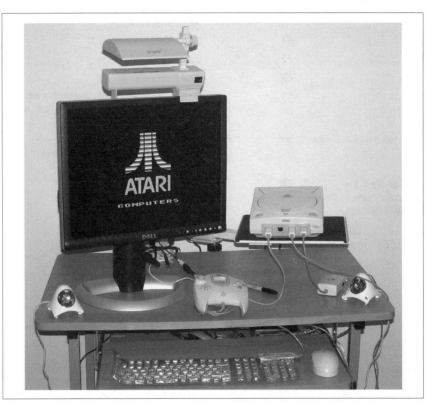

Figure 5-16. Atari!

Although the Atari800DC emulator boasts support for keyboards, I was unable to get it to work with my PC keyboard that was plugged into a Mad-Catz keyboard adapter. You will probably have better luck with a real Dreamcast keyboard. But even if you don't have a keyboard, you can get pretty far with the Atari800DC emulator—it's only slightly more painful than typing on a cell phone. You won't want to play Ultima IV this way, but it's fantastic for navigating through menus. Table 5-1 shows the Dreamcast controller and keyboard settings for Atari800DC.

Table 5-1. Atari800DC keyboard and controller settings

Controller button	Dreamcast keyboard button	Atari key
A	n/a	In game: joystick fire button; In emulator menu: select option
B	F4	Start
X	F2	Option
Y	F3	Select
L	F1	Bring up the emulator menu. Use this menu to load disks, cartridges, resert the Atari, and control various settings.
R (if you're in emulation)	n/a	Brings up the virtual keyboard. Use the joypad to navigate. Use A to send a key to the emulator.
R (If you're in the emulator menu or the virtual keyboard)	Esc	Leave menu
Start		Warm reset
Start+X	F5	Cold reset
Joypad		Joystick
n/a	F12	Reboot the Dreamcast
n/a	End	Help
n/a	Pause	Break
n/a	S3	Atari key

Apple][

The Apple][was one of the systems I wished I had when I was growing up. I remember seeing Wizardry I (Proving Grounds of the Mad Overlord) and realizing that if I had an Apple, I'd never need to leave the house. Apple][Soul Captor is the only Apple][emulator for the Dreamcast at the time of this writing, and fortunately, it's the only one you need.

You can download Soul Captor from a number of locations, including:

> *http://www.dcemulation.com/dcemu-apple2.htm*
> *http://consolevision.com/dreamcast/emus/apple2/*

Since the scrambled binary (*1ST_READ.BIN*) is already included in the binary download (*a2sc-bin-1.zip* at the time of this writing), you don't have to copy over a binary as you did with the Atari emulator from the previous section. Still, there's plenty to do:

1. Create a directory (such as *C:\Apple2*) and extract the Apple][Soul Captor binary distribution into this directory.

2. Add any additional disks to the *disks* subdirectory.

3. Update the *disks.xml* file to contain a list of all the *disks* in the disks sub-directory. You can either edit this in a text editor or run the *mkdisksxml. sh* shell script. Windows users will need a minimal Cygwin (*http://www. cygwin.com*) environment to run this script (to get to a directory on your disk drive under the Cygwin shell, use `cd /cygdrive/DRIVE_LETTER/path`, as in `cd /cygdrive/c/Apple2`).

Now you're ready to burn a Dreamcast CD from the contents of the directory you created. Make sure you select the one containing the top-level files, such as *IP.BIN* and *1ST_READ.BIN*. See "Burning Dreamcast CDs" earlier in this hack for more information.

Insert the CD you just burned into your Dreamcast, boot it up, and get ready to enjoy your Apple][experience. The main menu will let you start emulation, reset the emulator, load a disk, and load or save state to a memory card. Use the Dreamcast joypad to navigate the menu; press A to select and press B to leave the menu (after you load a disk by pressing A, you'll need to press B to leave the menu). Press Start to return to the main menu from within the emulator. Although Apple][Soul Captor doesn't have a virtual keyboard, you can usually press B or A on the controller to start a game, and the joypad works as a joystick once you're in a game.

Other Systems

There are a number of other emulators for the Dreamcast, in various states of development. Check out the sites listed in "Retro-Hack the Dreamcast" [Hack #50] to find emulators for the Amiga, Atari ST, Sinclair Spectrum, and more.

—*Brian Jepson*

Playing with Text Adventures
Hacks 63–67

You kids today are so spoiled! Back in the day, video games didn't have your so-called fancy graphics. In fact, many of them didn't have graphics at all! In this chapter, you'll learn all about text adventures, which also go by the high-falutin' name Interactive Fiction (IF). Some of them are the precursors to what are known today as point-and-click adventures, while some use the interactive storytelling concept to present narratives with branching paths, much like a Choose Your Own Adventure book.

Whether you want to play brand new IF or explore the classic original games, there are hacks here for you. You can even find out about massively multiplayer online text adventures that evolve and grow along with players. And if you think you'd like to try your hand at creating IF, you can learn how to do that here as well.

HACK #63 Play Interactive Fiction in One Minute

Enjoy quality text adventures quickly and effortlessly, no assembly required.

One of the best things about *interactive fiction*—the fancy-schmancy name for text adventures, but also a good catchall term for the type of game, since they don't always strictly rely upon text—is how easy it is to get up and running with a game. Installing an interpreter (the "platform" for the games) and getting some adventures for it [Hack #64] is much easier than poking around with MAME or emulating old operating systems.

For the moment, however, we'll set aside even operations as simple as those in favor of showing how you can get started with interactive fiction inside of a minute; no assembly required. All you need is a web browser, preferably one with Java enabled, and a capacity for lateral thinking.

Gameplay Basics of Text Adventures

Text adventures are the perfect videogames for people with poor hand-eye coordination: there's never anything rushing at you or any pressure to perform your next move, and the prompt will let you take all the time you need to enter your next command. If you can hunt and peck on a keyboard, you can play text adventures. The demands this sort of game makes are more mental than physical: it's a good thing that you'll usually have plenty of time and plenty of moves to find a solution, since puzzles in text adventures are usually more obscure than they might seem.

In fact, they can be surprisingly difficult when you consider how relatively limited your actions are within the game. Most text adventures recognize only very simple and fairly intuitive input; the hardest thing for the novice player to do might be to adapt to its unique grammatical structure, which is rarely similar to natural, everyday language. You can't, for example, tell the game you want to "scope out that girl over there." Leading articles are usually unnecessary (though often recognized if you can't help but include them), and the grammar you'll use is short and simple sentences like "look at girl," or "take sword."

Once you've got the basics down, it's best to start by using them to get a feel for your surroundings. Text adventure games are divided up into rooms, each one of which you can get a basic description of with the simple command "look." This initial, basic description will provide a number of hints and clues about objects in the room that might warrant further inspection, so you'll want to look closer by typing "look at [object]" or just "look [object]." It's only after you've thoroughly explored the room that you'll start to get an idea of what you should do there; every game has clues to its obstacles and puzzles, but they'll never announce themselves without a little digging.

When you've figured out what you need to do, it's helpful to remember a few commands that'll let you accomplish most of it. One especially important verb to remember is "take," which lets you pick something up (if it's portable, which not everything will be) and add it to your inventory. (If you forget what you're carrying, the "i" command will give a complete list of your inventory.) If you don't need it anymore or want to get rid of it for other reasons, use the verb "drop." If you're trying to put it somewhere specific, the syntax to use would go something like "put lotion in basket" or "put mickey into drink."

Once you've got that down, the rest should suggest itself—various other actions would be accomplished with syntax such as "glue hand to face" or "turn on doomsday device." One thing you would never do (at least in a well-written game), though, is "use doomsday device"—the "use" command is judged by almost every text adventure author to be too vague and all-encompassing, and to avoid players trying to cheat with a "use" shortcut, you'll usually have to be more specific. (That said, if you're stuck, try it, just in case the author has resorted to its... uh, use).

Once you've exhausted the possibilities for interacting with objects in a room—or once you think you have, anyway—it's time to move on to the next. The exits will always be noted in the room description, and to take one of them, you can type either "go [direction]" or simply "[direction]." If you wanted to climb a ladder, it would be either "go up" or "up," and to head through a north-facing door, the syntax would be "go north" or "north." (If you're really lazy, abbreviated versions of the cardinal directions such as "n," "w," "e," and "s" also work.)

The last major commands you're likely to need are related to conversation. Some games only support "talk to X," while others will allow you to "ask X about Y" as well as "tell X about Y."

More than any syntax or command lists, the main thing you need to know is that the solution is rarely obvious—what fun would the puzzles be otherwise?—and only by trying absolutely everything you can think of, no matter how little sense it might seem to make, can you make any progress. You can save at any point in a text adventure by typing "save," so if you're worried that what you're about to try might end your game, just save your progress first and then try it anyway. No matter how bewildered you may become, remember that there's a finite number of objects in your inventory, commands you can use, and things to do in each room, so something has to work. Keep trying!

Getting Your Game On

It's not hard to play and install text adventures: the download times for both the software to run them and the individual game files are short, and there are only two or three formats that the games are commonly released in. You don't even need that much, though, and here I look at a few games you can play with no installation necessary.

9:05. There are plenty of warnings surrounding this Java implementation of Adam Cadre's game 9:05, mostly due to the buggy nature of the interpreter. It's true that you wouldn't want to play many games in this format, but the online version of 9:05 (available at *http://adamcadre.ac/905.html*) makes a great starting point for a few reasons.

First, it's easy to jump right in and try a few moves. In fact, that's the stated purpose of the exercise—as Cadre says, "This page is here to serve as a preview of what interactive fiction looks like, for the uninitiated." If you're short on time, using someone else's computer, or just want to get a free preview before you devote any real effort to playing text adventures, a web-based trial game isn't a bad one.

Second, it's short. 9:05 is light on puzzles, and the whole game shouldn't take more than a few minutes, start to finish, even if you've never played any text adventures before at all. The tasks at hand aren't anything more complicated than removing your clothes and cleaning up before getting out of the house, and this is a good opportunity to learn the ropes of how to handle simple actions without having to worry about complex machinery or tricky commands.

Third, it's good. It's not deep, but the impact of 9:05's punchline comes across quite effectively, despite its brief length. This is your chance not only to see how to play text adventures, but also why to play them. Given a brief taste of what the text adventure format is capable of, you might be immediately hooked... and if you are, a good place to start is by replaying 9:05 again, which could result in a very different experience.

Galatea. Another good place to start for people new to the text adventure format would be Galatea, Emily Short's free-form piece based around conversation rather than puzzle-solving. It's not as no-nonsense as 9:05, but it's potentially more rewarding, and there are plenty of conversational paths and trees to explore, which lends itself to multiple replays.

The online version of Galatea, available at *http://jerz.setonhill.edu/if/gallery/galatea/index.html*, is attractively presented: the game itself, in a Java interpreter called ZPlet, takes up one frame, with the other frame devoted to supplemental information such as an explanation of the concept, suggested alternate conversation scripts to try once you've run out of ideas, and annotations and essays on the making of the game.

Once you've had your fill of Galatea, there are a few other online games hosted on the same server, all linked from *http://jerz.setonhill.edu/if/gallery/index.html*. The other text adventures in the gallery are Fine-Tuned: An Auto-Mated Romance, Metamorphoses, and of special interest to anyone curious about the format's history, Colossal Cave Adventure, the very first piece of interactive fiction ever written.

Mystery House Taken Over. Though it was the first of its kind to add simple graphics, Ken and Roberta Williams' Mystery House is still a text adventure at heart. Its interface consists of a parser that understands nothing more than simple two-word syntax for all commands, and though it has graphics of a sort, they're so sparse and abstract that it's just as easy to imagine what things really look like as it would be with pure text descriptions.

You can play the original Mystery House—albeit a version strangely stripped of its graphical complement—on the Web, but better still is the new collection of reinterpretations and reimaginings of the seminal adventure game available alongside it. The Mystery House Taken Over project (at *http://turbulence.org/Works/mystery/index.php*) uses the original 1980 game as a foundation upon which several of the most interesting creators of modern-day text adventures build new, strangely familiar edifices.

Like 9:05, you're free to download any and all of the Mystery House remixes available as part of the project; unlike 9:05, there's no drawback to playing them online using the Java interpreter. It's much more stable and easily used to play any or all of the projects anytime you feel like it. If you have to take a break during some of the more difficult versions, the Mystery House Java interpreter even lets you save your game.

The actual reworkings of Mystery House are many and varied; the Taken Over projects range from the silly and puzzleless (Adam Cadre's Mystery House Makeover) to the unsettling (Michael Gentry's You Wake Up Itching), from the faithful (Guy Minor's Mystery House: Occluded Vengeance) to the demented (Art Destroyer's Mystery House Nightmared). It's suggested that you play the original Mystery House first, with the included walkthrough if necessary, to get the most out of each successive mutation. Like 60-Second Shakespeare, the better you know the original, the funnier it gets.

Hacking the Hack

One of the best things about the Mystery House Taken Over project isn't just the wealth of interesting experimental versions of the original game, but the toolkit available from the same site. Once you become familiar with programming your own text adventures [Hack #67], download the Mystery House Taken Over Occupation Kit and take a stab at contributing your own reimagining of the Sierra classic. Who knows, future readers of this book might even see your effort up there along with all the rest!

—Nich Maragos

Download and Play Text Adventures

#64 Discover the ocean full of text adventures out there, then catch the best
ones.

The community of text adventure authors isn't huge, even by Internet sub-
culture standards, but they still produce enough output that someone brand
new to the format can feel bewildered about where to start looking. The central archive is vast and intimidating, and you might feel intimidated just figuring out which interpreter to choose. Fortunately, it's not as hard as it
seems.

If you want to download and play interactive fiction from your hard drive
rather than playing games via the web **[Hack #63]**, the first thing to do is install
what's known as a Z-Machine interpreter. Z-Machine clients run games
written in the Inform language, which is an open source version of the system used to write all the classic Infocom games **[Hack #65]** such as Planetfall,
Trinity, and A Mind Forever Voyaging. Not every game you'll come across is
written in Inform, but most of them are, and playing a few games that use
the Inform interpreter will teach you what you need to know when you go
looking for a TADS or Glulx interpreter. If you're looking for a list of all
known Z-Machine interpreters, you can get a pretty comprehensive one at
http://www.ifarchive.org/indexes/if-archiveXinfocomXinterpreters.html,   but
this page isn't exactly helpful when it comes to picking a game to play.

Baf's Guide

That's why you need Baf's Guide to the IF Archive, located at *http://www.
wurb.com/if/index/*. Every game mentioned in this section can be found at
Baf's, and there are enough pointers within the site to help you find what
you're looking for. You can search using a variety of criteria, including title,
star rating, language, genre, platform, or a stunning array of individual char-
acteristics—even if your tastes are as specific as "Lobjan-language games
based on Lovecraft horror written in GAGS with no puzzles, your choice of
protagonist gender, and containing a dragon," you can search by those
terms. You will not find anything you're looking for, but you can search by
those terms.

Before you go searching willy-nilly, though, there are a couple of worthy
directories to peruse first. The sidebar to the left has a section devoted to
"Comps/Awards," which you should consider making your first stop:
there's no such thing as an objective "best" IF, obviously, but the ones you'll
find in the competition winners section will at least have a high probability
of being very good.

There are many awards and competitions, but the two biggest are those listed underneath the general Comps/Awards category in the sidebar: the IF Comp and the Xyzzy Awards. Both competitions are open for anyone to vote, provided that authors don't vote for their own work. (The IF Comp is a bit stricter, with an automated frontend to ensure that judges play at least five games before judging; the Xyzzy Awards simply rely on the honor system.) The main difference is that the IF Comp is a pure reckoning of the best game, with the results released as a simple tally of the votes, while the Xyzzy Awards judge the submitted games in a variety of categories such as best writing, best setting, best NPCs, and best use of medium.

Both contest results are good for different reasons: if you're simply looking for the best text adventures, then the IF Comp listings are what you want. If you're looking for something specific from your text adventures, then the Xyzzy Awards can help, since they are broken out into separate categories. One caveat, though: since both the IF Comp and the Xyzzy Awards tend to be judged by people who are text adventure authors in their own right, and thus have fairly strong groundings in the medium, not every competition winner will necessarily be ideal for newcomers. Feel free to try out a few interesting-looking games, but if you get stuck or confused, don't be ashamed to set this section aside for later, and turn to a different sort of resource within Baf's Guide: the reviews.

One of the ways you can use the Guide is to look at only games that have been reviewed (try *http://www.wurb.com/if/game/reviewed* to go directly there). Though it has an obvious downside of leaving out quite a lot of games that no one has gotten around to writing about yet, the upside is that you get a little bit of opinion before downloading and playing the game. The reviews are all concise, usually 100 words or less, but they say enough to give you an idea of whether you'll be interested in playing it.

Other Sites

When it comes to the nuts and bolts of playing text adventures, Baf's Guide is pretty much all you need: all new text adventures make their way there eventually, and its ease of use means you'll be able to find them when they do. If you're interested in getting further into the text adventure community, though, there are other sites worth a look.

Brass Lantern

    Brass Lantern (*http://www.brasslantern.org*), founded by the organizer of the IF Comp awards, is a good source of news and articles relating not just to text adventures, but also the occasional graphical adventure such as the Myst series. Newcomers to text adventures will find the Beginner

Resources (*http://www.brasslantern.org/beginners*) section useful, while those with a little more experience in the format should check out its collection of editorials (*http://www.brasslantern.org/editorials*).

Xyzzy News

An online "magazine for interactive fiction enthusiasts," Xyzzy News (*http://www.xyzzynews.com*) runs news stories and other articles relating to text adventures, in addition to being the information clearinghouse for several competitions, not just the eponymous Xyzzy Awards. Back issues dating to 1995 are still available from the archives, which should help you get a sense of the reborn text adventure community's history from its own point of view.

rec.arts.int-fiction

Not technically a web site (though you can reach it through Google's newsgroup service at *http://groups.google.com/group/rec.arts.int-fiction*), this is nonetheless the place to go to get the freshest news and games as they happen. This is the source for the games archived on the IF Archive and organized at Baf's, and it's also a good place to find discussion both technical (authors recruiting testers, asking for help with a scripting language) and abstract interpretations of a particular game's story.

As when dealing with any other online community, it's a good idea to step back for a while and get a feel for the tone and feel of the place before posting, but once you feel comfortable doing so, go ahead and provide comments and/or bug testing for the authors who hang around the group. Like as not, they'll be grateful for the feedback.

Feelies.org

The Infocom creators that popularized text adventures often made a point of including strange widgets in the packaging of their games, such as the bit of fluff in the Hitchhiker's Guide to the Galaxy game. Though text adventures are no longer a commercial concern and have no packaging anymore, Feelies.org (*http://www.feelies.org*) aims to bring back *feelies* (a term for the physical detritus from the imaginary worlds in the game) for modern-day text adventure. If you're a fan of a particular game and want a memento of it, or if you plan to play it and want something to help you feel more immersed in that game's world, you might be able to find something in the catalog here.

All of these sites have their own sets of links, of course, so it won't take long to find even more information on the Web about text adventures and the people who make them, and even less time to get hooked on this unique, fascinating style of game. Happy hunting!

—*Nich Maragos*

HACK #65   Play the Best: Infocom Adventures

Collect and discover the cream of the crop of text games.

In the beginning, there was Adventure.

Widely accepted as the first text adventure game, Adventure (a.k.a. Colossal Cave) was written around 1975 by Will Crowther, programmer and spelunker. The game was very rudimentary, based on a map of a real-world cave system, but with certain elements of puzzle solving and treasure collection. The following year, the game was expanded extensively by Don Woods, and spread like wildfire across ARPAnet.

Among the people who quickly became fans of the game were Dave Lebling, Marc Blank, and Tim Anderson at MIT, who decided to set out to write a better game that drew on the same ideas. Along with Bruce Daniels, a fellow student, they completed the game over the next couple of years, eventually ending up with the first version of what is now known as Zork, the first Infocom title.

The original plan had been to simply call it a day once the game was complete, but a group from the MIT Laboratory for Computer Science decided that they wanted to set up a company together. With no plan for what to sell, they settled on the Zork game as their first product. It was also at this time that one of the greatest ideas of Infocom came into existence; in order to allow Zork to run across the range of home computers that were becoming available, they created the *Z-Machine*, a virtual machine that could be emulated across a range of hardware platforms, allowing a single version of the game to be produced and made available with the interpreter for each platform. It was this visionary step that allowed the game to be rapidly ported from PDP-11 to TRS-80 and Apple II, and that makes it possible to play the games on modern hardware.

Infocom went on to develop and publish some of the greatest and most groundbreaking pieces of interactive fiction ever made over the next few years, including two Zork sequels, Enchanter, Deadline (a mystery title), and the videogame version of The Hitchhiker's Guide to the Galaxy (in collaboration with author Douglas Adams).

It was in the mid-80s, however, that things started to turn sour. Although Infocom was still turning out some of the best interactive fiction available, much of the profits were pumped into a new piece of business software, a database called Cornerstone. At the same time, new generations of computer hardware were allowing graphical games to take over, a fact that Infocom never really seemed to come to terms with. As Cornerstone sank without a trace, Infocom was eventually sold to Activision, who hold the rights to their games to this day.

Activision pushed the company in what appeared to be more palatable directions to the modern gamer, introducing graphical interfaces in titles such as Beyond Zork and Zork Zero. But the time of the text adventure's popularity was drawing to an end, and despite producing consistently high quality games, commercial success slipped away. By 1989, the company's original staff had been decimated, and Infocom's time as the greatest purveyor of interactive fiction was over.

What Made Them Great

The caretaker at the school I went to once said something that seemed strange at the time. "I prefer radio to television," he said, "because the pictures are better." That contradiction lies at the heart of one of the main reasons for Infocom's success. The quality of writing in their games was consistently high, at a time when much of their competition in the text adventure field was limited to terse, single-sentence descriptions of locations. Take this example from the game Trinity:

> The temperature on this tiny platform is well below freezing. But it isn't just the cold that makes your teeth chatter when you look down that narrow stairway, thousands of feet high.

> Far below, the shadow of the structure stretches across the landscape. From this great altitude it looks like a dark finger, accusing a point on the east horizon.

The world that the player could imagine from the descriptions provided by the games was certainly more impressive than anything that computers of the time could display, and arguably still is, giving the lie to the old saying that a picture is worth a thousand words—roughly the number of distinct words in an average Infocom game, as it happens.

But it wasn't just the descriptions that made Infocom's games so good. The consistency of the worlds also set them above a lot of the competition. Ironically for a genre that had sprung from the map of a real-world location, a lot of early text adventures had very arbitrary maps that felt like a series of randomly selected rooms stuck together haphazardly. Not so Infocom titles; everything fitted together in a way that made sense within the context of the game setting, and a map of the game always made sense in a way that was not always the case for other titles in the genre. In fact a number of Infocom games came with convincing maps of the places they were set, which provided a useful tool for navigation within the game.

Within these worlds the puzzles—the meat of most interactive fiction—were also well thought out and integrated into the world. It's a lesson that a lot of game designers could learn from today, in their game worlds brimming over with color- and symbol-coded keys that must make it next to impossible for the villains to get around their homes. Where the path was blocked, it was normally in a more imaginative fashion, from the poodle yapping at the heels of your mailman in Wishbringer to the outright refusal of the game to allow you into the drive room in Hitchhiker's Guide to the Galaxy.

Puzzles in Infocom games were often considerably more complex than in other games of the time. Certainly they had their fair share of tasks that involved bringing an object to a location to gain passage, but there was so much more to some of the puzzles, from the time travel in Sorcerer which allows you to help yourself solve a puzzle to the interaction required by different specialist robots to accomplish tasks in Suspended, one of Infocom's quirkiest titles. A particular highlight of some games was the ability to solve the same puzzle in different ways: where there were multiple logical approaches to the same problem, often more than one of them would work. And even in those cases where they wouldn't, the games would sometimes acknowledge your ingenuity with a suitable response.

Puzzles, of course, couldn't be completed without a way of interacting with the game, and it was this interaction that was sometimes the worst enemy of the player in text adventures. Many games, including Adventure, had parsers that were limited to simple two-word instructions, and guessing the exact phrase required to carry out a particular action was often more infuriating than solving the puzzle itself. Infocom's parser was much more carefully crafted, and accepted input such as GET EVERYTHING EXCEPT THE RED KEY or PICK UP THE ZORKMID. BITE IT THEN PUT IT IN THE SMALL BOX. The ability of the games to understand more naturally phrased instructions made it far easier to concentrate on the task at hand, and removed another barrier between the player and the game world.

Packaging

One of the things that made Infocom's games so distinctive was their packaging, which often included a range of objects related to the game in some way, sometimes providing required information to solve the game, sometimes just adding atmosphere. It was yet another way of immersing the player further into the game, and often provided a form of copy protection as a handy side effect, as information found in the props would often turn out to be vital in completing the game.

The interesting pack-ins started with the mystery game Deadline, partly as a result of the input of Infocom's new advertising agency, and partly as a way to work around the space limitations of the game by taking essential background information and supplying it as hardcopy rather than within the text of the game itself.

Some of the more extravagant items are hard to come by in good condition these days. The mask that shipped with Suspended, for example, can add greatly to the value of the game. A few of the other interesting items you might come across in original Infocom games include:

- A scratch and sniff card in Leather Goddesses of Phobos, which gives off suitable aromas at various points in the game.
- A circus balloon in Ballyhoo—another tricky item to find intact.
- A matchbook (complete with scrawled phone number) in The Witness.
- A calendar celebrating the life and times of the Flathead dynasty in Zork Zero.

Buying Infocom Games

Unfortunately, laying your hands on Infocom games has become increasingly difficult of late. The rights to the games are currently held by Activision, which is not currently selling them in any form. They did release the first three Zork titles as freeware, but the software they released only runs on Windows 95 and above. You can download the games at the (unofficial) Infocom home page (*http://www.csd.uwo.ca/Infocom/*).

Fortunately for the eager collector, Activision also released a number of compilations which can provide a good way of building up a collection quickly. The first of these are the two Lost Treasures of Infocom collections. Volume one contains twenty games, including the five Zork titles, The Hitchhiker's Guide to the Galaxy, and the Enchanter trilogy. Volume two contains eleven of the remaining titles, most notably Trinity, Bureaucracy, Nord and Bert, and A Mind Forever Voyaging. These two compilations come in sturdy cardboard boxes with a nicely printed instruction manual containing copies of all of the important contents from the original release. Later, The Masterpieces of Infocom was released, a single CD containing 33 Infocom games with documentation provided on the disc in PDF format.

The bad news is that none of the games are commercially available any more, and that you need to make sure you have the right documentation from the original set (or the duplicates from the Activision compilations) to play the games through to completion. But there's some good news too.

The good news is that because of the nature of Infocom's games, the platform for which you get the games is not all that important. Provided you have some way of reading the discs, you should be able to convert the data into a format suitable for running on your machine of choice. The Interactive Fiction Archive at *http://www.ifarchive.org* has converters for Apple II, Atari and C64 versions of the games, and the data files needed to run the games are openly available from the disc on most other platforms. You can also find interpreter software for your platform of choice, from Gameboy Advance to Windows XP, at the archive site.

The best way to hunt down Infocom games these days is probably online. eBay is an obvious first port of call. A simple search for Infocom should turn up most of the matches, but don't forget to search for individual games by name as well. As always with eBay, the harder the listing is to find, the more likely you are to pick up a bargain.

You'll also find a number of Infocom fan sites online, some of which have trade or for sale sections. You're less likely to find real bargains that way, but if you want to be sure of what you're getting it's a good way to go.

The Games

Here are brief descriptions of a few of the best games that Infocom produced. Although virtually any Infocom game is a worthwhile purchase, these are among the ones that stand out as the best of the best.

The Hitchhiker's Guide to the Galaxy. The babelfish vending machine from The Hitchhiker's Guide to the Galaxy is probably the most famous puzzle in the history of interactive fiction, and deservedly so. Even people who have never played a text-based game in anger have heard of it. One vending machine, one dressing gown, and a miscellany of items grabbed from Arthur Dent's now-demolished home on his now-demolished planet, and all you need to do is get a fish out of the vending machine and into your ear. It's actually not that complex a puzzle, but it'll have most people tearing their hair out in frustration, while at the same time realizing that the fault is theirs, not the game's—the highest praise that a puzzle can receive.

This is almost certainly one of Infocom's highest points, and the people behind it are a big part of that. Steve Meretzky, one of Infocom's most prolific developers, and Douglas Adams, the author of the original radio play and book worked together on this one, and it shows in the quality of the writing, the understated humor, the ingenious and appropriate puzzles, and the all-round feeling of craftsmanship to the title.

There's also a certain level of defiance of convention to the game. At one point it will refuse to allow you to carry out a relatively innocuous action, then deliberately lie to you about the contents of a room. At another, a typo or misunderstood sentence will take on real significance for the inhabitants of another galaxy. To play the game online, head over to *http://www. douglasadams.com/creations/infocomjava.html*. All you'll need is a browser with Java support.

It says something about the quality of this game that over two decades after its original release, the BBC are using a graphically updated version of the game to promote the new Hitchhiker's Guide radio series. At the time of writing it is still available on the BBC web site and provides a great way of getting into one of Infocom's best titles for free.

The original packaging included a Don't Panic button, destruction orders for your home and planet, a microscopic space fleet, some fluff (the true significance of which is only made clear upon playing the game), and a pair of peril-sensitive sunglasses. Oh, and no tea. None of these contents are required to play the game through to completion.

Trinity. Trinity, by Brian Moriarty, is widely seen as one of the highlights of Infocom's output. It starts out in what appears to be the real world, but as World War III breaks out you are transported into a strange fantasy world faintly reminiscent of a darker version of Wonderland. If you can make sense of this strange new world then perhaps you can do something about the impending nuclear catastrophe.

Along with some of the best writing that Infocom had to offer, the game has a lot of extra comments for people who can recognize the references to places and people real and fictional scattered throughout the game.

There are some wonderfully twisted puzzles to solve, including a remarkable piece of coding that allows you to switch the whole world around to a mirror image of itself, including the map, by navigating a Klein bottle. And what other game allows you to attempt to pay Charon (the ferryman of the Styx) with a credit card rather than the customary silver coin?

Along with the game, the box contained a comic about the history of the atomic bomb, a map of the Trinity site, a fold-out sundial, and instructions for making an origami crane. There are important clues to be found in the comic book.

Planetfall. Planetfall was most notable for containing one of the most endearing and well-realized non-player characters (NPC) in text adventures. Floyd the robot was brought alive through cunning coding and great characterization. He reacted to your actions and the environment, and you ended up feeling guilty if you ever turned him off, and genuine emotion when he showed his truly heroic nature later in the game. It says a lot about the appeal of Floyd that Stationfall, the sequel to Planetfall, was billed as the return of Floyd, rather than of your character. And deservedly so.

It's not all about Floyd, though. The way in which you're thrown into the game's setting with very little knowledge of what's going on, and slowly build up a realization of what your goal is as you discover more of the background to the facility you find yourself in, is masterfully implemented. You're never led by the hand, but there's always something to point you in the right direction—even if you don't work it out in a single play-through, you can get a better sense of the world for your next attempt.

In the packaging you'll find a Stellar Patrol recruitment leaflet, a Stellar Patrol ID card, three postcards from a range of scenic planets, and some extracts from your diary. None of this is vital to completing the game.

A Mind Forever Voyaging. One of the features of Infocom games that makes them so appealing is the desire of the authors to push back the boundaries of the interactive fiction genre, to try something entirely new. Steve Meretzky's A Mind Forever Voyaging is one of the better examples of this. Set in a research lab in the near future, you play the part of a computer running simulation software for a social engineering plan in the final stages of evaluation. As a computer, you have no physical presence in the world, just access to a small number of communication nodes from which you can observe and communicate with the outside world, and a number of programs you can access and give simple commands. Enter the simulation, and you get to play the part of a citizen in the world governed by the Plan, exploring a simulated city of the future, first directed by the scientists at the facility, later by your own curiosity.

The most noteworthy point about the game from a pure gaming point of view is that this is a text adventure with maybe two puzzles in the whole game, neither of which is more than a couple of simple actions. Because in this case it's not about solving puzzles—it's about the social commentary provided by the ongoing simulations and the political responses to your discoveries.

It's a more short-lived experience than a lot of Infocom titles: you'll inevitably make your way through the majority of the game without anything to hold you back. But it's well worth seeking out as one of the better examples of a title that genuinely lives up to the title *interactive fiction*.

As always, the packaging for this game was lavish, with a color map of the city in which the game is set, a copy of "Dakota Online" magazine, and a pen. Above all, however, you'll need to make sure that if you're buying this title it comes with the decoder ring that was part of the original package. Without it you'll never be able to enter the simulation that makes up the majority of the game.

Other Highlights

Selecting a handful of Infocom games to recommend is always difficult, because a lot of worthy titles will always fall by the wayside. A few of the other great games that I can't let pass without at least a brief mention:

- Suspended is another title that tries to do something very different, with the user's interaction with the world taking place through six very specialized robots, each with their own sensors and capabilities. It's definitely not a game for everyone, but it stands out from the crowd and pushes the genre in new directions.

- The Enchanter trilogy (Enchanter, Sorcerer, and Spellbreaker) are set in a fantasy world with an ingenious set of magical spells for you to learn and use. The interaction between these spells can lead to some intriguing puzzles. The later games in the trilogy are among the most difficult titles Infocom produced, with some complex but extremely satisfying problems to solve.

- Leather Goddesses of Phobos is a humorous and slightly risqué pulp space opera adventure, which offers a series of lewdness settings (though at the end of the day all of them are comparatively civilized). The game features some great pulp writing and settings, as well as the odd addition of interactive smell, with various points in the game prompting you to use the scratch and sniff card shipped with the game.

- Nord and Bert Couldn't Make Head or Tail of It is another quirky title that throws the player into a series of short mini-adventures, each of which is based around a different style of wordplay, from spoonerisms to trite sayings. The traditionally solid Infocom parser is taken to a new level in this game, as it has to recognize the topics of the different adventures along with common variations.

—Adrian Jackson

Get Covered in MUDs

#66 Discover massively multiplayer online text adventures.

Over the past several years, the electronic gaming community has been aglow over the advent of graphical Massive Multiplayer Online Role-Playing Games (MMORPGs). From Ultima Online and Everquest to World of Warcraft, these games have been renowned for their ability to draw their players into playing them for days on end. All of these modern graphical MMORPGs owe a huge debt of gratitude to those little games spawned on a college campus back in 1978, the simple MUDs, the predecessors to every

MMORPG on the market today. These MUDs and their immediate progeny are still available even now, appealing to a niche market of enthusiasts.

About MUDs

So what is a MUD? The acronym typically stands for *multi-user dungeon*, but you may also hear some people refer to the D as meaning *dimension, diversion, domain,* or even *delusion*. Regardless, a MUD simply refers to a text-based environment where players create their own characters and interact with others. While there are non-game MUDs out there, we're going to ignore them—most MUDs are games. Many MUDs are done in the fantasy genre and focus on powering up your character via hacking-and-slashing, but those are not defining traits for these games. Science-fiction genre games are also enormously popular, and there are even some games rooted in historical events. One sub-genre of MUDs, MUSHs (Multi-User Shared Hallucinations), focuses more on social interaction rather than on having the highest stats, and its players create their own content.

Though the onset of graphical based MMORPGs have cut into the numbers of MUD players, these games still attract a notable following. A popular claim among MUD players is that the human imagination is the most advanced graphical engine possible, and I've heard many people describe how pure text creates a level of immersion absent from graphical games.

MUDs divide up their areas into smaller sections called rooms, much like most single-player text adventures did. A typical room has a room title, a description of the room and people/objects inside of it, and lists what directions you can move your character in. Note that a room does not need to be an actual room; it can be in the middle of a desert or in the middle of a forest, like in the following example:

```
[Woodland Clearing, Altar]
The sunlight pierces through the blanket of tree leaves above onto
a simple altar crafted from marble. A gentle breeze rustles the
foliage every so often.
You also see Bob the Barbarian and a bag of gold.
Obvious exits: north, east, up.
```

Most MUDs are totally free to players, meaning as long as you have a computer with an Internet connection and an appropriate client, you can play them wherever, whenever. These games also have very tiny player bases—probably 50 at most. The larger MUDs will cost you money, but in return, you will get better customer support and additional in-game features, and in general they will be far more polished. The standard for these games is to offer a 30-day free trial.

Before Playing a MUD—the Setup

Before you actually start playing a MUD, you'll have to find one you like, then learn a little more about it.

Find a game. There are by some estimates around 3000–5000 MUDs running today. The most frequently updated lists are at MudConnect (*http://www.mudconnect.com*) and Top Mud Sites (*http://www.topmudsites.com*). If you're looking for a game outside of the fantasy genre, you may have to scavenge a little harder, but it shouldn't take you too long. The topics range from MUDs based on the Lord of the Rings to Star Trek and X-Men and everything in between.

Start reading the game's web site. Your fellow players and the GameMasters (developers/support staff for the game, a.k.a. GMs or Gods) for your chosen MUD will all have myriad assumptions about you as a new player (newbie) to their game, but the one thing they will all share is a presumption that you have the aptitude and desire to do a lot of reading. Otherwise, why on earth would you be playing a MUD instead of the latest installment of Halo or Grand Theft Auto?

See what character classes and races are available. Read how combat works. Get a feel for the game's economic systems and political climate. Most importantly, read the rules on player conduct. Some games allow player killing (PK'ing), some don't, and others allow it only under very specific circumstances. Many games have very strict policies against *multiplaying* (controlling multiple characters at the same time). Almost all prohibit executing programs where your character does certain actions while you're off doing something else away from your keyboard, commonly referred to as *botting* or *AFK* (away-from-keyboard) *scripting*.

Find a client you like. Most MUDs will offer an applet or tell you the URL/port code that you can use to access their game via Telnet or your own client on their respective web pages. If you can possibly avoid it, do not use Telnet, as the most you can do is type out commands and see a very fixed number of lines back. The specialized applets offered with most games are also usually lacking, though there are some exceptions. However, those applets will typically only work with one game, so if you decide to play another game, you will have to recreate all of your settings again, a lot of which would probably be reuseable your next game.

If you decide to look for your own MUD client, there are some features that you should look for at a bare minimum. First is the ability to create logs of your play sessions for later reference. Second, you need the ability to create your own triggers/macros. This way, you don't have to get carpal tunnel syndrome from typing attack commands repeatedly. Third is the ability to highlight or to filter strings of text. Highlighting is invaluable for calling your attention to certain text strings when you're in areas with high scroll rates, or where text shows up on your screen very quickly. Filtering also helps with this and it also lets you blacklist players that are annoying.

One of the most well-known third-party client programs is zMUD (*http:// www.zuggsoft.com*). It provides advanced script creation support, map creation, multiple windows, multiplaying, and even links to MudConnect so that all you have to do is point and click to access a plethora of MUDding goodness. While it costs $30, you get to try it for free for 30 days, and any upgrades thereafter will be free.

Creating Your First Character

Set aside a couple of hours in the early evening hours for your first login. MUDs are nowhere near as time-intensive as many of the graphical MMOR-PGs out there, but you ought to set aside time in case you are instantly hooked. You should also have some paper and a pencil for scribbling down notes.

The best time to log into a game for the first time is slightly before the evening hours for whatever time zone most of the game's players live (typically the United States). If you're logging in from within the States at 8PM to an Australian or British MUD, don't be surprised if you don't see anyone there, because the players for that game will be asleep. Peak hours for most of these games is during prime time; logging on beforehand should give you plenty of time to create your character, get adjusted to some of the commands, and then do some solo exploration before people log in en masse after work or school.

When you first log into a MUD, you will be prompted to create your character name and your password. Some MUDs require that you email the administrator to get access; others will let you log in immediately.

Exercise the same common sense you would when creating a password for these games as you would when creating a password for anything else in your life: create a unique password for each character/game you try out and keep it to yourself. Make passwords from combinations of letters and numbers that mean something only to you. I've met too many people who gave out their passwords to their bestest friend ever who later whined to their respective game's Gods or GameMasters that their character was "hacked."

When you're thinking of your character name, remember that first impressions are everything. In the absence of seeing an avatar, the only thing that another player will see when you first walk by is something like:

```
>Milnar has just entered the area.
```

"Ah," that player will think. "There's a newbie who's at least trying. I shall go up to meet him." Okay, they wouldn't think *exactly* that, but since MUDs are in general small, close-knit communities, they'd do their best to make you feel welcome.

Conversely, if that same player saw:

```
>Lorddarthvader has entered the area.
```

...their response would range from ignoring you outright to calling for a GM. They'll definitely inform their friends that a *n00b* (a new person who's probably going to be a major annoyance) has entered the area. You've committed the sin of naming yourself after a ridiculously famous character from Star Wars, which even in a Star Wars themed MUD would be forbidden, and topped it off with the title "lord". Many games reward titles to their own players after they've accomplished certain tasks.

For those of you who have trouble coming up with names, much less names that would be in-genre for your particular game, there are multiple name generators online. One of the best ones is the Fantasy Name Generator (*http://rinkworks.com/namegen/*).

Once you've selected your character name, it is time to finish creating your character! Your game should handwalk you through the creation process, giving you prompts in case you ever get stuck. Some games choose to put you through a character generator and then spit your character out into the live game. Others have an integrated tutorial process where you learn the basic commands for movement and interacting with objects as you define your character's appearance/history.

Taking the First Few Steps

Congratulations on finally making it through all that character creation/tutorial stuff! You are now at the bottom of the player totem pole. This should be a temporary state.

The creators for your MUD are well aware that you want to jump right into their game. Resist that temptation and scour the help files for the following information. The 20 additional minutes you spend now reading up on this information will save you a lot of time and frustration later.

If the game features combat, check and see what the penalties are for death. As a beginning player, whatever death penalties your game has will be very light, but those penalties generally will become very harsh as you advance a couple of levels. It's best to know what these are beforehand. See what commands display information about your health if that wasn't covered during the tutorial.

Also, see what commands are used for chat channels. Learn under what circumstances you can use each particular one. Many MUDs feature some sort of newbie channel where newbies can ask questions. Don't be embarrassed about using it—that channel is there for you! Most experienced players on your MUD will be more than happy to tell you where the popular hangouts are, where to do things at your given stage of the game, and anything else you may want to know.

Common MUD Commands

This is far from an exhaustive list, but it should cover your immediate needs until you meet other people in the game who can tell you about all the various chat channels and attack commands for your particular game.

- HELP: Self-explanatory—gives you information on how to play your particular game. You will be using this one a lot. If the information you get from this is sparse, that's a sign that you should be playing a different MUD.
- WHO: See how many people are online. Some games allow you to see the character names of those people as well as any GMs that want players to know they're around.
- SAY: Allows you to talk in your present room.
- SHOUT: Allows you to communicate to many nearby rooms. Use this sparingly, as many people do not appreciate anyone taking up excess air space.
- LOOK: Look around the area. Commonly abbreviated as l (a lowercase L).
- NORTH/SOUTH/EAST/WEST: Travel in each of the main cardinal directions to another room. Abbreviated to n, s, e, and w, respectively.
- UP/DOWN: Move up or down. Abbreviated as u and d, respectively.
- INFO/SCORE/SKILL: See your character's present statistics.
- INV: Displays your inventory.
- QUIT: Log out.

A few don'ts when you ask for help. Don't ask for free handouts; you will almost never get them, and will certainly cause yourself to be alienated by other players. Don't type in all caps, as this is considered yelling. Finally, don't repeat the same question over and over in rapid succession. Ask a question once—if someone knows the response, they will answer you fairly quickly. If no one responds and there's chatter on the channel, repeat or rephrase your question politely after a couple of minutes .

Scribble down a list of the commands that you've learned so far and what they do. Yes, you could refer back to the help files for that information, but you learn the commands much faster if you make your own cheat sheet.

Finally, now that you've done all that, go out, explore, and have fun! If it helps you, sketch out your own map as you slowly start exploring. I found that graph paper helped enormously when sketching areas out. See if you can access any in-game maps. Note the locations of stores and other major buildings. Hook up with other novices or find a friendly older player who can show you the ropes. Make lots of friends. What's the point of playing a multiplayer game solo, anyways?

Best of luck playing your first MUD!

—*Carol Van Epps*

HACK #67 Write Text Adventures with INFORM

Create your own journey through a land of words.

Text adventures (also known as *interactive fiction*) have been around for decades. While these are broad terms, they usually conjure thoughts of a large array of sectioned-off areas, each with its own unique description, items, and traversable paths. Without a vivid imagination and a keen eye for detail, forays into text-based worlds are brief, painful experiences.

Although it's certainly possible to build a text adventure from scratch, there's no need to reinvent the wheel if you're looking to make a traditional "go north, look, get key"-style game. If that sounds good, then you have your pick of several tools. One of the best is INFORM, a powerful and highly customizable design system that consists of code libraries with pre-written commands and a game-writing language. To write games with INFORM, you'll need to download the libraries and a compiler, available for all platforms at the INFORM homepage: *http://www.inform-fiction.org/*. You should also download the manual, since it will come in handy when you want to move beyond basic rooms and items.

To actually *play* your creations, you'll need to download the INFORM interpreter [Hack #64].

Remember the Rules

Whether you're a first-timer or a veteran author with dozens of games under your belt, it's good to keep a few basic rules of text-adventure writing in mind when you start a new project.

Be detailed, not wordy. Short, custom descriptions for items and clever sentences for nonstandard actions are more than enough to satisfy a player and draw them into the game.

Remember the role of imagination. Your descriptions are going to paint a different picture for everyone no matter how detailed they are, so don't let them run on for pages. Unless her looks are important to the story, describe that princess as having "the most beautiful body you have ever laid eyes on," rather than going on for several sentences about the mole on her cheek.

Make sure the game is always winnable! If the player picks up a carrot and eats it, only to realize later that they needed it to catch a rabbit, make sure they can either get another carrot or find another way to trap the rabbit. Leaving them no recourse but to restore a saved game is poor design; the player is punished not by the elements of the world, but by a lack of vision on the author's part. In other words, every possible action should kill the player, win the game, or move them somewhere along the path to victory (even if it's back a few steps).

Plan Out Your World

Planning is always essential to developing a game. This is especially true with INFORM; each room allows for movement in the eight cardinal directions, up/down, and in/out. Carefully mapping out your game, as shown in Figure 6-1, before you start coding will give you a valuable reference and minimize dead-ends. Your game will undoubtedly evolve throughout the process, so keep the map current and ensure your digital and paper versions match up.

You'll be focusing on how to code, not write, so the first game will be a painfully boring example program containing the basics elements of a text adventure: a few rooms, a puzzle that requires an item to be solved, a key, and a locked door.

Create the Game

Everything in an INFORM game, from the most detailed room to the humblest item, is called an object. The INFORM libraries define a myriad of properties that can be assigned to objects, and depending on which ones

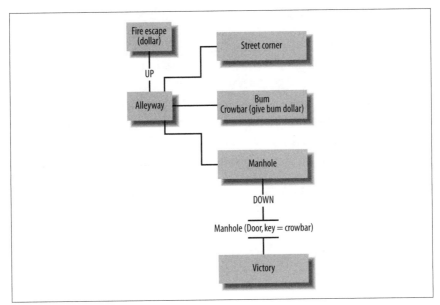

Figure 6-1. Map of the example game

you set, it can become a room, an item, an NPC, or something you create yourself.

This game will place the player in a small city alley; the player must find some money, give it to a bum in exchange for a crowbar, and pry open a manhole to enter the sewers.

The INFORM skeleton. Here is the skeletal source code for this game:

```
!% -D

!Define constants
Constant Story "City Adventure";

Include "Parser";
Include "VerbLib";

!Game code goes here

[ Initialise; ];

Include "Grammar";
```

The first line is a special case; letters following the !% are read in as compiler switches (-D is debug mode). All other lines starting with ! are treated as comments.

In the next section, you define any constant values you wish to use throughout the game. Some of these are built into INFORM, such as Story (the name of your game). Others include Headline (a brief description shown at the start of the game) and MAX_SCORE (the maximum amount of points a player can earn).

The next two lines are critical; they load in INFORM's text parser and command library. You can't do much in a text game if the game can't understand your input!

Next comes the actual game, followed by the Initialise routine (be careful, the spelling *has* to be British). Initialise is run at the start of the game and can be used for giving the player items, setting their initial location, and generally whatever your game requires.

Finally, the grammar library is included. Due to dependency issues, the Parser, VerbLib, and Grammar libraries must always be included in that order, with Parser and VerbLib coming before the game code, and Grammar at the end.

Make some objects. Fire up your favorite text editor and type in the code from the previous section, then save it as an INF file (such as *city.inf*). You're free to compile it at this point, but it'll only result in the player standing around in the dark. So head to the !Game code goes here line, delete the comment (if you even bothered to type it), and create the game's rooms like so:

```
Object the_alley "An alley"
    with description "This is a small back alley.",
    has light;
```

Though a good game would be a bit more descriptive, this room will serve our purposes nicely. The first line tells the compiler that you're about to create a new object, followed by its *internal name*, "the_alley", and *external name*, "An alley." The internal name is used to refer to the room within the source file, while the external name is what the player sees. This system makes it possible to have the player see multiple rooms with the same name; a handy feature for mazes, forests, or other areas where unique room names aren't necessary.

The with and has keywords both start lists of various object properties. The first property you need to define is description; what the player sees when they look at the room, item, etc. We also illuminate the room using the light property.

Add in the remaining rooms:

```
Object fire_escape "Fire escape"
    with description "You're way up high. The floor wobbles unsteadily.",
    has light;
```

```
Object street_corner "6th & Elm"
    with description "Cars rush back and forth. Forget about crossing.",
    has light;

Object bum_town "Pat's cardboard box"
    with description "A surly bum named Pat lies asleep here.",
    has light;

Object manhole_room "Manhole"
    with description "There's a manhole at this end of the alley.",
    has light;

Object win_room "You win!"
    with description "You descend into the sewers, smiling happily.
       You win!",
    each_turn [; deadflag = 2;],
    has light;
```

each_turn is a loop-like structure that executes every turn the player is in the
room. In this case, it sets deadflag, a built-in player property, to 2, which
indicates that the player has won the game. By default, deadflag is set to 0
(the player is alive). Setting it to 1 kills the player.

Move down to the Initialise routine and change it to:

```
[ Initialise; location = the_alley;];
```

Save the game as *city.inf*. Open a shell/terminal window (or Command
Prompt under windows) and make sure that:

- The Inform library (*English.h*, *Grammar.h*, and so forth, which are contained in a Zip file that you can get at *http://www.inform-fiction.org/*), and the *city.inf* source file are all sitting in your current directory.

- The Inform compiler is located in your $PATH (%PATH% on Windows).

Then, compile the game. Here is how the compilation looks on Unix, Linux,
or Mac OS X (Windows will be similar):

```
$ inform city.inf
Inform 6.30 (27th Feb 2004)
$
```

That's it—no news is good news.

Now you can run the game (*city.z5*) with an INFORM interpreter. You'll
find yourself stuck in the alley; you can "look" to your heart's content, but
that's about it. The next step is to connect the room. Replace the definition
of the alley with this (the new lines are shown in bold):

```
Object the_alley "An alley"
    with description "This is a small back alley. A fire escape is
       accessible immediately above you, and exits lead off to the
       east, southeast, and northeast.",
```

```
    u_to fire_escape,
    ne_to street_corner,
    e_to bum_town,
    se_to manhole_room,
    w_to "There's nothing but a brick wall that way."
    has light;
```

If you compile and run the game again, you'll be able to move from the alley to another room, but not vice-versa. Go back to the source file and connect the street corner, bum, and manhole rooms back to the alley. Remember: you have twelve total connections available: the eight cardinal directions (n_ to, s_to, e_to, w_to, nw_to, ne_to, sw_to, se_to), up/down (u_to, d_to), and in/out (in_to, out_to). For example, to complete the manhole room, you'd change the definition to:

```
Object manhole_room "Manhole"
    with description "There's a manhole at this end of the alley.",
    nw_to the_alley,
    has light;
```

To add more detail to the environment, you can also display a custom message if the player tries to go down a nonexistent path (such as west in the alley).

There's nothing that stops you from making strange and nonsensical connections, like going *up* to the fire escape from the alley, and then *east* from the fire escape back to the alley. This is usually a bad idea; it'll be hard for both you and the player to keep an accurate map of the game world. Confuse the player with a cryptic message or difficult puzzle, not random room connections.

At this point, the world is complete; compile the game and you can roam anywhere you like... except the win_room.

Add in items. Now that the basics are in place, you can add the items. You can create them anywhere in the source file, but it's best to separate them from the rooms.

INFORM describes items for you; during play, items appear after a room's description as "There is also a/an X here."

You need to create four items: A dollar to give to the bum, the bum himself (whom I've named Pat), a crowbar to pry open the manhole, and the actual manhole, which leads to the final room and ends the game. The dollar and crowbar are just generic items that sit in the player's inventory, while the manhole actually functions as a door, and requires some special properties.

Note that in addition to defining an internal and external name for each item, you can type in a room name on the first line to set its initial location:

```
Object dollar "dollar" fire_escape
    with description "It looks like it's been in circulation for quite
        a while.",
    name 'dollar' 'bill' 'buck' 'washington',
    has;

Object crowbar "crowbar"
    with description "It's old and rusty, but it still does everything
        it was made to do.",
    name 'crowbar' 'bar',
    has;

Object manhole_lid "manhole" manhole_room
    with description "The center reads, 'City Sewage'",
    name 'manhole' 'hole' 'portal',
    with_key crowbar,
    door_dir d_to,
    door_to win_room,
    has scenery door openable lockable locked;

Object bum "Pat" bum_town
    with description "He reeks of alcohol and potato chips.",
    name 'bum' 'pat' 'drunk' 'vagrant',
    life [;
        Give:
            if(noun == dollar)
            {
                move dollar to self;
                move crowbar to player;
                "Pat grunts and rolls over, revealing his crowbar.
                You take it.";
            }
            else "Pat doesn't want that.";
    ],
    has scenery animate proper;
```

You will also need to connect the manhole room to its door (the manhole lid). You can do that by adding the line shown in bold to the manhole room's definition:

```
Object manhole_room "Manhole"
    with description "There's a manhole at this end of the alley.",
    nw_to the_alley,
    d_to manhole_lid,
    has light;
```

Here's a breakdown of how the items were defined in the preceding code:

name

> The name attribute allows the player to refer to an item by more than its in-game name. While you don't need to go crazy, put yourself in the player's shoes and think of at least one easy-to-use shorthand name. Be extremely careful with the syntax: use single quotes, one space in between names, and a comma at the end.

object manhole_lid

> The manhole is a lockable door, and as such has several attributes that define it as such. The first is its key (in this case, the crowbar), followed by which direction it's blocking (down), and where it leads (the "You win!" room).

> door, openable, lockable, and locked are also door-related properties that should be self-explanatory. Leaving any one of them out will render your door useless.

scenery

> scenery takes care of two things: it prevents the player from picking up the object, and it removes the "There is also a manhole/bum here." line. Since both the room name and description allude to the object's existence, it's unnecessary (and awkward) for the player to see the extra line. You can still look at and interact with them like any other item.

life

> The large block of code following Pat's declaration is a routine that allows you to interact with him. life is a built-in INFORM routine; here, you use it to make Pat react to the player. Give indicates the command Pat reacts to, while if(noun==dollar) checks to see if the player is trying to give him the dollar. If she is, Pat takes the dollar and gives the player the crowbar via INFORM's move function. Otherwise, Pat declines.

animate

> animate tells INFORM that Pat is a living creature, which will change the game's default responses when you interact with him, while proper indicates Pat is a proper noun and should be referred to by name, with no articles in front.

The game is now complete; you can wander all over our little world, give poor Pat some money and triumphantly enter the sewer. You can go back and add in more rooms, make Pat react to more commands, or take what you've learned and start bringing your own ideas to life.

Here is a walkthrough of this simple game. Note that this game takes some artistic license with the meaning of the word "unlock":

```
City Adventure Release 1 / Serial number 050621 / Inform v6.30
Library 6/11 SD

An alley
This is a small back alley. A fire escape is accessible immediately
above you, and exits lead off to the east, southeast, and northeast.

>u

Fire escape
You're way up high. The floor wobbles unsteadily.

You can see a dollar here.

>take dollar
Taken.

>d

An alley

>e

Pat's cardboard box
A surly bum named Pat lies asleep here.

>give pat a dollar
Pat grunts and rolls over, revealing his crowbar. You take it.

>w

An alley

>se

Manhole
There's a manhole at this end of the alley.

>unlock manhole
(with the crowbar)
You unlock the manhole.

>open it
You open the manhole.

>d

You win!
You descend into the sewers, smiling happily. You win!

    *** You have won ***
```

```
In that game you scored 0 out of a possible 0, in 11 turns.

Would you like to RESTART, RESTORE a saved game or QUIT?
```

Amazingly enough, we've barely scratched the surface of INFORM's capabilities—it's possible to kill the player with traps or deadly items, have the game respond to commands with custom messages, award points for getting items or accomplishing tasks, and even add to the code libraries and make your own commands! With INFORM, your imagination is the only limit. To take your game to the next level, be sure to read the Inform Designer's Manual (*http://www.inform-fiction.org/manual/*).

—Matt DelGiudice

Playing with DOS

Hacks 68–71

In this age of user-friendly operating systems, automatic upgrades, and slick graphical user interfaces, isn't there a part of you that longs for the simplicity and the pliability of the good old C:\> prompt? Many of us are schooled in the ways of Disk Operating System, or DOS, the simplistic but powerful OS that used to run our lives before Windows 95.

Sure, maybe all things considered you'd rather not go back. But perhaps you want to find some of the old DOS games that you remember so fondly. Or maybe you still have the floppies (yes, floppies) sitting around, but need a solution that will let you actually play the games again on your modern, superfast hardware. Or maybe you're interested in writing your own DOS game. If that's the case, then the hacks in this chapter will satisfy all your primal urges.

Run DOS Without Microsoft

#68

Put a freeware DOS onto your computers.

Among the various permutations of Windows, XP offers the best mix of DOS compatibility and system stability. However, you will still run into a lot of problems running your favorite old DOS applications [Hack #70] even under Windows XP. And if you're running Mac OS X, Linux, or an earlier version of Windows, you may run into more trouble.

If so, there are a couple of solutions. DOSBox [Hack #69] will let you run most applications without grief, and it should be your first stop.

But for pure DOS goodness, nothing beats running DOS right on the bare metal. Dig that 386, 486, or Pentium out of your closet, and get ready to boot it, old school style.

FreeDOS

If you want a DOS for your computer, and you'd prefer to use *libre* software, FreeDOS is just what you need. Even if you are in need of a DOS just because you can't find your old DOS boot disks, FreeDOS is *probably* just what you need. It offers excellent compatibility, is actively supported and developed, and has advanced features such as power management and IDE DMA support. You can read all about FreeDOS and download it at *http://www.freedos.org*.

This Old Box

If you want to run FreeDOS on a real computer, you're going to need the right equipment and software:

1. If your FreeDOS computer can boot or read from a CD-ROM, all you need is another PC with a network connection and the ability to burn a CD-ROM. Download the FreeDOS CD-ROM image and burn it to a CD. You may want to burn it at a low speed, since the compatibility between new and old CD drives can be hit and miss.

2. If your FreeDOS computer has a CD-ROM but can't boot from it, you'll need a way to write a disk image to a floppy. You can use *rawrite* (Windows, DOS) or *dd* (Linux and Unix) to write the image. If all your network-connected machines are floppyless, consider booting your FreeDOS computer into whatever operating system it has, transferring your floppy images over, and writing the images to floppies there. Download the FreeDOS CD-ROM image and burn it to a CD, and also grab the 1.44MB floppy image and write it to a floppy.

3. If your FreeDOS computer has no CD-ROM, you'll need to write a full set of FreeDOS images to floppies (see the `disksets` subdirectory of the FreeDOS site).

In this hack, I'll choose door number 2, not just because it has elements of both 1 and 3 and thus economizes on the size of my examples, but because my 486, a Compaq luggable (see Figure 7-1), can't boot from its CD-ROM drive.

Partitioning. When I started to consider doing a clean install of DOS, I took a look at the network card that was working so nicely. The external SCSI controller and internal IDE adapter were living in such harmony under Debian GNU/Linux that I couldn't bring myself to blow away the Linux installation I had. So, I decided to steal a little disk space from my swap partition.

Figure 7-1. My new DOS box

 If you just want to use your whole disk, use the FreeDOS installer to configure your partitions. But I suggest that you put a Linux system on the same machine, even a really tiny one. It could make it easy to maintain your system later.

First, I logged in as *root*, turned off the swap, fired up *fdisk*, and looked at my partitions:

```
debian:/home/bjepson# swapoff -a
debian:/home/bjepson# fdisk /dev/hda

Command (m for help): p

Disk /dev/hda: 64 heads, 63 sectors, 619 cylinders
Units = cylinders of 4032 * 512 bytes

   Device Boot    Start      End    Blocks   Id  System
/dev/hda1   *         1       16     32224+  83  Linux
/dev/hda2           558      619    124992   82  Linux swap
/dev/hda3            17      557   1090656   83  Linux

Partition table entries are not in disk order
```

Next, I deleted the swap partition, recreated it with a smaller size, and used the unused space to create the fourth primary partition as a FAT partition:

```
Command (m for help): d
Partition number (1-4): 2

Command (m for help): n
Command action
```

```
   e   extended
   p   primary partition (1-4)
p
Partition number (1-4): 2
First cylinder (558-619, default 558):
Using default value 558
Last cylinder or +size or +sizeM or +sizeK (558-619, default 619): 600

Command (m for help): n
Command action
   e   extended
   p   primary partition (1-4)
p
Partition number (1-4): 4
First cylinder (601-619, default 601):
Using default value 601
Last cylinder or +size or +sizeM or +sizeK (601-619, default 619):
Using default value 619

Command (m for help): t
Partition number (1-4): 2
Hex code (type L to list codes): 82
Changed system type of partition 2 to 82 (Linux swap)

Command (m for help): t
Partition number (1-4): 4
Hex code (type L to list codes): 6
Changed system type of partition 4 to 6 (FAT16)
```

Then I checked to make sure the partitions looked correct, and wrote the partition table to disk:

```
Command (m for help): p

Disk /dev/hda: 64 heads, 63 sectors, 619 cylinders
Units = cylinders of 4032 * 512 bytes

   Device Boot    Start      End    Blocks   Id  System
/dev/hda1   *         1       16     32224+  83  Linux
/dev/hda2           558      600     86688   82  Linux swap
/dev/hda3            17      557   1090656   83  Linux
/dev/hda4           601      619     38304    6  FAT16

Partition table entries are not in disk order

Command (m for help): w
The partition table has been altered!

Calling ioctl( ) to re-read partition table.

WARNING: Re-reading the partition table failed with error 16:
Device or resource busy.
The kernel still uses the old table.
The new table will be used at the next reboot.
```

```
WARNING: If you have created or modified any DOS 6.x
partitions, please see the fdisk manual page for additional
information.
Syncing disks.
```

Finally, I rebooted, and then fixed up the swap file:

```
debian:/home/bjepson# swapoff -a
swapoff: /dev/hda2: Invalid argument
debian:/home/bjepson# mkswap /dev/hda2
Setting up swapspace version 1, size = 88764416 bytes
debian:/home/bjepson# swapon -a
```

Keeping the existing Linux system on the Compaq gave me another advantage: when I need to to copy files over the network, I can boot into Linux, copy the file over, and easily move stuff to my C: drive.

Installing FreeDOS. I'll need a CD image and floppy image to install Free-DOS. On one of my modern PCs, I downloaded the FreeDOS CD image (*fdbootcd.iso*), burned it to a CD-ROM, and inserted it into my Compaq's CD-ROM drive.

I went back to my soon-to-be a dual boot FreeDOS/Linux box and downloaded the FreeDOS floppy image (*fdos1440.img*), wrote it to a floppy disk with dd if=fdos1440.img of=/dev/fd0, and rebooted with that floppy in the drive.

As it turned out, the FreeDOS installer got as far as formatting my C: drive, but could not recognize my CD-ROM drive. Here's another advantage to having Linux on the other partition. Since the FreeDOS installer can work directly off the ISO image, I solved the problem by booting into Linux and copying the ISO image over to my C: drive:

```
debian:/home/bjepson# mount /dev/hda4 /mnt/
debian:/home/bjepson# cp fdbootcd.iso /mnt/
debian:/home/bjepson# umount /mnt/
debian:/home/bjepson# reboot
```

That was a quick and easy solution. But there are other solutions for problems booting from CD-ROM. When the Free-DOS boot floppy first starts up, you could select the Smart Boot Manager to see if it will detect your CD-ROM. You could also choose to start the FreeDOS installer and then load a driver floppy, assuming you can find one for your hardware. But, this trick (booting into Linux, downloading some DOS games [Hack #70], copying them over to the DOS partition) will come in handy if I decide I want to run some cool DOS games. And why else would I be doing this?

Then, I went through the FreeDOS installation again, and it found the ISO image I had copied over and ran through the installation.

You might be done now. But if like me, you're adding FreeDOS to a machine currently running Linux, you'll need to configure your bootloader to be able to boot DOS. On my system, I needed to add the following to */etc/lilo.conf* (you may also want to check that the prompt option is enabled so you don't have to press the Shift key to get the menu):

```
other=/dev/hda4
  label=FreeDOS
  table=/dev/hda
```

Next, I had to run the *lilo* command as *root* for this change to take effect):

```
debian:/home/bjepson# lilo
Added Linux *
Skipping /vmlinuz.old
Added FreeDOS
```

Once this was done, I rebooted, selected FreeDOS at bootup, and enjoyed DOS in all its glory!

Hacking the Hack

One problem remained: my CD-ROM drive still didn't work.

I know from having run MS-DOS on this machine that I need two drivers to use my CD-ROM drive: *ASPI2DOS.SYS* and *ASPICD.SYS*. The trick is finding them; you may need to use Google to find the right DOS drivers for your hardware (FreeDOS is compatible with regular DOS drivers). The good news is that these files are available on any Windows 95 or 98 boot floppy. Even better, you can boot from that floppy, watch as the drivers load (it loads a mess of SCSI drivers) and figure out which one you need.

The next step was to copy the files to my C: drive (I put them in *C:\BJ*, using my initials for the location of drivers I've installed; you will come up with something more clever), and edit my *CONFIG.SYS* file to load them. Free-DOS uses a funny syntax with its menu system. A ? followed by a number indicates that the item should only be loaded when the user has selected the corresponding menu option. So ?12DEVICE=FOO indicates that FOO will only be loaded if the user chose 1 or 2. I added these two lines to *CONFIG.SYS*, right after the line that loads EMM386:

```
12?DEVICE=C:\BJ\ASPI2DOS.SYS
12?DEVICE=C:\BJ\ASPICD.SYS /D:FDCD0001
```

FDCD0001 is one of device names that ShsuCDX (FreeDOS' equivalent of MSCDEX) looks for when it's run from *AUTOEXEC.BAT* (FreeDOS should have configured it as such, but there's no harm in double-checking). With these two lines added to my *CONFIG.SYS*, my CD-ROM drive is successfully configured as the D: drive.

—Brian Jepson

HACK #69 Run DOS Games

Get DOS games running correctly under your current operating system.

With the widespread acceptance of DirectX, running games on a Windows machine has become very easy and straightforward. Generally, you need only run a setup program and double-click on the resulting icon to start the game. However, running games on a PC has not always been so simple an affair. Conventional memory, extended memory, expanded memory, sound card IRQs and DMAs, mouse drivers, file buffers, boot disks and myriad other configuration details conspired to thwart a DOS gamer's best efforts. Sometimes, getting a DOS game to run was a game in and of itself.

While Windows has freed users from the hassle of having to remember specific hardware settings when running games, it has done nothing to ease the task of running old DOS games. In fact, Windows NT/2000/XP have eschewed the DOS-based nature of their predecessors in favor of a pure Windows-only OS which only makes running already finicky DOS games even more difficult. Thankfully, there are ways to circumvent these issues and bring your favorite DOS games back into service.

When DOS Roamed the Earth

Sometimes, running a DOS program is as easy as simply running an executable. More often than not, the process is a bit more involved. As developers sought to offer games with more graphics, sounds, and features, the number and complexity of settings users had to adjust to support these features increased. This complexity showed up particularly in the realm of sound card configuration and memory management.

In the pre-Windows 95 world, installing a sound card often involved running a DOS utility that would have you configure various hardware settings for the sound card, usually its port address, IRQ, and DMA. Later, when installing a DOS game, you would have to remember these settings as well as your sound card model. If you happened to have a non-standard sound card installed, you would have to know which major soundcard's interface and settings it emulated for the purpose of DOS gaming.

Memory management under DOS can also be a complicated affair. DOS has four major types of memory: conventional memory, upper memory, expanded memory, and extended memory.

Conventional Memory

The first 640K of memory. This memory is primarily used for loading programs. It is also known as base memory.

Upper Memory Blocks

The 384K of memory immediately following the 640k of conventional memory. It is generally used for storing the BIOS and video RAM. This and conventional memory make up the 1MB of RAM, which early PCs designers reasoned, for the foreseeable future, would be more than enough for most peoples' purposes.

Expanded Memory

A method for addressing memory above the DOS 1MB limit that temporarily writes the contents of memory higher than 1MB to a portion of upper memory that can be accessed and manipulated by DOS programs.

Extended Memory

A later and more natural method for accessing memory above 1MB that involves more direct access than expanded memory. However, many DOS programs require expanded memory so memory managers, like *emm386.exe*, often emulate expanded memory when needed.

Many later DOS games have particular requirements about how much conventional memory is available (some as much as 600K of the total 640K) and how extended or expanded memory are made available. To free up conventional memory MS-DOS 6 included *memmaker.exe*, a program that attempts to push device drivers and other memory-resident programs out of conventional memory and into upper memory. Several DOS games use their own extended memory managers and require that MS-DOS's default extended memory manager, *emm386.exe*, have certain options disabled or not be loaded at all.

Sometimes all the memory and driver tweaking required to get certain DOS games running would leave you with a system unsuitable for running other software. At times like these people would create *boot disks*. Boot disks are system disks with all the tweaks and settings necessary to get a DOS game running and can be used to start the computer in a condition ready to run particular DOS games. Some game installers even offered the option to automatically generate a boot disk for the user. However, sometimes additional tweaking was needed.

Even with a DOS game successfully running, later computer users, especially those with Pentiums and higher, would find that their games simply ran too fast. The solution to this problem generally involved using a CPU slowdown utility like Mo'Slo (http://www.hpaa.com/moslo/).

Many of these issues apply to PCs running Windows 98 and earlier because one always had the option of rebooting to directly to DOS if a program wouldn't run in Windows. Since Windows XP is not built on DOS, it's not possible to reboot the machine directly to DOS. In fact, the Windows XP command prompt is also an MS-DOS emulator. Unfortunately, this DOS emulator is limited in terms of features useful for getting old DOS games running properly. The solution is to use a DOS emulator more suited to the task.

Running DOS Games Using DOSBox

While it is possible to run many DOS games in Windows XP's native DOS emulator, you may never be able get them to run at a reasonable speed, even using slowdown utilities like Mo'Slo. A better solution is to use a DOS emulator designed for running DOS games.

DOSBox is a DOS emulator that is available on multiple platforms, including Windows, Mac, and Linux. It emulates various hardware, memory and graphics settings and helps circumvent a lot of the messy details involved in running a DOS game on Windows. It also allows the user to control its emulation speed and to tune the performance of the DOS game it is running.

The installer for DOSBox can be acquired from the Downloads section of the DOSBox web site (http://dosbox.sourceforge.net). As this writing, the latest Windows version of DOSBox is Version 0.63. Once downloaded, the installer can be used to install DOSBox on your system.

As an example, let's walk through the steps necessary to get Champions of Krynn, a 1990 title from SSI's "Gold Box" series of Advanced Dungeons & Dragons simulators, running under Windows XP. We'll be installing Champions of Krynn from the Advanced Dungeons & Dragons Gold Collectors CD which contains unmodified "Gold Box" titles.

Using the install program included on the Gold Collectors CD, install Champions of Krynn (under Windows XP, not DOSBox) to the default directory on the hard drive (*C:\WIZWORX\COK*).

You are now ready to run Champions of Krynn. Technically, you can run it with WinXP's native DOS emulator but it will run *very* fast and music will probably not work. DOSBox will provide a much more satisfying experience. You can start DOSBox by selecting the DOSBox icon from the Start Menu. Once DOSBox has started you will see the screen shown in Figure 7-2.

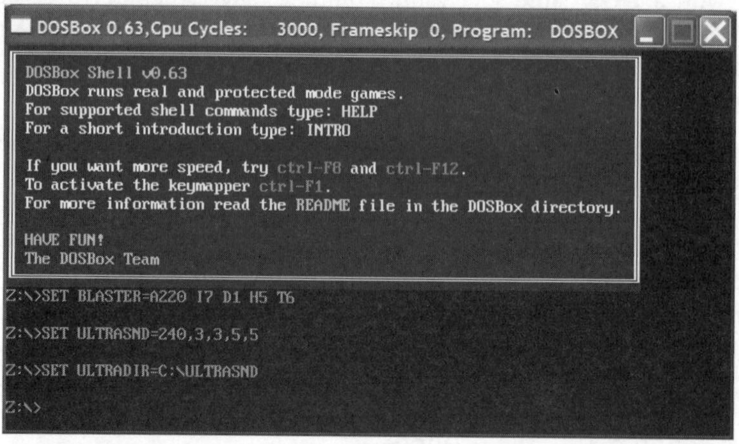

Figure 7-2. Starting up DOSBox

In order to access directories on your hard drive, they must be made visible to DOSBox by using the *mount* command. The *mount* command maps a directory on your real hard drive to a drive letter in DOSBox. Type the following command:

```
mount c C:\WIZWORX\COK
```

This command mounts the Champions of Krynn directory (*C:\WIZWORX\ COK*) to the C: drive in DOSBox. You can then change to that drive and get a directory listing with the following commands:

```
c:
dir
```

You should receive output similar to what you see in Figure 7-3.

From here, run *START.EXE* to start Champions of Krynn. Upon startup the game, it queries for information regarding graphics and sound. Tell it to use EGA graphics (the best available) and an Adlib sound card (one of the cards emulated by DOSBox.) The next settings are for mouse/joystick use and the location of the save directory. These are up to the user. Enter your choices and you'll see a splash screen like the one in Figure 7-4.

Champions of Krynn is running, at a decent speed no less. This is all well and good, but there are a few tweaks we can do to make the experience a little more pleasant.

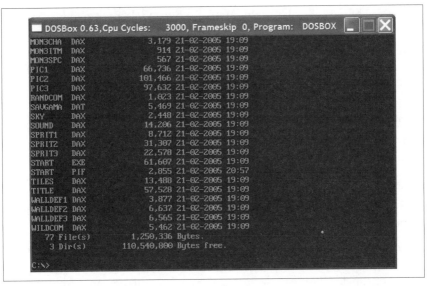

Figure 7-3. Partial dir listing for Champions of Krynn

Figure 7-4. Champions of Krynn, back from the dead

Tweaking DOSBox for Speed and Convenience

Right now, you need to go through several steps to start a DOS game using DOSBox. Also, the game is confined to a relatively small window. It would be nice to be able to start a game in DOSBox with custom settings merely by double-clicking on a single icon. With Windows batch files and some simple command-line parameters, you can.

First create a new text document on your desktop and rename it *run_cok. bat*. Right-click on this file and select Edit. In the window that opens enter the following, then save the file:

```
cd C:\Program Files\DOSBox-0.63
dosbox C:\WIZWORX\COK\START.EXE -fullscreen -exit
```

Now, when you double-click on *run_cok.bat*, it will change to the DOSBox install directory (*C:\Program Files\DOSBox-0.63*) and run DOSBox with the given settings. The first parameter tells DOSBox to automatically mount and start the Champions of Krynn executable. The optional -fullscreen and -exit parameters tell DOSBox to run in fullscreen mode and to automatically exit once Champions of Krynn is done running.

Now you're ready to enjoy Champions of Krynn as it was meant to be enjoyed. Possibly even better. Note that, should a DOS game be running too slowly or quickly, you can decrease DOSBox's emulation speed by pressing Ctrl-F11 or speed it up by pressing Ctrl-F12.

 Even with all this tweaking, there is one inconvenience you can not avoid: manual-based copyright protection. Many DOS games enforce copyright protection by referencing content in their printed materials, usually in the form of a question whose answer is contained somewhere in the game's instruction manual. If you don't happen to have a particular DOS game's manual, you may be able to find a digital copy on its install disk or on the Web.

Running Games with Proprietary Memory Managers

While the preceding steps should cover most older DOS games, DOS programs that use large amounts of RAM may require a few extra steps to run under DOSBox. Let's take a look at an example involving Ultima 7: The Black Gate, a game known for both quality gameplay and a frustrating start-up process (due in no small part to its custom memory manager, Voodoo).

The Ultima 7's installation progresses mostly without incident from the Complete Ultima 7 CD and you should be able to run the installer directly from the CD in WinXP. The installation program queries for sound card brand and settings. By default, DOSBox emulates a SoundBlaster 16 at port 220 with IRQ 7 and DMA 1. The closest match in the install program is a Sound Blaster Pro with the same settings. The installer will then complain about your PC being in protected mode and offer to make a boot disk. We will ignore the warning and the offer and solve the problem in a much cleaner way.

First, let's try running Ultima 7 using the same method we used for Champions of Krynn. Start up DOSBox from the Start menu and mount the Ultima 7 directory (*C:\ULTIMA7*). Next, try starting Ultima 7 by typing ultima7 at the C: prompt. The message shown in Figure 7-5 appears.

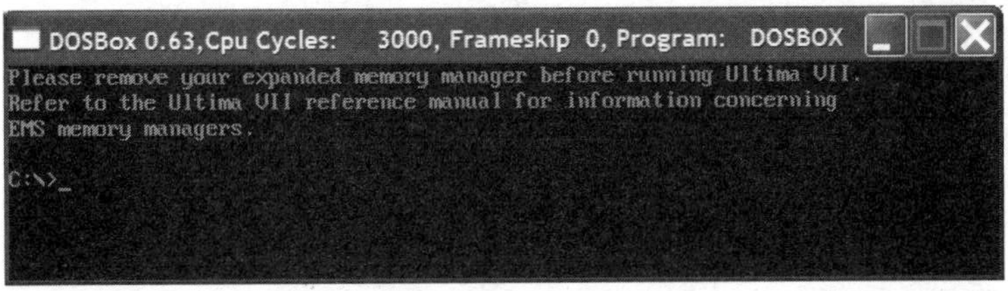

Figure 7-5. Ultima 7 can't run with other EMS managers

It seems that Ultima 7 can't run in DOSBox because of the way it is handling expanded memory. Luckily, DOSBox's memory handling can be changed by editing its configuration file. The default configuration file, *dosbox.conf*, can be found in the DOSBox directory (*C:\Program Files\ DOSBox-0.63* for Version 0.63 of DOSBox). Since we don't want to change the DOSBox configuration for all the programs it runs, we'll make a copy of the configuration file and call it *dosbox_u7.conf*. Now, open the new configuration file and locate the following section:

```
[dos]
# xms -- Enable XMS support.
# ems -- Enable EMS support.

xms=true
ems=true
```

Disable EMS support like so:

```
[dos]
# xms -- Enable XMS support.
# ems -- Enable EMS support.

xms=true
ems=false
```

Disabling EMS support is essentially the same as running *emm386.exe* without EMS support and allows Ultima 7's Voodoo memory manager full reign of memory handling.

Tweaking Speed

You can also set DOSBox's initial emulation speed and frame skipping to values that work best for your computer by changing the settings in the following sections of the configuration file:

```
[render]
# frameskip -- How many frames dosbox skips before drawing one.
# aspect -- Do aspect correction.
# scaler -- Scaler used to enlarge/enhance low resolution modes.
#   Supported are
#   none,normal2x,advmame2x,advmame3x,advinterp2x,interp2x,tv2x.

frameskip=0
aspect=false
scaler=normal2x

[cpu]
# core -- CPU Core used in emulation: simple,normal,full,dynamic.
# cycles -- Amount of instructions dosbox tries to emulate each millisecond.
#       Setting this higher than your machine can handle is bad!
# cycleup  -- Amount of cycles to increase/decrease with keycombo.
# cycledown  Setting it lower than 100 will be a percentage.

core=normal
cycles=3000
cycleup=500
cycledown=20
```

Now that the new configuration file is ready, you can pass in the name of the file as a runtime parameter. As with Champions of Krynn, you must define a batch file to run Ultima 7 using custom DOSBox settings. Create a file called *run_u7.bat*, open it for editing, and add the following:

```
cd C:\Program Files\DOSBox-0.63
dosbox C:\ULTIMA7\ULTIMA7.COM -exit -fullscreen -conf dosbox_u7.conf
```

The -conf parameter allows you to specify a configuration file to use instead of the default *dosbox.conf*. In this case, we use *dosbox_u7.conf*. Now that the batch file is ready, you can double-click on *run_u7.bat* and see what happens (see Figure 7-6). Now that's a sight for sore eyes.

Running Games that Require CDs

Instead of having the player keep hard copy manuals on hand for reference, some later DOS games implemented copyright protection by requiring that a game CD be inserted in order to be played. Playing a CD-based game in DOSBox requires a few extra steps to have DOSBox recognize a CD-ROM drive. Let's take a look at one such game and see how we can get it running.

Figure 7-6. Ultima 7, up and running

Privateer, a 1993 space-flight sim from Origin Systems, was released along with Strike Commander on a single CD. In order to play the game, users must install it and, as most of the game's data files stay on the CD, have the CD in their computer.

As before, begin the process by running the install program from the Privateer/Strike Commander CD. Set the music and sound card values, remembering that DOSBox emulates a Sound Blaster 16 at port 220 with IRQ 7 and DMA 1. Once installation is complete, you must continue on to the process of getting DOSBox ready to run Privateer.

Like Ultima 7, Privateer uses its own proprietary memory manager, called JEMM. Also like Ultima 7, Privateer requires that you disable DOSBox's EMS emulation by changing the line ems=true to ems=false. Once you make the change to the configuration file, save it as *dosbox_priv.conf*.

To get DOSBox to run Privateer with these new settings, create a batch file called *run_priv.bat* containing the following:

```
cd C:\Program Files\DOSBox-0.63
dosbox C:\PRIVATER\PRIV.EXE -exit -fullscreen -conf dosbox_priv.conf
```

The batch file automatically starts Privateer using DOSBox. However, when you try it, you'll notice that something is wrong, as shown in Figure 7-7.

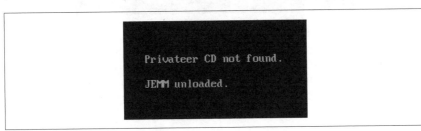

Figure 7-7. Privateer can't run if DOSBox can't see the CD

DOSBox is unable to locate the Privateer CD because it has not been told to mount the CD-ROM drive. To mount a CD-ROM drive in DOSBox, you use the *mount* command as in the following example:

```
mount d d:\ -t cdrom
```

As with mounting hard drive directories, this mounts the CD directory in the second parameter as the drive letter identified by the first parameter. Many DOS games assume that D: is the CD-ROM drive, so you should mount the CD-ROM drive as the D: drive in DOSBox. The -t cdrom parameter flags the mounted directory as a CD-ROM drive (otherwise, DOSBox would treat it as a hard drive).

It would be nice to not have to explicitly mount the CD-ROM drive each time you run Privateer. Fortunately, you can modify *run_priv.bat* to have DOSBox run the *mount* command before attempting to run Privateer as seen here:

```
cd C:\Program Files\DOSBox-0.63
dosbox C:\PRIVATER\PRIV.EXE -exit -fullscreen -conf dosbox_priv.conf ↵
-c "mount d d:\ -t cdrom"
```

The -c "mount d d:\ -t cdrom" parameter that we have added tells DOS-Box to execute the command mount d d:\ -t cdrom before running *PRIV. EXE*. Additional commands can be specified using the additional instances of the -c parameter. Now that you've made the change, save the file, double-click *run_priv.bat*, and you should see the screen shown in Figure 7-8.

Figure 7-8. Privateer, ready for action

You're now ready to re-live the 90s and enjoy Privateer in its full glory. There is, however, one more step you can take to further streamline your experience. You can try hacking Privateer so that you don't have to have the CD inserted to play.

Hacking the Hack

The process for executing a no-CD hack on a game varies wildly depending on how CD dependence is implemented. Some games contain a reference to the CD in a configuration file. In the case of Privateer, this data can be found in *PRIV.CFG*. Opening up *PRIV.CFG* with Notepad reveals the following:

```
=D:priv.tre
```

It usually takes a bit of guesswork to figure out what data in a configuration file means. In this case, it's fairly obvious that it's referring to a file on the D: drive called *priv.tre*, which happens to be Privateer's primary data file. This suggests a certain course of action. First, copy *priv.tre* into the Privateer directory (*C:\PRIVATER*). Next, modify *PRIV.CFG* like so:

```
=C:priv.tre
```

Finally, you should no longer need the -c "mount d d:\ -t cdrom" when running DOSBox, so remove it from *run_priv.bat*. Now, when you run the game, Privateer will check the C: drive for *priv.tre* and you should no longer need a CD to play.

With DOSBox and some creative configuration, you can get most DOS games to run as conveniently as games designed for Windows. Remember, if you have trouble getting a DOS game to run or to stop requiring a CD, do a Google search for advice, maybe entering *"name of game* dosbox help." Chances are someone else has been working on the same problem.

—Robert Ota Dieterich

Rediscover Classic DOS Games

HACK #70

Remember that game? You know, the one with the thing that stayed on the ground and the thing that went up in the air with the beeps and the boops?

DOS games were a funny affair. If you were a home computer fan from the days of 8-bit home computers like the Atari, C64, and Apple][, you probably thought it was an odd transition to go from all that color and sound to a computer with no sound card and, at best, four washed-out pastel colors. But then you picked up an EGA card. And then a Soundblaster. And next thing you know, you had a CD-ROM drive in your computer. Sure, it was a few hundred dollars above and beyond the original cost of your computer, but you finally had sixteen colors on your screen and multichannel sound.

Of course, if you were one of the lucky owners of a PC that had fancy audio and graphics features out of the box, you started having fun before the rest of us. Who can forget the venerable Tandy 1000, which had the graphics and sound capabilities of a PCjr, but stuck around a bit longer? In fact, if you run the installers for some classic DOS games, you'll still see a configuration option for Tandy Graphics.

There were plenty of games to be had on the shelves of video game stores back then, but there are plenty of classics that weren't quite as mainstream. If you hounded the bulletin boards back in the old days, you might remember such classics as Sopwith and Alley Cat.

Once you know how to get FreeDOS [Hack #68] running on your old hardware, or after you've settled into DOSBox [Hack #69] as your DOS environment of choice, you're ready to dig up the classics and return to the day when shareware games splashed their ordering information on screen as soon as you chose "quit".

The Old Days of DOS

Two of my favorite video games of all time are CGA classics. In Bill William's Alleycat (Figure 7-9), you played a cat that jumps around an alley, avoiding dogs, catching mice, trying to stay in one piece, and maybe meeting up with your girlfriend. Most of the action takes place in the alley, but once you jump into an open window, you'll find yourself avoiding a broom. Get to the right place, and you'll be taken to a mini-game (for example, jumping into the fishbowl transports you to a large pool where you're avoiding electric eels and trying to eat fish).

You can find Alleycat at a number of sites listed in the section "Finding the Classics".

Sopwith, shown in Figure 7-10, is a classic that puts you in the cockpit of a prop plane and pits you against cows, birds, and other players. You can find Sopwith at *http://www.classicgaming.com/sopwith*. The author of Sopwith, Dave Clark, has released the source, and lots of great stuff has followed. Sopwith.org is the main site for all things Sopwith. Pick up a copy of the game or one of its variants, and even a map editor so you can make your own levels. And don't miss Sopwith 3, a modern remake that maintains the classic look. CGA never looked so good.

As EGA and VGA took hold, DOS games started to get much better. Apogee's shareware Commander Keen series was, for many people, the first time an IBM PC game could feel like a real video game system. It may have not been Nintendo, but many long nights have been sacrificed to this series.

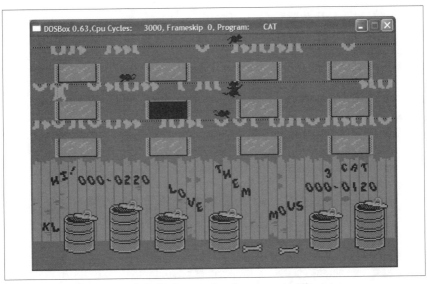

Figure 7-9. Hopping around clotheslines and garbage cans in Alleycat

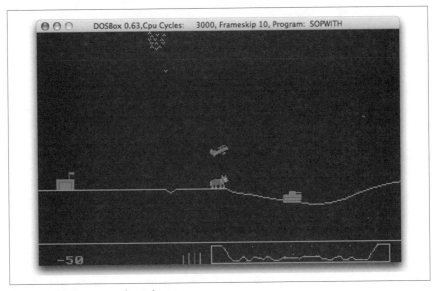

Figure 7-10. Step away from the cow

Finding the Classics

If there's an old game you remember, chances are pretty good you can find it out there. If it's a shareware or freeware game, you shouldn't have any trouble finding it online. There are a few sites out there that catalog these classics:

The DOS Games Archive

This site (*http://www.dosgamesarchive.com/*) has a catalog of games with links to downloads. You can filter by shareware, freeware, and demo games, as well as the genre of game you're interested in. In addition, this site features interviews with DOS game developers, discussion forums, a newsletter, and more.

DOS Games

At the time of this writing, DOS Games (*http://www.dosgames.com/*) boasted links to 400 classic DOS games. You'll find them organized by genre here, along with descriptions and downloads.

FreeDOS Links

FreeDOS [Hack #68] is a retro-DOS geek's best friend. They also have a great set of links to DOS games and other resources.

> One of the great things about old shareware and freeware is that the creators of these games meant for them to be distributed far and wide, so you don't have to explore the dark corners of the Internet to find games to play. This approach works fine as long as you can still find the person you're supposed to pay when it comes time to unlock the rest of the shareware game you're addicted to.

I don't mean to ignore all the commercial games that were available. Some of the earliest games I played included the Ultima series and Sierra On-Line's King's Quest, Gold Rush, and Manhunter. Fortunately, many of these games are available in CD-ROM collections. Although you will probably have trouble finding these games on the shelves in mainstream video game stores, they can often be found in the bargain bin or on auction sites such as eBay.

To get a (usually) daily dose of yesteryear, there are a couple of weblogs that I find essential. Abandonia (*http://www.abandonia.com/*) posts a screenshot and game description to their home page on a daily basis. Virtual PC Guy (*http://blogs.msdn.com/virtual_pc_guy/*) is Ben Armstrong, a Program Manager on Microsoft's Virtual PC team. He posts a mixture of technical stuff about Virtual PC and Virtual Server, but frequently posts some tips about getting an old DOS or Windows game running under Virtual PC.

—*Brian Jepson*

Write a DOS Game

Put your old game programming books to good use.

Many of the most fondly remembered games in video game history were DOS games. Scorched Earth, Lemmings, the Ultima series, King's Quest, The Secret of Monkey Island, Warcraft, and many others have brought countless hours of entertainment to gamers everywhere. But, why should it stop there? With just a compiler, a decent game programming library, and a little ingenuity, you can create your own games to run in DOS alongside the giants of yesteryear.

Enter DJGPP and Allegro

DJGPP (DJ's GNU Programming Platform) is a free C/C++ development system for MS-DOS. It began in 1989 in response to a comment by Richard Stallman that *gcc*, the standard UNIX C/C++ compiler, could not be ported to MS-DOS due to the limits of DOS's 16-bit architecture. DJ Delorie took this statement as a challenge and began working on his port of *gcc* to MS-DOS. Since then it has become a stable and feature-rich product with a wide array of support programs and code libraries.

Allegro is a game development library developed for DJGPP that has since been ported to multiple operating systems. It wraps routines for handling 2D graphics, sound, input, and networking in a series of simple-to-use functions. Not only does Allegro simplify development by abstracting what would otherwise be complex, hardware-specific code, it also allows easier porting of projects to other operating systems supported by Allegro.

Both DJGPP and Allegro can be found at *http://www.delorie.com/djgpp/*.

Installing DJGPP

Using the Zip Picker at *http://www.delorie.com/djgpp/zip-picker.html*, you can download the portions of DJGPP that meet your needs. You can also download utilities to aid in program development like RHIDE, an integrated development environment similar to the Borland DOS IDE. Once you have answered the questions on the Zip Picker page, you will be presented a page of all the DJGPP packages you need. Download all of these packages to the same directory. As DOS development tends to involve a fair bit of navigation through a text console, it's probably best to use an easy to reach directory like *C:\DJGPP*.

Once you have downloaded the packages, go to your DJGPP directory and unzip all the files. Be sure to preserve directory structures when unzipping the packages. If you need an unzipping utility, you can use unzip32, also available at *http://www.delorie.com/djgpp/*.

The final step in the installation is to define DJGPP's environment variables. These can be edited in Windows XP by right-clicking on My Computer → Properties. In the System Properties window, select the Advanced tab, then the Environment Variables button. From here, you can define new variables for the current user or the entire system. Define the variables shown in Table 7-1.

Table 7-1. Environment variables for DJGPP

Variable name	Variable value	Example
DJGPP	[DJGPP directory]\DJGPP.ENV	*C:\DJGPP\DJGPP.ENV*
PATH	[DJGPP directory]\BIN	*C:\DJGPP\BIN*

To make sure that the installation was successful, try compiling and running a simple "Hello World" program. You can run RHIDE by browsing to the *bin* directory in your DJGPP directory and double-clicking on *rhide.exe*. Create a new file by selecting New from the File menu. In the window that opens, enter the following:

```
#include <stdio.h>

int main(void) {
    printf("Hello World!");
}
```

Save the file, giving it a name like *hello_world.cpp*, then compile it by pressing F9. You should see a screen similar to Figure 7-11.

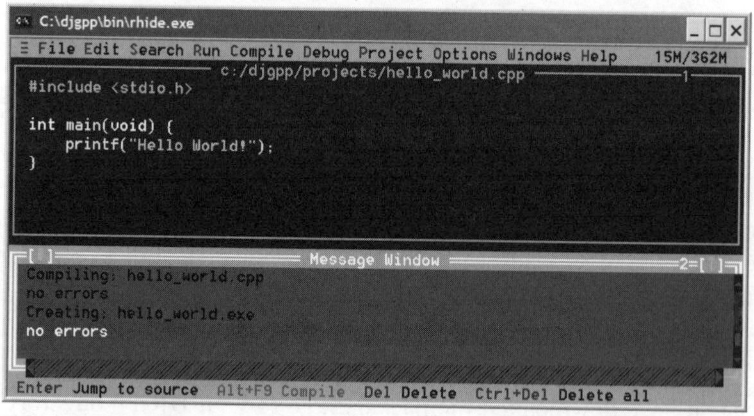

Figure 7-11. Not the Blue Screen of Death

Once it's done compiling, bring up a DOS prompt by selecting DOS shell from the File menu. From here, type the name of the file without an extension (i.e., just *hello_world*), and you should see output like that shown in Figure 7-12.

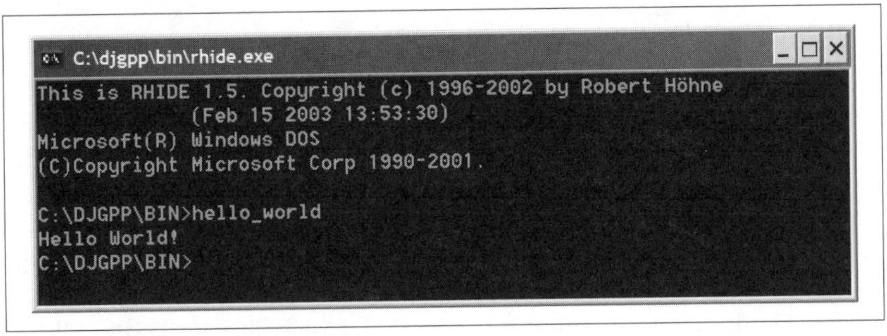

Figure 7-12. Hello DJGPP!

Installing Allegro

If you haven't already done so, download the Allegro package from the DJGPP site and unzip it in your DJGPP directory. Next, from a command prompt, go to the Allegro directory (*C:\DJGPP\allegro*, for example) and type make. The make command will automatically start compiling and building the Allegro library. Once it's done, type make install and press Enter to finish the process.

You are now almost ready to start using Allegro, but first you need to configure RHIDE so that it knows where to look for Allegro's library files. Under the Options menu, select Libraries. Mark the checkbox next to one of the open spaces and enter "alleg". Click OK and you should be ready to start compiling code with Allegro.

Hello Allegro!

In order to make sure the Allegro installation completed successfully, you can run the graphical equivalent of a Hello World program: turning the screen a hideous shade of magenta! To accomplish this task, enter and save the following code into a new file:

```
#include <allegro.h>

int main(void) {
  allegro_init();
  set_gfx_mode(GFX_AUTODETECT, 640, 480, 0, 0);
  install_keyboard();

  bool game_over = false;
  while(!game_over) {
```

```
      if(keypressed( )) {
        game_over = true;
      }

      clear_to_color(screen, 5);
    }

    allegro_exit( );
  }
```

Though this might seem like a lot to take in at once, it's really a fairly simple "Hello Allegro" program. The #include <allegro.h> includes the Allegro header file in your code and allows you to access Allegro's functionality. The function call to allegro_init( ) initializes Allegro and must be called before any other Allegro functions. The set_gfx_mode(GFX_AUTODETECT, 640, 480, 0, 0) call sets the screen to 640 x 480 pixels using the default graphics device. Similarly to allegro_init( ), install_keyboard( ) initializes Allegro keyboard functionality and must be called before executing keyboard-related functions. The body of the program is a loop that ends when a key is pressed, signaled by the keypressed( ) function. It also uses the clear_to_color(screen, 5) call to clear the screen and set it to the aforementioned magenta color. In this case, screen is a special variable automatically defined by Allegro and 5 is the index number corresponding to magenta in an 8-bit (256 color) palette. Finally, allegro_exit( ) cleans up after Allegro and is called just before the program ends.

If everything went correctly you should be able compile this program, run it, and be presented with a magenta screen that remains until you press a key. It's not much, but the development of many great games began with a blank, single-colored screen.

Handling Images with Allegro

While magenta-colored screens are well and good, they really need something else to bring out their full potential. In this case, externally-loaded images will do nicely. Start off by making a medium-sized bitmap in your favorite image manipulation tool (the GIMP, available at *http://www.gimp. org*, works quite nicely) and save the image as *hello_allegro.bmp* in the same directory your "Hello Allegro" executable resides.

Now, it's time to add a bit of code (shown in bold) to the previous example to take advantage of the new image file:

```
#include <allegro.h>

int main(void) {
  allegro_init( );
  set_gfx_mode(GFX_AUTODETECT, 640, 480, 0, 0);
  install_keyboard( );
```

```
BITMAP* imgHello = load_bitmap("hello_allegro.bmp", NULL);

int x = 0;
bool game_over = false;
while(!game_over) {
  if(keypressed()) {
    game_over = true;
  }

  clear_to_color(screen, 5);

  blit(imgHello, screen, 0, 0, x, 100, imgHello->w, imgHello->h);
  x++;
}

destroy_bitmap(imgHello);

allegro_exit();
}
```

The new code loads the image file *hello_allegro.bmp* into imgHello via the load_bitmap( ) routine. It also initializes a variable called x which is used in the blit( ) call to animate imgHello moving across the screen. blit(imgHello, screen, 0, 0, x, 100, imgHello->w, imgHello->h) copies a rectangular region from imgHello to the screen. The first two 0s represent the coordinates on imgHello from which copying begins, (0, 0) in this case. The x and 100 are the coordinates on the screen to which imgHello should be copied; thus, increasing the value of x causes the image to move right across the screen. The final two values are the width and height of imgHello. The values for imgHello->w and imgHello->h were defined when *hello_allegro. bmp* was first loaded. Finally, destroy_bitmap(imgHello) deletes the reference to the image data, which is important for preventing memory leaks.

When you run this program, you'll notice that the image appears and moves across the screen like it should, but flickers terribly. This is because you are able to see the image as it is being erased by clear_to_color( ) before being redrawn in its new position by blit( ). The solution is to implement double-buffering, a staple of 2D graphics programming. Double-buffering essentially consists of copying your graphics to a separate buffer bitmap not seen by the user. Once all the graphics for that frame are copied to the buffer, its contents are copied to the screen. The modifications (shown in bold) needed to implement double-buffering can be found in the following code:

```
#include <allegro.h>

int main(void) {
  allegro_init();
  set_gfx_mode(GFX_AUTODETECT, 640, 480, 0, 0);
  install_keyboard();
```

```
BITMAP* buffer = create_bitmap(640, 480);
BITMAP* imgHello = load_bitmap("hello_allegro.bmp", NULL);

int x = 0;
bool game_over = false;
while(!game_over) {
  if(keypressed()) {
    game_over = true;
  }

  clear_to_color(buffer, 5);

  blit(imgHello, buffer, 0, 0, x, 100, imgHello->w, imgHello->h);
  x++;

  blit(buffer, screen, 0, 0, 0, 0, 640, 480);
}

destroy_bitmap(imgHello);

destroy_bitmap(buffer);
allegro_exit();
}
```

The new code in this selection creates a new BITMAP called buffer with the same dimensions as the screen. Now, instead of clearing the screen to magenta and blitting imgHello to the screen, the code clears and blits to buffer instead. Once the drawing is complete, blit(buffer, screen, 0, 0, 0, 0, 640, 480) copies the buffer to the screen. Of course, destroy_bitmap() is used to dispose of buffer before exiting the program.

Now, when you run the program, the image shown in Figure 7-13 should move across the screen completely flicker-free. Not bad for a little extra code.

At this point, you may be curious about how to handle non-rectangular images like cars, spaceships, or anything other than boxes seen from straight above. This can be done simply by using draw_sprite() instead of blit(). The draw_sprite() routine behaves similarly to blit() except it doesn't draw pixels that are the designated transparent color, color 0 for 8-bit images or RGB(255, 0, 255) for 24-bit images. You can find out more about this and other Allegro functions in the documentation found in the *docs/* directory of your Allegro installation.

Handling Input with Allegro

A game is nothing without interactivity. With that in mind, Allegro provides multiple means to receive human input from keyboards, mice and joy-

Figure 7-13. Hello Allegro!, indeed

sticks. You have already seen very basic keyboard handling in the previous examples. The following code sample expands on the previous programs by allowing you to move the image freely around the screen:

```
#include <allegro.h>

int main(void) {
  allegro_init( );
  set_gfx_mode(GFX_AUTODETECT, 640, 480, 0, 0);
  install_keyboard( );

  BITMAP* buffer = create_bitmap(640, 480);
  BITMAP* imgHello = load_bitmap("hello_allegro.bmp", NULL);

  int x = 0;
  int y = 0;
  bool game_over = false;
  while(!game_over) {

    if(key[KEY_LEFT]) {
      x--;
    }
    if(key[KEY_RIGHT]) {
      x++;
    }
    if(key[KEY_UP]) {
      y--;
    }
    if(key[KEY_DOWN]) {
      y++;
    }
    if(key[KEY_ESC]) {
      game_over = true;
    }
```

```
    clear_to_color(buffer, 5);
    blit(imgHello, buffer, 0, 0, x, y, imgHello->w, imgHello->h);

    blit(buffer, screen, 0, 0, 0, 0, 640, 480);
  }

  destroy_bitmap(imgHello);

  destroy_bitmap(buffer);
  allegro_exit();
}
```

Much of this code should look familiar. The major difference is the use of the key array defined by Allegro. Each index of the key array contains a value representing the state of a key on the keyboard, either true for a depressed key or false for an unpressed key. You can reference particular keys using the Allegro-defined key constants, like KEY_ESC, KEY_A, KEY_UP, etc. The program uses the key array to increment or decrement the values of x and y based on the arrow keys and to exit the program when Esc is pressed. The values of x and y determine the location of the image, which therefore appears to move as the arrow keys are pressed. Congratulations, you now have the beginnings of a very basic, but infinitely expandable, DOS game.

Organizing Projects with RHIDE

Before you go rushing off to create your masterpiece, I'll leave you with one last note. One of the most useful features of RHIDE is its ability to organize multiple source files into a single project. This is an essential feature when working on any non-trivially large program. By using the Project menu to define a project, you can associate multiple source files with the project and have them be compiled and linked together automatically by RHIDE. The resulting executable will also be created in the same location as the project file. This is great when you want to make sure your executable and data files are in the same place. Now, get out there and make some games!

—*Robert Ota Dieterich*

## CHAPTER EIGHT

Playing at Game Design
Hacks 72–80

Anybody can create a retro game!

The preceding paragraph might have caused you to scoff with derision, or roll your eyes at the very thought, or even drop the book on the floor, exclaiming, "Not me!" But yes, it's true. Whether you're a seasoned programming expert or a total game design virgin, you're sure to find a hack in this chapter that interests you and gets you creating your very own game.

For beginners, there are game-design utilities like ZZT and Adventure Game Editor that will let you piece together your own retro-styled creations—all you need is above-average intelligence, which you clearly have since you purchased this volume. (Thanks for that!) And if you're looking for a real challenge, use later hacks in this chapter as your introduction to programming for systems like the Atari 2600 and Game Boy Advance.

Who knows, with the things you learn here you might even be able to sell your creations!

HACK #72 Design Games with ZZT

Use a retro game to quickly and easily make new retro games.

What do the names "Tim Sweeney" and "Epic Megagames" mean to you? For most people reading this book, they probably conjure up images of Unreal Tournament.

Not so for me.

When I hear those names, I instantly flash back to 1993. It's seventh grade, and I'm making my own video games using ZZT. Sweeney's creation, the very first game released under the Epic Megagames name, was an unassuming piece of software from the outside. You could play a top-down action/adventure/puzzle game that used ASCII text for all of its graphics. Register the program by sending Tim a few bucks, and he'd send you a disk with three more adventures.

But underneath that façade, Sweeney's game had a feature that made ZZT much more than a simple adventure game. Instead of pressing P at the title screen (shown in Figure 8-1) to play the game, you could press E and make your own game using the simple and fun (if not always intuitive) game design tool.

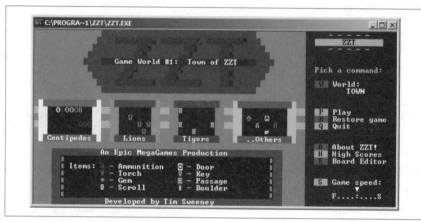

Figure 8-1. The title screen of ZZT

Immediately, ZZT fans were making and sharing their own games, and the popularity of the software grew and grew even as Epic had completely moved on to bigger and better games. Intrepid hackers started devising their own tools that pushed the boundaries of the ZZT design tool, making it do things it was never intended to. Soon, Sweeney's own games looked old hat next to what some people were churning out. Eventually, Epic released the full version of the game as freeware.

What's amazing is that ZZT is still going strong today. In fact, there are many different web sites where you can learn more about how to use the program, download a wealth of different games (some amazing, some awful), and find utilities that help you create better-looking and better-playing software. Some of the best are:

http://zzt.the-underdogs.org

> A great starting place for all sorts of ZZT information, z2 offers nearly everything you could want. Download ZZT, read tutorials on the creation engine, and sift through a catalog of downloadable games. I especially like the "Featured Games" section that lists twenty of the best games available.

http://www.chocobo.org/~butz/zzt.htm

One of the oldest (if not the oldest) ZZT web sites, this is the home page of "Duky, Inc.," a ZZT "company" created by a fan named Luke Drelick. Yes, nearly everyone established their own "companies" back in the day with which to brand their games. The site contains about 287 ZZT games.

http://kevedit.sourceforge.net/

KevEdit is a ZZT world editor that was last updated in 2002, just in time to release a Windows XP version. I recommend that you start out using the standard ZZT editor, but if you do start getting into ZZT development you may want to check out this one's advanced and streamlined features.

Jumping Into ZZT Editing

The old adage proves (mostly) true with ZZT: the less complex a game editor is, the more limited its functions. Actually, I don't know if that's an old adage. I may have just made it up right now. But it seems to be true. You have to understand that when you create a ZZT game, you're creating a top-down action/adventure title in which the main form of interaction with objects is either shooting or touching.

Now, the reason I said *(mostly)* is because once you learn the ins and outs of ZZT, you can start to experiment and stretch the limits of the engine to create things that were never supposed to be. Dedicated fans have made shooters, falling-object puzzle games, and thoughtful role-playing games in which not a single shot is fired.

But for starters, we're going to make a game in which you kill some things, and then win.

Running ZZT. You can get the full version of ZZT for free from just about any web site that deals with it, like z2. Unzip the archive to a new directory on your computer. If you download any games (the files will have the *.zzt* extension), just unzip them and put them into the same directory as you put the program.

After you install, run the *zzt.exe* file; you'll page through a screen of options asking you to select an input method (keyboard is best for editing) and color versus monochrome. (Hey, it was a valid question in 1991.) You'll see the title screen. You can press P to play Town of ZZT, but if you want to try out other games that you've downloaded, press W to select a world.

A list similar to Figure 8-2 will pop up. (If you've downloaded the Yoshi games that I made back in the day, it'll be *very* similar to the figure.) Notice

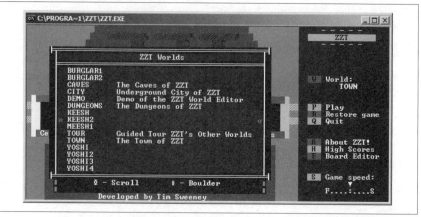

Figure 8-2. Selecting a world on the ZZT title screen

that there's a demo of the ZZT world editor, called DEMO, in the list. Check this out later. You'll also want to play a bit of Town of ZZT to get an idea of what you can make very easily using the tools provided.

Your first board.   For now, just press E to enter the board editor. You'll see the screen in Figure 8-3.

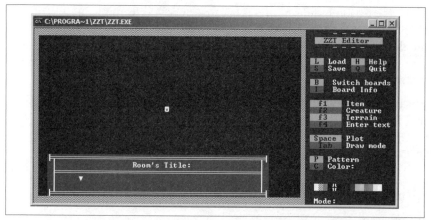

Figure 8-3. The ZZT editor starting screen, and your first big decision

You'll need to enter a title for the room your player is starting in. For purposes of keeping our marketing department happy, name it Retro Gaming Hacks. The player will never see this designation, so use your room names for your own organizational purposes.

This would probably be a good time to mention that a ZZT game is, in effect, a series of interconnected boards. When your player is in one board, that is all the program is ever dealing with. You can cause events to happen across boards by turning flags on and off, but that is the only means of communication.

Apart from flags, the only information that is carried across boards are the player's stats—health, ammo, money (called *gems*), etc. Apart from that, the player is only dealing with one board at a time. This is helpful because you're only editing one board at a time. So let's start with this one.

In general, creating your game board is like using a paint program. You move the cursor around the screen shown in Figure 8-4 and drop terrain (walls, bricks that you can shoot through, lines, water, etc.), enemies, and other objects exactly where you want them during the game. Let's add some enemies for our player to shoot. Press F2 to bring up the creatures menu, and add a Ruffian by pressing R. Next you'll set some variables that determine how the enemy acts.

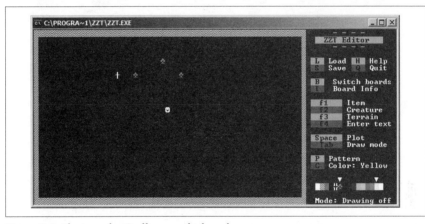

Figure 8-4. Placing a few Ruffians on the board

If you save your game now by pressing S, then choosing a filename of up to eight characters, you can exit to the title screen and try playing your game. What will probably happen is that the Ruffians will immediately assault your player, disappearing as he touches them. He'll take 10 damage per hit. What a fun game! Let's add some ammo so our player can actually fight back. Press F1 and add some. (In the game, you shoot by holding the shift key, then tapping a directional arrow.) Also add some gems, which give the player back 1 HP each.

We don't really need all this space for our killing spree, so let's make the room smaller by adding walls. If you press P in the editor you'll see an arrow in the bottom left hand corner cycle through the different patterns you can draw with. If you press Tab, you'll be in draw mode. So press P once to switch to the wall pattern that makes up the border of the room, and draw some more walls for the player. Then move to the empty space outside those walls, and press X to fill it in (see Figure 8-5).

 I'm actually breaking a cardinal rule of ZZT game development in the interest of expediency here. In general, it is considered extremely poor craftsmanship to leave the default yellow border on your ZZT boards. Usually you'll want to start off a board design by moving the cursor to the board, moving the pattern selector to the blank space, and pressing X to fill the area with empty space.

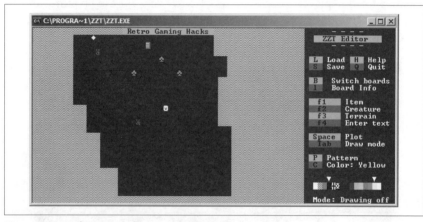

Figure 8-5. ä is for ammo; that's good enough for me

Not much of a game yet, is it? Notice the three-lined object in Figure 8-5. That's a passage, which transfers the player to a new board. Before we place it we'll have to actually make a new board, though. Press B and choose the last option. You'll have to name the new board. Now press B to switch back to the Retro Gaming Hacks board. Place a passage with F1 and point it towards the new board in the menu that pops up.

 There are some interesting rules for passages. If there is an identically-colored passage in the destination room, the player will appear there. If not, the player will appear at the default starting location for the board, which is where the player is placed in the editor. By default, it's the center of the screen. You can change that by putting him in a new place with the F1 menu.

The first thing I'm going to do is create a Scroll (off the F1 menu). Scrolls are one-time-use items that display a text message to the player. Once you place it, you'll input the text you want it to display. You can edit it later by pressing Enter when the cursor is over the scroll, as shown in Figure 8-6. (This goes for just about everything else you place.)

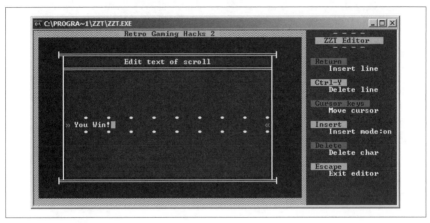

Figure 8-6. Editing the text of the scroll

ZZT-OOP. For most of the other things you can add to a ZZT game—different types of walls, enemies, and other pre-programmed objects—simple experimentation will help you learn what they do. Just throw a bunch of them on a board, save the game, then play it to see what happens! But to make real ZZT games you have to learn ZZT-OOP, or Object Oriented Programming.

Now, I know I said this was easy. And it really, truly is. ZZT object programming uses real English words that mean what they say (for the most part). We're going to put a simple object into this next room, somewhere near the scroll. An Object is in the Creatures menu, which you access by pressing F2. Hit O to place it. You'll first be asked to pick which of the 255 ASCII characters you want to represent the object. If it's a person, choose one of the two smiley faces.

When you do, you'll see a text entry box much like the one you used on the Scroll. If you enter just text in here, the object will start talking as soon as you enter the room. But you don't want that, you want him to talk when you're touching him. So you enter the following code, as shown in Figure 8-7:

```
@Pat
#end
:touch
```

```
Buh, I am Pat. Touch me again to win.
#zap touch
#end
:touch
#endgame
```

Figure 8-7. Entering code in ZZT-OOP

Odds are, you can figure out exactly what each of these lines of code do just by reading through them. But let's go line-by-line for the slower kids in the back of the class.

When you preface a line with @, you're giving the object a name. This name will show up when the player interacts with the object (in the space where "Edit Program" appears in Figure 8-7). But it's also important because other objects on the same board will be able to interact with Pat only if he has a name. This can only appear on the first line of the program:

```
@Pat
```

When you enter a room, all objects immediately start executing their programs. If you want Pat to speak only when spoken to, you'll have to cause his program to end before he can stir up any trouble. When you preface a line with #, you're giving the program a command:

```
#end
```

A line with a : in front of it means that the following section of the program will only execute when a certain message is sent. In this case, if the player touches the object, the code below this line will run:

```
:touch
```

If you enter a line as plain text, with no symbol preceding it, it will appear as plain text. In the case of a human object, the player will assume that the character is talking to him:

```
Buh, I am Pat. Touch me again to win.
```

If you want Pat to say something different the next time you touch him, you'll have to get rid of that first :touch condition. This command will do that:

```
#zap touch
```

Note that if you don't put an #end command here, the program will continue to execute, skipping right past that :touch conditional and ending the game. Stop it before it does:

```
#end
```

This second touch message will never execute unless the first one is zapped:

```
:touch
```

The game will end, the player's high score will be saved, and he will have to press Escape to quit to the title screen:

```
#endgame
```

Further Reading

There is a tutorial for newbies on z2 (*http://zzt.the-underdogs.org/index. php?p=newbie1*) that goes into a lot more depth than I have here. It also assumes that you're going to download and use some of the utilities that allow you to have more colors and more options for your editing process. I think that's a little too complex for your first game, but otherwise the tutorial is excellent and explains many of the other functions of the ZZT-OOP programming language that you'll need to use.

In ZZT there is an internal Help file that you can access at any time by pressing H in the editor. The folks at z2 have transcribed it all into HTML for easier reading at *http://zzt.the-underdogs.org/index.php?p=zoh*.

And of course, as I mentioned earlier, a great way to learn about what you can do with ZZT is to play others' games. You can always check out the crappy Yoshi games I made when I was in middle school, as seen in the eye-catching Figure 8-8.

Yoshi and the Attack of the Mind-Warping Fingernails, with yellow borders, wasteful board design, and in-jokes only understood by about three people in my middle school! Amazing, isn't it? How about that "To Level 1 Map" label? That's some non-invasive level design right there, no?

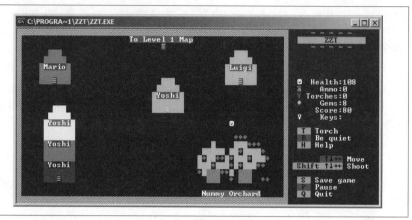

Figure 8-8. The map screen for my first ZZT game

I'm half impressed and half mortified that you can still get these games all over the Internet today. In any case, it's probably best if you check out some titles on z2's featured games list, like Burglar (Figure 8-9).

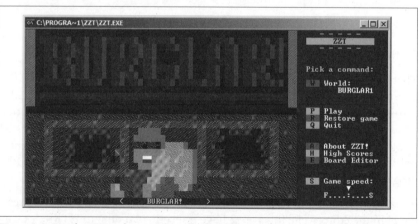

Figure 8-9. Burglar! Note the exceptionally detailed art

HACK #73 Use Freeware Game Creation Tools

Find utilities that will let you assemble pre-fab games for fun and/or profit.

So you want to make your own video game, but you don't have any programming or artistic skills? Hey, there's nothing wrong with that—you don't have to be a math nerd or expert painter to come up with a good game design. You just need imagination. But if you want to bring it to life, you'll need some help.

That's where game creation software comes into play. There are many utilities out there that provide you with tools you can use to make your own game without ever typing in a line of code. Of course, your designs will be limited by the capabilities of the program, but if you're just interested in dipping a toe into the game design waters to see how you like it, this is the best way to get started.

Elsewhere in this chapter, I've discussed a few game creation utilities in depth—how to make top-down action adventures using only text-based graphics [Hack #72], how to make a game your friends can play using the Web [Hack #74], and how to create an old-school point-and-click adventure [Hack #80]. In this hack, I'll talk briefly about other utilities that are available, in the hopes that you'll find one suited to your own great idea.

> An extensive list of game creation utilities like the ones listed next is available at *http://www.ambrosine.com/resource.html*.

Game Maker

> Official home page: *http://www.cs.uu.nl/people/markov/gmaker/index.html*
> Platform(s): Windows
> Price: Free, with optional 15 euro ($20) registration for extra features

If you know your way around a computer and can master most software applications within a few minutes, Game Maker (Figure 8-10) might be your cup of tea. It's currently at version 6.0 and the web page is constantly being updated, which means that you're not downloading a program that's fallen into disuse.

Many tutorials are available on the site. They usually contain text documents in Adobe Acrobat PDF format, sample game files that can be loaded up in Game Maker and messed around with, and sample sprites and graphics that can be loaded into your game so you don't have to do all the work.

There is a tutorial for starting-from-scratch beginners who just want to jump in and make a simple game to get accustomed to the program. But there are also tutorials for intermediate and advanced users that focus on the specific types of games that Game Maker can help you put together, from scrolling shoot-em-ups to Zelda-style RPGs to platform games... even first-person shooters (though that does require the registered version of the software and some deep knowledge of the program's features).

Even better, you can get some sample games made with Game Maker to see immediately what it's capable of. Some games are only available as standal-

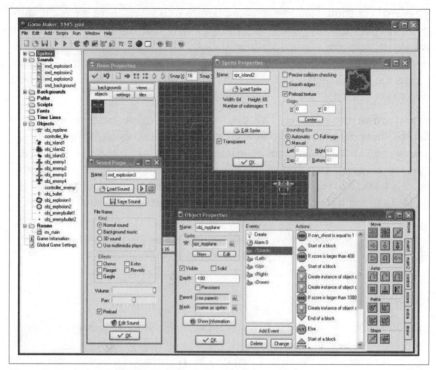

Figure 8-10. Game Maker's interface

one programs, but some (including a few that were used as final class projects for a game creation course at the University of Utrecht, which was taught by the program's creator Mark Overmars) are available as Game Maker project files, so you can open them up and look at how the effects were done. Even more games are available at *http://www.gamemakergames.com/*.

When you're finished with your own game, you can save it as a standalone program and do whatever you want with it—give it to your friends, sell it… or start your own game company around it if you think it's good enough!

Stagecast Creator

Official home page: *http://www.stagecast.com*
Platforms: Windows, Macintosh, Unix
Price: $49.95 (evaluation version available for free download)

Is Game Maker is way too complicated for you? Looking for a much simpler game creator? Are you an educator looking for a program that will let you teach younger children about game making, but something that's flexible enough so that teenagers and adults can enjoy it as well? Then Stagecast Creator might be the answer.

Stagecast lets you create interactive games, stories, and simulations with graphically-oriented tools. Games are saved as Java applications, which means they can be played over the Web or distributed separately. The official web site features sample games for play, as seen in Figure 8-11.

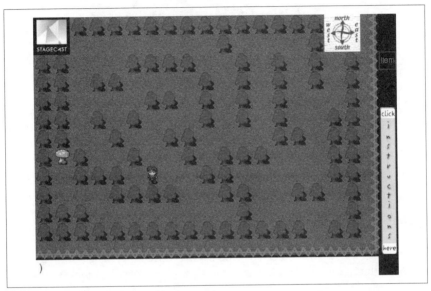

Figure 8-11. Eliot's Duck, a Stagecast sample game

Gamers might find the software generated by Stagecast to be clunky and limited, but teachers will find it to be a valuable tool. Also available on the site are various education packages that include multiple copies of the software at a discount, teachers' guides, and other resource material for class-rooms.

> A brief introduction and tutorial for Stagecast is available on the web site of the cable TV station G4: *http://www.g4tv.com/techtvvault/features/29542/Make_Your_Own_Computer_Games_and_Sims.html*.

RPGToolkit

Official home page: *http://www.toolkitzone.com*
Platform(s): Windows
Price: Free (open source)

Fancy making a Final Fantasy? Dare to create a Dragon Quest? The open source project RPGToolkit (*http://www.toolkitzone.com*) lets you make role-playing games just like the ones you grew up playing. Create a lengthy adventure with all the cute sidekicks, battles, and teenage angst you can whip up!

A Word About RPG Maker

RPG Maker is a very popular RPG creation utility published by the Japanese company Enterbrain. It has a rather large fan base among English-speaking role playing enthusiasts because some clever hackers have translated some of the Japanese PC releases, like RPG Maker 3000, into English.

Unfortunately, as the RPG Maker series is a retail product sold in Japanese stores, it is a violation of copyright to distribute it. Still, if you do buy a Japanese version of the game, you can find the translation patches online. Try doing a Google search for rpg maker translation.

There are indeed official English versions of the program that have been released, but they are only available for the PlayStation and PlayStation 2 systems. If creating a console RPG sounds like fun to you, look for RPG Maker and RPG Maker 2 at your favorite video game shop.

The first game (for PSone) lets you create sprite-based old-school RPGs. The second (on PS2) lets you create simplistic 3D adventures. The advantage to using the PS2 version is that you can use any USB keyboard for text entry, whereas the PS1 game uses only the standard controller, making for a long and laborious process if you make a text-heavy RPG (and really, what RPG isn't?).

A sequel that promises major improvements, RPG Maker 3, is due from publisher Agetec in 2005.

Much like Game Maker, a lot of the creation is done using graphical menus (see Figure 8-12) and windows. You can use all sorts of pre-programmed events to save time, but if you want to carefully plot out all of the things that happen during battles and event scenes, you'll need to learn to use the internal programming tool, called RPGCode.

A quick-start guide that walks you through creating a basic game, as well as extensive documentation of the rest of RPGToolkit's features, are available at *http://tk3.toolkitzone.com/help/*.

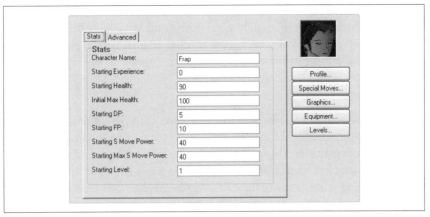

Figure 8-12. RPGToolkit's character editing window

 ### HACK #74 Design Web-based Flash Games

Bring your retro game concepts to life with animation.

If you're looking to expose your games to as many people as possible, Macromedia's Flash is one of those rare cross-platform tools whose reach extends as far as the eye can see. You need a Gamecube to play Smash Bros. You need an Xbox to play Halo. You need a Windows PC to run an *.exe*. With Flash, all you need is a web browser. Anyone who has access to the Internet (certainly a sizeable percentage of gamers) can experience your vision without the need for specific hardware or expensive upgrades.

While Flash's Interactive Development Environment (IDE) makes it easy to keep track of the objects you're working with, it is by no means a substitute for coding. The latest version of Flash MX, without writing any of your own code, gives your applications about the same capabilities as Flash 1.

You can download a free, 30-day trial of Flash MX from *www.macromedia. com* (you'll have to register). It's fully functional, comes with plenty of helpful tutorials and documentation, and any games you create will remain playable forever. If you find that you want to continue using Flash after the trial expires, you can purchase a copy from Macromedia for $400. This hack is going to assume you're familiar with basic Flash terms such as the stage, timeline, panel, as well as the standard drawing tools and their various settings. If you're already scratching your head, spend some time with the samples Macromedia provides. You can find them under the Help menu, or in the *FL_Getting_Started.pdf* file bundled with the installer.

Before you get started creating a game, familiarize yourself with the Flash IDE—it's fully customizable, and it's to your benefit to take advantage.

Since I cut my teeth on Flash 5, I've reconfigured several keyboard shortcuts on my personal copy to match what I'm familiar with (I'll be using the default shortcuts, so you won't have to change anything if you're using a freshly-installed copy of Flash).

Set the Stage

You need an actual game before you can have multiple difficulty levels and realistic explosions. So before you even open Flash, spend some time brainstorming and planning the overall structure of your game. The idea is to come out with clear ideas for what objects are required, what properties they will have, and what actions they need to be able to do. Don't get bogged down with programming details during the planning stage; record your ideas in clear, readable English (or whatever your native language is). Right now, an object is something that appears in your game (e.g., a car), properties are things describing it (e.g., speed, acceleration), and actions are what it's capable of (e.g., turning, braking).

For this hack, we'll be building an extremely simple game skeleton somewhat reminiscent of Missile Command. There will be no focus on graphics or sound—they can be added in at any time with virtually no effort. It won't look like much, but the finished product will be a complete, easily upgradeable game that encompasses all the major aspects of game design.

Game requirements.   Remember, there's no code being written at this point. Write down your ideas in plain language so everyone involved in the project can understand what needs to be done. Our game will need:

A goal
> There has to be a point to playing a game. What fun is a game with no direction? "Beat the high score" and "Save the princess" are good goals, but "Stomp on enemies" isn't. The goal for this game is to shoot enough enemy missiles to save the city.

Score
> The player's score will be the determining factor for whether they've won, lost, or are still playing. The score should increase when the player destroys a missile and decrease if the player misses one.

Missiles
> Missiles should start offscreen and make their way from the top of the screen to the bottom. Since they're moving objects, they need to keep track of their speed and acceleration. This implementation will also include a wait timer, so there isn't a constant rain of missiles. If clicked, the missile is destroyed, and the player gets a point. If it makes it to the bottom, the player loses a point.

That's all this hack's example requires, but for a complete game you design, this is the point in the process when you should list sounds, animations, difficulty levels, and other aspects. For larger projects, it may help to list the objects first, and come back to fill in their properties and actions later.

Now that we have a clear description of what we need, it's time to bring our idea to life! If you haven't already, open up Flash and create a new Flash Document. Make sure the Library panel is visible (press F11 if it is not).

Conceptually, a game is nothing more than a list of different possible scenarios (more commonly called "states"). Each state is connected to one or more other states, and the game moves between them via the player's actions. Figure 8-13 shows an RPG character exploring a town. States are represented in boxes, actions in ovals.

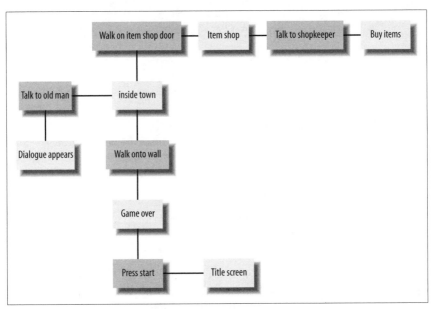

Figure 8-13. Different game states while exploring a town

Prepare the elements. The concept of states translates very well into Flash; each game state should be a single frame on the main timeline. This game will have three states, so click on Frame 1 and push F6 twice to insert two new frames. Using the Properties panel (located at the bottom of the screen by default), name the three frames "game," "win," and "lose" respectively as shown in Figure 8-14.

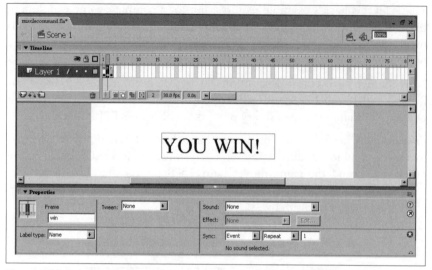

Figure 8-14. Labeling the "win" frame

 Get in the habit of giving frames meaningful names. It's easy to remember that "win" is frame two at first, but as you build games with more and more states, it gets difficult to keep track of everything. Moving a single frame to a new position would require you to change every reference to it. By naming important frames, you'll be able to access them no matter where they go.

Go to the "win" frame and use the Text tool to write "You win!" in the middle of the stage. The font, size, and color are up to you. Go to the "lose" frame and do the same thing, this time writing "You lose!"

Next up is drawing the missiles. Click on the "game" frame and draw a square or circle. You can use whatever colors you like, but make sure the shape is filled with a solid color. Alternatively, you can import a graphic by pressing Ctrl+R (Command+R on the Mac). Once your graphic is ready, use the Arrow tool to select it and press F8 to convert it to a Symbol. Name it "missile" and set its behavior as "Movie Clip." Drag it to the top of the game's work area, just above the stage. Finally, using the Info panel, change the Missile's length and width to 50 pixels by 50 pixels.

The last bit of prep work is setting up the score display. Use the Text tool to write the word "Score" in the upper-right corner of the stage. Below it, make a Dynamic Text box by selecting "Dynamic Text" from the Properties panel. Now would be a good time to save the file.

Begin Coding

Now that you've laid the foundation, it's time to whip out some Actionscript and make those missiles fire.

From its humble beginnings in Flash 4, Actionscript has evolved into a robust, sophisticated language that has turned Flash from an animation studio to a jack-of-all-trades web-programming tool. Its syntax is based on JavaScript, but it has some unique points as well (describing them goes beyond the scope of this hack; check out the Flash documentation for more info). Flash MX 2004 is the first version to feature Actionscript 2.0, which boasts full object-oriented programming capabilities. While we won't need these advanced features for this simple game, they are invaluable for large-scale web applications and heavy-duty game engines. It wouldn't hurt to take a look at the built-in Actionscript references; they're located under the help menu and in the *FL_ActionScript_Ref.pdf* file bundled with the installer.

Since Actionscript can be used with Frames, Buttons, and Movie Clips, knowing where to use it is just as important as how:

- Actionscript on Frames should be restricted to initializing variables and writing functions. Be sure to consider the scope of your code; global functions and variables belong on the main timeline, while properties specific to a Movie Clip belong within that Movie Clip.

- Actionscript on Buttons, naturally, is for player-triggered events. Actionscript's event handlers can only react to mouse clicks and key presses, so their use is limited to simple actions like jumping to a particular frame, or sending and receiving data across the Web.

- Movie Clips are like Flash Movies unto themselves, and should be thought of as such. They're clickable, so they can be used like buttons to react to user input. However, their true strength lies in the ability to listen for and react to various events and changes within the movie itself.

Set up global variables. Click on Frame 1 of the main timeline and open up the Actions panel (Press F9 if it's not visible), and type the following (the commented line numbers are for your reference and don't have to be included in your code):

```
stop();      //Line 1
score = 0;   //Line 2
```

The stop() function on the first frame is crucial. Try compiling the movie (Press Ctrl+Enter on Windows, Command+Return on the Mac) without it—the game will immediately play to its end and the player simply sees "You lose!" Not exactly the kind of game that keeps players coming back, right? Remember, Flash is an animation tool at its core, so it treats everything as a movie. stop( ) only halts playback; code will continue to execute and Movie Clips will continue to play.

Head back to the stage and click on the Dynamic Text box you made earlier and take a look at the Properties panel. Notice the var field? You can bind a Dynamic Text box to any variable in your project, such as the number of frames it contains or the X position of a button. You will be assigning the player's score to this one, so click the var field and type in "score". Press Ctrl+Enter (Command+Return on the Mac) at this point to compile the movie to an *.swf* file. You should see "SCORE 0" in the upper-right corner of the movie as shown in Figure 8-15.

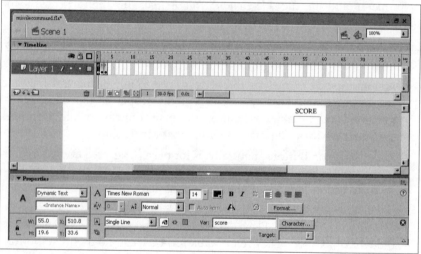

Figure 8-15. Setting the Dynamic Text field to display the score

Launch the missiles. As fun as having a working scoreboard is, it'd be nice if the player could somehow get points. This requires the missiles to be operational, so go back to your project and double-click on the missile. You're now in symbol-editing mode, and the timeline has changed from the main movie's to the missile's. Click frame 1 of the missile's timeline and add the following code:

```
velocity = 1;                          //Line 1
acceleration = .5;                     //Line 2
timer = Math.floor(random(29));        //Line 3

function fire( )                       //Line 4
```

```
{
}

function resetMissile( )          //Line 5
{
}
```

velocity refers to the initial speed of the missile. In Flash, positioning is all done in pixels, so a velocity of 1 means that whenever the missile moves, it will move by one pixel.

acceleration is the rate at which the missile's speed is increasing. Whenever the missile accelerates, its speed will increase by two.

timer is used to delay the missile's launch by a small amount of time. This prevents multiple missiles from all falling at the same time, and adds a general element of randomness to the game.

fire( ) will eventually control the missile's descent. It will be called when timer reaches a certain value.

resetMissile( ) will eventually re-initialize the missile to a random position and fire it again. It will be called when the player clicks the missile, or when it reaches the bottom of the screen.

Return to the main timeline for a moment by clicking Scene 1 above the timeline. Select the missile (only click once!), go to the Actions panel, and type:

```
onClipEvent(enterFrame) //Line 1
{

    if(this.timer == 30) //Line 2
       {
           this.fire( );   //Line 3
       }
    else this.timer++;    //Line 4
}

  on(press)               //Line 5
  {
    resetMissile( );      //Line 6
    _parent.score++;      //Line 7
  }
```

What's with all this on stuff? They're called *handlers*—Flash elements that sit around waiting for a particular event to happen. When it does, they "handle" it by executing their code. The onClipEvent handler is one of the most useful and powerful features of Movie Clips—if the clip is on the stage, the code within the handler executes every frame of the movie. Meaning, if your frame rate is 20 frames per second, the code will execute 20 times per second. Handlers are what allow a game to remain playable even though playback has been stopped; i.e., even though the movie is paused on frame one, it's still running at 20 fps, so buttons remain clickable, and Movie Clips continue to run.

The generic on handler is strictly for reactions to user input. press refers to the Movie Clip or button in question being clicked on.

So what exactly happens? Here's how it all goes down:

- Line 1 specifies that the following code should be executed on every single frame of the movie.
- Line 2 checks to see if this particular missile is ready to fire. If so, fire( ) is called and the missile is set into motion.
- Line 4 increments the timer if it's not time for the missile to launch.
- Line 5 reacts to the user clicking on the actual body of the missile.
- Line 6 calls resetMissile( ), which resets each missile's variables to their initial values and repositions it at the top of the screen.
- Line 7 increases the player's score by a point. _parent refers to the main timeline, where the score variable resides.

> When working with object paths in Flash, it's always better to use relative, not absolute, references. The main timeline is also accessible with _root, however, it's preferable to use _parent. If your game were to be loaded dynamically into another Flash movie, any calls to _root wouldn't work. Similarly, when working with Movie Clips and objects, use this to refer to an internal property or method. Your code will be much easier to read and you'll avoid problems with duplicate variable names.

Double-click on the missile to re-enter symbol editing mode, and click on frame 1. Go to the body of the fire( ) function and type in:

```
this.velocity += this.acceleration;    //Line 1
this._y += this.velocity;              //Line 2

if(this._y > Stage.height)             //Line 3
{
    _parent.score--;                   //Line 4
    resetMissile( );                   //Line 5
}
```

- Line 1 increases the speed of the missile's descent.
- Line 2 moves the missile down the stage, towards the bottom.

- Line 3 checks to see if the missile has hit the bottom of the stage. It's preferable to use Stage.height instead of an actual number in case you change the movie's dimensions later.

- Line 4 subtracts a point from the player's score, as a penalty for letting the missile hit.

Last but not least, we have resetMissile( ). The program simply reuses each missile clip once it's been destroyed or reached the bottom. Go to resetMissile( )'s body and enter the following code:

```
this._x = Math.floor(random(Stage.width) - this._width);   //Line 1
this._y = -(Math.floor(random(100) + this._height));        //Line 2
this.vel = 1;                                                //Line 3
this.timer = Math.floor(random(29));                        //Line 4
```

- Line 1 moves the missile to a random position on the X-axis. By default, a Movie Clip's origin is its upper-left corner, so the - this._width ensures that the entire missile will be onscreen.

- Line 2 puts the missile somewhere between 50 and 150 pixels above the stage. This will cause some missiles to be faster than others when they hit the screen, adding a bit of variety to the game.

- Line 3 resets the missile's velocity.

- Line 4 resets the missile's timer to a random value.

The game is nearly complete! This is an excellent time to test the movie, so press Ctrl+Enter (Command+Return on the Mac) and grab your mouse. If you typed everything correctly, your "missile" should repeatedly drop from the top of the screen. You may be able to see it reappearing and sitting still after each cycle; Flash zooms out and shows offscreen objects in the test environment. This will also affect the Stage's width and height variables, so select "Show all" from the View → Magnification menu, or press Ctrl+3 (Command+3 on a Mac).

The missile's movement probably seems slow and choppy. That's because the velocity, acceleration, and timer were all written with a frame rate of 30 fps in mind, which is the standard minimum frame rate for games today. To change your game's frame rate, go back to the work area and hit Ctrl+J (or Command+J on Macintosh) to access the Document Properties shown in Figure 8-16. Change the frame rate to 30 and close the window. You can also change the background color, if you wish.

To increase the difficulty, click on the missile, copy it, and paste two of them onto the work area. Spread them out across the top of the stage, and test your movie again. A little harder now, right?

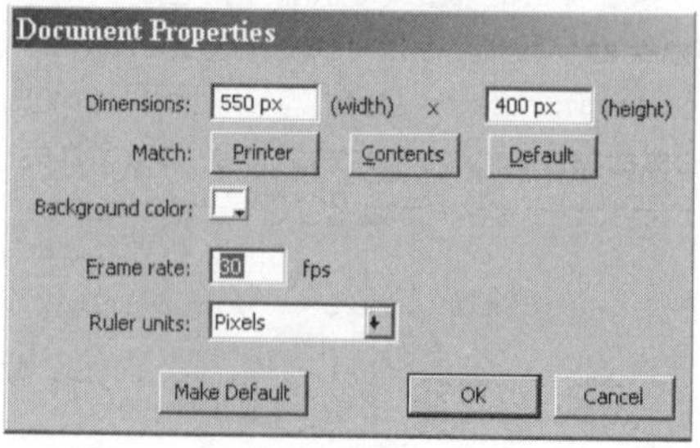

Figure 8-16. Changing the game's frame rate

Make the Game Winnable

Looking at the current state of our project, it does everything required, except accomplish the goal. In its current state, the game isn't winnable or losable. To remedy this, you need to constantly keep an eye on the player's score and take them to the win/lose frames once it passes a certain threshold.

You could do the score checking in fire( ) or the on handlers of the missile, but that results in a poorly organized code structure that'll be hard to update. You would have to make sure all your missiles had the new score checking code, and if you decided to change the conditions for winning and losing, you'd have to go back and edit them all. The better (and most common) solution is to make a movie clip whose sole purpose is to check the score. This "action clip" will allow you to complete the game and keep the code separated logically.

Go to the Library panel (Press F11 if it's not visible) and click the File-Plus icon in the lower-left corner. You'll be prompted to name your new symbol; call it "checker" and make sure its behavior is set to Movie Clip. You'll be taken into symbol-editing mode once you hit OK. Draw a small box somewhere in the middle (size and color are unimportant), and then head back to the main timeline. Drag "checker" from the library onto the work area (keep it offscreen), click it, open up the Actions panel, and type:

```
onClipEvent(enterFrame)
{
    if(_parent.score >= 5)
    {
        _parent.gotoAndStop("win");
    }
    else if(_parent.score <= -5)
    {
        _parent.gotoAndStop("lose");
    }
}
```

There's no new code here; every frame, the "checker" clip looks at the score and directs the player to the "win" or "lose" screen if their score is high or low enough. Press Ctrl+Enter/Command+Return once more and enjoy the completed game!

Hacking the Hack

This game isn't much to look at (see Figure 8-17), but remember, replacing and updating graphics in Flash takes seconds. A small face-lift gives the game a lot more credibility; you can draw directly in Flash, or press Ctrl+R (Command+R on the Mac) to import a picture. Use some graphics to replace the black squares and make a background (see Figure 8-18), and spice up the win/lose screens!

Figure 8-17. Our missile game, before updating the graphics...

Figure 8-18. ...and after

Other things to consider are explosion animations for the missiles, multiple difficulties, or moving to a new level with more missiles after reaching a certain score. With the knowledge of how to apply game programming principles to Flash, it becomes trivial to add the "complex" features that supposedly make the game what it is. As long as you keep your code well organized and have a clear vision for your game, there's no limit to what you can do with Flash.

—Matt DelGiudice

Create Your Own Atari 2600 Homebrew Games

Join a vibrant scene devoted to creating and distributing new Atari 2600 games.

Even though the Atari 2600 is one of the oldest game consoles around, it has a vibrant homebrew scene. These coders produce a remarkable amount of new material, with everything from RPGs to bizarre puzzle games up to altered updatings of classics. Best of all, the Atari 2600 scene seems to exist in an atmosphere of harmony and mutual understanding, with no beefs, group wars, or other shenanigans.

This hack is excerpted from Chapter One of *Gaming Hacks*, by Simon Carless (O'Reilly, 2004).

How can you learn how to create new game levels, or even entire games, for the 2600? Good question.

Creating Homebrew 2600 Games

Suppose you're fed up with merely playing homebrew marvelousness (though shame on you if you are). Maybe you want to create your own levels for games. Maybe you want to go whole hog and code entire homebrew titles from scratch. Either way, there are several resources available.

Using 2600 custom level creation tools. If you just want to mess around with level design, Atari Age runs a series of excellent contests in which you can create new levels for games under development. Often, the finished and produced homebrew cart will include the winning levels. More importantly, entrants often make their tools available for others after the contest closes.

In particular, the Indy 500 XE Track Designer (*http://www.atariage.com/ features/contests/Indy500XE/index.html*) is a lot of fun, if you're a wannabe race driver. Figure 8-19 shows the "easy-to-use Windows-based track editor that allows the easy creation of new tracks, loading and saving of tracks... and the ability to generate a binary so you can immediately test your creations." On a very similar note, the Combat Redux Playfield Design tool (*http://www.atariage.com/features/contests/CombatRedux/index.html*) works similarly.

It's a whole lot of fun to block out a level and then test it straight away in an emulator.

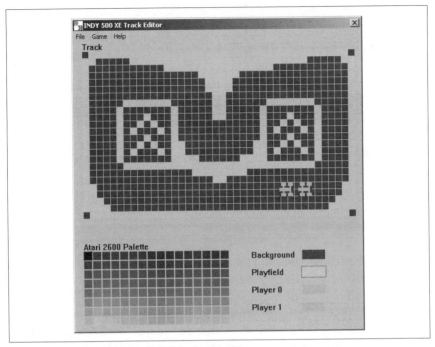

Figure 8-19. Designing a track with Indy 500 XE

These two appear to be the only fully-featured level design tools currently available. Other tools require complex, time-consuming binary hacking (*http://www.atariage.com/software_hacks.html?SystemID=2600*) or are more unwieldy and general, such as Hack-O-Matic II (*http://www.dacodez.tk/*). However, it looks like the development community may produce further advanced tools, with an Adventure dungeon editor under serious development as we write, and more tools planned.

Changing graphics in existing games. We mentioned before that binary hacking is a can of complex, time-consuming, and unwholesomely difficult worms, especially if you want to rewrite large chunks of the game. If you'd rather mess around a little with an existing ROM, perhaps changing the sprites in your favorite 2600 game, that's somewhat simpler.

Adam Trionfo's Changing Atari VCS Graphics—The Easy Way (*http://www. gooddealgames.com/articles/changing_atari_vcs_graphics_the_easy_way.pdf*) is a perfect beginner document. It modifies a Space Invaders ROM, explaining how to use two programs called ShowGFX and EditGFX (available from *http://www.lizardmaster.com/tlm/dev.cfm*) to create plain text files listing all of the vital information in the 4096-byte ROM. The magic is in the following DOS command:

```
C:\> showgfx spaceinv.bin 0 4096 > spaceinv.txt
```

You can then load the text file and look for the graphics hidden within the information, since it's a pixel by pixel representation of each space invader. The tutorial points out you can change the player's ship (which actually appears upside-down, as do many of the other sprites in 2600 game ROMs) to a smiley face simply by replacing the appropriate Xs in the text file and then converting the text file back to a binary again with the following command:

```
C:\> editgfx spaceinv.txt testspac.bin
```

You can then run the binary in an emulator or via another method of your choosing.

Coding 2600 titles from scratch. The exhaustive Atari Age even has the last word with regard to coding resources, with an excellent 2600 coding page (*http://www.atariage.com/2600/programming/*) which links to Kirk Israel's superlative "2600 101" (*http://www.atariage.com/2600/programming/2600_101/*) basic tutorial. The intro notes that the Atari 2600 is "a very quirky beast [since] it has very little memory or other resources to work with" before explaining the vagaries of the game system. You'll obviously need to program using assembly language all the way—no wimpy C++ here.

If you want specific coding tools, try the DASM Assembler (*http://www. atari2600.org/dasm/*) or the Distella disassembler (*http://www. atari2600collector.com/distella.htm*). They're both excellent tools, providing plenty of functionality considering the age of the console. Adam Trionfo's previously mentioned tutorial actually helps a great deal by describing ways you can disassemble existing Atari 2600 ROMs and then change their content.

Many homebrew developers also provide their source code for free, with highlights including the source to SCSIside (*http://www.pixelspast.com/games/ scsicide/scsi131.s.txt*) and Space Treat Deluxe (*http://www.atariage.com/2600/ archives/source/SpaceTreatDeluxe_source/index.html*). Sorting through someone else's successful game code should help you out.

As for already-produced homebrew titles, to find Atari Age's list of 2600 homebrew games, go to the search page (*http://www.atariage.com/software_ search.html?SystemID=2600*) and pick Homebrew from the Rarity dropdown menu and hit the Search button.

Although Atari Age has the best overall set of homebrew games, links, and info, Erik Eid has the best single Atari homebrew web page (*http://www.wwnet.net/~eeid/station26/homebrew.html*). It lists the available homebrew 2600 games with basic info about each title. Though it's slightly out of date at the time of writing, it provides a good general look at the diversity of the 2600 scene.

The Best 2600 Homebrew Games

There are a few homebrew titles in particular worth singling out. All of these games may be available in cartridge form, but they're also freely downloadable and playable on emulators or on the hardware itself via suitable peripherals.

SCSIcide by Joe Grand. This ingenious, surreal action title from 2001 lets you assume "the role of a hard drive read head and your mission is to read the color-coded bits of data as they scream past you on ten separate data tracks." It's especially fun because of the bright, fast-moving blobs of color. The genuine cartridge version also uses the paddle controller. Learn more at *http://www.pixelspast.com/games/scsicide/index.php?ID=games&subID=scsicide*.

Marble Craze by Paul Slocum. This advanced split-screen game uses dual paddle controllers to simulate vertical and horizontal tilting of a playfield to move the titular marble around the world. Because it required the use of paddles, it was unplayable in emulators until recently. Fortunately, with the help of the Stelladaptor Atari controller to PC plug-in (*http://www.atariage.com/store/product_info.php?products_id=267*), you can now play it on an emulator, so download the ROM release. Oh, and any game with a random Super Mario Kart reference is fine by me—one of the levels is called "Rainbow Road." See *http://www.qotile.net/marble.html*.

Oystron by Piero Cavina. A relatively ancient homebrew title from 1997, this fast-paced arcade title may remind you of other classic games while demonstrating a twisted style all its own. The bright sprites with the clever color variations are also neat. The homepage includes *.BIN* files containing many of the early prototypes for the game; it's great to see how it progressed over time. Download it from *http://www.io.com/~nickb/atari/oystron.html*.

Warring Worms by Billy Eno. This is a souped-up version of the classic Snake-style game, with trailing tails, missiles, 256 game types, and both one- and two-player modes. Being able to pass through your opponent's tail by firing is a neat twist and the basic gameplay is as super-addictive as ever. This 2002 release is definitely a homebrew to try, so head on over to *http://www.baroquegaming.com/projects/WarringWorms/warring_worms.htm*.

Skeleton+ by Eric Ball. This conceptually fun 3D maze game has skeletons galore for you to find and destroy, a corresponding undead locator, and even pseudo-stereo sound—on appropriately modded 2600s—so you can tell where the skeletons are coming from. This is addictive and rather scary, provided that pixelated zombies (as seen in Figure 8-20) fit your idea of terrifying. I dare you to visit *http://www.atariage.com/software_page. html?SoftwareLabelID=2381.*

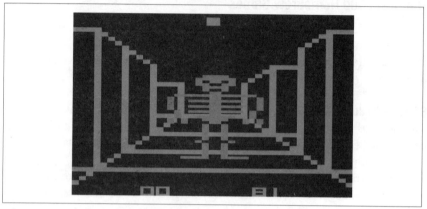

Figure 8-20. A not-so-scary skeleton

The ultimate accolade for homebrew creators came in 2003, when the Game Boy Advance version of the Activision Anthology game (*http://www. metacritic.com/games/platforms/gba/activisionanthology/*) featured several homebrew Atari 2600 games, including Climber 5, Okie Dokie, Oystron, Skeleton+, Space Treat Deluxe, Vault Assault, and Video Euchre. Although only the GBA version had these homebrew Atari treats on it—avoid the PlayStation 2 version, they're not on there!—it's well worth seeking out to see some homebrew classics in portable form, in a wonderful piece of re-appropriation by the games industry.

As well as those titles, there are a multitude of other neat possibilities including both released games and forthcoming gems. Check out the homebrew games currently in progress and download early demos from the Atari Age In Development page (*http://www.atariage.com/development_list.html*).

In particular, Paul Slocum's upcoming Homestar Runner RPG (*http://www. qotile.net/rpg.html*) is an excellent example of retro fun with a modern twist. This Atari 2600 homebrew title has official endorsement from the creators of the cult webtoon. It includes turn-based gameplay and the ability to fight bad guys from other Atari 2600 games—a mouthwatering prospect for those addicted to the Homestar Runner (*http://www.homestarrunner.com/*) humor factory.

Whether writing an entire game or not, you may still want to test out your works in progress (or other people's in-development or completed titles!) on an actual, honest-to-goodness Atari 2600. That's where putting your home-brew games onto a real Atari 2600 cartridge comes into play—read how to do it in *Gaming Hacks* (O'Reilly).

—*Simon Carless*

Program for the Game Boy Advance

HACK #76

Make your own portable playthings.

What budding game programmer doesn't fantasize about seeing one of his own creations on a console or portable gaming device? Thanks to extensive game development communities and the efforts of independent program-mers, this fantasy is no longer such a pipe dream.

In addition to being the prime platform for game companies to re-release their classic 8 and 16-bit titles, the Game Boy Advance has also become a major center for independent, amateur, and homebrew development. The relatively low cost and ease of development for the Game Boy Advance (GBA) has made it a common entry point into console-based programming. In this hack, I'll show you what tools you'll need for development and show you the first steps in writing a program that will use some of the GBA's video modes.

Welcome to the GBA Dev World

To develop games for a console, you typically need a development license from the console vendor and the accompanying software development kit, or SDK. Often the prices for such licenses run into the several thousands of dollars or more. Luckily for hobbyist GBA developers, there is a free alterna-tive available for those who do not have that sort of spare cash lying around. DevKit Advance is a free GBA development kit developed by volunteer pro-grammers. It allows you to compile and link source code into a format understandable to a Game Boy Advance.

Most programming for a GBA is done in C/C++, with some assembly thrown in for the brave and performance-conscious. Unlike the PC world, where most code is compiled for processors in the x86 family, GBA code must be compiled for an ARM processor. This is the main reason you need a special SDK to write software for a GBA. Thankfully, the tools necessary for GBA development, from compilers to image conversion tools, are readily available on the Internet.

Assembling Your Tools

The first thing you will need for your new Game Boy Advance development shop is the SDK. DevKit Advance (*http://devkitadv.sourceforge.net/*) can be downloaded at *http://sourceforge.net/project/showfiles.php?group_id=67315*. For most development in C++ you will need to download the following files to the same directory on your hard drive—I use *C:\gbadev* (the actual names are version-dependent, so the file names may vary):

> *agb-win-core-r5.zip*
> *agb-win-binutils-r4.zip*
> *agb-win-gcc-r4.zip*
> *agb-win-newlib-r4.zip*
> *agb-win-libstdcpp-r4.zip*
> *agb-win-patch-r4.zip*

Once these files are downloaded, unzip them while making sure to preserve their directory structure. They should all unzip to a subdirectory called *devkitadv*.

While it's certainly possible to write all your code in a simple text editor like Notepad or vi and then compile it manually using DevKit Advance's compiler and linker, it's probably wise to use some sort of Integrated Development Environment (IDE) to organize your projects. But if you want to use the command-line tools this way, you'll need to follow the instructions in *devkitadv\windows.txt* to prepare your environment. Since that document assumes you will be using *C:\devkitadv*, you may want to move the *devkitadv* subdirectory to the root of your hard drive so you don't have to adjust the instructions.

Emacs, Eclipse, and Microsoft Visual Studio are all workable solutions for making development more convenient. The Newbie's Guide to Game Boy Advance Development by VerticalE provides a good tutorial for how to set up Visual Studio 6.0 to work with DevKit Advance, and it can be found at *http://www.gbadev.org/download.php?section=docs&filename=NGGBA.zip*.

If you plan to develop without an IDE, you may wish to visit a few tutorials on using makefiles and a GCC-like compiler, like the one used in DevKit Advance. The following sites should offer enough information to get you started:

> *http://galton.uchicago.edu/~gosset/Compdocs/gcc.html*
> *http://users.actcom.co.il/~choo/lupg/tutorials/writing-makefiles/writing-makefiles.html*

To test your new creations, you can either copy your newly compiled GBA ROMs to a flash cart and run it on a GBA or you can use a GBA emulator.

Ideally, you should do both. An emulator allows you the convenience of quick testing from your PC while flash cart testing will show you how your program runs on real hardware and expose problems not evident on emulators (which are generally more forgiving).

You can find information on purchasing and using GBA Flash carts at *http://www.linker4u.com/* and *http://www.lik-sang.com/*.

There are several free GBA emulators [Hack #44] available on the Internet. A fairly decent list of them can be found at *http://www.devrs.com/gba/software.php#emus*. I find that Visual Boy (*http://vba.ngemu.com/*) works well for my purposes.

You will also need tools that allow you to convert images and sounds to a format usable by a GBA. You can download graphic conversion utilities at *http://www.gbadev.org/tools.php?section=gfx* and you can download sound conversion utilities at *http://www.gbadev.org/tools.php?section=sou*. For the purposes of this hack, I use Digital Inline's pcx2gba 1.10a and Warder1's GBA Map Editor beta 4 for graphics conversion.

Getting Dirty with the Code

The first step performed by almost any GBA program is to set the video mode. The video mode determines how and in what format graphics are presented on the GBA screen. The GBA has four backgrounds (or layers) on which graphics can be displayed and six video modes that define how the backgrounds can be used. The six video modes can be divided into two different types: tiled and bitmapped. The different video modes are listed in Table 8-1.

Table 8-1. The GBA video modes

Video mode	Type	Backgrounds
0	Tiled	All four BGs are static and available.
1	Tiled	BG0, BG1, and BG2 are available.
		BG2 is scalable and rotatable.
2	Tiled	BG2 and BG3 are available.
		Both are scalable and rotatable.
3	Bitmapped	BG2 is 240x160 pixels in 15-bit color.
4	Bitmapped	BG2 is 240x160 pixels in 8-bit indexed color and features a frame buffer for better animation quality.
5	Bitmapped	BG2 is 160x128 pixels in 15-bit color and features a frame buffer for better animation quality.

Tiled modes allow graphics to be made out of arrays of smaller graphics. This allows large graphics to be stored and executed efficiently as long as they are made up of repeatable tiles. Bitmapped modes allow a background to be accessed directly as an array of bytes. They can be used for displaying highly detailed images at the cost of speed and storage size. Bitmapped modes only use BG2.

To change the video mode, and several other video related settings, you write data to the video control register. As far as GBA programming goes, registers are particular sections of memory where certain events are to happen if data is placed there. The video control register lives at memory location 0x04000000, so to change video settings, you would use code similar to the following:

```
*(unsigned short*)0x04000000 = <value>;
```

This line essentially says to set the unsigned short (a 16-bit value) at memory location 0x04000000 to whatever value you specify. The value you specify is a 16-bit number whose component bits reflect various settings including the video mode. The lowest three bits of the value determine the video mode. Refer to Table 8-2 for the video modes and their corresponding values:

Table 8-2. Values for setting the video mode

Video mode	Hexadecimal	Binary
0	0x0	000
1	0x1	001
2	0x2	010
3	0x3	011
4	0x4	100
5	0x5	101

For example, to set the video mode to mode 3 you would write the following:

```
*(unsigned short*)0x04000000 = 0x3;
```

You can also combine these video mode values with values representing other settings in the video control register. Bit 10, for example, determines whether or not BG2 is enabled. Because you are setting the GBA to mode 3, you will need BG2 to be enabled. BG2 can be enabled with the value 0x400, which you can combine with the value for mode 4 by using a logical OR, like so:

```
*(unsigned short*)0x04000000 = 0x400 | 0x3;
```

Table 8-3 provides a list of useful values that can be set in the video control register.

Table 8-3. Useful video control register values

Function	Hexadecimal	Binary
Display frame buffer (in modes 4 and 5)	0x10	1 0000
Clear Screen (turns screen white by clearing the video buffer)	0x80	1000 0000
Enable BG0	0x100	1 0000 0000
Enable BG1	0x200	10 0000 0000
Enable BG2	0x400	100 0000 0000
Enable BG3	0x800	1000 0000 0000
Enable Sprites	0x1000	1 0000 0000 0000

To really understand how this works, you will need a thorough understanding of binary and hexadecimal numbers and binary operations. You can visit *http://www.edmagnin.com/CSIS240/reference.html* for more information about binary and hexadecimal. Also, the tutorials at *http://gbajunkie.co.uk/* provide a useful set of macros for changing settings with the video control register.

With all this information, you are ready to write an extraordinarily simple GBA program. Copy the following code, save it, and then compile it:

```
int main(void) {
    *(unsigned short*)0x04000000 = 0x3 | 0x400 | 0x80;
}
```

If you are using the command-line compilers, save this program as *hello.c*. Then, compile it and prepare the ROM image with these two commands:

```
gcc -o hello.elf hello.c
objcopy -O binary hello.elf hello.gba
```

You can adapt these two commands for the remaining examples in this hack.

As you can see, this code is a simple one-line program that sets the video mode to Mode 3, enables BG2 and clears the video buffer. If you were successfully able to compile this program, you should be able to run it on a GBA or GBA emulator. When you run it, you should see a blank screen appear on your GBA or emulator. Not exactly brain surgery, but from here on in, things get interesting.

Managing the Video Buffer

To display something on the GBA's screen you must put data in a particular section of memory called the video buffer. In the case of the GBA, the video buffer is the 96KB large section of memory starting at 0x06000000. Those familiar with programming using graphical DOS modes like 13h will find the process of accessing the video buffer quite familiar.

In general, you can display something on the GBA screen by using code similar to that used to set the video control register. However, it is useful to write functions to abstract the process, as most people would find it easier to think about graphics in terms of pixels than memory coordinates. The following code is an example of a function for writing a particular color (r, g, and b) to a particular pixel (x and y) in mode 3:

```
void SetPixelMode3 (int x, int y, int r, int g, int b) {
    unsigned short color = (b << 10) | (g << 5) | r;

    unsigned short *pixelAddress = (unsigned short*)0x06000000;

    pixelAddress = pixelAddress + (240 * y) + x;

    *pixelAddress = color;
}
```

Mode 3 uses 15-bit true color, so the color of any pixel is determined by a 15-bit value. The video buffer in Mode 3 is actually be made up of 16-bit values, but seems to ignore the highest bit just fine. With this in mind, the code casts the color as an unsigned short, which happens to be a 16-bit number, and casts the pixel address as a pointer to an unsigned short. In terms of code, this is accomplished by the << operator which is used to shift the value of b 10 bits higher and the value of g 5 bits higher. The values for r, g and b are then all combined using a logical OR operation. The construction of a 15-bit color is shown in Figure 8-21.

To determine the address at which to place the color, keep in mind that the video buffer is a continuous array of memory starting at 0x06000000. In the case of Mode 3, which is 240×160 16-bit values, every 240 16-bit values can be thought of as a horizontal line on the screen, as seen in Figure 8-22.

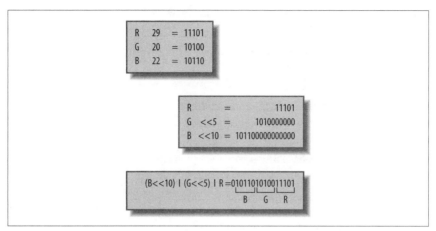

Figure 8-21. Construction of a 15-bit color

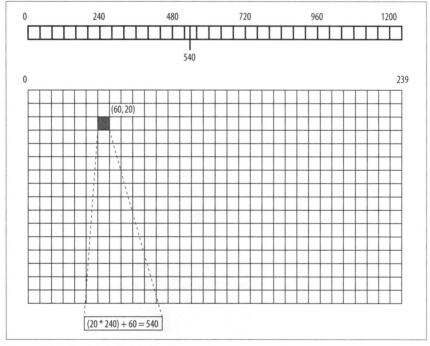

Figure 8-22. The Mode 3 video buffer

Therefore, from the starting address of 0x06000000, the memory address at which to place a pixel is y times 240 (the number of values or pixels per line) plus x. With that in mind, try compiling and running a program that takes advantage of this new function, such as the following:

```
void SetPixelMode3(int x, int y, int r, int g, int b) {
    unsigned short color = (b << 10) | (g << 5) | r;

    unsigned short *pixelAddress = (unsigned short*)0x06000000;

    pixelAddress = pixelAddress + (240 * y) + x;

    *pixelAddress = color;
}

int main(void) {
    *(unsigned short*)0x04000000 = 0x3 | 0x400;
    int i;

    //Draw horizontal red line
    for(i = 0; i < 100; i++) {
        SetPixelMode3 (10 + i, 10, 31, 0, 0);
    }

    //Draw diagonal green line
    for(i = 0; i < 100; i++) {
        SetPixelMode3 (10 + i, 10 + i, 0, 31, 0);
    }

    //Draw vertical blue line
    for(i = 0; i < 100; i++) {
        SetPixelMode3 (10, 10 + i, 0, 0, 31);
    }
}
```

When you run this program on a GBA or emulator, you should see something similar to Figure 8-23.

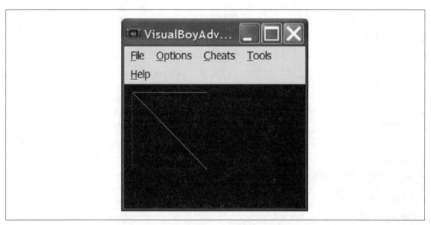

Figure 8-23. Hello, Mode 3

Displaying Images on a GBA

Pushing pixels is a decent way to start, but, for real power, you need to be able to load external images and to use double-buffering for smooth animation. For that, we will harness the power of Mode 4. While it's certainly possible to animate and load external images using Mode 3, it's lack of a secondary region on which to draw graphics before displaying them results in flickering animation. Also, the 8-bit palette-based color system of Mode 4 allows you to save a lot more images to memory compared to Mode 3.

The first step in loading an image on a Game Boy Advance is to create an image that can be easily converted into a format usable by a GBA. You will be using the pcx2gba utility (see "Assembling Your Tools," earlier in this hack) to convert graphics, so first use your preferred image editor create a graphic in PCX format. Mode 4 uses 8-bit color, so the PCX will have to be a 256-color indexed image. To fill the screen, the image should be 240 pixels by 160 pixels. Save your graphic as *my_pic.pcx* in the same directory as *pcx2gba.exe*. From a DOS prompt, go to the pcx2gba directory and execute the following command:

```
pcx2gba TXT4 my_pic.pcx my_pic.h mypic
```

This command tells pcx2gba to convert *my_pic.pcx* into *my_pic.h*. There are several different formats a GBA can use for graphics; TXT4 tells pcx2gba to convert into a header file that can be included directly in a GBA program's C/C++ code. The mypic argument is the name used for the data structures defined in the new header file (*my_pic.h*), which contains an array of data for the image palette, mypicpal, and the actual image data, mypicdata.

To add the newly converted image to a GBA program, you include it in your source file using a #include directive. Then you add it to your project or link it at compile time. To actually display the image on the screen, you must first copy the color palette into the palette memory of the GBA, which is located at 0x05000000. Then, like in Mode 3, you copy the image data into the video buffer, starting at 0x06000000. In Mode 4, however, bear in mind that the video buffer takes up half the space it does in Mode 3, because it uses 8-bit versus 16-bit color. You will copy half as much data to fill the video buffer.

The following code displays the picture defined in *my_pic.h* on the screen:

```
#define USHORT unsigned short
#include "my_pic.h"

int main(void) {
    *(unsigned short*)0x04000000 = 0x4 | 0x400;
```

```
    int i, x, y;

    unsigned short *gbaPalette = (unsigned short*)0x05000000;
    for(i = 0; i < 256; i++) {
        gbaPalette[i] = mypicpal[i];
    }
    unsigned short *gbaScreen = (unsigned short*)0x06000000;
    for(y = 0; y < 160; y++) {
        for(x = 0; x < 120; x++) {
            gbaScreen[(y * 120) + x] = mypicdata[(y * 120) + x];
        }
    }
}
```

The header created by pcx2gba defines the image and palette as arrays of
type USHORT. This is not defined by default, so first you must define it as
being an unsigned short. Next you need to include the header with the picture data. As before, a simple setting at memory address 0x04000000 sets the
video mode, this time to Mode 4. The next section of code defines a pointer
to memory address 0x05000000, the GBA color palette. The program then
copies the 256 color entries from the palette in *my_pic.h* into the GBA palette. The final block of code does a similar operation, except it copies from
the image data in *my_pic.h* into an array starting at the beginning of the
video buffer. You may notice that x only iterates to 120 even though the
screen is 240 pixels wide. In Mode 4, each pixel is 8 bits long, however the
unsigned shorts used to store the image are 16 bits long. Each unsigned
short houses the data for two adjacent pixels. So, instead of copying one
pixel at a time 240 times, the program copies 2 pixels at a time 120 times.
When you compile and run this program, you should see the image you created show up on the GBA's screen.

Mode 4 has half as much memory allotted to the video buffer as Mode 3.
The other half is used to implement a frame buffer, a secondary buffer of
memory in which to place graphics. You can place images in the frame
buffer just as you would to the video buffer. The advantage is that you control when the frame buffer or the video buffer is displayed. This is useful
when drawing a complex image or when performing animation. You can
wait until your image is ready to be displayed before finally displaying it.
Whether the frame buffer or the video buffer is displayed is determined by
the fifth bit of the video control register. The frame buffer can be made visible in Mode 4 like so:

```
*(unsigned short*)0x04000000 = 0x10 | 0x4 | 0x400;
```

The following code illustrates putting a second image (create *my_pic2.h* as
you did with *my_pic.h*) into the frame buffer and rapidly switching between
the frame buffer and the video buffer:

```
#define USHORT unsigned short
#include "my_pic.h"
#include "my_pic2.h"
#define VCOUNT (*(volatile unsigned short*)0x04000006)
#define vsync() while (VCOUNT != 160);
typedef enum bool { false, true } bool;

int main(void) {
    *(unsigned short*)0x04000000 = 0x4 | 0x400;
    unsigned short *gbaPalette = (unsigned short*)0x05000000;
    bool flipped = false;
    int i, x, y;

    for(i = 0; i < 256; i++) {
        gbaPalette[i] = mypicpal[i];
    }
    unsigned short *gbaScreen = (unsigned short*)0x06000000;

    for(y = 0; y < 160; y++) {
        for(x = 0; x < 120; x++) {
            gbaScreen[(y * 120) + x] = mypicdata[(y * 120) + x];
        }
    }

    unsigned short *backBuffer = (unsigned short*)0x600A000;
    for(y = 0; y < 160; y++) {
        for(x = 0; x < 120; x++) {
            backBuffer[(y * 120) + x] = mypic2data[(y * 120) + x];
        }
    }
    while(1) {
        vsync();
        if(flipped == false) {
            *(unsigned short*)0x04000000 = 0x10 | 0x4 | 0x400;
            flipped = true;
        }
        else {
            *(unsigned short*)0x04000000 = 0x4 | 0x400;
            flipped = false;
        }
    }
}
```

The code is fairly straightforward, but there are a few interesting points to note. First, in this scenario both images share the same palette. In fact, only my_pic1's palette is actually loaded into memory at 0x05000000. In order for both pictures to look right, you have to make sure they have the same palette when you create them in an image editor. Alternatively, you could load each images' palette just before you display it. This, however, can slow things down and cause odd color distortions on the displayed image as the palette is being changed.

The second point to note is the vsync( ) call. On a GBA, like a monitor, there is a brief period of time during which nothing from the video buffer is being drawn on the screen. It is best to make changes to the video buffer during this time to avoid odd effects (e.g., shearing) as you switch from one image to the next. Calling vsync( ) aligns you with the period of time, so you can start writing to the video buffer immediately after you call it and, hopefully, finish before the video buffer is drawn on the screen. The following clever bit of code, cribbed from Dev'rs GBA Dev FAQ (*http://www.devrs. com/gba/*) implements the vsync( ) call:

```
#define VCOUNT (*(volatile unsigned short*)0x04000006)
#define vsync() while (VCOUNT != 160);
```

Essentially, like the video control register at 0x04000000, there is a value at memory location 0x04000006 that indicates what line of the screen is currently being drawn. If you wait until the final line of the screen has just been drawn, line 160 in the case of Mode 3 and 4, you can begin modifying the video buffer during the brief interval when the screen is not being displayed.

—Robert Ota Dieterich

Add Tiles and Sprites to Your GBA Game

H A C K
#77   Make your portable masterpiece come alive with tiled graphics.

Writing directly to the video buffer with bitmapped video modes on the Game Boy Advance **[Hack #76]** is all well and good, but uses a lot of memory and can be slow if you want to try any sort of complicated animation. The reason game consoles and portables are able to produce such brilliant visual effects, despite their low hardware specs compared to PCs, is because of their highly specialized graphics hardware.

In the case of the GBA, and most consoles made for 2D graphics, this comes in the form of specialized handling of tiled graphics. In this hack, I'll show you how to use tiled graphics to reduce the amount of memory taken up by an image and increase the speed at which it can be displayed.

The first step in getting a GBA to display tiled graphics is, of course, to create the graphics it will be using. Tiles are essentially 8×8 squares that can used to draw a larger image. Larger and non-square tiles can be made up of multiple 8×8 tiles. Figure 8-24 shows a set of eight 16×16 tiles or, from the GBA's perspective, thirty-two 8×8 tiles.

Once you have a usable set of tiles, it's time to make the map data that will actually tell the GBA which tile to display where. There are several tools available on *http://www.gbadev.org/* for creating map data, one of which is Warder1's GBA Map Editor. When you launch Map Editor, two windows

Figure 8-24. Graphic tiles

open up. One is the Tools window, where you can load a bitmap containing all your tiles. The other window is the GBA Map Editor itself, which you can use to paint your map by using the tiles that are loaded in the Tools window. The maps you create with this tool can be saved in its proprietary format and loaded again later to be edited. To make use of map data on a GBA, you can export the data to either a C source file that you can include in your project or into a bitmap, which you can run through a different image-to-map converter should you desire.

> Note that the GBA Map Editor's Export to C functionality seems to have a bug where it sometimes only exports half of the map data to the C file. This can occasionally be solved by re-exporting the data or switching to a higher resolution map.

Load the Map into Memory

Once your map data is converted to a GBA-friendly format, you will need to convert your tile graphic as well. As with images to be loaded in bitmapped video modes, the tile graphic must be converted into palette data and pixel data. Assuming you've converted the graphic of your tiles to a 256-color PCX, you can convert it with pcx2gba, like so:

```
pcx2gba SPR4T my_tiles.pcx my_tiles.h my_tiles
```

> To make a quick and dirty set of tiles, create a 64x32 pixel PCX file similar to the one shown in Figure 8-24, using the graphics editor of your choice (The Gimp, *http://www.gimp. org*, is a great, free choice). To compile the examples in the rest of this hack, be sure to read "Program for the Game Boy Advance" **[Hack #76]** first.

As before **[Hack #76]**, this command converts *my_tiles.pcx* into an array of palette data named my_tilespal and an array of pixel data named my_tilesdata, both in a file called *my_tiles.h*. The SPR4T parameter tells the program to cut the data into a series of 8x8 tiles with the conversion.

With all the data converted to a format usable by the GBA, it's time to actually load it. The first step is to change the video mode and load the palette data. These steps are pretty similar to what you have seen before.

```
#define USHORT unsigned short
#include "my_tiles.h"

int main(void) {
  *(unsigned short*)0x04000000 = 0x1 | 0x400;
  int i;

  unsigned short *tilePalette = (unsigned short*)0x05000000;
  for(i = 0; i < 256; i++) {
      tilePalette[i] = my_tilespal[i];
  }
}
```

The first section of code, of course, changes the video mode. This time, I am using Mode 0 and intend to write to BG2, so I make sure it is enabled. The palette for background tiles goes to the same location in memory that the color palette for bitmapped video modes does, so the palette loading code is virtually the same.

Next, the program loads the pixel data for the tiles and the map data. This is where things get interesting. Both the tile data and map data must be loaded into the same 64KB region of memory, which starts at 0x06000000. Also, the GBA requires that the tile data be aligned to a 16KB region called a Character Base Block, which is indexed from 0-3, and that the map data be aligned to a 2KB region called a Screen Base Block, which is indexed from 0-31. These blocks basically serve as flag posts marking where in memory the background should look for its map and tile data. Later, when you actually display the background, you will use the indexes of the Character and Screen Base Blocks to tell the GBA where to look for the relevant tile and map data. Finally, it's very important that the Character Base Blocks and the Screen Base Blocks being used do not overlap. If they do, you will get corrupted tile and map data. Figure 8-25 illustrates the concept of Character Base Blocks and Screen Base Blocks.

The following code shows how you can load the tile data into properly aligned Character Base Blocks. You'll need to add these variable declarations to the top of the preceding example:

```
int tile_setCharBaseBlock = 1;
unsigned short *tileData =
  (unsigned short*)( 0x06000000 + (tile_setCharBaseBlock * 0x4000) );
```

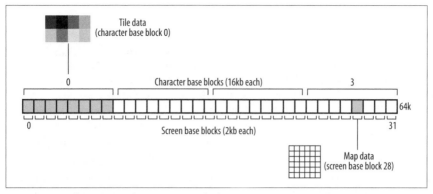

Figure 8-25. Character and Screen Base Blocks

And add the following for loop immediately after the for loop you use to load the palette:

```
for(i = 0; i < (my_tiles_WIDTH * my_tiles_HEIGHT) / 2; i++) {
    tileData[i] = my_tilesdata[i];
}
```

The first thing this segment of code does is to set the variable tile_setCharBaseBlock with the index of the Character Base Block you intend to use since you will need it later. The second line creates a pointer to the start of video memory (0x06000000) then adds 16KB (0x4000) times the index of the base block you intend to use. After that, the code follows standard procedure to load data from one part of memory to another.

This example performs a similar task for the map data:

```
#define USHORT unsigned short
#define u8 unsigned short

#include "my_tiles.h"
#include "my_map.c"

int main(void) {
  *(unsigned short*)0x04000000 = 0x1 | 0x400;
  int my_mapScreenBaseBlock = 28;
  int i;
  unsigned short *myMapData = (unsigned short*)my_map;
  unsigned short *tileMap =
   (unsigned short*) ( 0x6000000 + (my_mapScreenBaseBlock*0x800) );
  for(i = 0; i < (64 * 64) / 2; i++) {
      tileMap[i] = myMapData[i];
  }
}
```

To create your map, fire up the GBA Map Editor, create a new 512×512 map, and select Tiles → Load Tiles from the Tools window to load your tiles bitmap (you will need to convert your *.PCX* tile file into a *.BMP* first). Then, return to the GBA Map Editor main window, paint your map, and use the File → Tools → Export to C menu to create the *my_map. c* file used in the preceding example.

To make sure there's no chance of collision with the previously loaded tile data, this code prepares to write to Screen Base Block 28. Because the map data imported from the GBA Map Editor is an array of 8-bit values, the second line casts it to 16-bit values in order to make it easier to load. Similar to the tile data loading code, the third line calculates the address at which to write as 0x06000000 plus the Screen Base Block index times 2048, or 0x800 in hexadecimal. The map data you're loading was exported as a 64×64 array of 8-bit values. Because we are loading it as 16-bit values, which are twice as large, we iterate through the loop half as many times had we been moving one 8-bit value at a time. The GBA is optimized to write 16-bit values, so it's important to do so whenever possible.

Display the Map

With your tiles and your map data loaded, it's time to actually start displaying them. The GBA can have up to four background layers, depending on the video mode. Mode 1 allows BG0, BG1, and BG2 to be used, with BG0 and BG1 being static and BG2 being a rotation/scaling background. Each background has a 16-bit value in memory known as the background control register. By writing certain values to one of these registers, you can change the settings of that particular background. Table 8-4 lists the memory addresses for the four background control registers.

Table 8-4. Background control registers

Background	Location in memory
0	0x4000008
1	0x400000A
2	0x400000C
3	0x400000E

Setting the background control registers can be done in a fashion similar to setting the video control register, as in the following code snippet, which loads the map into BG2:

```
*(unsigned short*)0x400000C = (tile_setCharBaseBlock << 2) |
  (my_mapScreenBaseBlock << 8) | 0x80 | 0x8000;
```

Like the video mode changing code, this code is largely composed of using logical ORs to combine various key values into one value. New here are the operations tile_setCharBaseBlock << 2 and my_mapScreenBaseBlock << 8. These operations take the base block values saved from loading the tile and map data and shift them to the proper bits to have them identify the relevant Character Base Block and Screen Base Block when placed in the background control register. Incidentally, assuming Mode 1, the preceding code sets the background to be a 512×512 pixel background using 256-color tiles. Table 8-5 lists several useful values for configuring a tiled background.

Table 8-5. Background configuration values

Function	Hexadecimal	Binary
Priority 1 (display order)	0x0	0
Priority 2	0x1	1
Priority 3	0x2	10
Priority 4	0x3	11
8-bit Color	0x80	1000 0000
16-bit Color (static backgrounds only)	0x0	0000 0000
Dimensions 256x256 (static) 128x128 (rotation/scaling)	0x0	00000 0000 0000 0000
Dimensions 512x256 (static) 256x256 (rotation/scaling)	0x4000	0100 0000 0000 0000
Dimensions 256x512 (static) 512x512 (rotation/scaling)	0x8000	1000 0000 0000 0000
Dimensions 512x512 (static) 1024x1024 (rotation/scaling)	0xC000	1100 0000 0000 0000

The following complete example combines everything you've seen so far to display a map on the screen:

```
#define USHORT unsigned short
#define u8 unsigned short

#include "my_tiles.h" /* 64x32 pixel pcx, converted by pcx2gba */
#include "my_map.c"   /* 512x512 tile map, exported by the map editor */

int main(void) {

  int tile_setCharBaseBlock = 1;
  int my_mapScreenBaseBlock = 28;
  int i;
```

```
/* Initialize the display */
*(unsigned short*)0x04000000 = 0x0 | 0x400;

/* Load the palette */
unsigned short *tilePalette = (unsigned short*)0x05000000;
for(i = 0; i < 256; i++) {
    tilePalette[i] = my_tilespal[i];
}

/* Load the tiles */
unsigned short *tileData =
  (unsigned short*)( 0x06000000 + (tile_setCharBaseBlock * 0x4000) );
for(i = 0; i < (my_tiles_WIDTH * my_tiles_HEIGHT) / 2; i++) {
  tileData[i] = my_tilesdata[i];
}


/* Load the map */
unsigned short *tileMap =
  (unsigned short*) ( 0x6000000 + (my_mapScreenBaseBlock*0x800) );
unsigned short *myMapData = (unsigned short*)my_map;
for(i = 0; i < (64 * 64) / 2; i++) {
    tileMap[i] = myMapData[i];
}

/* Load the map into BG2 */
*(unsigned short*)0x400000C = (tile_setCharBaseBlock << 2)
    | (my_mapScreenBaseBlock << 8) | 0x80 | 0x8000;

}
```

The Refreshing Taste of Sprites

A game without sprites is essentially a stage without any actors. Being the 2D graphics maverick that it is, the GBA has a lot of specialized functionality centered around sprites. Sprites are, like tiled backgrounds, images made from series of 8×8 tiles. The GBA can store up to 128 sprites, which can be between 8×8 pixels and 64×64 pixels in dimension. Sprite pixel data and palette data are stored in different parts of memory than background tile pixel and palette data, so you can have different palettes for your sprites and backgrounds.

Creating the graphics for a sprite is relatively straightforward. You need only remember to keep the dimensions within the 8×8 to 64×64 bounds and the color depth to 16 or 256 colors. Converting an image to be used by the GBA can be done with pcx2gba, using the same method used to convert background tile images.

This section assumes a *.PCX* file called *pat.pcx*, and a corresponding header file called *pat.h*. You could generate the correct files using *pat.pcx* as input with this command:
```
pcx2gba SPR4T pat.pcx pat.h pat
```

Now to the actual displaying of sprites. As always, the program begins by setting the video control register with the requisite values. The following line of code sets the GBA to Mode 1 and enables sprites:

```
*(unsigned short*)0x04000000 = 0x1 | 0x1000 | 0x40;
```

The extra 0x40 at the end is another setting value related to sprites. In memory, sprites can either be stored in a 2-dimensional array or a 1-dimensional array. By default, the GBA stores sprites in a 2D array, but often it can be easier to access them in a 1D array. ORing 0x40 into the video control register causes the GBA to store sprites in a 1D array.

Loading sprite pixel and palette data follows the familiar pattern of moving the data to designated areas of memory—in this case, 0x05000200 for sprite palette data and 0x06010000 for sprite pixel data. The following code loads the palette and data for a sprite named pat (be sure to have a line with #include "pat.h" at the top of your source file):

```
unsigned short *spritePalette = (unsigned short*)0x05000200;
for(int i = 0; i < 256; i++) {
    spritePalette[i] = patpal[i];
}

unsigned short *spriteData = (unsigned short*)0x06010000;
for(int i = 0; i < (pat_WIDTH * pat_HEIGHT) / 2; i++) {
    spriteData[i] = patdata[i];
}
```

For actually controlling where a sprite is displayed, the GBA uses a section of memory called the Object Attribute Memory (OAM). This memory serves a similar purpose to the background control registers. Values placed into OAM define how sprites behave. OAM allots 8 bytes to each of its 128 sprites. The size of each entry in OAM makes it difficult to handle settings through a single variable. The easiest way to handle it is to define a data structure that is 8 bytes long.

The OAMSprite structure, below, defines a structure whose data consists of an array of four unsigned shorts. Being that each unsigned short is two bytes long, this adds up to eight bytes.

```
struct OAMSprite {
    unsigned short reg[4];
};
```

This structure also lines up nicely with the locations in memory where various important bits of sprite information are located. The Y and X values of the sprite, along with a few key configuration values, are located in reg[0] and reg[1], respectively. The location of the sprite data in memory to be used by a given sprite can be referenced with reg[2]. The final variable, reg[3], can be used to access various functions related to rotation and scaling.

At this point, it's possible to display a sprite with code similar to the following:

```
OAMSprite pat;
int x = 24;
int y = 86;
pat.reg[0] = y | 0x2000;
pat.reg[1] = x | 0x8000;
pat.reg[2] = 0;

unsigned short *OAM = (unsigned short*)0x07000000;
unsigned short* spritePtr = (unsigned short*)&pat;
for(int i = 0; i < 4; i++) {
    OAM[i] = spritePtr[i];
}
```

As you can see, this code assigns values to the OAMSprite pat. The x and y values can go straight into reg[1] and reg[0] along with a couple of values for configuration. In this case, 0x2000 indicates that pat has 256 colors and 0x8000 indicates that pat is 32x32 pixels in dimension. The value in reg[2] is set to the index of the start of the sprite's image in the tile pixel array. In this case, 0 refers to the first tile. When the sprite is ready to be displayed, it is copied over into OAM, at memory location 0x07000000. Table 8-6 contains a few useful values relating to sprites in OAM.

Table 8-6. OAM values

Attribute	OAMSprite variable	Hexadecimal	Binary
16 Colors	reg[0]	0x0	00 0000 0000 0000
256 Colors	reg[0]	0x2000	10 0000 0000 0000
8x8	reg[1]	0x0	0000 0000 0000 0000
16x16	reg[1]	0x4000	100 0000 0000 0000
32x32	reg[1]	0x8000	1000 0000 0000 0000
64x64	reg[1]	0xC000	1100 0000 0000 0000
Horizontally Flipped	reg[1]	0x1000	01 0000 0000 0000
Vertically Flipped	reg[1]	0x2000	10 0000 0000 0000

Handling Input

The GBA has 10 different buttons that can be used for input: the four directional keys, A, B, L, R, Start and Select. The state of these ten buttons is contained in a 16-bit value located at 0x04000130. The lowest ten bits of this value indicate the state of each button, equaling 0 if the button is being pressed and 1 if it is not, as shown in Figure 8-26.

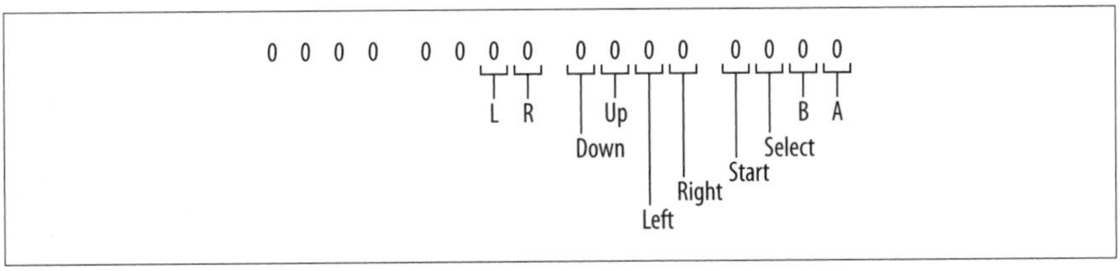

Figure 8-26. The key register

To determine if a particular button is being pressed, you can compare the value at 0x04000130 with a number corresponding to the bit you want to check using a logical AND operation. The number 0x2, for example, is the result you get when only the second bit in a number is 1 and, therefore, corresponds to the B button. A logical AND can be performed with the value at 0x04000130 with the following snippet of code:

```
*(unsigned short*)0x04000130 & 0x2
```

This expression returns a 1 if the second bit of both numbers is 1. Because a button press is indicated by a value of 0 in the appropriate bit, this is actually the opposite of what you want. So, you negate this expression to get something like this:

```
if( !( *(unsigned short*)0x04000130 & 0x2 ) ) {
    //Button B is being pressed
}
```

Table 8-7 contains a list of values that can be used to identify each button in an expression like the one above.

Table 8-7. The buttons on a GBA

Button	Hexadecimal	Binary
A	0x1	1
B	0x2	10
Select	0x4	100
Start	0x8	1000
Right	0x10	1 0000

Table 8-7. The buttons on a GBA (continued)

Button	Hexadecimal	Binary
Left	0x20	10 0000
Up	0x40	100 0000
Down	0x80	1000 0000
R	0x100	1 0000 0000
L	0x200	10 0000 0000

For further information on GBA programming, be sure to visit *http://www.gbadev.org/* and *http://www.devrs.com/gba/*. Also see "Play Homebrews on your GBA" [Hack #46] if you want to play your game on real hardware. With what you've now seen, and what you can find on those sites, you will have enough information to put together a rudimentary GBA game with graphics and input.

—*Robert Ota Dieterich*

HACK #78 Put Your Homebrews on Cartridges

Start your own homebrew retro-game assembly line.

So you've developed your own homebrew game for the Atari 2600 [Hack #75] or maybe another classic system. You've probably spent a significant amount time developing your game by using an emulator. Frankly, though, nothing beats the sight and sound of the real thing, and you'd be hard-pressed to sell just your ROM file through digital distribution. It's time to bestow that game of yours to the world in a real, physical cartridge, and for-tunately for you, it isn't all that difficult to do!

Before I begin, here are some definitions you should know:

ROM (Read Only Memory)
> A generic term used to describe the program file, or the physical chip the program file is stored on. The ROM chips in game cartridges are usually *mask ROMs*, the programming for which was stored as a result of the manufacturing process. Mask ROMs cannot be erased or repro-grammed.

PROM (Programmable Read Only Memory)
> A ROM chip that can be programmed to hold data. PROMs are avail-able in many different sizes and configurations.

EPROM (Erasable Programmable Read Only Memory)
> A ROM chip that can be erased with UV light and reprogrammed many times. An EPROM will have a clear window in the center, usually cov-ered with a sticker or label to protect from accidental erasure.

EEPROM (Electronically Erasable, Programmable Read Only Memory)
A ROM chip that can be erased and programmed electronically. An EEPROM might store high-score data or other data persistent between operational sessions.

PCB (Printed Circuit Board)
The physical circuit board that chips and electronic components are attached to.

Package
Describes the size and arrangement of a ROM or other computer chip. The most common package for older chips is dual in-line package (DIP), a large rectangular shape with 2 rows of pins.

Pinout
Term that describes the configuration and functions of the connecting pins on a chip, cartridge, etc.

Cartridge PCBs

Before the homebrew scene began to flourish, there was really only one method of obtaining PCBs: removing the ROM chips from existing games and replacing them with reprogrammed ROM chips. Recycling original PCBs is still a viable option today, but if you're going to assemble a large number of game cartridges, then you've already got a lot of work ahead of you. Add to that the wear and tear that recycled PCBs experienced in their previous life as Combat or Pac-Man, and you've quickly built up a case for using new PCBs instead of old ones. New PCBs are available for many platforms, including the Atari 2600, 5200, Colecovision, and Vectrex. Most are available for only a few dollars, and unlike some recycled PCBs, new PCBs are typically made to use more commonly available ROM chips. If you do choose to recycle PCBs, you'll need to desolder the original ROM chip, clean the board and contacts, and add your own ROM. Some game system manufacturers used proprietary ROM devices, and depending on the particular game platform, you may have to add some additional logic chips to your PCBs. For example, the Atari 2600 uses ROMs chips with an *active high* chip select (CS) line. Modern PROM and EPROM devices use *active low* CS, requiring the signal be inverted for correct operation. New 2600 PCBs will have a place to insert an inverter chip, whereas recycled PCBs usually won't have such a provision.

When developing your game, you may have been required to make some choices for bankswitching schemes, mappers, etc. When selecting a new PCB or finding a donor candidate for recycling PCBs, you'll need to be sure the PCB logic meets the requirements of your program file. For example, a

2K/4K PCB for the 2600 won't work at all for a 32K ROM with F4 bank-switching. Ideally, you should choose your hardware before programming your game, that way you know of your requirements ahead of time.

If you've decided to release a homebrew on a less common system, such as the Sega Master System or Arcadia-2001, then you've got a bit of extra work ahead of you. You'll want to spend some time examining the cartridge pinouts, how the factory ROMs are installed, and whether there is a comparable drop-in replacement EPROM available. You may have to alter the PCB slightly to accept a different type of EPROM. Fortunately, the hardware specifications and pinouts of most game systems have been documented by other enthusiasts, so it should be a trivial matter to search around and find some hardware information for your particular platform.

Do-It-Yourself PCBs

If new PCBs aren't available for your system but you're still interested in using new hardware, you can always have new PCBs manufactured. There are many companies that will produce custom PCBs in bulk at very reasonable cost and even provide free software for designing the board layout. Try *http://www.pcbpro.com* for starters. You could even subsidize your project by having extra PCBs made and reselling them to other homebrewers.

If you're truly masochistic, you could make your own by purchasing blank PCBs, photoresist film, etchant, a UV light, drill press, bit, jig saw, etc. It'll take forever, the results will be inconsistent, and you'll still spend a lot of money. This may be an option if you want to produce a single PCB "proof" to ensure your circuit design works, but for a large run of PCBs it won't be worth the effort for anything but the smallest of production runs.

ROMs: New or Used?

Unless your game concept is "Nihilistic Screaming Lines" for the Atari 2600 or "Ultimate Please-Insert-Cartridge" for the Colecovision, you'll need to store your game data on something. I talked about PCBs first because the available PCB options will determine the appropriate type of ROM chips that you will need to obtain.

The least expensive way to obtain ROM chips is through recycled electronics. These are usually EPROMs and are sold as "pulls." Most electronic parts vendors (try the ones listed at *http://www.arlabs.com/sources.htm*) sell pulls for no more than $1-$2 each, and sometimes less than that. If you want to hunt for your own EPROMs, check out used computer stores or university surplus stores. You may be able to find a stack of old hardware full of EPROMs for dirt-cheap. Just peel back the labels to read the part codes.

New ROMs are also available from electronics vendors. If they're available, PROM chips will usually be cheaper than EPROM chips. Once they're written they can't be changed, but most people won't buy a homebrew game and tear it open to reprogram it. New PCB vendors frequently stock ROM chips in the appropriate sizes, too.

 Some older EPROM chips may have the same number as a standard EPROM but have a different pinout. For example, the Texas Instruments TMS2716 has a different pinout than a standard 2716 ROM. If in doubt, try doing a Google search for the EPROM part number to see if there are any variations.

Erasing and Programming ROM chips

Programming (also called "burning") ROM chips is a fairly easy process. There are many value-priced EPROM programmers that can handle a wide variety of EPROM types. Some currently available budget-oriented programmers include:

Willem EPROM Programmer, www.willem.org, 37–80 euros ($45–$100)
Available in kit form or preassembled, the line of Willem EPROM programmers is geared towards someone with greater familiarity with EPROM technology. They are one of the least expensive options, but they also require some technical proficiency to use; many of the settings for various EPROM devices are made via jumpers and DIP switches. The Willem is capable of programming a wide variety of devices by default, and adapters are available for additional devices. Zero Insertion Force (ZIF) sockets are optional. Software is free, and source code is available.

SPEP Plus, Futurelec, www.futurelec.com, $79.95
The SPEP Plus EPROM programmer handles most 27-series EPROM devices. It has a parallel port interface, ZIF socket, and comes with software and a manual.

The Pocket Programmer 2, Transtronics, Inc., www.xtronics.com, $149.95
The Pocket Programmer is a parallel port programmer with a built-in ZIF socket. In its default configuration it is capable of programming a wide variety of 8-bit EPROM devices. EPROM device selection is done fully in software. Adapters are available for additional devices and packages. Free software updates are provided for one year.

Figure 8-27 illustrates various types of ROM chips you might use. From left to right: a 2Kb 2716 EPROM, a 32Kb 27c256 EPROM, a 1Mb 27c1001 EPROM, and a 27c2048 2Mb 16-Bit non-erasable PROM.

Put Your Homebrews on Cartridges

Figure 8-27. Various ROM chips

Erasing Used EPROMs

EPROMs can be erased by exposing them to a source of UV light. There are a wide variety of EPROM erasers available, starting at about $50. Most of them have a small drawer that can accommodate several chips and have a built-in timer. The actual amount of time it takes to erase an EPROM will vary depending on manufacturer. Place your EPROMs into the eraser and set the timer for 1–2 minutes. Once the timer expires, remove the EPROM, insert it into your programmer, and perform a *blank check*. If the check passes, the EPROM has been erased and is ready for reprogramming. If the check fails, place the EPROM back into the eraser and expose it for a few more minutes. Keep track of how much time it takes to reach full erasure, and erase remaining devices for the total time plus an additional 1–2 minutes.

 An EPROM can be permanently erased if overexposed to UV light. When testing for erasure time, only erase in increments of a few minutes. Otherwise, you could end up with an EPROM that can never be reprogrammed.

Programming ROM Devices

Once you've obtained your ROM chips, it's time to program them with your game code. Insert your PROM or EPROM into the programmer and select the appropriate device type. You may want to perform one last blank check to make sure the ROM is ready to be programmed. Next, load the binary image of your game software into the programming buffer and program the device. If the software doesn't automatically verify the ROM contents, there is usually an option to verify the ROM against the contents of the program buffer. It's a lot easier to verify a good program at this stage than after you've assembled a cartridge and discovered that it doesn't work correctly.

Soldering ROMs to PCBs

Once your game has been programmed to the ROM chip, it's time to solder it in the PCB. Be sure to insert the chip on the PCB correctly; a ROM chip inserted backwards will not work, and if it is powered up in that state, it will probably damage the chip.

If you don't have a soldering iron, look for one around 15 to 30 watts and with a grounded plug. If you're planning to solder a lot more in the future, you may want to invest in an iron with a variable temperature control.

If you've never soldered before, you'll want to practice on some old hardware first, like an old VCR or radio. There are many good soldering tutorials available on the Internet; search around and find one that matches your learning style. Practice removing components and then re-soldering them back on. If you can successfully re-solder removed components and the device still works, then you're in business!

Cartridge Cases

Well, your PCB has to go in something, right? If you're recycling PCBs, they'll go right back in to the cartridge case they came from. If you're buying new PCBs, they're made to fit into a particular style of case, usually first-party cartridge cases. The PCB vendor will be able to tell you which cases are appropriate.

Also available for a few platforms are brand new cartridge cases. For example, new Atari 2600 cases can be had in the original black color, or you can jazz up your title and use other colors like red, blue, and clear. See *http://www.vgwiz.com* for more details on new 2600 cases.

If you're going to reuse original cartridge cases, you'll need to first prepare them by removing all of the labels. On some cases, the adhesive may have become so brittle over the years that the labels will fall right off. On others, you'll have to coax the label off with plastic-safe solvent and/or a hair dryer. Lighter fluid works well for releasing the adhesive from the plastic shells. Let the fluid soak into the label for a few minutes and then starting at one corner, slowly peel the label off. Other household products, such as WD-40 and Goo Gone, can help greatly in removing labels and cleaning label residue.

Once the old label and adhesive residue has been removed, disassemble the casings and thoroughly clean them with warm, mildly soapy water. Some of these old games have seen serious duty in attics, garages, flea markets, and kids' hands. You might be surprised at the amount of grime that has accumulated over the years. Some cartridges may have integrated dust shields and springs, so make a note of how everything goes back together.

When the cases are nice and clean, you can either use them as-is, or you can spice them up with a few coats of plastic-bonding paint. Be sure to use a paint that's intended for plastic as cartridges get a fair amount of wear from being inserted and removed, and conventional paints may chip or flake off. Try painting a sample cartridge and inserting and removing it several times to make sure the paint holds fast.

Final Steps

Once your cases are prepared, ROMs programmed, and everything soldered to your PCBs, it's time to reassemble and test everything. Always test each cartridge before sending them out. Testing finished cartridges en masse should only take a few minutes of your time; it's just not worth the hassle and headaches if your customer receives a non-working cartridge.

Now that you've assembled and tested your cartridges, maybe it's time to add a label, set of instructions, or even an outer box. See [Hack #79] for some ideas on how to make your game look just as, or even more, professional than original games!

—Luke Sandel

HACK #79   Create Packaging for Homebrew Games

Make lots of money off your creations with slick package designs.

Many of the people that purchase homebrew games are just as much collectors as they are gamers. For a collector, the nostalgic feeling of opening a brand new game title is a tremendous rush. If you've invested the time to create a homebrew game that you're truly proud of, you owe it to yourself to spend the extra bit of time required to round out your product with good quality packaging and artwork. Collectors will love you for it!

In this section, I will cover some options for producing labels, boxes, and manuals—from simple, do-it-yourself options to professionally produced packaging.

Now, maybe you're more of a programmer than an artist. That's okay—all is not lost. There are services dedicated to helping homebrew authors create artwork, publish, and even market their productions!

Before we get started, I'd like to go over a few printing terms that you'll need to be familiar with:

Bleed
:   A term used to describe printing that goes right to the edge. Artwork printed *full bleed* will have no borders visible.

Coverage
:   How much area is occupied by printing. A sheet of paper with "test" written in 12-point font has a very low amount of coverage. That same sheet of paper with a photograph printed right to the edges has a high amount of coverage.

Weight
:   Typical measurement of the thickness of paper or cardstock. A more precise measurement is the grams per square meter, or *gsm*.

Developing Eye-Catching Artwork

Think back to the last time you stood in the store perusing the latest titles. Maybe this was back in 1982, or maybe it was last week. Either way, artwork plays a prominent role in grabbing the attention of the would-be buyer.

The question remains: how do you get great artwork if you're not an artist? It may be easier than you think. You can always ask an artistically inclined friend or relative, or if you're a member of an on-line gaming forum, you could hold a contest. Some homebrew production services may be able to design artwork to your specifications.

Many of the original fonts used for packaging are available for download. For example, Ergoe, Hammerfat, and MumboSSK were used on original Atari labels and are available from the *http://www.AtariAge.com* web site.

While you could devote an entire book, nay an entire collegiate discipline, to developing good package art, this chapter is more about materials and printing. However, I would like to include a few notes on the preparation of your artwork:

- When preparing artwork for print, try to err on the side of excessively high quality rather than low. If using a scanner to prepare artwork, the minimum for acceptable quality is 300DPI, but shoot for an output resolution around 600DPI.

- If using non-industry standard software to prepare artwork, try and export your final product as a PDF or other industry standard file type.
- Be sure to ask permission before using any copyrighted materials in your artwork.

Printing: Types and Benefits

The method of printing your artwork will depend heavily on a few factors:

- How many copies do you plan on producing?
- How much do you plan on selling the game for?
- What kind of quality are you looking for?

Inkjet printing

> *Price*
>
>> For a small, low-coverage production run, inkjet is probably the best option. Inkjet printers are commonplace and inexpensive, and even large-format inkjet printers can be had for less than $300. If your artwork has a large amount of coverage, you'll find yourself changing expensive ink cartridges often. Beware of cheaper inkjet cartridge refills—they often use lower quality ink that will fade more easily and produce substandard results.
>
> *Quality*
>
>> Inkjet quality is highly dependent on the printer itself and the paper used. Inkjet prints have a tendency to smudge if exposed to moisture, so it isn't the best choice if you have a full bleed manual.
>
> *Overall Appearance*
>
>> Appearance can range from poor to excellent depending on printer or paper. Inkjet prints will also take on the properties of the paper used; glossy paper produces glossy prints, matte paper produces matte prints.

Laser printing

> *Price*
>
>> If your artwork has a large amount of coverage, it will probably be cheaper to have laser prints made. Print shops like CopyMax and Kinko's have high quality color laser printers and generally reasonable deals on bulk purchases.
>
> *Quality*
>
>> Laser prints are sharp and high quality. They don't run or bleed onto skin or fabric. Modern color laser printers are of superior quality to all but the most expensive of printing presses.

Overall Appearance

Laser prints are acceptable for most tasks. However, color laser printers that use fuser oil will create shiny prints, and differing colors may appear to have different levels of reflectivity. These artifacts are usually only apparent when viewing the subject at an angle. Recent color laser technology has negated the requirement for fuser oil, and these reflectivity artifacts will not appear.

Offset, or press printing

Price

This is positively the most expensive route and should only be considered on very large product runs or when maximum quality and precise color are required. The bulk of offset printing costs are from the job setup; the price will drop exponentially as the production quantity increases.

Quality

Offset printing may or may not produce the highest quality output; quality is highly dependant on the technology of the press. Always ask to see samples, and if you can find out the model of the press, you can do some research to find out if it's a quality machine.

Overall Appearance

Offset printing offers a wide variety of inks and appearances. The results may range from mediocre to excellent. Offset printing does offer some features unavailable on inkjet or laser, like the ability to use precise *spot match* colors.

Material Selection

There are a lot of choices for labels, paper, and cardstock for producing labels, manuals, and boxes. You'll want to be sure to choose acid-free paper stock and acid-free adhesives for labels. The cost difference should be negligible, but the long-term storage implications of choosing non-archival quality materials will be disastrous. Manuals should be stapled with stainless steel staples to prevent rusting in humid climates.

Printing Labels

Printing labels is fairly easy. With full-sheet labels available, it is a relatively straightforward process to print your labels and cut them out, either with scissors or with a professional press-type cutter.

Depending on the game system and cartridge shells that you're using, you may desire rounded corners for your labels. If you have a lot of patience you can round them by hand with scissors, but the work is tedious and the results will be inconsistent. If you want a professional appearance, you may have to do a little research and see if you can order labels in the required size or have them die-cut. Talk to a local printing shop and see what kind of options they offer.

Printing Manuals

The simplest booklet-style manual uses an 8.5×11 sheet, folded in half. This creates a simple booklet that uses center stapling. Printing, folding, and stapling by hand would be possible, although you should add a few small marks to indicate the stapling area in the center of your manual booklet. If you have more than a few pages or are using a heavy paper stock, the edges will begin to fan out and require trimming to look professional.

Many copy/print shops have a booklet-making machine that can fold, staple, and then trim the edges to produce a consistent, clean-edged manual. It shouldn't cost more than $1 per manual for the service, and you'll save yourself a lot of time and headaches.

For paper stock, the bare minimum weight you should use is 24lb—anything lighter and text on the opposite pages will show through, or if you use inkjet printing, you'll see the ink bleed through the page. A 32lb bright white stock should provide a reasonable base for any printing method and be strong enough to hold up through repeated readings. If you decide to print manuals on colored stock, be sure to limit the color selections of your print or prepare to spend a bit of time viewing proofs to ensure the results are acceptable.

Printing Boxes

A game box is going to be the most difficult part of the packaging to produce. You'll need to decide on the dimensions of the box and if you want to cut, fold, and glue them yourself.

Use a ruler and a sharp hobby knife to cut the box out of the cardstock. Buy a lot of extra blades and change them at the first sign of dullness. You can try scissors, but you may end up bending the edges and corners of the boxes.

Before folding an edge, hold a ruler against the edges and score them on the inside of the box with a butter knife or other dull-edged object. This will help create a smooth, straight fold. Don't score too hard, though, or you might mar the outside of the box. If your boxes are being printed professionally, they may have a service available to pre-score the fold lines.

A local or Internet-based print shop may be able to provide a complete box producing service. Be sure to get several quotes since prices may vary considerably. If you're only planning a small run of games, producing boxes can be an expensive option, but if you're making 100–200 games, the price per unit will drop dramatically.

An appropriate minimum weight for cardstock is 67lb, but an 80lb or 110lb may be more suitable. If your paper supplier lists the weight in gsm, aim for stock within the area of 200gsm. The heavier the stock, the more resistant to damage it will be, but the more difficult it will be to produce clean, straight folds. If the boxes are laser printed, you may experience some flaking at the folds if the stock is too heavy. If possible, have some proofs made up at varying weights and see what works best for your production. Pre-scoring will help prevent edge flaking.

Alternatives and Exemplary Examples

Not everyone that has released a homebrew title has walked the conventional path. There have been some wonderfully creative and unique ideas used for homebrew game packaging. For example, keeping with the hard-drive-adventure theme of Joe Grand's 2600 release of SCSIcide, the game cartridge was packaged in a static-free bag—a simple yet clever idea. Other clever packaging concepts are shown in the following figures.

Alex Herbert's Vectrex release of Protector was shipped in a heavy, textured box, shown in Figure 8-28. A foil-inlay "Baiter" graced the front of the box, and a small numbered sticker was placed on the back to indicate the unique production number (100 were made, sequentially numbered). Included inside: a single-sheet instruction manual, a colored translucent plastic screen overlay with reverse-printed text and graphics, and a white cardboard insert to hold the cartridge securely in the center of the package. The original selling price was £31.18 (around $50, including postage, at the time). These days you'd be hard pressed to find one selling for less than $200.

George Pelonis's Vectrex release of "I, Cyborg" was packaged (see Figure 8-29) in a hinged, black plastic box just slightly larger than the cartridge itself. A label was affixed to the box lid, and a mini instruction manual was included inside. It is a great example of simple, tasteful, and unique packaging.

All of Eduardo Mello's Colecovision releases have included offset printed boxes, manuals, and labels. Mello has even had new cartridge casings made with his handle "Opcode" embossed into the back, as shown in Figure 8-30.

Figure 8-28. Protector's box design

Figure 8-29. I, Cyborg's cartridge, manual, and case

Final Recommendations

While some of you may be hardcore do-it-yourselfers, you can really save a lot of time and money *and* add to the quality of your work by sourcing your printing to a print or copy shop. If you're looking for color laser prints, the cost/quality edge clearly lies with those that have professional equipment. If

Figure 8-30. Opcode's embossed cartridge design

you add up the price of a color laser printer, toner, and paper stock, you'll find that most print shops are quite competitive. Plus, if you do the work, then you'll eat the cost of misprints, proofs, paper jams, etc. If they produce it, you only pay for what they deliver.

Always produce around 10-20 units of overage (e.g., if you're producing 100 games, have 110 boxes/manuals/labels produced). That way you have something to fall back on should a box or manual become damaged, either during assembly or after shipment to your customer.

Regardless of who produces the packaging, always spot check inkjet prints for smudges, lines, and fading. Check laser prints for smudging and overall consistency. If you run a heavy cardstock through a laser printer and the fuser isn't hot enough, the toner can brush right off of the page (and onto your hands and clothing).

With a little effort, you're sure to produce a game that sells fast and becomes a point of pride with collectors around the globe. Good luck!

—*Luke Sandel*

HACK #80   Create Your Own Adventure Game

Use Adventure Game Studio to make a classic point-and-click.

Hey, remember point-and-click adventure games? I sure as heck do. Classic series like Sierra's King's Quest and Leisure Suit Larry, and of course LucasArts' Monkey Island and Sam and Max, were the reason I counted myself among the PC gamers in the nineties. The genre never had to die, but die it did as Sierra and Lucas quit producing adventures after games moved to 3D and the market for hand-drawn games dried up.

And so, the point-and-click became pointedly retro. But hope is not lost. If you've read *Gaming Hacks* (O'Reilly), you've learned how to run classic LucasArts adventures on your modern-day PC. And in this very book you've already seen how to run your classic Sierra games on your Game Boy Advance [Hack #47]. But what if all these retro puzzlers aren't satisfying your need for adventure? Well, have you ever thought of making your own?

"Nonsense," you say. "I have no programming knowledge whatsoever." Maybe so, but this hack is dedicated to proving that you don't need it. As long as you're a relatively intelligent individual (and you must be if you're reading this) you can use Adventure Game Studio (AGS) to create your own point-and-click adventure in whatever style you please. And the program will even distill your game down to a single executable file so you can distribute the game freely (or commercially, if you really think you have something people would pay for). In this hack we'll create a very basic adventure in just under an hour. Ready... go!

First, head to the AGS project's official home page, *http://www. adventuregamestudio.co.uk*, to download the game engine. Note that it requires Windows 95 or greater, but a Linux port of the game engine is available, meaning that you can run any of these games on Linux (but not Mac, sadly). Unzip the *ags_262.zip* archive to a new directory, then run *agsedit.exe* to launch the program.

At the first menu, choose to create a new game. Use the Default Game template rather than the Blank Game, and name it whatever you want. If you want the game to run under DOS, keep the filename to eight characters or less. You'll then be asked to pick the game's resolution. For purposes of this hack, stick with the ultra-old-school 320x200 resolution. Once you do that, you'll see the program's main menu, shown in Figure 8-31.

Holy cats, that's a lot of checkboxes! Here's some good news: you can ignore them all for right now. You are, however, going to mess around with your game's color mode. In the left menu tree, click on Palette. By default the game is in 256-color mode, but you have to pick each color individually. Let's not bother: click on "Change game's colour depth" and select 16-bit color. Now you can use whatever hues you want, at a minimal sacrifice to game speed.

Now let's create a room. Minimize AGS and open up your favorite paint program. Start with a canvas that's 320 pixels wide by 200 pixels tall (that's

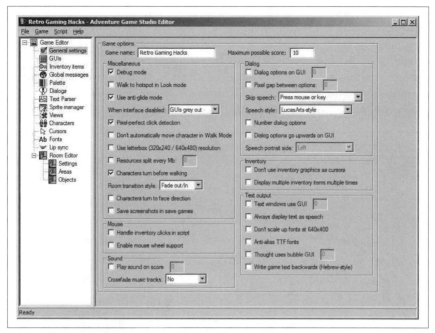

Figure 8-31. Adventure Game Studio's game settings menu

the resolution you chose for the game, remember). Now get to drawing. For the purposes of this hack, I suggest drawing a path leading into a forest, as seen below. Save it as a bitmap file (not *.jpg*). If you're not even this artistic, you can download my ultra-snazzy sample image, shown in Figure 8-32, at this book's web site (see "How to Contact Us," in the Preface).

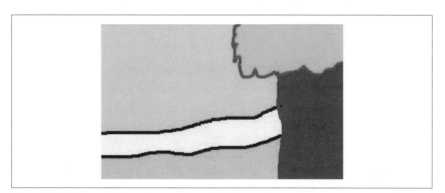

Figure 8-32. My very first adventure game background

Back in AGS, click on the Settings tab under Room Editor in the menu bar. Click the picture of a tree to import your saved bitmap as a room (see Figure 8-33). It will appear in the black area below all the buttons and such.

Those yellow lines over it can and should be dragged around—they represent the edges of the room, the point at which the player will be transported to a new screen. (Hypothetically, of course, since you're only making one screen.) The left line should already be in place, since the left exit is at the far left of the screen. Place the right line so it roughly lines up with the entrance to the forest. The top and bottom lines can go anywhere as long as they're not inside your yellow path.

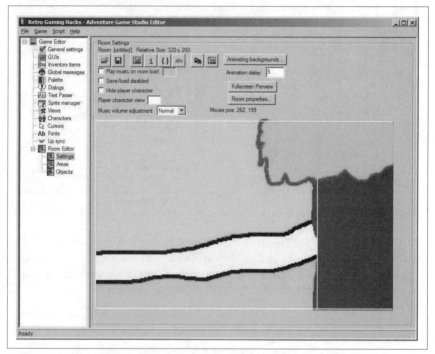

Figure 8-33. The Room Settings menu. Click and drag the yellow lines to demarcate the edges of your room.

Now it's time to define where the player can walk around. Click on the Areas tab in the left menu, and you'll see a dialog box that says Show This Room's: Hotspots. I'll come back to this later, but first click on the Hotspots drop-down box and select Walkable Areas (see Figure 8-34). Now it's just like using a paint program. Using the Line, Free Draw, and Fill tools, fill in your yellow path with blue. Use the Line tool to outline the walking area, then use Fill to get the whole thing (if your whole map turns blue, you didn't outline the area properly—hit Undo and make sure your lines are connected).

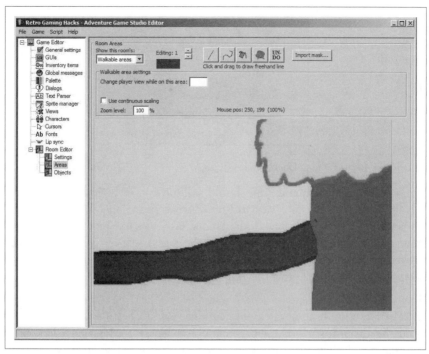

Figure 8-34. Walkable areas, all filled in

Now save your room by clicking File/Save Room As. Name it *room1*—or
anything, really. Next, you're going to make sure the character starts off in
the right place. Move your mouse over the walkable area and find where
you'd like the character to be standing when the game starts. Note the X and
Y coordinates that the game gives you under the heading "Mouse pos"
("pos" stands for *position*).

In the left-hand menu tree, click Characters and you'll see the default character, Roger, so kindly provided for you in the Default Game template.
You'll see boxes labeled "Starts At," so enter the X and Y coordinates that
you just made a note of.

Now you're ready to test the game. First, save it by clicking File → Save
Game. Before you test, click File → Preferences, and change the Game Testing State box to "Force Windowed." This will make the game open up in a
window rather than going fullscreen. If you'd like to see your adventure in
fullscreen mode, leave this box as is and click File → Test Game. Try things
out yourself for a while! You haven't added interactivity, but you can move
the mouse to the top of the screen to access the GUI buttons (see
Figure 8-35), or you can right-click the mouse to cycle through the standard
Walk/Look/Talk/Use icons. Try them on Roger!

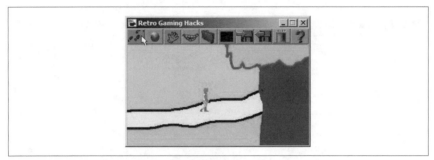

Figure 8-35. Retro Gaming Hacks: The Adventure

Fun, eh? No, not really. But you should still have some of your hour left, so let's add things to do. Go back to Room Areas and change that dialog box that says Walkable Areas back to Hotspots. Use the same paint-style tools to draw a filled box around the leaves of the trees. Above, you'll see an up arrow and a down arrow. Click the up arrow and you'll be making a second hotspot. Go ahead and draw this one in the tree's trunk.

Now you'll add interactivity to these hotspots. Click the down arrow to go back to Hotspot 1, then click Interactions. Right click Look At Hotspot. From the drop-down box, select Game → Display a Message. Click Edit Message, then click New Message (see Figure 8-36), then type what you want the game to say when you look at the green tree branches. Insert an environmental message or poke gentle fun at the extremist sect of the environmental movement—it's up to you.

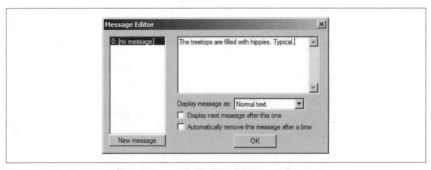

Figure 8-36. Message editor

Now go back and do the same thing all over again for Hotspot 2 in the tree trunk. But this time, write the message "The trunks seem to want to talk to you." Get it? It's a clue as to what you should do next! You're writing a real adventure game now!

So you want to make the trunks chat you up. Go back to the Interaction Editor and click the Talk to Hotspot line. Add in a Game → Display a Message for whatever you want the wise old tree trunks to say. Then we'll reward the player. Right click the Display a Message line that's just been created, and select Add another interaction after this. Choose Add Score on First Execution.

Click "Change," then change the Value field (shown in Figure 8-37) to 5. You're giving the player five points for being smart enough to talk to trees! You've made an adventure with puzzles, scores, and everything! Too bad it's not fun unless you really, really dislike hippies. And even then.... But save the room, save the game, and try it out (check the results in Figure 8-38)! And if you want to play my version (and discover the hidden surprise I left in there without telling you), download it at this book's web site (see "How to Contact Us," in the Preface).

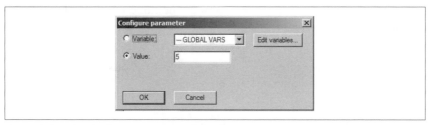

Figure 8-37. The Configure parameter dialog box

Whew! You've created your own adventure game in just under an hour or so. If you'd like to see where many, many, many such hours can get you, check out the awesome Award Winning games section at *http://www. adventurestudio.co.uk*. And to continue with your training, you might start with the lengthy beginner's tutorial at *http://www.bigbluecup.com/acintro. htm*. Happy adventuring!

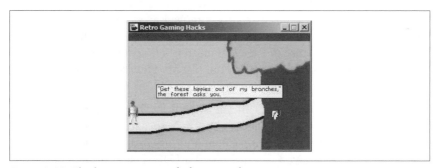

Figure 8-38. The forest is angry with the unseen hippies

Playing Around with Other Neat Stuff

Hacks 81–85

With all this talk of retro gaming hacks (by which I am referring to the past four hundred pages or so, which you should check out if you haven't already), you might have noticed there was one thing missing. That's hacking the games themselves.

In this fragrant potpourri of a chapter, we present to you several hacks dedicated to cracking the secrets of some of the most famous retro games of all time, like Pac-Man and Super Mario Bros.

HACK #81 Learn the Patterns of Pac-Man

Smash your high scores and become a Pac-maniac.

When Pac-Man descended on the world's arcades in 1980, it was responsible for the loss of more quarters and hours than any game before it. The colorful maze game with its iconic characters and catchy music was simple to learn but impossible to master.

Or was it? Not long after the game became popular, Pac-Man addicts started to realize that the behavior of the dastardly ghosts that populated the dot-filled maze was not random. The ghosts moved according to certain rules, and if the player followed specific patterns through the maze he would not be hurt. This led to the rise of Pac-Man masters who could spend hours on a machine for a single quarter...and to the rise of "How to Win at Pac-Man" paperbacks that sold millions.

You can't find those paperbacks on sale in your local supermarket anymore, but you can still learn the secrets of the Pac-Man patterns on various web sites like *http://www.hanaho.com/pacman* and *http://www.upcweb.com/D3B/ Downloads.aspx*, where you can download a PDF version of the book *How to Break a Million at Pac-Man*.

In this hack, I'll cover some of the general rules for patterns, peculiarities of ghost behavior, and other tidbits you'll want to know. Then, I'll take you step-by-step through a pattern, described at the Hanaho web site, that will take you unharmed through the first half of the first Pac-Man board.

General Pac-Maneuvers

Never hesitate

This is one of the most important things you need to know—patterns don't work if you slow down, stop, or accidentally go the wrong way while trying to execute one. If you make a wrong turn, the pattern will no longer work. To make sure you always maintain top speed, remember to hold the joystick in the direction you want Pac-Man to turn before he reaches the intersection. Pressing it after he hits the corner and comes to a stop may be just enough time to ruin the pattern.

The bottom of the screen is death

It's no coincidence that every Pac-Man pattern starts off by collecting most if not all of the bottom row of dots. You don't want to be down in the bottom two rows with ghosts on your tail; there are few exits. Clear them while Pinky and pals are safely inside the pen.

Go up the staircases and around the T

When building your own patterns or just trying to stay alive, the "staircase" pattern as shown in Figure 9-1 is an excellent way to keep the ghosts guessing. Just tromping down one long hallway will make you a sitting duck. Also, note the T-shaped maze piece in the upper middle of the board. Ghosts will almost never go up the stem of the T, so if you're being chased, that's a good place to lose them.

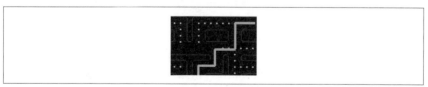

Figure 9-1. A sample "staircase" path

Find the safe spot

Figure 9-2 shows a spot where Pac-Man will be safe from ghosts for an unlimited amount of time—perfect if you need to wipe sweat off your hands, go to the bathroom, or eat a sandwich in the middle of a high score attempt. There are two caveats, however—for the space to be safe you must enter it from the south, and only when none of the ghosts are looking directly at Pac-Man (watch the pupils of their eyes). Note that in the picture Pinky is looking at Pac-Man, so he is actually not safe.

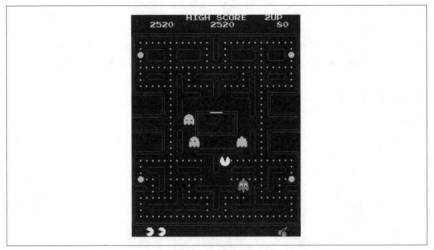

Figure 9-2. The "safe" spot

A Sample Pac-Man Pattern

The following patterns work only on the original arcade version of Pac-Man! The home versions of the game, like the ones on the Namco Museum discs **[Hack #16]** are completely reprogrammed, and arcade patterns will rarely work. The general tips mentioned in the previous section should still be helpful, but don't come crying to me if the patterns won't work on your Game Boy Advance Pac-Man Collection.

The pattern described forthwith will bring you through the first half of the first level of any standard Pac-Man coin-op. It's easy to learn, 100% effective, and very impressive to onlookers (you'll see why in a bit). Here's the first and easiest part:

1. Start out by moving left. Head down the second corridor, then left again. Grab the whole bottom row, then come back to the starting position in a mirror image of the way you came, as shown in Figure 9-3.

2. Head "up the staircase" in a zig-zag pattern alternating up and left. Circle around to the right side of the T, then come down it. Circle around the ghost pen. At this point you should be where Pac-Man is in Figure 9-4. Now it gets exciting, because the ghosts will be closing in on you. Head down past the energizer…

3. Then circle back up and left to grab it. If you've done the pattern perfectly you will have performed a crowd-pleasing escape from the ghosts. Now do the "double staircase" as shown in Figure 9-5 and you should easily catch between three and four ghosts as they run away.

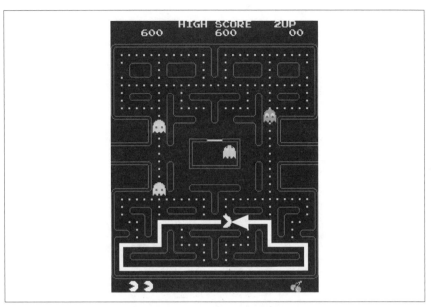

Figure 9-3. The opening pattern

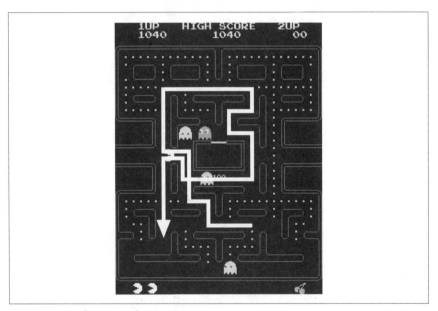

Figure 9-4. Circling around

You're on your own from here on out, but with three energizers and all "safe" dots left, you should have no trouble completing the level.

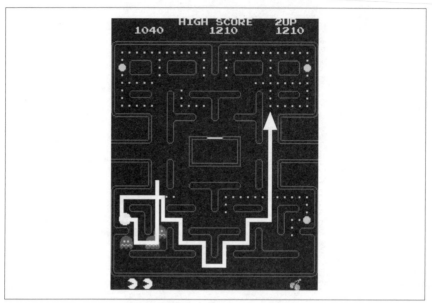

Figure 9-5. Setting yourself up for success

Show Off with Super Mario

Find the Minus World, get 100 lives, and other tricks.

Anyone who grew up with the Nintendo Entertainment System remembers hearing the stories. There was some kid in your class at school whose brother, or cousin, or out-of-town friend had found out a way to get *a hundred lives* in Super Mario Bros. Or had jumped over the flagpole. Or, most unbelievable of all, had walked through a wall and discovered a secret Minus World.

Luckily, most of us could use our playground smarts to sniff out such obvious B.S. I certainly heard my share of Nintendo whoppers back in the day. But in the case of Super Mario Bros. most of the secrets turned out to be true. Little did we know as we traded gossip at recess that there was already a best-selling book in Japan that explained everything. Similarly successful books followed quickly in the United States.

Eventually, thanks to the proliferation of early NES tip books and magazines, the hundred-lives trick and the Minus World became common knowledge. But unlike the massive wealth of pre-programmed cheats and tricks that infest games today, the Super Mario Bros. tricks were inadvertent bugs and exploits that the programmers never imagined. They were also difficult to pull off, meaning that Mario mastery, even today, can be an impressive parlor trick to perform in front of your friends. And with retro games making a comeback, you never know when you will be called into service.

Here, then, are the secrets to Mario mastery; the tricks and tips that, with practice, will bring you up to the average gameplay level of an American nine-year-old circa 1986. (That's a lofty goal, mind you.)

Get 100 Extra Marios

Throughout the game—firstly and most conveniently in World 3-1—as Mario comes to the staircase of blocks that ends the level, you'll see two Koopa Troopa turtles marching down the steps. You might see this as just another obstacle in your path, but in reality these little turtles are the secret to your near-eternal life. Poor Mario begins his adventure with a mere three lives in reserve, but at the end of this crucial trick, you can amass upwards of 128 extra chances—more than enough to beat the game a few times over!

1. First, make your way to the staircase at the end of World 3-1. As shown in Figure 9-6, there will be two Koopa Troopas tromping down the steps—jump over the first one and stand in place on one step, waiting for the second.

2. As the Koopa Troopa nears the step directly above the one you're standing on, jump straight up as shown in Figure 9-7. When you land on the Koopa, his shell should stay in place on one step. (If not, commit suicide by jumping into the pit at left, and try again.)

3. As you come down on the Koopa (see Figure 9-8), tap the A button continuously and you should begin to jump off the shell repeatedly as it bounces off the step.

4. If you can keep up the jumping, you'll start earning extra lives (designated by the 1UP symbol) for every time you stomp the Koopa, as Figure 9-9 shows.

This trick is not a "bug" so much as it is an exploit of a documented feature. If Mario can stomp many different enemies (or in this case, one enemy, over and over) without hitting the ground, he will earn successively more points and then extra lives for each enemy.

However, Mario was not supposed to have this many lives! After you leave World 3-1, you'll notice that the hex codes that display Mario's remaining lives have gone out of whack and now only display bizarre graphics. And if you get more than 128 lives, the program won't be able to count them— and you'll get a Game Over the next time you die.

Figure 9-6. Here they come

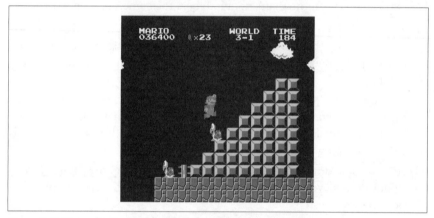

Figure 9-7. Stomp him!

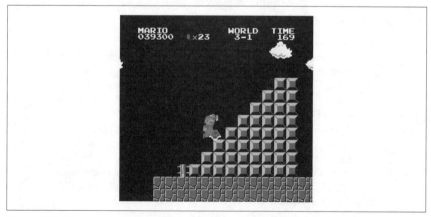

Figure 9-8. Start tapping

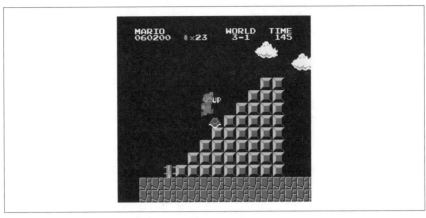

Figure 9-9. 1UP, and 1UP, and...

Enter the Minus World

Here's an even tougher trick. Luckily it takes place early in the game. At the end of World 1-2, the first underground level, Mario is "supposed" to enter a horizontal green pipe that takes him above ground and to the end of the level. The not-really-a-secret about this place is that if Mario rides the orange lifts up to the ceiling, he can walk over the pipe and into the Warp Zone where he can immediately skip to the beginning of World 2, 3, or 4. But there's a totally different place to go as well, if you know how to find it.

1. First, get to the end of World 1-2. Instead of going through the pipe, stand on top of it, on the left side, as shown in Figure 9-10.

2. Jump straight up and smash the brick above your head. You can break any brick to the left of this as well, but do not break the brick adjacent to the pipe! (See Figure 9-11.)

3. Here's the tricky part. Stand on the left side of the pipe and make Mario crouch by pressing down. Now, in a crouched position, jump straight up into the gap. Gently ease Mario into the lower-right corner of the block you left by the pipe, as shown in Figure 9-12.

4. It may take more than a few tries for you to get the feel of it, but eventually—I swear this is true—Mario will be sucked backwards through the brick (see Figure 9-13), the pipe, and the wall. No image trickery here! See that pipe to the right? Enter it immediately after Mario comes out the other side. Don't walk too far to the right, or the pipe will become a standard warp to World 4.

5. Holy what the heck! As soon as you go down the pipe you'll see the screen in Figure 9-14. You'll enter World negative 1, or the Minus World. It's disappointing, though—just an underwater level that loops over and over. The only way out is to get a Game Over.

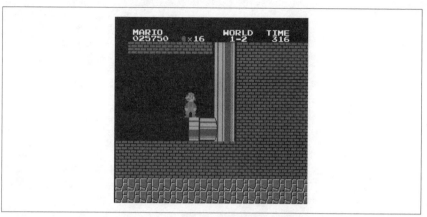

Figure 9-10. Stand here

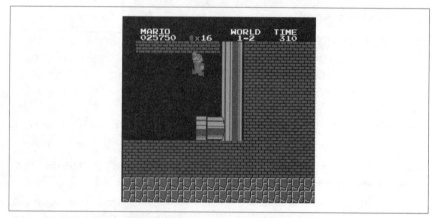

Figure 9-11. Smashy smashy

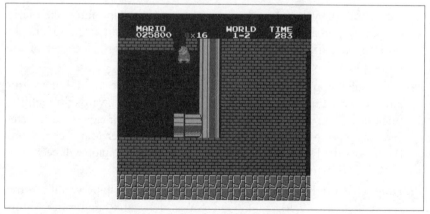

Figure 9-12. Touch the lower left corner of the brick

To get sucked backwards through the bricks as shown in Figure 9-13, be sure to jump straight up, then ease Mario over to the right. You don't want to hit the bottom of the brick, or else you'll smash it and you won't be able to do the trick.

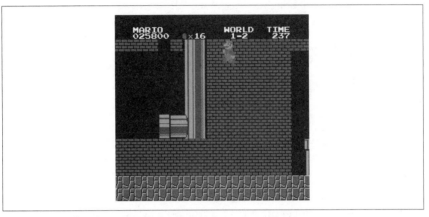

Figure 9-13. Whoosh!

Figure 9-14. Welcome to the Minus World

The Minus World is actually a bug, discovered soon after the game's Japanese release. But it became so popular that the designers, when porting the game to the Famicom Disk System [Hack #8] a year later, decided to make it into a feature. The method for entering is the same, but the Minus World is a series of three bizarre (but completable) levels. Finishing them will bring you back to the title screen, where by way of reward you will be able to press the B button to jump to any level in the game. This special Minus World was not put into any later edition of Super Mario Bros.

Jump Over the Flagpole

At the end of each level in Super Mario Bros. is a flagpole. Jump off the top of the staircase just right by getting a running start then leaping at the last second, and you can hit the very top of the pole for 5000 points. Rumors abounded that it was possible to jump over the pole in certain levels— though nobody knew what could possibly await on the other side.

Eventually, it was found that by using the pulleys and platforms in World 3-3, Mario could get high enough to clear the pole. Make your way to the pulleys at the end of the level. Stand on the left platform, and the right one will begin to rise up as you fall. Right before the right platform touches the pulley (and both platforms fall off), jump from the left to the right, then bounce off the far right edge of the right platform. If your timing and accuracy are perfect, you'll clear the top of the flagpole!

Unfortunately there's nothing on the other side. The background scenery will repeat endlessly until time runs out. Oh well... they can't all be winners.

Hack the Leisure Suit Larry Games

HACK

#83

Find hidden nude scenes, easter eggs, and secret tricks in the risqué adventure series.

By the late eighties, graphic adventure games—cartoonish quests filled with brain-bending puzzles—were well on their way to becoming one of the most popular game categories available for the exploding personal computer market. Game publisher Sierra On-Line, having pioneered the genre with the ubiquitous King's Quest, continued to grow the genre with titles like Police Quest, Space Quest, and a game called Leisure Suit Larry In The Land of the Lounge Lizards.

This groundbreaking game, filled with bawdy humor and adult situations, followed the adventures of a perpetually dateless, out-of-style, balding disco-hall getabout named Larry Laffer as he attempted to work his sleazy yet lovable self into the hearts of beautiful women. With each new entry in the popular series, Larry's creator Al Lowe and his team of misfits hid all sorts of surprises, from more revealing artwork of the games' leading ladies to tricks and cheats that let the impatient player bypass some difficult moments.

In this hack, I'll run down some of the best tricks and secrets hidden in the Leisure Suit Larry games. Just be warned that if you don't already have the games, tracking down original copies can be extremely difficult as Sierra no longer publishes them. Try searching the online auction site eBay (*http://www.eBay.com*) to find the games; add the phrase -magna to the end of your search string to filter out the recent Leisure Suit Larry game, Magna Cum Laude, from the results.

 If you've got some classic Larry games but are having trouble getting them to run properly on your computer, try some of the solutions offered in [Hack #69].

Leisure Suit Larry in the Land of the Lounge Lizards

Larry's very first outing took him to scenic Lost Wages in search of romantic fulfillment. Shockingly, he sort of found it.

Defeat the "Age Quiz". To prevent impressionable young persons from getting into the first Larry game, the humorous "age test" shown in Figure 9-15 was administered before the game began.

Figure 9-15. Leisure Suit Larry's age quiz

Questions mostly concerned items of topical interest circa 1987, the sort of things adults would know but kids wouldn't. The only problem is that nowadays, even the over-18 crowd would wrestle with questions like:

Who has not been a U. S. Attorney General?

1. John Mitchell

2. Sam Shepard

3. Ramsey Clark

4. Herbert Browner

The answers to all of the age-test questions are available on Al Lowe's web site (*http://www.allowe.com/Larry/1questions.htm*). But there is another trick you can use, left in by programmers sick of answering their own questions every time they felt like starting a game up. Press Alt-X to bypass the quiz entirely. In the re-released 1991 VGA graphics version of the game, you must press Ctrl-Alt-X to get around the quiz.

Turn off the hot tub bubbles. Near the end of the game, you'll get into a hot tub with Eve (see Figure 9-16), Larry's dream woman. While you're chatting with her, try typing in the command turn off bubbles to see what happens. In the point-and-click VGA version of the game, you'll see a button on the hot tub that you can press to achieve the same goal. We'd show you the results, but this is a family publication.

Figure 9-16. Hm... if only that water level were a little lower

Leisure Suit Larry Goes Looking For Love (In Several Wrong Places)

Larry starts out in his first sequel living with Eve, but she soon kicks him out of the house. He sails away on a cruise ship to places unknown.

Bypass the copy protection. Larry's second game featured no age test, but it did include a copy protection scheme that sought to prevent those who had not purchased the game legally from getting past the title screen.

In the game's manual were color pictures of sixteen cartoon beauties (okay, some of them were a little scary-looking), each with a phone number written beneath her portrait. Before the game could begin, you had to input the girl's phone number.

You can find pictures of all sixteen girls at Al Lowe's site (*http://www.allowe. com/Larry/2women.htm*), but where's the hack in that? Moreover, the pictures were designed such that if the manual were to be photocopied, it would be difficult to tell the black-and-white, blurry images apart. This had the unintended side effect of making it difficult to figure out the woman in question even with an original manual!

A better way to get past the copy protection—although it only works on version 1.002.000 of the software—is to input Al Lowe's birthday as the last four digits of the number: 555-0724.

Leisure Suit Larry 3: Passionate Patti In Pursuit of the Pulsating Pectorals

You think that I'm making these titles up, but I'm not. In Larry 3 you alternated between playing as the man himself and his undercover-agent girlfriend Patti as they investigated mysterious happenings on Nontoonyt Island (say it out loud).

Defeat the age quiz (again). Larry 3 brought back the dreaded Age Quiz, with questions designed to confound and stump any young child or innocent adult who dared fire up the *Larry3.exe*. This time around, you could still play the game if you failed the questions, but the game's naughtiness level would increase or decrease depending on how well you did. If you want to skip the quiz, press Ctrl-Alt-X and you'll be able to set the rudeness level. Set it all the way to 5 to enjoy the game as it was intended!

Get around the copy protection. Larry 3 employed a novel means of copy protection. If you pirated the game, you would be able to play through the first few screens, thus giving you a taste of the full product. But you wouldn't be able to get very far without having the manual handy, as the maitre d' of the club (shown in Figure 9-17) requires a ticket number printed on a random page. If you input the wrong number, the game will end immediately—hope you saved beforehand, butterfingers!

Since designer Al Lowe has provided a full list of the ticket numbers on his home page (*http://www.allowe.com/Larry/cluescheats.htm*), I don't feel particularly bad about printing them in Table 9-1.

Figure 9-17. I'm guessing it's not 6

Table 9-1. The ticket numbers

Page	Ticket number
3	00741
5	55811
6	30004
8	18608
11	32841
12	00993
15	09170
18	49114
19	33794
22	54482

There is another bit of copy protection for which the manual is needed, but since it also constitutes a puzzle in the game that requires a bit of lateral thinking, I won't spoil it here. If you're stumped (or don't have the manual), check out the URL listed in the previous paragraph. (And while you're there, read the informational section about the design of the Nontoonyt jungle maze for some insight into a truly retro gaming hack!)

Leisure Suit Larry 5: Passionate Patti Does a Little Undercover Work

Wait a minute... Leisure Suit Larry 5? What happened to 4? If you play this adventure, you'll find out. Or not.

Bypass the copy protection (yet again). Larry 5's copy protection works much the same way as Larry 3's—you'll be able to play a bit of the game, but you won't get far without the manual. This time, however, the copy protection isn't an easily-copied list of numbers. You have to enter in a series of meaningless symbols that coincide with an airport check-in computer's travel arrangements.

A large, easy-to-read image of the symbol list is available, again, at designer Al Lowe's site (*http://www.allowe.com/images/L5cpyprot.gif*).

See more of Chi Chi. When you first meet the dental receptionist Chi Chi (shown in Figure 9-18) towards the end of Larry 5, you might be wishing that her uniform wasn't so expertly tailored. Clicking on the button using the "touch" cursor won't initially work, but if you're persistent and click her about seven times, you'll get some surprisingly risqué results.

Figure 9-18. Drat that pesky button

Find Leisure Suit Larry 4. When you begin the game, walk over to the desk and pick up the xylophone. After you pop Chi Chi's buttons, use the mallet from the xylophone on the second cactus from the left in the office bathroom. Actually, I'm just kidding. There is no Larry 4, and no hack will ever uncover one!

Leisure Suit Larry 6: Shape Up Or Slip Out!

Larry invades a health spa in Larry 6, which represented a return to form for the series after the disappointingly simple fifth installment. For the first time, the game saw an optional release on CD-ROM, which featured full voice acting.

Peek into the women's shower room. This is one of the most infamous Easter eggs hidden in the Larry games. You can't get into the womens' showers, but you can see what lies inside. Go into the mens' shower room and look on the wall for a discolored tile. Take it off the wall, look in the resultant hole, and a brief cutscene (that I cannot show you) will play automatically.

Take Cav's shirt. Make absolutely sure to save your game before you attempt this Easter egg, as Cav—the buffed and physically imposing aerobics instructor—will literally kill Larry if he dares to take her shirt away. After you get her membership card (this is a necessary part of the game), you can remove her shirt if you try enough times (like with Chi Chi). Just don't come crying to me when you're dead.

Leisure Suit Larry 7: Love For Sail!

For the beautifully redesigned Larry 7, a CD-only game with animation rivaling television cartoons and all sorts of new features, the design team included several difficult-to-find but highly amusing Easter eggs. In fact, it's possible to see practically every female in the game (see Figure 9-19) in a less-than-clothed state.

Figure 9-19. If only there were some way to "push" those plants out of the way...

Many of the eggs revolve around use of the mostly optional text-entry system, which was rejected as obsolete after Larry 3 but brought back because of the wide variety of commands (and resultant jokes) it allowed for. Since the methods for performing the Easter eggs are lengthy and complicated (and available at Al Lowe's web site, of course: *http://www.allowe.com/Larry/7eggs.htm*), I won't go into the details. Suffice it to say that they really pulled out all the stops!

As I mentioned earlier, there is another Larry game now available for PC, PlayStation 2, and Xbox, called Leisure Suit Larry: Magna Cum Laude. There aren't too many Easter eggs in the game, since it is more of a collection of minigames and less of a puzzle-solving title. But if you look closely, you'll be able to re-enact the famous shower sequence in full 3D. And you might even see some of the girls from Larry 2 in the sorority house.

Play Retro Versions of Modern Games
HACK #84

Play the games of today, just without that pesky third dimension.

Part and parcel of the retro game revival phenomenon are modernized versions of classic games. Updated with new, slick graphics and/or expanded gameplay, modern versions of retro games bring the classic gameplay to a new audience. These can be official, like the *Arrangement* versions of Namco arcade games in more recent editions of Namco Museum [Hack #16], or unofficial, like the fan creations collected at the site Retro Remakes (*http://www.retroremakes.com*).

But that's not what I'm going to talk about in this hack.

No, this section is about hacks that are the exact opposite of what you'd typically think of as a "retro remake." These hackers look at games like Metroid Prime or Halo and think to themselves, "This is a great game... but it would be even better if it was done in 2D with 256 colors." They're taking modern games and stripping away the glitz, making them retro in the process.

Since the projects described in this hack tend to skirt the boundaries of copyright and fair use, it's very possible that by the time you read this, one or more of the projects may have been shut down. Caveat lector.

Ocarina of Time 2D

One of the most famous (or infamous) 2D-ification projects was housed at *http://www.oot2d.com* before creator Daniel Barras took the site down sometime in 2004. As the name implies, Ocarina of Time 2D is a DOS version of the Nintendo 64 smash hit The Legend of Zelda: The Ocarina of Time, done up in 16-bit Super Nintendo style, as shown in Figure 9-20.

Those familiar with the game know that this is an ambitious project (too ambitious, if the fact that the site has been taken down is any indication). If you want to try a very simple demo that Barras crafted in the PC game

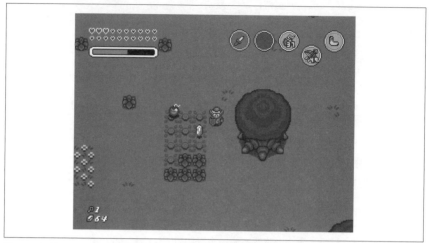

Figure 9-20. Ocarina of Time 2D

creation software Game Maker [Hack #73], it is available for download at Zelda Dungeon, along with other fan-made Zelda games (*http://www. zeldadungeon.net/FG.php*).

Metroid Prime 2D

Another retro remake crafted in Game Maker, Metroid Prime 2D is an attempt to create a traditional side-scrolling Metroid game from the 3D, first-person GameCube entry in the series. This sounds like an even harder task than Ocarina of Time 2D, but this project seems to stand a much better chance of being completed since there is a team of upwards of two dozen people working on every aspect of the game.

On the official web site (*http://www.mp2d.co.uk*) you can see much of the work in progress. The hundreds of artwork and music files being used in the game are available to view, and there are a few very brief concept and physics demos as well. The team hopes to release the first official demo—featuring the "frigate sequence" (see Figure 9-21) that was used to demo the original title—soon.

Codename: Gordon

While the preceding projects surely raise the eyebrows of Nintendo's legal team, not all fan-made games are frowned upon by the copyright owners. Consider Codename: Gordon, a 2D version of the popular FPS Half-Life. Half-Life's developer Valve decided to support the creators of the game, making it available through their Steam digital download service along with other Half-Life and Counter-Strike games. Figure 9-22 shows Codename: Gordon.

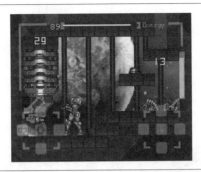

Figure 9-21. Metroid Prime 2D

Figure 9-22. Codename: Gordon

The official web page for the project (*http://www.halflife2d.com*) is temporarily unavailable as of this writing, but you can get the game at classic PC
game repository Home of the Underdogs (*http://www.the-underdogs.org/
game.php?id=4882*). And if you've got a Steam game like Half-Life 2
installed, you'll see Codename: Gordon available in Steam's Play Games
window. One word of caution, as Underdogs points out: though this ador-
able-looking shooter would seem to have low system requirements, it in fact
requires a 1.6 gigahertz processor or higher to run. It is written in Macromedia Flash [Hack #74].

Similar in concept, but not officially supported, is Halo:
Blood Covenant, a 2D shooter based on the popular Xbox
title. You can see screens and download a demo at *http://
www.consoletroopers.com*.

Doom 2D

This is easily the oldest retro remake covered in this hack, as it was originally released in 1996—and in Russian, at that! Yes, it's a 2D, side-scrolling shooter based on the seminal FPS, Doom. You can download an English-translated version at Home of the Underdogs (*http://www.the-underdogs.org/game.php?id=2828*). The levels are based on the original game's, and there's even a two-player deathmatch mode, shown in Figure 9-23.

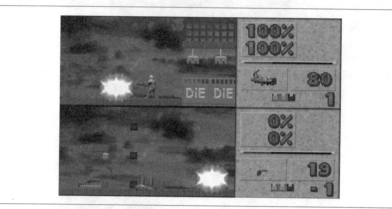

Figure 9-23. Doom 2D in deathmatch mode

If you want to go even more retro, there's always Doom: The Roguelike (*http://chaos.magma-net.pl/doom/*), a top-down dungeon-exploration/shooter game with RPG elements that uses ASCII text characters for all its graphics. The name comes from the classic computer adventure game Rogue, which DTR's graphics and gameplay mimic.

> More information on Rogue and roguelikes, including information on how to develop your own, can be found at *http://www.roguelikedevelopment.org*.

Grand Theftendo

And now for something completely different. Although many of the preceding projects stem from popular console games, all of them are programmed for the PC. Not so Brian Provinciano's Grand Theftendo (*http://www.grandtheftendo.com*). A remake of Grand Theft Auto III for the Nintendo Entertaiment System, Grand Theftendo (shown in Figure 9-24) is easily the most interesting retro remake out there.

In addition to programming the game itself, Provinciano has released a program called NESHLA, or NES High Level Assembler, which is an open-

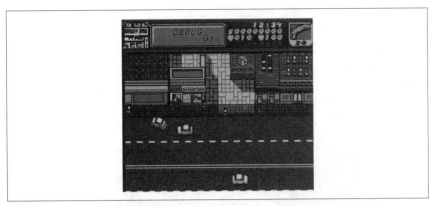

Figure 9-24. Grand Theftendo

source 6502 assembler for the NES that promises to make life easier for would-be NES homebrew programmers. Check it out at *http://sourceforge. net/projects/neshla*, and maybe you'll be making your own NES games in due time.

HACK #85   Remix Your Retro Sounds

Capture audio from your favorite game, and tap your inner DJ, musician, or just be that guy with the annoying ringtone.

As simple as the sounds are, audio has always been a critical component of retro gaming. If you've played MAME without the necessary samples [Hack #28], you knew something was missing. To make the experience perfect, the sound needs to be there.

If you ever wanted to bottle up the arcade experience and take it with you, audio is your opportunity. With some clever software that "hijacks" the output of your sound card, you can turn the audio from any game into an MP3 file. Then, what you do with it is limited by your imagination, and probably the court decision du jour about music sampling.

Capturing Retro Audio

One of the problems with capturing the audio from your games is that the sound is coming *out of* your audio hardware, not into it. The way around this is to pick up a piece of software that takes the sound as it goes to your speakers and makes a parallel recording of it in an audio file.

On the Mac, the top choice is Rogue Ameoba's Audio Hijack (*http:// rogueamoeba.com/audiohijack/*), a $16 shareware application that's simple to use. On the PC, I suggest Total Recorder (*http://www.highcriteria.com/*), which is $12. Both Audio Hijack and Total Recorder have evaluation versions available so you can try before you buy.

With Audio Hijack, you need to drag the application you want to record to the Audio Hijack main window. Click the Hijack button to launch the application, click Record in the Audio Hijack window and start playing the game. Figure 9-25 shows an Audio Hijack session with MacMAME.

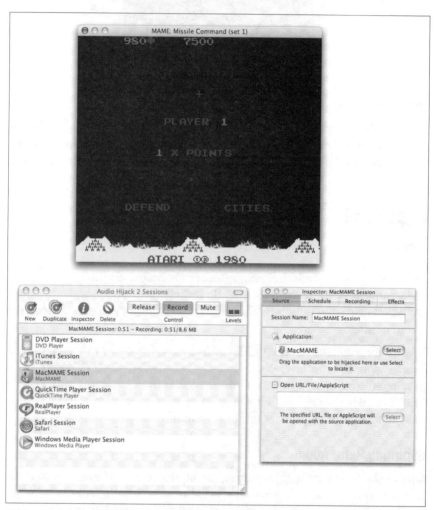

Figure 9-25. Recording the sounds of Missile Command

When you're done, click Record again to stop recording, and use the release button to stop Hijacking the audio. Audio Hijack will save the sound to your desktop, using a name such as *MacMAME Session 20050628 2112.aiff*.

It's a bit simpler on Windows with Total Recorder: start recording and play your game. Total Recorder will capture all audio that comes out of your PC. When you're done, you can save the audio in MP3 or WAV format.

The reason it's easier is that Total Recorder replaces your sound driver with its own, and redirects the sound to the real card at the same time it's recording. You shouldn't even notice this, but if you go to your Sounds and Audio control panel, you'll see that "Playback through TotalRecorder" is specified as your output device. Total Recorder lets you change its settings so that the Total Recorder audio device is only active while you are using Total Recorder, but you'll need to launch Total Recorder before you launch the programs you want to record if you use this option.

Edit Your Audio

After you've saved your sound into an MP3 or WAV, you'll no doubt have some sound at the beginning and end that you don't want. The top-notch (and free) Audacity (*http://audacity.sourceforge.net/*) comes to the rescue, whether you are on Mac OS X, Windows, or even Linux and Unix. You can open a file in Audacity, and select the segment of sound you're interested in, as shown in Figure 9-26.

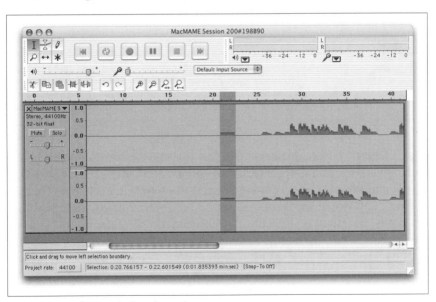

Figure 9-26. Selecting the bit of sound you want

Once you've isolated the bit of sound you want, choose File → Export Selection as MP3. The first time you export to MP3, you'll get some instructions for finding the add-on library you need to create MP3s. Follow the instructions, and you'll be on your way.

The fun with Audacity doesn't end here: it's a full featured audio editing application. Want to add echo, compression, or even a wahwah sound? Select the segment of sound you want to modify and choose an effect from the Effect menu. Be sure to try the GVerb effect, which lets you specify a room size, reverb time, and more. There are more plugins available at the Audacity home page.

Do Something Cool with It

Now that you've got MP3s of your retro sound effects, you can do what you want with them. Pull them into GarageBand and lay down some rad tracks. Weave them into the background of your mixes so they are barely perceptible, but leave your audience with a longing for the old arcade.

I'm no musician, and I'm no DJ; I'm but a man of simple needs. So I'm going to beam that sound over to my cell phone and set it as a ringtone. Since my cell phone (a Nokia 3650) doesn't support MP3 files, I had to use File → Export Selection as WAV to create a file that it would use.

 Some phones use even more exotic audio formats. One of the easiest ways to convert your MP3s or WAVs to the right file type is to use Mobile PhoneTools (*http://www.bvrp.com/ eng/products/mobilephonetools*), a $40 application that can create ringtones (among its many other talents) for a wide variety of cell phones.

After I had my *missile_command.wav* file, I beamed it over to my cell phone using Bluetooth, and it appeared on my phone as a message and opened up in a sound player. On my phone, I saved the sound (by selecting Options → Save), and exited the sound player (so the sound file wouldn't be in use when my phone rang). Finally, I went into the Profiles utility, and set *missile_command.wav* as my ringtone. When you hear me coming, reach for your trackball!

—*Brian Jepson*

Index

We'd like to hear your suggestions for improving our indexes. Send email to *index@oreilly.com*.

P

packaging homebrew games, 406–413
Packrat Video Games web site, 3
  emulators, 145
Pac-Mac Arrangement (Namco), 68
Pac-Man
  Coleco, 42
  hacking, 420–423
  JAMMA connectors, 44
  Namco, compilation including, 68
  Namco/Jakks Pacific, 58
  patterns, 420
    sample of, 422
  (see also Jr. Pac-Man), 11
paddles
  Atari, 13, 55
  Atari 2600, 10
Palm, Atari Retro, 66
Pangolin, MAME arcade vector
    graphics, 136
PayPal, 2
PC Atari emulator, installing, 144
PC computers
  Atari paddles on, resource for, 13
  blueMSX Colecovision
    emulator, 153
  early, playing with, 241–289
    Apple][systems, 241–257
    Commodore 64, 257–266
  Intellivision emulators, 147
  running DOS (see DOS)
  running Windows (see Windows)
  Vectrex, emulating on, 39
  (see also computers)
PC Engine, 34
  Japanese games for, 35
PC joystick controllers, 16
PC2JAMMA project web site, 44
PCAtari emulator, 144
PDAs, classic games on, 197–206
PDP-1 computer, 275
PDP-11, 298
PDRoms web site
  Atari 2600, 145
  freeware, 152
    NES-compatible games, 159
  homebrew games, 195
  MAME ROMs, 110
Peasant's Quest (Homestar Runner), 77

Pentium III processors, blueMS
    emulator, 153
Pentium Pro processors, MAME version
    for, 85
performance
  blueMSX emulator, 153
  MAMEoX emulations on Xbox, 108
  NEStra emulator, 174
  Virtual Colecovision, 153
Perry, Dave, 277
Philly Classic gaming convention, 5
Phoenix (Arcade Legends/Radica), 62
PhotoGuide Japan web site, 36
Pimp's Quest (Newgrounds), 76
Pitfall! (Activision), 67, 83
Pitfall! (Activision), Jakks Pacific
    version, 58
Planetfall (Infocom), 303
Play-Asia retailer, 35
Play-Asia web site
  Neo Fami systems on, 20
  PokeFami on, 27
Players switch, later models of pong
    systems, 8
playing
  arcade games on computers, 84–136
    Linux, 96–104
    Macs, 91–96
    in MAMEoX, 107
    Windows, 84–91
    Xbox, MAME, 105–108
  classic games, 13–17, 137–240
    on handhelds, 197–206
    on Windows, 142
  with DOS, 321–348
  with early PCs, 241–289
    Apple][systems, 241–257
    Commodore 64, 257–266
  at game design, 349–419
  MAME, 87
    anywhere, 133–136
  retro games in DOS, 337–340
  text adventures, 295–297
Playstation 2 (Nintendo)
  Activision Anthology, 67
  Namco Museum, 68
PlayStation (Nintendo), Japanese games
    for, 34
plug-and-play, Intellivision systems, 148
Pocket PC, Atari Retro, 66

Colophon

Our look is the result of reader comments, our own experimentation, and feedback from distribution channels. Distinctive covers complement our distinctive approach to technical topics, breathing personality and life into potentially dry subjects.

The image on the cover of *Retro Gaming Hacks* shows two Atari 2600 joysticks. These joysticks, which were released with the original Atari console in 1977, have become icons of console gaming. While the ergonmics of the joysticks may be questionable, their simple utilitarian design—one button to shoot and one stick to move—offers a sturdy control device for gamers everywhere.

Philip Dangler was the production editor and proofreader for *Retro Gaming Hacks*. Derek Di Matteo was the copyeditor. Darren Kelly and Claire Cloutier provided quality control. Nancy Crumpton wrote the index.

Ellie Volckhausen designed the cover of this book, based on a series design by Edie Freedman. The cover image is an original photograph by Kevin Thomas. Karen Montgomery produced the cover layout with Adobe InDesign CS using Adobe's Helvetica Neue and ITC Garamond fonts.

David Futato designed the interior layout. This book was converted by Keith Fahlgren to FrameMaker 5.5.6 with a format conversion tool created by Erik Ray, Jason McIntosh, Neil Walls, and Mike Sierra that uses Perl and XML technologies. The text font is Linotype Birka; the heading font is Adobe Helvetica Neue Condensed; and the code font is LucasFont's TheSans Mono Condensed. The illustrations that appear in the book were produced by Robert Romano, Jessamyn Read, and Lesley Borash using Macromedia FreeHand MX and Adobe Photoshop CS. This colophon was written by Philip Dangler.

Better than e-books

Buy *Retro Gaming Hacks* and access the
digital edition FREE on Safari for 45 days.

Go to www.oreilly.com/go/safarienabled
and type in coupon code 2RFS-8TGE-22TG-K1ER-166B

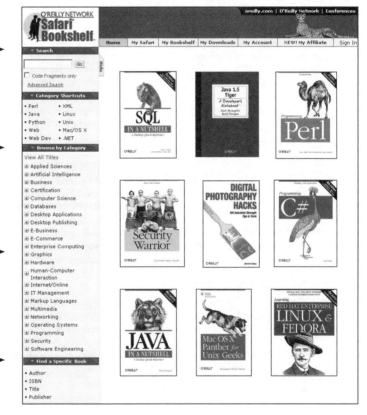

Keep in touch with O'Reilly

Download examples from our books

To find example files from a book, go to: *www.oreilly.com/catalog* select the book, and follow the "Examples" link.

Register your O'Reilly books

Register your book at *register.oreilly.com* Why register your books? Once you've registered your O'Reilly books you can:

- Win O'Reilly books, T-shirts or discount coupons in our monthly drawing.
- Get special offers available only to registered O'Reilly customers.
- Get catalogs announcing new books (US and UK only).
- Get email notification of new editions of the O'Reilly books you own.

Join our email lists

Sign up to get topic-specific email announcements of new books and conferences, special offers, and O'Reilly Network technology newsletters at:

elists.oreilly.com

It's easy to customize your free elists subscription so you'll get exactly the O'Reilly news you want.

Get the latest news, tips, and tools

www.oreilly.com

- "Top 100 Sites on the Web"—PC Magazine
- CIO Magazine's Web Business 50 Awards

Our web site contains a library of comprehensive product information (including book excerpts and tables of contents), downloadable software, background articles, interviews with technology leaders, links to relevant sites, book cover art, and more.

Work for O'Reilly

Check out our web site for current employment opportunities:

jobs.oreilly.com

Contact us

O'Reilly Media, Inc.
1005 Gravenstein Hwy North
Sebastopol, CA 95472 USA
Tel: 707-827-7000 or 800-998-9938
    (6am to 5pm PST)
Fax: 707-829-0104

Contact us by email

For answers to problems regarding your order or our products:
order@oreilly.com

To request a copy of our latest catalog:
catalog@oreilly.com

For book content technical questions or corrections: **booktech@oreilly.com**

For educational, library, government, and corporate sales: **corporate@oreilly.com**

To submit new book proposals to our editors and product managers:
proposals@oreilly.com

For information about our international distributors or translation queries:
international@oreilly.com

For information about academic use of O'Reilly books:
adoption@oreilly.com
or visit:
academic.oreilly.com

For a list of our distributors outside of North America check out:
international.oreilly.com/distributors.html

Order a book online

www.oreilly.com/order_new

Our books are available at most retail and online bookstores.

To order direct: 1-800-998-9938 • *order@oreilly.com* • *www.oreilly.com*

Online editions of most O'Reilly titles are available by subscription at *safari.oreilly.com*